THE GARDENER'S HINT BOOK

THE
GARDENER'S
HINT BOOK

CHARLES L. WILSON

Illustrated by
James W. Lockyer

jD| JONATHAN DAVID PUBLISHERS INC. Middle Village, New York 11379

THE GARDENER'S HINT BOOK

To my beloved Miriam

Acknowledgment

This book is a compilation of hints discovered by gardeners and scientists through years of experience. The origin of most of these ideas is impossible to trace and acknowledge. I have drawn heavily from bulletins issued by the U.S.D.A. and State Agricultural Experiment Station and from the works of numerous garden writers. The patience and competence of Jim Lockyer in making the illustrations are gratefully acknowledged. My wife, Miriam, provided the encouragement, typing, and love that made it all possible.

Library of Congress Cataloging in Publication Data

Wilson, Charles L
  The gardener's hint book.

  Bibliography: p.
  Includes index.
  1. Gardening. I. Title.
SB453.W549   635   76-26893
ISBN 0-8246-0210-2

Table of Contents

Preface

All gardeners have at times admired the green grass, lush vegetables, or thriving trees and shrubs of a neighbor. Why is his garden so beautiful? What does he know that I don't? *The Gardener's Hint Book* shares with you the secrets of admired gardeners from around the world and, whether you are a beginner, or an expert, you will find herein numerous suggestions to improve your gardening.

The Gardener's Hint Book is a practical book. Each of its 12 chapters —which cover the basic aspects of gardening—is preceded by an overview. Each chapter overview outlines the basic principles and procedures necessary to succeed in the aspect of gardening discussed in that chapter. The overviews are by no means exhaustive. What they do is highlight those details which need attention if success is to be expected. They provide the perspective which every potential gardener should have before beginning work. They are useful as checklists which can be consulted before, during, and after the planting season to assist in ordering supplies, carrying out maintenance, and trouble shooting. The overviews also provide the jumping off point for further reading.

The major portion of the book is composed of practical hints and suggestions. Each hint consists of a bit of information essential to successful gardening or provides an alternative to established gardening practices. Learning by trial and error in gardening is often expensive and always frustrating. It may be necessary to wait for a year to pass before another attempt can be made. *The Gardener's Hint Book* aims to reduce the uncertainty so many gardeners have about what they are doing.

In addition to the hints and tips presented in each chapter, a number of useful tables and charts are included throughout. The appendices in the back of the book contain additional useful information.

Until recently, two basic gardening "philosophies" have been espoused: *organic gardening*—relying on rotted organic materials (such as manure) and other nonchemical means for fertilization and pest control; and *scientific gardening*—relying largely on synthetic chemicals for fertilization and pest control. In the wake of the ecology debate, the two were cast as arch rivals with organic gardening being overglorified and scientific gardening overcriticized. In fact, farmers have been practicing each in conjunction with the other for years. The farmer who discards his animal manure in the cause of chemical fertilization is as rare as the farmer who uses animal fertilizers exclusively.

The Gardener's Hint Book doesn't advocate either school of thought. It intends to make you neither an "organic" gardener nor a "scientific" gardener, but a "successful" gardener. To do so, it recommends both organic and chemical fertilizers, weed killers, insecticides and fungicides, depending on their availability, need, and cost.

—Charles L. Wilson

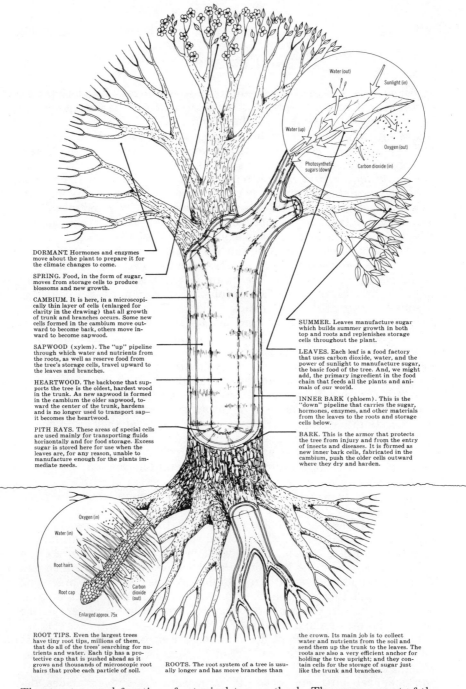

DORMANT. Hormones and enzymes move about the plant to prepare it for the climate changes to come.

SPRING. Food, in the form of sugar, moves from storage cells to produce blossoms and new growth.

CAMBIUM. It is here, in a microscopically thin layer of cells (enlarged for clarity in the drawing) that all growth of trunk and branches occurs. Some new cells formed in the cambium move outward to become bark, others move inward to become sapwood.

SAPWOOD (xylem). The "up" pipeline through which water and nutrients from the roots, as well as reserve food from the tree's storage cells, travel upward to the leaves and branches.

HEARTWOOD. The backbone that supports the tree is the oldest, hardest wood in the trunk. As new sapwood is formed in the cambium the older sapwood, toward the center of the trunk, hardens and is no longer used to transport sap—it becomes the heartwood.

PITH RAYS. These areas of special cells are used mainly for transporting fluids horizontally and for food storage. Excess sugar is stored here for use when the leaves are, for any reason, unable to manufacture enough for the plants immediate needs.

Within the circular inset (leaves):
Water (out)
Sunlight (in)
Water (up)
Oxygen (out)
Photosynthetic sugars (down)
Carbon dioxide (in)

SUMMER. Leaves manufacture sugar which builds summer growth in both top and roots and replenishes storage cells throughout the plant.

LEAVES. Each leaf is a food factory that uses carbon dioxide, water, and the power of sunlight to manufacture sugar, the basic food of the tree. And, we might add, the primary ingredient in the food chain that feeds all the plants and animals of our world.

INNER BARK (phloem). This is the "down" pipeline that carries the sugar, hormones, enzymes, and other materials from the leaves to the roots and storage cells below.

BARK. This is the armor that protects the tree from injury and from the entry of insects and diseases. It is formed as new inner bark cells, fabricated in the cambium, push the older cells outward where they dry and harden.

Within the circular inset (roots):
Oxygen (in)
Water (in)
Root hairs
Root cap
Carbon dioxide (out)
Enlarged approx. 75x

ROOT TIPS. Even the largest trees have tiny root tips, millions of them, that do all of the trees' searching for nutrients and water. Each tip has a protective cap that is pushed ahead as it grows and thousands of microscopic root hairs that probe each particle of soil.

ROOTS. The root system of a tree is usually longer and has more branches than the crown. Its main job is to collect water and nutrients from the soil and send them up the trunk to the leaves. The roots are also a very efficient anchor for holding the tree upright; and they contain cells for the storage of sugar just like the trunk and branches.

The structure and function of a typical tree or shrub. The arrangement of the "up" and "down" pipelines differs somewhat in annual flowers and vegetables.

Introduction

Many dedicated gardeners lack a theoretical and scientific understanding of gardening. Theory, they claim, belongs in the classroom. Furthermore, it makes a generally pleasant undertaking unpalatable. Yet, almost every gardener has *some* theoretical knowledge, and experienced and successful gardeners have, for the most part, grasped well the scientific principles of gardening. In order to make informed decisions about problems he encounters, the experienced gardener has found that knowledge indispensable. For this reason, you are encouraged to read the few pages that follow.

The Gardener's Hint Book does not purport to be a science textbook. You will not be burdened with endless pages of scientific jargon; but neither should you be shortchanged. If you are to do much gardening and expect to be successful, a basic understanding of the workings of plants is essential. With this in mind, this introduction is divided into three sections: 1) How a plant is constructed and functions, 2) How a plant grows, and 3) How a plant's environment affects its growth. The scientific information set forth in these sections will sometimes be clarified with practical implications.

HOW A PLANT IS CONSTRUCTED AND FUNCTIONS

Almost every plant has three main parts: *roots,* which anchor the plant and draw nutrients and water from the soil; a *stem* (sometimes more than one), which supports the leaves and fruit, carries water and nutrients upward, and carries sugar manufactured in the leaves downward; and *leaves,* the food manufacturing part of the plant.

The existence of the three parts is obvious in most cases. All plants have roots, though some branch more and extend more deeply than others. All have stems: the trunk of a tree is as much a stem as the stem of a marigold. And all have leaves—grass plants, maple trees, evergreens and ferns included—though their shapes and sizes vary radically. When thinking in terms of function, the structural differences between plants lose their significance. The only major difference, then, between a small azalea bush and a large oak tree is that the azalea has many small stems while the maple has one thick trunk. Despite structural differences, it is important to remember that *all* plants have roots, stems, and leaves.

The Roots

We sometimes fail to realize just how large a part of every plant is buried in the ground. The roots of a houseplant extend down only a few inches. A mature oak tree, however, has roots which may extend as far down as ten feet, and a weeping willow tree has roots which sometimes extend as much as 50 feet beyond the tree's trunk.

A plant's roots play a major part in anchoring it to the soil. By clinging to the soil, its roots help a plant resist the wind and hold itself upright. There are no support posts for plants in the natural state and those plants whose roots cannot provide sufficient anchorage to combat the elements do not survive.

Roots also serve to absorb water and nutrients—which are needed for a plant's growth and development—from the soil. In order to function, a plant requires nitrogen, phosphorus, potassium, and other trace elements. Most of these nutrients dissolve in soil water, are absorbed into the roots by tiny, delicate terminal root fibers, and are then drawn up through the main stem to the plant leaves.

Let us examine a root under the microscope. At the very end of the root's tip is a *cap* which serves as a protector. The delicate cells of the root tip divide rapidly, producing new cells and causing the root to grow through the soil. Behind the growing point of the outer cells of the root tip are *root hairs*—horizontal extensions which penetrate the soil. Much of the intake of water and nutrients is done by the root hairs, which incidentally, are very delicate and quickly die if allowed to dry out.

The roots are nourished by carbohydrates transported from the leaves and nutrients found in the soil. Like all living plant cells, they require oxygen to help release the energy stored in the carbohydrates. The parts of the plant above the ground have relatively little difficulty in obtaining the needed oxygen from the air. But, oxygen can become very scarce in soil, particularly when the soil is heavy or flooded. A lack of available oxygen in the soil can cause a plant to die.

Most plants have a "will to live," and most root systems will try to adapt to the soil conditions. In general, plants growing in light, sandy soils will develop deeper, more branched root systems than they would in heavier soils. This adaption is a combination of convenience and necessity: light, sandy soils provide poor anchorage and contain less moisture than heavy soils. The roots must sometimes travel great distances to obtain adequate water and nutrients. But sandy soil is easy for the roots to penetrate.

Heavier soils are dense and moist. The soil resists the spreading of the roots. If the heavy soil contains sufficient nutrients for the plant, a relatively compact root system will develop. If the nutrient supply is inadequate in the immediate vicinity of the plant, the roots must work hard to push through the compacted, clay soil. If they make it, the plant will flourish; if not, the plant will decline as the demands of the expanding leaf network for more and more raw materials go unanswered.

Occasionally, a plant that has struggled to survive for years will suddenly flourish. Not uncommonly, this is the result of the persistence of a root system that has finally pushed its way through stubborn clay to lighter, more yielding soil.

With the above in mind, it is easy to understand several basic planting procedures. Unless a transplanted plant has grown in a container or is very small, it has probably lost a substantial part of its root system—and the all-important root hairs—when being dug up and moved. Plants are generally tough and will regenerate a replacement root system within a year **if** the following steps are taken:

1) The remaining roots are not allowed to dry out. This is especially crucial when dealing with bare-root stock. Exposure to the air for even short periods of time can kill dormant, bare-root stock. Gardeners must be careful not to leave roots exposed to sun and wind while they dig their planting holes.

2) The branches of the plant are pruned back. Removal of part of the branches lightens the work load of the functioning roots. The branches *will* grow back.

3) An adequate hole is dug and filled with well-conditioned, fertile soil. The bigger the hole, the better: it should always be twice the size of the root zone. Peat moss should be added to the hole—not because it nourishes the tree, but because it readily absorbs and holds moisture and provides minimum resistance to the regenerating and expanding root system.

4) The plant is watered sufficiently. Although the smaller root system of a transplant can only handle a limited amount of water at any moment, sufficient water must be available to the roots when it is needed. To facilitate the water intake of transplanted bare-root stock, dead roots are removed and live ones pruned back an inch or so to remove dried out tissue.

The Stem

The stem of a plant extends from ground level to the point where the leaf stem *(petiole)* joins the leaf to the branches. A *branch* is an extension of the main stem; a *leaf stem* is an extension of the leaf. (Not all plants—e.g. pines—have leaf stems.)

A major function of the stem and its extensions is support. The stems of most plants stiffen sufficiently to keep the plant erect and hold its leaves up to the sun. The stems of most trees and shrubs have a woody content which helps support the plant. The stems of non-woody plants—such as annual flowers and vegetables—usually stiffen enough to provide support for their life span.

Some plants would "prefer" to be erect but lack the necessary strength in their stems. Nature has supplied some of these plants (usually climbers) with *tendrils,* or holdfasts, which help the plant cling to an outside body. Grape vines, cucumber plants, and ivy will all climb up a trellis if provided.

Sometimes, of course, we want plants to do things that they weren't created to do. Tomato plants, for example, would be perfectly happy lying on the ground. But, because they yield better fruit when staked, we provide both the support (a pole) and the fastener (wire or string). The shaping of fruit trees has become an art form of sorts. But, fruit trees don't particularly want to be shaped like candelabras, and if that is the appearance we desire, we must provide the support.

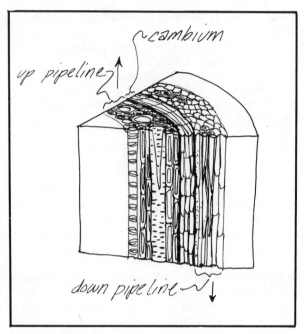

A cut-away of a stem. The cambium is flanked by the "down" pipeline to the out-side (right) and the "up" pipeline to the inside (left). The unmarked area to the right of the "down" pipeline is the bark and the unmarked area to the left of the "up" pipeline is the heartwood.

Visualize the inside of a stem as a series of hollow cylinders of varying thickness fitted one inside the other. Some of the cylinders serve as pipelines which carry water and nutrients, as well as food that has been stored in the roots, from the roots, up to the leaves. Other cylinders carry sugar, hormones, enzymes and other materials from the leaves to the roots and storage cells below.

The *cambium layer* is a microscopic layer of cells from which all stem growth originates. New growth on the *inside* of the cambium layer adds to the thickness of the "up" pipeline; new growth on the *outside* of the cambium layer adds to the thickness of the "down" pipeline. The cambium layer itself always remains the same thickness.

The arrangement of the "up" and "down" pipelines in trees and other woody plants is different than the arrangement in most vegetables and annual flowers. A tree adds new cylinders of growth to its "up" and "down" pipelines each year. These new layers appear on either side of the cambium layer. In time, the layers farthest from the cambium stop func-tioning as pipelines, and begin to contribute to the tree's support. The nonfunctioning part of the "up" pipeline becomes part of the dark inner core of the tree (the heartwood); the nonfunctioning part of the "down" pipeline adds to the thickness of the bark. The continuous thickening of the inner core of woody plants provides additional support as the plant matures. The continuous thickening of the bark obscures pruning cuts and small bruises.

The "up" and "down" pipelines in vegetables and flowers are arranged in bundles scattered throughout the stem tissue. This is best seen in the celery plant, whose stringly parts are bundles of "up" and "down" pipelines.

A plant cannot live if the entire circumference of the cambium layer has been severed. It is important to remember that if mice and other rodents, which often chew (girdle) the bark of a tree, succeed in severing the cambium layer around an entire plant, it will die. Repellent chemicals and fences are used as preventive measures.

The Leaf

The leaf is a food factory. It is essential to the growth and development of the entire plant, including the roots, that its leaves function efficiently. We, as animals, take our food "premade," primarily in the form of carbohydrates, fats and proteins. A plant requires the same types of food, but must manufacture that food from simple substances taken from the soil and air.

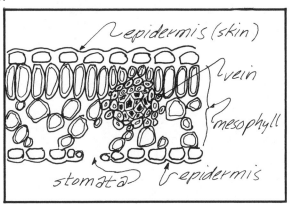

The structure of a leaf blade.

A leaf has two main parts: the *blade* and the *petiole*. The petiole connects the leaf to the stem and contains the "up" and "down" pipelines that connect the leaf and blade to the main stem. It is in the blade that the process of food manufacture, called *photosynthesis*, takes place. Photosynthesis involves fusion of a gas (carbon dioxide from the air) and water (from the soil) to form a carbohydrate. The source of energy for this process is the sun.

How is the blade of a leaf able to carry out photosynthesis? If you cut across a leaf, you will find that it is composed of three layers. The top and bottom layers, called the *epidermis* (or skin), are one-cell thick. Between the skin layers is a multi-celled layer where photosynthesis occurs. Carbon dioxide gas enters the skin layer through small pores, called *stomates,* and fuses with water that has been transported through the petiole. Carbohydrates, laden with energy from the sun, are formed. These manufactured carbohydrates are then sent down the leaf, through the petiole, and into the stem or roots via the "down" pipeline. Here, they are either stored or utilized as energy.

Not all water that is supplied to the leaf is used for photosynthesis. Much of it is lost to the atmosphere through the *stomates* in a process called *transpiration*. Transpiration can be compared to human perspiration; its purpose is to rid the leaf of excess moisture. As long as the plant can replace the evacuated water, no difficulty exists. Problems arise when water is given off by leaves exposed to the sun at a time when the roots are unable to replenish the water supply. Such a condition sometimes exists in winter when the sun draws moisture from the leaves while the moisture around the roots is frozen. It is a cause of winter kill.

The manufacture of carbohydrates is important to plants. When the carbohydrates are broken down, they release the energy imparted to them by the sun. The decomposed carbohydrates combine with other nutrients absorbed by the roots to make essential proteins. In turn, these proteins form enzymes and membranes which make up the structure of the plant.

Though they look markedly different, the leaves of a maple tree, a pine tree, a cucumber plant, and a rubber plant all have the same fundamental structure and function. The leaves of a plant are arranged to most efficiently capture the sun's rays. It is the superior effectiveness of certain plants in trapping the sun's rays which allows them to live in more limited light conditions than others.

The question of sunlight needs is not a by-the-way-consideration in choosing a plant. It is vital! Certain plants, such as rhododendrons and azaleas, cannot tolerate excessive sunlight. Their leaves are constructed in such a way that excessive sunlight destroys the food making cells in the leaves. Some plants—the hemlock and yew are examples—function effectively in full *and* reduced sunlight. Most deciduous trees require full sunlight.

HOW A PLANT GROWS

Now that you understand how the three primary parts of a plant function individually, let us discuss how they work together to enable a plant to grow. It must be understood that a plant *must* grow—even if only a fraction of an inch per year—to live. A plant that has stopped growing is dead.

All plants theoretically begin with a seed. Other means than seed propagation (called *vegetative propagation*) are sometimes used. For our understanding, though, let us start with the seed.

The emergence and development of a full-grown plant from a tiny seed is miraculous. Within the seed there exists a preformed miniature plant (*embryo*) consisting of a root, stem, and seed leaves *(cotyledons)*. When the seed is placed in soil, moisture enters the seed and initiates growth of the embryo. First, the root grows through the seed coat and establishes

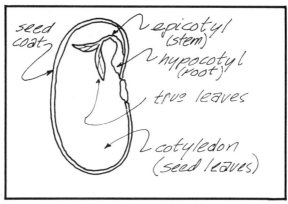

An ungerminated seed.

contact with the soil. Then, the tip of the stem extends upward with the seed leaves, at which time the seed coat is shed. It is at this point in its development that the seedling is seen emerging through the soil with its seed leaves.

As the seedling develops, the tip of the stem continues to grow, shedding its seed leaves and forming true leaves. At the same time, the first roots of the seedling, grow further downward. The growing stem and roots develop lateral branches which add to the plant body. The growing root surface is able to supply the plant with increasing amounts of water and nutrients, while the growing leaf surface is able to manufacture increasing amounts of food.

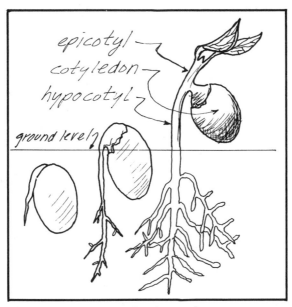

A germinating seed.

We discussed above how the *thickness* of a stem increases with the addition of new growth on the inside and outside of the cambium layer. But, how do stems grow *taller?* Will the low branches on a stem become the top branches as the plant matures? The answer is "no." The upward and outward growth of a plant takes place from the *tips* of its branches. For this reason, it is always suggested that the low branches on a shade tree be pruned to the height desired. They will remain the same height from the ground for the lifetime of the tree.

At the tip of each branch, and along its side, are clusters of actively dividing cells, much like those of the cambium. Each cluster, or *growing point,* is enclosed in the buds of all perennial plants. (It also exists in the tip of plant embryos *in the seed.*) During the growing season, the growing point, which is covered during the dormant season, is exposed at the tip of each bud. As new cells are produced, the bud extends in length and the newly formed cells become part of the branch. It becomes obvious that the growing points of plants should not be brushed against or bruised unnecessarily. Destroying a few crucial buds can misshape a potentially beautiful tree.

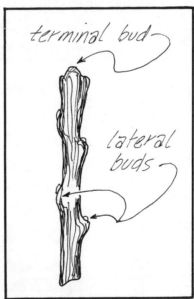

The terminal and lateral buds of a branch.

Growing points are classified as *terminal growing points,* located at the very tips of upright branches, and *lateral growing points,* located along the sides of branches. The shape of a plant depends on the relationship of the terminal growing points to the lateral growing points. In plants having one main stem or trunk (most trees), the bud sitting atop the highest branch—known as the *leader*—is crucial. A plant whose terminal growing point is very aggressive, and whose lateral growing points are not, will be very tall and spindly. A plant that has equally strong lateral and terminal growing points will be very bushy. When the main terminal grow-ing point of some plants is destroyed, a lateral growing point may assume dominance and serve as the main terminal growing point. It will, however, take time for this dominance to assert itself. For this reason, a good deal of consideration should be given before pruning a tree's main terminal bud.

The time to enter dormancy is usually signalled to the plant by a shortening of day length and a drop in temperature. In temperate climates, most plants lose their leaves in the fall and cease to grow during the winter months. Growing points (both terminal and lateral) are formed during the summer, but remain inactive during that year and throughout the winter. In warmer climates, the period of dormancy is shorter.

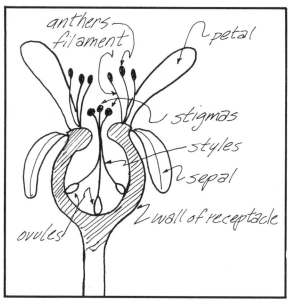

A flower. The male part—the stamen—consists of the anther and the filament. The female part—the pistil—consists of the stigma, the style and the ovule.

As gardeners, we are particularly concerned with our plants' flowers and fruit. Flowers and fruit are related: fruit develops from the enlarged seed-containing ovaries of flowers. Although in some cases they are small and inconspicuous, most plants produce flowers.

Flowers are produced by special buds which contain growing points with the ability to form the flower parts. Flower buds are generally plumper than the more pointed growth buds. Their formation is in-fluenced by the plant's nutrition and general vigor.

Plants have a limited amount of energy. How this energy is used deter-mines whether the plant will devote itself primarily to growth or to flower and fruit production. Plants tend to put their energy into growth. For this reason, fruit trees and roses are pruned radically and suckers are removed from tomato plants. By pruning off this vegetative growth, energy is diverted to flower and fruit production.

Once flower buds have opened and flowers have fully formed, *pollination* is the next important step in a plant's life cycle. In flower gardens, we are not concerned with pollination because the flowers themselves are the object. But, in vegetable and fruit gardens, it is another matter. If pollination does not occur, there will be no fruit production. Some plants are pollinated by bees, others by wind, and some are self-pollinating. Pollination can be promoted by planting cross-pollinating plants in parallel rows, or by placing honeybee hives in the garden area.

The plant's life cycle is completed with the formation of seed inside the fruit. Much of the plant's energy is sapped by the seed production process. Therefore, it is wise to clip off flowers in flower gardens before they "go to seed," and, thereby, save energy which can be used for the production of more flowers.

Some plants have a definite life expectancy; others can live indefinitely. Annuals germinate, flower and produce seed all in one year. Biennials generally produce vegetative growth one year, then flower, produce seed, and die the second year. Perennial, non-woody plants, such as asparagus, can live indefinitely, but generally succumb to one problem or another after several years. Trees and other woody plants have an unlimited life expectancy. Each year, they "lay down" a new plant over the old one by the action of the cambium. Some trees can live to be hundreds of years old. Their ultimate death is a result of disease, insect infestation or structural damage rather than the expiration of an alloted number of years.

HOW A PLANT'S ENVIRONMENT AFFECTS ITS GROWTH

In plant paradise, all soils would contain an unlimited amount of those nutrients needed by plants to thrive; the proper balance of rainfall and sunlight, warmth and cold would exist; the soil would have exactly the right texture to allow the roots to anchor and feed properly; and insects and disease would not exist. It is just this kind of paradise that every gardener is trying to create for his plants.

Climate

For the home gardener, ensuring proper moisture is not a problem. A spigot is usually accessible. He need only consider the moisture requirement of a plant if a larger scale garden is planned where supplemental watering is impractical.

Climate is the most difficult thing for a gardener to work around. Each plant has its sunlight requirement: from mere daylight to full sunshine. When choosing plants, the simple and hardfast rule is: if the light demands of a plant can't be approximated, don't include it in your garden.

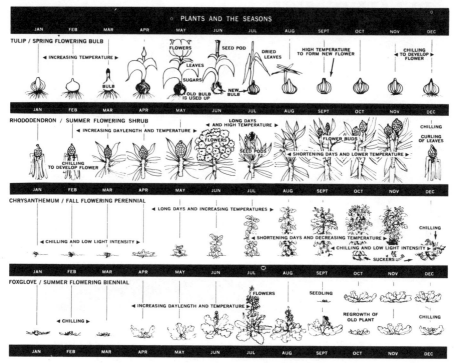

How varying day lengths and temperatures affect four different plants.

The rules dealing with *hardiness* (the ability of a plant to withstand cold) are more flexible. Plants have a minimum temperature below which their tissue will die. However, many plants—roses and strawberries, for example—are grown out of their natural climate range by providing winter shelter, which can consist of wind shields and a heavy mulch around the roots.

For certain plants, a minimum amount of cold is required for the plant to function normally. A pear tree, for example, requires approximately 1,200 hours of temperatures below 45 degrees F. to allow the proper period of dormancy without which fruit won't be produced. Many field crops, such as lettuce and cabbage, will not do well in consistent 90-degree temperatures. Excessively warm temperatures are a factor in choosing plants.

Elements in the Soil

It is below the soil line where a gardener has the most control over good plant growth. Plants require certain basic elements, found in the earth, to survive. All plants require relatively large quantities of nitrogen, phosphorus and potassium. These are knows as *macroelements,* and are often symbolized on fertilizer bags as N, P, and K respectively. There are

RELATIVE SIZE

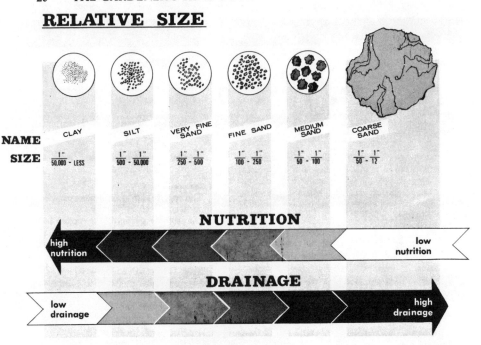

Soil particles range from very fine clay to coarse sand. A particle of sand is at least 1,000 times larger than a particle of clay.

also at least 13 trace, or *microelements*—including iron, manganese and magnesium—which plants need in smaller quantities. Very often, soil contains a sufficient supply of microelements. Where deficient, they are easily supplemented.

Though plants cannot grow without adequate water and nutrients, two factors greatly influence the ability of plants to *utilize* the water and nutrients *even when available:* soil texture and acidity.

Soil Texture

The fact that soils have different textures is a hard one for many gardeners to grasp. Although gardening catalogues and books abound in such terms as "heavy clay" and "sandy loam," it is doubtful that they have much significance to most gardeners. Soil texture is critical to plant growth, and it is worth a few minutes of time to see why.

Many of us have difficulty understanding the importance of soil texture because we fail to realize that the roots of a plant must take up oxygen *from* the soil and release carbon dioxide *to* the soil. If this exchange is not carried out, the plant will die. To accomplish this oxygen-carbon dioxide exchange, there must be somewhere for the oxygen to come from and somewhere for the carbon dioxide to be released. This "somewhere" is the space between the particles of soil.

Soil is composed of a variety of variable-sized particles. The larger particles are called *sand;* the smaller ones are called *silt,* or *clay.* The relative number of large to small soil particles determines soil texture.

A soil which is predominately composed of large sand particles is called a light or sandy soil. Light soil has relatively large spaces between its particles and allows an easy exchange of oxygen and carbon dioxide. The space between particles also prevents water from "standing" in the soil, thus providing good drainage. Good drainage facilitates the all-important oxygen-carbon dioxide exchange. Light soil is also more suitable for root growth. On the other hand, light soil has poor nutrient and water-holding capacity, making it very difficult for the roots to absorb sufficient quantities of the raw materials needed by the plant.

A soil which is predominately composed of clay, or silt particles is called a *heavy* or *clay* soil. Heavy soil has very small spaces between its particles, limiting the amount of oxygen available to the roots and making it difficult for the roots to expel carbon dioxide. The small spaces between the particles trap water, resulting in poor drainage and further limiting the room available for oxygen and carbon dioxide. It is harder for roots to grow in this more compacted soil. On the other hand, heavy soil has good water and nutrient-holding capacity and, consequently, is more fertile.

The ideal garden soil is a mixture consisting of 10% to 20% clay and 80% to 90% sand. A mixture of this kind—known as *sandy loam*—provides a compromise between the better drainage and gas exchange capability of a pure sand soil and the superior water and nutrient-holding capacity of a pure clay soil. If you have such a soil, you are lucky; if not, you can help create it.

Exactly how soil textures differ will not become clear until you have examined several types. A good way to do this is to collect at least two soil samples. The hint on page 32 outlines a simple procedure whereby the different components of the soil can be isolated. Following this procedure on several soil samples will sensitize you to soil texture and, hopefully, encourage you to test and improve your own soil before planting.

Heavy soils can be improved by adding such organic amendments as compost, peat moss or leaf mold. The organic material creates air pockets between the clay particles. Inorganic amendments, such as sand, perlite (expanded pumice), vermiculite (expanded mica), and haydite (volcanic gravel) will also improve heavy soils. Light soils, too, can be improved by adding organic amendments. The amendments will fill the spaces between sand particles and trap nutrients and water.

How much amendment should be added? In almost pure sand or almost pure clay soils a 50-50 mixture of amendment and soil should be made. Average soils require a mixture of 25% amendment and 75% soil. Since organic amendments are helpful to all types of soil, it is a good rule of thumb to add one part of organic matter to every three parts of soil in all planting holes.

Acidity and Alkalinity

The concept of soil acidity and alkalinity is confusing to many gardeners. Simply explained, all soil contains *decomposed* water in the form of hydrogen ions and hydroxide ions. If the hydrogen ions dominate, the soil is said to be *acid*. If the hydroxide ions dominate, the soil is said to be *alkaline* (or sweet). If a soil contains an equal quantity of hydrogen and hydroxide ions, it is said to be *neutral*. A scale of 1 to 14 has been set up to measure relative acidity. A pH (an abbreviation for *potential of hydrogen*) between 1 and 6 represents an *acid* soil. A pH between 8 and 14 represents an *alkaline* soil. A soil with a pH of 7 is neutral.

The relative acidity or alkalinity of a soil is crucial: there is a direct relationship between the pH rating of a soil and the availability of the soil's nutrients to a plant. Even if all the proper nutrients are present in a soil, they *may not* be available to a plant if the pH is much too high or much too low. The reason for this is that a pH at either extreme chemically binds the nutrients to the soil.

Excessive soil acidity or alkalinity generally exists in areas of high or low rainfall. Areas of low rainfall have excessive amounts of calcium in the soil, which creates an alkaline condition. In areas of high rainfall, most of the alkaline materials have been washed out of (leached) the soil, leaving an acid condition. Most plants flourish in a slightly acid soil (pH 6 to 7). However, some plants (e.g. azaleas and rhododendrons) are acid-loving and others (e.g. currants and gooseberries) are alkaline-loving.

Excessively acid soils can be made less so by adding agricultural lime. Excessively alkaline soils can be made more acid by adding sulfur (or a sulfur compound, such as aluminum sulfate) or acid peat. A soil test will determine how much to add. The popular practice of indiscriminately adding lime to the soil is a foolish one.

Fertility

Most soils do not provide enough nutrients to maintain the lush growth that we demand of our plants. Deficiencies can be corrected by the "shotgun approach," in which a combination fertilizer is applied in the hope of eliminating any existing deficiencies. A more intelligent approach is to have the soil tested, and apply only those nutrients of which the soil is deficient.

Soil deficiencies can also be detected by noting deficiency symptoms on growing plants. The following chart gives some specific symptoms and their remedies. Reading deficiency symptoms correctly demands a certain amount of experience and is something which the novice gardener might not want to trust himself to do.

Nutrient deficiencies can be corrected by applying either organic or commercial (chemical) fertilizers. Organic fertilizers should usually be

Nutrient Deficiency Symptoms

Plant roots absorb mineral elements from the soil and use them for plant growth. A lack of any needed mineral will cause poor development and result in sick plants. This table gives some specific deficiency symptoms and their causes.

	DEFICIENT NUTRIENT				
SYMPTOM	Nitrogen	Phosphorus	Potassium	Iron	Magnesium
Sickly, yellowish-green color of leaves	X				
Slow growth, dwarfing	X	X		X	
Drying of lower leaves	X		X		
Purplish leaves, stems, and branches		X			
Poor flower production		X			
Mottling, spotting, streaking, or curling of leaves, starting on lower leaves			X		
A general loss of green color on lower leaves, veins remain green, streaking of yellowish-green throughout foliage					X
Foliage pale yellow, general chlorosis, veins remain green until leaf turns nearly white				X	

supplemented by commercial fertilizers since the decomposition process which organic fertilizers must undergo generally consumes some of the soil's nutrients.

Commercial fertilizer bags are marked with groups of three numbers: 5-10-5, 8-8-8, 10-10-10, etc. From left to right, these numbers designate the percentage of nitrogen (N), phosphorus (P), and potassium (K) in the bag. (Potassium is also designated as potash.) These numbers refer only to the three major elements needed by all plants. If some of the trace elements, such as iron or magnesium, are needed, additional applications must be made. The fine print on the fertilizer bag will tell whether or not trace elements have been included.

Apply fertilizers according to soil test recommendations. If equal amounts of nitrogen, phosphorus and potassium are needed, 8-8-8, 10-10-10, 13-13-13, or any other balanced fertilizer can be applied. (The only difference between 8-8-8 and 10-10-10 is that the latter is more concentrated than the former. If precision spreaders are not available, it is sometimes more convenient to use a less concentrated fertilizer (which is more easily controlled). If one or more of the three basic elements (N,P,K) is not needed, specialized preparations are available. Consult the Appendix for additional information on fertilizers.

Organic fertilizers can generally be mixed with soil when planting. More care must be taken with commercial fertilizers; direct contact with plant parts causes burning. Commercial fertilizers should always be spread as evenly as possible to minimize burning.

Pest Control

Even when a plant is located in a soil containing the proper nutrients and texture, is exposed to the proper amount of sunlight, and receives the proper amount of moisture, all of the work will have been for nothing if insects, disease, and weeds are not controlled.

The Gardener's Hint Book contains suggested chemical, biological and mechanical means to control specific insects and diseases. But, the first step toward pest control is identification of the problem. Once the problem has been determined, remember never to apply a chemical treatment without reading the label on the container. The result might be worse than the original condition.

The need for an all-purpose pesticide that will control *most* insects and diseases often arises. The following is a mixture recommended by the Extension Service of the University of Arkansas:

Substance	Form	Amt./3 gals.
Methoxychlor *or*	50% wettable powder	6 tablespoons
Sevin (carbaryl) *plus*	50% wettable powder	9 tablespoons
Malathion *plus*	25% wettable powder	6 tablespoons
Captan *plus*	50% wettable powder	9 tablespoons
Benomyl	50% wettable powder	½ of 1 tablespoon

Weeds can take all of the joy out of gardening. They not only reduce the beauty of a garden, but sap the soil of needed nutrients and moisture.

The cheapest and simplest way to control weeds is to remove them manually or with a hoe. The task can be eased if a power cultivator is available. Applying mulches—such as pine bark, black plastic, stone chips, and wood chips—will control weeds, conserve moisture, and sometimes improve the appearance of a landscape. If the situation dictates it, use a chemical weed control *(herbicide)*. *However,* herbicides can sometimes retard or kill the plants they aim to help, so *never* use a weed killer unless you are sure that it is recommended for your situation.

Having read this far, you are ready to busy yourself with some gardening. The rest of the book contains practical hints geared to taking the guesswork out of gardening. I think that you will find the information helpful and easy to understand.

Happy gardening!

CHAPTER ONE

Designing and Executing a Landscape

Overview

Outdoor living has become an important part of the American lifestyle. To enjoy it to the fullest requires careful planning of outdoor areas. In effect, when a yard is landscaped, outdoor "rooms" are being created. It is, therefore, necessary to develop a "floor plan," similar to one that would.be prepared for a house. The first step in preparing such a plan is to **sketch the house and lot on a large sheet of paper** and experiment with various arrangements of the outdoor areas.

It is important—especially in built-up areas—**that landscapes blend in with the environment.** A thoroughly modern landscape—no matter how well designed—will look out of place among a row of early American landscapes. There are, however, means of compromise. Don't be overly bound by tradition.

A convenient way to decorate an outdoor area is to **use the landscape to mirror the house style.** A colonial landscape featuring boxwoods (or yews), lilacs, English hawthorn, and wisteria, would greatly enhance an early American style house. Exotic trees—such as the purple-leaf beech, the empress tree, and the weeping mulberry—blend well with the ginger-bread trim on Victorian houses. Victorian houses also provide a nice background for magnolias, rhododendrons, and other showy, broad-leaved trees and shrubs. Contemporary homes can be landscaped according to a variety of themes. The "desert" (using rocks, gravel, and plants), "oriental" (using rocks, small paths, miniature plants, and bridges), and "natural" (using native plants) themes are favorites. It is important that whichever theme is chosen be carried through to completion. **Mixed-style landscapes rarely succeed.**

By first developing an overall plan, harmonious results will be achieved. Probably **the greatest obstacle to achieving a successful landscape is impulsive buying;** a beautiful plant bought on impulse and planted at random in an area with which it is incompatible creates difficulties. Once the plant has become established, most of us lack the heart to uproot it, regardless of how it affects the overall landscape. Remember, **it generally takes a number of years to complete a landscape.** So, avoid impulsive buying.

In planning, first **determine your personal needs.** Consider the family activities. Is a play or rest area needed? Do you want a flower or

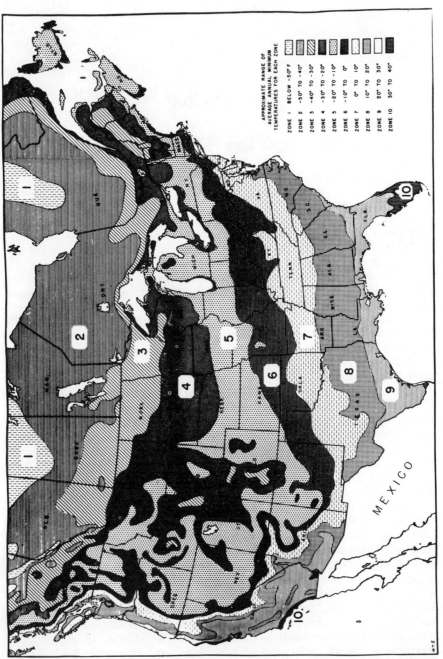

Plant hardiness zone map.

In purchasing plants, especially by mail, hardiness zones are often referred to. In most cases, it is unwise to purchase a plant if you live in a lower-numbered zone than the plant is adapted.

vegetable garden? If your house has already been landscaped, it will be necessary to decide to what extent you are willing to alter what already exists.

Play areas should be grassed, partially shaded, and observable from the house. Plan the area so that it can be easily altered as the children grow up.

Flower and vegetable gardens should be located where they receive full sunlight most of the day. They also require fertile, well-drained soil.

Outdoor patios should be situated where there is good access to food preparation areas in the house.

As the outdoor areas are arranged, consider their appearance both from the house and from the street. **Try to achieve a measure of balance in your planning.** Curved lines are natural and restful, whereas angular lines, unless perfectly executed, can be unnerving.

Check the drainage and soil fertility before undertaking any large landscaping projects. Plants cannot be expected to survive unless these two factors are favorable. If drainage is poor, it may be necessary to lay underground tiles and gravel to allow escape for excess water. If the soil is too heavy or too light, it can be improved by the addition of organic matter and sand.

Don't destroy surrounding woods when building a house. Instead, work with the woodland, carefully shaping it to meet your needs. Otherwise, you may learn too late that mature trees are usually irreplaceable within a lifetime.

After the landscape has been designed and the soil prepared, it is time to select appropriate plants. **Choose only plants that are adapted to your geographic region** and your own site. Even if you plan to do all landscaping yourself, it would be sensible to go over your list of plants with an expert before buying.

Remember that **plants grow, so give them room.** If you don't care for the bare look around a seedling, consider surrounding it with a flower bed until the tree begins to assume size.

Grass is the most common choice for covering the yard, but consider such alternatives as pachysandra, myrtle, juniper, mulches, gravel, brick tile, wood, and slate. Don't be one of those people who plants a new lawn every year even though soil conditions are not suited to a lawn.

Landscaping can often be frustrating, with novel ideas slow in coming. To stimulate your imagination, **study other well-landscaped areas for ideas.** Free advice is available from local nurserymen and extension horticulturists. If you can afford them, landscape architects can enhance your property's beauty and value.

Fences, paths, walls, pools, and patios can add variety and beauty to your home and garden. Design such structures to be both functional and aesthetically pleasing.

Walls constructed of stone, brick, masonry, and wood can be attractive and fulfill a useful purpose in preventing erosion. **If walls are not constructed properly, they may require considerable maintenance.** No matter how high the wall, a foundation at least 12 inches deep is required to assure a firm base for the wall. The foundation can be constructed out of poured concrete or packed stone. In cold northern climates, dig to below the frost level. Walls should be at least 6 inches thick. Reinforcing is required if the wall is more than 5 feet high. Do not use bricks for retaining walls unless they are less than 3 feet high and the ground behind them is stable.

Fences should be constructed out of sturdy and durable materials. Set posts into the ground at least 3 feet deep and about 8 feet apart. Use nothing less than a 2-inch by 4-inch rails and stringers for fencing. If the fence is to remain unpainted, redwood and cypress are the materials of choice. Never use fir, hemlock, spruce, or ponderosa pine where there will be alternate wetting and drying of the wood. The design and type of fence you choose should blend with the architectural design of your house and garden. Otherwise ordinary homes can be made attractive by the choice of a proper fence. On the other hand, improperly chosen fences can detract from the natural design of some homes.

In constructing paths and walks, follow the natural traffic patterns in your yard and garden. Flagstone paths and walks are preferred to masonry; they appear more natural. Good drainage is necessary beneath walks or paths. Unless the soil is extremely sandy, a 10- to 12-inch base of cinders or gravel should be placed under flagstone or masonry walks, paths, and patios.

A small garden pool can make an attractive addition to a garden. Be sure that it blends into its surroundings. Pre-fabricated plastic or metal pools are recommended. It is possible to build your own pool by digging a hole, adding drainage material, and forming the walls with concrete. But inasmuch as leakage often results, such construction is not recommended.

Section One

GENERAL ADVICE

Advice on Landscaping

Your tax dollars pay the salaries of experts who can offer good, free, technical advice on landscaping. Look under "United States Department of Agriculture" in the telephone directory to locate your local County Agricultural Extension Service. This service can put you in touch with a horticulturist with whom you can confer on landscaping, and who will provide you with a variety of free or low-cost publications. Large urban areas, such as Manhattan in New York City, often do not have Extension services. For those who live in these areas, help is usually available from adjoining counties.

✓   ✓   ✓

Ask Landscape Contractors for Specifications

Misunderstandings sometimes arise when home owners do not ask landscape contractors for specifications. Make sure there is a *written* agreement between you and the contractor before proceeding with work of any kind. The price quoted should include details on grading, tilling, fertilization, seeding (specifically stating seed mixture and amount), and exact plant types and sizes.

✓   ✓   ✓

Check Ordinances on Swimming Pools

If you are planning construction of a swimming pool, check for possible local restrictions. Some communities have requirements for fencing, water filtration, and insurance which can greatly increase the final cost of construction.

✓   ✓   ✓

Restrictions on Fences and Hedges

Some communities have restrictions on the use of fences and hedges along property borders. Common restrictions involve height and type of construction. Some areas ban fences entirely. A thorough check of existing restrictions can save money and time.

✓   ✓   ✓

Landscaping Small Lots

Small lots require extra special planning. Keep service areas, including driveways and trash storage areas, to a minimum and locate them on the north side of the house. Leave the sun-filled southern areas for gardening.

✓   ✓   ✓

Gardening on Corner Lots

With proper planning, corner lots offer a unique opportunity for private gardening. They allow for the arrangement of house and garage so that each faces a different street. The L-shaped barrier that is formed is an ideal place for a private garden. Planned otherwise, a corner lot can become quite public.

✓   ✓   ✓

Garages on Small Lots

Where a garage is situated is important for conserving space. When garages face the street, they occupy the least space. If garage doors do not face the street, considerable potential garden space is taken up by the driveway.

✓   ✓   ✓

Look Critically at Your Landscape

You are not married to your landscape. Cast an occasional critical eye at it and, if a plant has lost its appeal or ceased to perform its function, consider eliminating or replacing it. Do the same with plants that require more care than you can give.

Section Two

PREPARING FOR LANDSCAPING

Grading

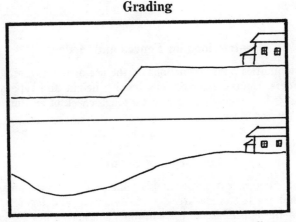

If lawns are not graded properly, rapid water run-off, causing erosion, will result. After the grass grows in, it will be exceedingly difficult to mow without scalping the lawn. To avoid problems caused by abrupt changes in grade (top illustration), sharp edges should be rounded (bottom illustration).

✔   ✔   ✔

Save Topsoil

Bulldozers generally make 2 visits to home construction sites: the first when the machine excavates the foundation and the second when the yard is filled and graded. During the first visit, topsoil should be piled conveniently so that it can be respread on top when the land is graded.

✔   ✔   ✔

Grading with an Extension Ladder

Grading doesn't always require the use of costly machinery. If the soil is loose, light grading can be done with a 10- or 15-foot section of an exten-

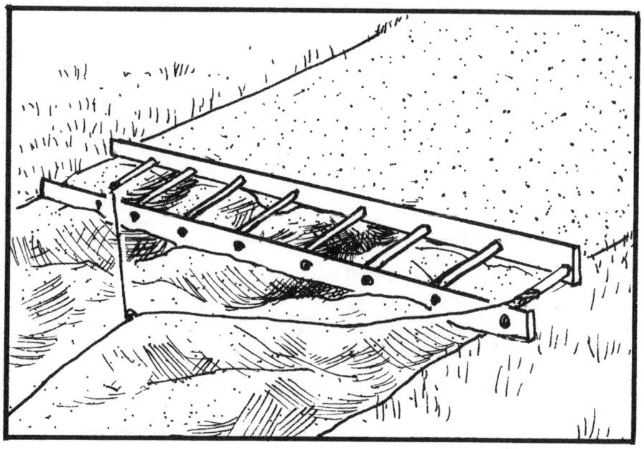

sion ladder. Tie a rope to the top rung (at the side rail) and tie the other end to the lowest rung. By dragging the ladder section sideways, the high places will be shaved off. Loose dirt is picked up between the two side rails, carried along, and automatically dumped into the low spots.

✓ ✓ ✓

Taking a Soil Sample

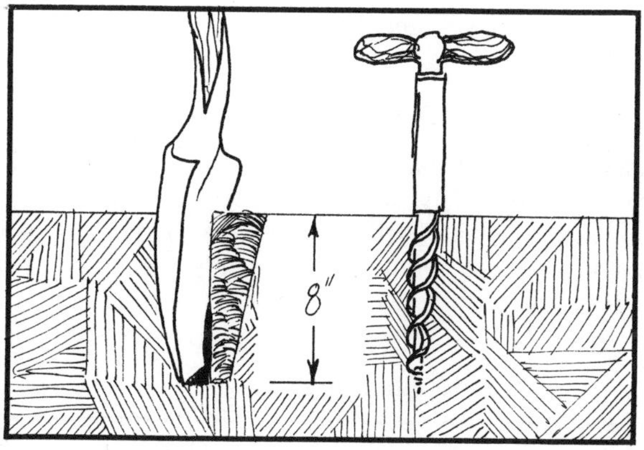

It is important to test your soil very early in the landscaping process. The procedure used to take a soil sample can affect the soil analysis. Don't just scoop up surface soil. Take a cross section sample about 8 inches deep, using a shovel or soil augur. Take a half dozen or so random samples throughout the garden areas and mix them. Place a ½-pint sample in a plastic bag, which can be mailed in a cardboard box or book mailer.

✓ ✓ ✓

Testing Soil Texture

It is important to know the texture of a soil so that you can choose adaptable plants for your garden. The soil texture is determined by the

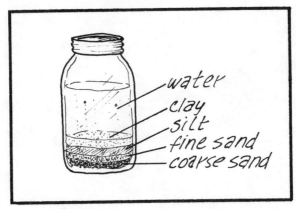

size and arrangement of its particles. To test a soil for its texture, put ¼ cup of soil in a pint jar. Fill it almost to the top with water. Seal and slush the mixture lightly for 30 seconds. Slush it once again and set it aside until the water clears (about 3 or 4 days).

Compare the widths of the various layers. If the soil contains more than 50% sand, it is light, sandy soil. If it contains more than 50% silt (extra fine clay particles) and almost no clay, it is a heavy, silt loam. If it contains more than 25% clay and 25% silt, it is a clay soil. An ideally-textured soil contains 40% sand, 40% silt, and 20% clay.

✦   ✦   ✦

Black Soil Isn't Always Fertile

Most people think that black soil is always fertile. This is not necessarily true. Blackness in soil merely means that the soil contains carbon. It is possible that a black soil was fertile at one time but has been robbed of its nutrients by repeated crop production. The only way to be certain of a soil's fertility is to test it or to observe how crops grow in it.

✦   ✦   ✦

Standing Water

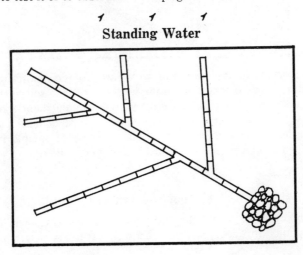

If you find that water does not drain from your property after rainy weather, consider laying drainage tile underground to carry the water away. An efficient way of achieving good drainage is to arrange the tile in a herringbone pattern as illustrated. Tile should be placed in ditches deep enough not to interfere with cultivation (at least 8 inches) and should slope toward the drainage ditch or gravel pit. One-half inch should be left between tile sections for water to enter. The tiles should be covered with a minimum of 2 inches of gravel before soil is added to fill in the ditch. Field tile for this purpose can be purchased from building suppliers. Perforated plastic tubing can also be used.

Section Three

ESTABLISHING OUTDOOR AREAS

Consider the View from Your House

Too often, we landscape more for the pleasure of our neighbors than ourselves. View your land from inside your house as well as from the street. Design areas that make pleasing scenes from windows and doors. Before deciding on a landscape, view the area from every angle—indoors *and* outdoors. You will find that it will take several viewings to know your property well.

✓   ✓   ✓

Plant Cautiously at Driveway Entrances

Tall plants at driveway entrances can obstruct the view of drivers leaving and entering. Plant only low-growing plants within 15 feet of driveway entrances. Residents on corner lots also have a special responsibility not to obstruct the view of intersections from the road. Keep all plants, walls, and fences well below eye level for at least 15 feet back from an intersection.

✓   ✓   ✓

Face Flower Borders South or Southwest

Most flowers need full sunlight. To get maximum sunlight, flower borders should face south or southwest. If this is not possible, keep the background of the border as low as possible to let in light.

✓   ✓   ✓

Gardening on the South Side of Houses

Spring can be brought to your home earlier by planting very early blooming bulbs, perennials, and shrubs on the warmer south side of the house.

Crocuses, snowdrops, winter jasmine, and other early bloomers planted here can be enjoyed a full week or two in advance of those planted elsewhere. Chrysanthemums and other late flowers also escape frost longer when planted on the south side of buildings.

↗   ↗   ↗

Fit Flower Beds into Surrounding Landscape

Flower beds or borders are much more attractive if they fit well into the surrounding landscape. One way to accomplish this is to choose flower colors that blend with the blooms of nearby trees, shrubs, and vines. White flowers of candytuft and white dwarf iris blend nicely with a background of white flowering bridal wreath. Pleasurable effects can be created by allowing peonies and bearded iris to harmonize with nearby climbing roses.

↗   ↗   ↗

Athletic Courts Should Be North-South

The direction in which you arrange an athletic court is important. Courts for tennis and basketball should be oriented north-south, rather than east-west, so that the low morning or afternoon sun does not annoy the players.

↗   ↗   ↗

Outdoor Areas Detached from the House

Most outdoor terraces and patios are attached to the house. Don't overlook the possibility of establishing such areas in other parts of the yard. Sometimes, outdoor patios are very functional if built around a large tree which supplies shade and shelter. Such areas can be selected to provide more privacy than patios attached to or near the house.

↗   ↗   ↗

Construct Patios at House Level

Plan on constructing patios at the same level as the door leading into the house. Considerable traffic occurs between the house and the patio, and transporting food, furniture, etc., on level ground is both safer and easier.

↗   ↗   ↗

Avoid Square and Rectangular Patios

Add interest to your landscape by making the patio a shape other than the traditional square or rectangle. Curved lines are more interesting and blend better with natural landscapes. If you plan on screening in your patio, though, it would be better to stick to a square or rectangular shape. Screening a curved patio will be prohibitive.

↗   ↗   ↗

Leave Access to the Back Yard

When designing large lots, planners often neglect to consider access to the rear for trucks, large machines, or vehicles. If an extension of the driveway is undesirable, a 10-foot-wide swath of lawn should be left free of shrubbery to allow passage.

✓   ✓   ✓

Wait before Constructing Outdoor Barbecues

Permanent outdoor barbecues can sometimes become a permanent obstacle. It is well to utilize inexpensive portable grills for a season. Test different areas of the yard for the best location.

✓   ✓   ✓

Avoid Brightly Colored Outdoor Furniture

Brightly colored garden furniture has recently been introduced. Such furniture competes with flowers and should be avoided. The safest colors to use are those that blend with nature: tints of gray or green, buff, or slate blue.

✓   ✓   ✓

Accent Garden Textures with Lights

Many interesting textures in a garden can be accented by using lights. Patterned tree bark or masonry can be emphasized by placing a light source parallel to the trunk and 4 to 10 inches from the surface, aimed at an angle. Trees with unusual textured bark include: paper birch, saucer magnolia, and red birch.

✓   ✓   ✓

Lighted Lily Pads for Pools

An attractive way to light a pool for evening enjoyment is to use lighted lily pads. A lighted lily pad consists of a light bulb in a waterproof socket placed beneath an artificial floating lily leaf. They are available at major garden centers.

Section Four

DESIGNING A LANDSCAPE

Consider Maintenance before Buying

Some landscape plants require much more care than others. Consider this when selecting plants so that gardening will be a joy rather than a chore. Which hedge plants you select, for example, should be determined with maintenance responsibilities in mind. Privet is sometimes selected because it is inexpensive. However, it requires pruning at least twice a year. The slightly more expensive tallhedge requires no special care after planting.

✓   ✓   ✓

The Importance of Proportion

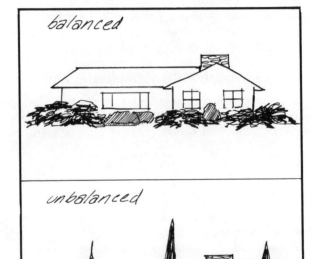

Houses, plants, and other structures should be kept in balance with one another. For example, landscape a ranch house with informal spreading shrubs, such as spreading yews, which carry out the visual horizontal lines of the house. Upright shrubs would conflict with the horizontal lines of the house. Tall trees around such a house would dwarf it.

✓   ✓   ✓

The Importance of Repetition

The same plants, groupings of plants, or texture combinations should be used more than once within a landscape. Such arrangements add unity and cohesion. In repeating plantings, however, avoid perfect balance—that is, plantings that are mirror images of one another. Such arrangements give a

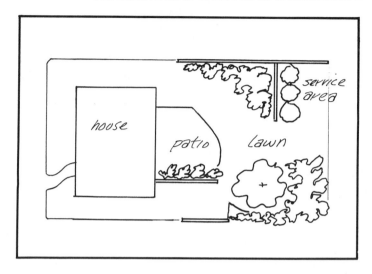

formal, unnatural effect. In the illustrated landscape, the curved lines of the groups of plants roughly correspond to those of the patio. Had the planting areas mirrored the patio exactly, a less pleasing result would have resulted.

✓   ✓   ✓

The Importance of Plant Forms

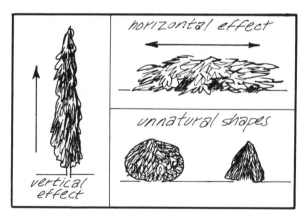

The form or shape of a fully developed plant must be borne in mind when selecting plants to be used in the landscape. A column-shaped plant, for instance, draws the eye upward. A creeping plant draws the eye to the ground. Round or pyramidal shapes look unnatural in most landscapes and should be used sparingly.

✓   ✓   ✓

EVERGREEN

CONIFERS

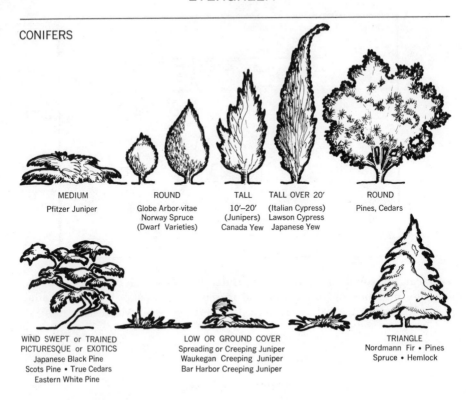

MEDIUM	ROUND	TALL	TALL OVER 20'	ROUND
Pfitzer Juniper	Globe Arbor-vitae Norway Spruce (Dwarf Varieties)	10'–20' (Junipers) Canada Yew	(Italian Cypress) Lawson Cypress Japanese Yew	Pines, Cedars

WIND SWEPT or TRAINED PICTURESQUE or EXOTICS
Japanese Black Pine
Scots Pine • True Cedars
Eastern White Pine

LOW OR GROUND COVER
Spreading or Creeping Juniper
Waukegan Creeping Juniper
Bar Harbor Creeping Juniper

TRIANGLE
Nordmann Fir • Pines
Spruce • Hemlock

BROADLEAF EVERGREENS

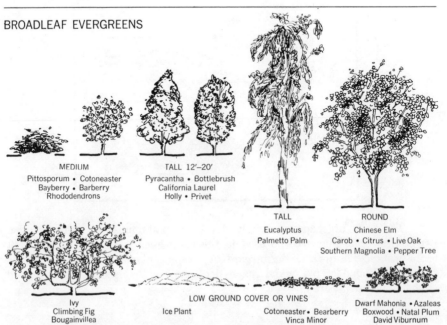

MEDIUM
Pittosporum • Cotoneaster
Bayberry • Barberry
Rhododendrons

TALL 12'–20'
Pyracantha • Bottlebrush
California Laurel
Holly • Privet

TALL
Eucalyptus
Palmetto Palm

ROUND
Chinese Elm
Carob • Citrus • Live Oak
Southern Magnolia • Pepper Tree

Ivy
Climbing Fig
Bougainvillea

LOW GROUND COVER OR VINES
Ice Plant

Cotoneaster • Bearberry
Vinca Minor

Dwarf Mahonia • Azaleas
Boxwood • Natal Plum
David Viburnum

The drawings on these pages offer specific plants according to plant shape.

DECIDUOUS

TREES

ROUND—GLOBE—SHAPED

Arnold Crabapple • Japanese Maple
Mulberry • Green Ash • Pistachio
Hawthorne Sycamore

FASTIGIATE TREE OR COLUMNAR TREE

Dawyck Beech • Siberian Crabapple
English Oak • Poplar • Sargent Cherry
Sentry Ginkgo • Lombardy Poplar
Pyramidal European Birch
Linden

BROAD OVAL TREE

Bradford Pear
Sugar Maple • Labarnum
European Mountain Ash

FAN SHAPED—HORIZONTAL BRANCHING

Flowering Dogwood
Silk Tree • Redbud
Amur Maple

CONICAL TREE OR TRIANGLE

American Sweetgum
Pin Oak

SHRUBS

LOW 1½′–5′

February Daphne • Bush Cinquefoil
Anthony Waterer Spirea
Japanese Barberry

MEDIUM 5′–12′

Snowball • Forsythia • English Privet

TALL 12′–18′

Crapemyrtle • Spindle Tree
Russian Olive • Lilac

LOW, GROUND COVER OR VINES

Prostrate Pyracantha

Lantana

GROUND COVER 6″–18″

Cranberry Cotoneaster
Carpet Bugle • Memorial Rose
Aaronsbeard St. Johnswort

VINES

Wisteria • Passionflower • Bittersweet
Virginia Creeper • Clematis • Grapes

Avoid Unnatural Accents

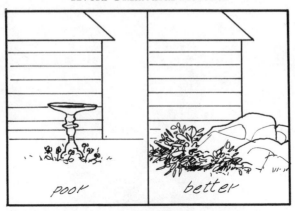

Gardens and yard areas can sometimes be enhanced by the addition of an artifact as a point of interest. However, don't use artifacts such as sundials, gazing globes, birdbaths, statues, or other mass-produced, commercial products as primary focal points. Simple fountains, colorful plants in wooden tubs, and large, interestingly-shaped rocks are more appropriate to preserve a natural environment.

Designing with Goose-Eggs

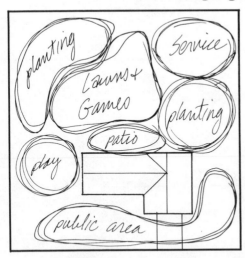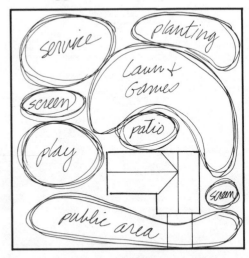

After you have decided in a general way on the outdoor areas you want, experiment on paper with their arrangement. A simple way to do this is to make goose-egg sketches to block out the different areas. Experiment with a variety of arrangements (two examples are shown). Ask yourself whether the various areas that you have sketched are compatible with each other. If they are not, rearrange them to suit. Your arrangement must take into account the terrain of the lot and any existing plantings. Think of the traffic patterns from area to area as you would the traffic patterns in your house. Give this stage of landscaping much thought. It is easier and less expensive to rearrange plants on paper than to do so after they have been planted.

Working Out a Landscape

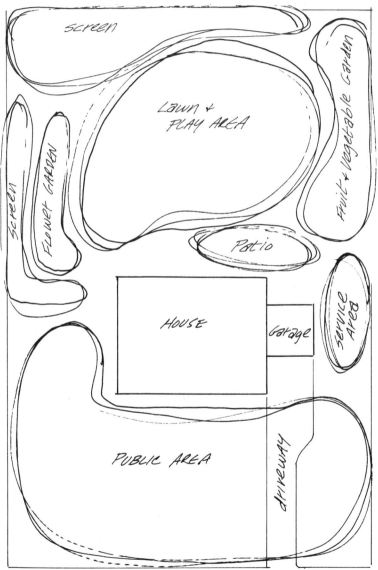

A goose-egg study for a 160 x 240 foot plot.

Once the arrangement of outdoor areas has been decided, you are ready to choose specific plants for these areas. Your choice of plants is limited to those that suit your climate as well as your budget. Study the plants that have been used in other landscapes in your neighborhood or locale. Check with the local nurseryman as to what plants are available and what he

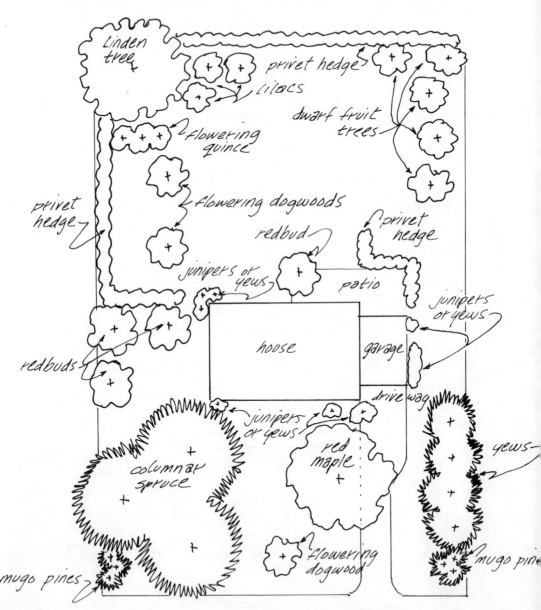

One way of carrying out the preceding goose-egg study.

recommends. In general, the public area of a landscape should contain one or more large shade trees; service areas should be screened with dense plantings or fencing; the lawn and game area should be grassed and left open; gardening areas should receive full sunshine.

To give a specific example, assume that you have studied your area and

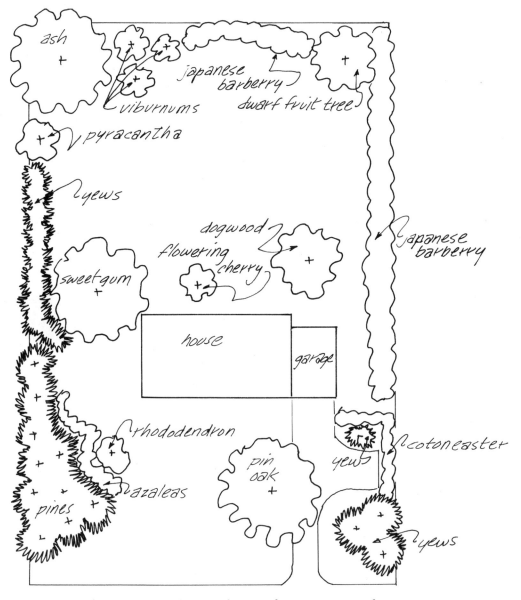

Another way of carrying out the preceding goose-egg study.

come up with the illustrated goose-egg study for a plot 160 feet by 240 feet. You must now block out the area to scale (graph paper is useful), and choose specific plants. The choice is almost without limit. Two possibilities are offered here. One suggestion: in sketching out areas, be sure to outline the area the plant is expected to cover *when it matures*. This will avoid the all too common picture post card house which turns into a jungle.

↗   ↗   ↗

WHAT SHALL I PLANT?
Five Possibilities for Each of Ten Situations

For a Quick-Growing Screen
Arborvitae
Canadian hemlock
Douglas fir
Norway spruce
Poplar

For a Formal Clipped Hedge
Amur maple
Arborvitae
Canadian hemlock
Privet
Yew (upright)

For an Informal Hedge
Forsythia
Honeysuckle (bush)
Juniper
Lilac
Yew (spreading)

For a Wet Location
Canadian hemlock
Red maple
Viburnum
White ash
Willow

For a Dry Location
Goldenrain tree
Hackberry
Scarlet oak
Tatarian honeysuckle
White pine

Berry Bearers
Cotoneaster
Euonymus (various varieties)
Flowering crabapple
Mountain ash
Viburnum

Small or Dwarf Border Plants
Andromeda
Cotoneaster
Euonymus
Juniper (spreading)
Pachysandra

For Partially Shaded Locations
Azalea
Canadian hemlock
English ivy
Holly
Rhododendron

For Smoky and Dusty Areas
Austrian pine
Ginkgo
Locust
London planetree
Norway maple

Trees for Streets
American linden
Kwanzan flowering cherry
Red oak
Sugar maple
White ash

More possibilities will be found in the chapters ahead.

Plants Attractive to Birds

Sunflower—*Helianthus* spp.
Bird use: 52 species
Ornamental value: Tall annual plant; has large yellow flowers.
Adaptation: Well-drained soil; sun.
In bloom: June–August. *Ripe seed:* August–September
Height: 4 to 8 ft.
Sources: Commercial seed stores.

Crabapple—*Malus* spp.
Bird use: 29 species
Ornamental value: Small to medium-size trees; showy, white to pink blooms; red, purple, orange, or yellow fruits.
Adaptation: Well-drained soil; sun and light shade.
In bloom: April–May. *In fruit:* September–April
Height: 10 to 30 ft.
Sources: Commercial nurseries, grafting, budding.

Elderberry—*Sambucus* spp.
Bird use: 50 species
Ornamental value: Tall shrubs; flat, whitish flower clusters; red to purple-black fruits.
Adaptation: Moist to well-drained soil; sun to shade.
In bloom: May–July. *In fruit:* July–October
Height: 5 to 8 ft.
Sources: Commercial nurseries.

American Cranberrybush—*Viburnum trilobum*
Bird use: 28 species
Ornamental value: Tall upright shrub; showy flat clusters of whitish flowers; glossy scarlet fruit clusters.
Adaptation: Deep, moist to well-drained soil; sun to light shade.
In bloom: May–June. *In fruit:* September–May
Height: 8 to 12 ft.
Sources: Commercial nurseries, some State nurseries, wild transplants or cuttings.

Cherry—*Prunus* spp.
Bird use: 49 species
Ornamental value: Variable forms; shrubs, small to large trees; small fine-toothed leaves, yellow in fall; showy white flower clusters or drooping spikes; small, bright-red to black fruits.
Height: shrub, 5 to 15 ft.; tree, 20 to 75 ft.
Adaptation: Moist to dry soil; sun to light shade.
In bloom: April–June. *In fruit:* Variable with species, June–November.
Sources: Commercial nurseries, wild transplants.

Wild Plum—*Prunus americana*
Bird use: 16 species
Ornamental value: Large shrub to small tree; suited to large yards or fields; spreads by suckers to form clumps; fragrant pink and white flowers; hardy red or yellow fruits.
Adaptation: Moist to well-drained loamy soil; sun.
In bloom: April–May. *In fruit:* July–October
Height: 10 to 30 ft.
Sources: Commercial nurseries, wild transplants.

Cotoneaster—*Cotoneaster spp.*
Bird use: 6 species
Ornamental value: Medium-size shrub; usually planted as a hedge but also as ground cover; dark-green leaves turning red-gold in fall; small pink or white flowers; showy red, orange, or black fruits.
Adaptation: Moist to well-drained soil; sun.
In bloom: May–June. *In fruit:* September–November
Height: 2 to 10 ft.
Sources: Commercial nurseries.

Tatarian Honeysuckle—*Lonicera tatarica*
Bird use: 18 species
Ornamental value: Large shrub; pink to yellow-white blooms; yellow to red fruits.
Adaptation: Well-drained to dry soil; sun to light shade.
In bloom: May–June. *In fruit:* July–September
Height: 5 to 15 ft.
Sources: Commercial nurseries.

Redcedar—*Juniperus virginiana*
Bird use: 25 species
Ornamental value: Medium-size coniferous tree (many varieties); dense, green to blue-green needles; small, dusty-blue, berrylike cones.
Adaptation: Moist to dry soil; sun to light shade.
In bloom: April–May. *In fruit:* September–May
Height: 15 to 40 ft.
Sources: Commercial nurseries, some State nurseries, and wild transplants.

Know the Mature Height and Spread of Plants

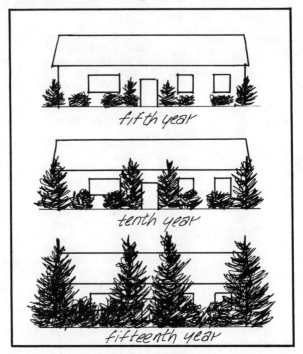

Although landscape plants may be in good proportion with a house when they are planted, they may later "swallow" their surroundings. Study the mature height and spread of plants, and choose them with this information in mind. The illustrated example shows what happens when height and spread is not considered.

Use Plants to Hide Awkward House Angles

Most houses have certain unbalanced or poorly designed elements, but they can be made more attractive by hiding or softening these areas with trees or shrubs. Examples of poorly designed elements include: poorly proportioned or blank walls; large porches; unattractive angles, jogs (recesses), or changes in roof lines; strong vertical chimney lines contrasting with dominant horizontal lines of the house; and jogs that have a "tacked on" appearance. The diagram shows a way in which unpleasing roof lines can be softened.

Landscaping a Ranch Style House

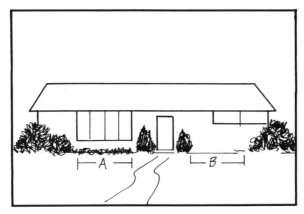

The tendency in landscaping ranch style houses is to cover the entire front with shrubs which tends to smother the house. Continuous plantings are not necessary unless the foundation is high and unsightly. A more open planting design is presented below: (A) under a large window, ground cover can be used to tie the corner plantings together; (B) grass can be allowed to extend to the house.

Landscaping Split Level Houses

Plants for split-level houses need to be chosen in scale with the "low side" (right) and the "high side" (left). A small tree on the high side, ties the house to the landscape and gives it balance.

✔   ✔   ✔

Trees That Frame a House Should Be in Balance

It is important that you choose trees that at maturity will be in proportion to the size of your house. Small trees around a large house make it appear even larger. Large trees around a small house make it appear smaller.

✔   ✔   ✔

Landscaping Two-Story Houses

Tall two-story houses can be made to look longer and wider by the proper choice and arrangement of landscape plants. This look can be achieved by extending the corner plantings beyond the house and arranging them toward the street. The planting at the corner of the house should be ½ to ⅔ of the distance to the second story. Gradually increase the height of the other plants as they extend away from the corner, ending in a small tree.

Such an arrangement draws the eye toward the front door and reduces the impact of the tall house.

*   *   *

Landscaping Long Lots

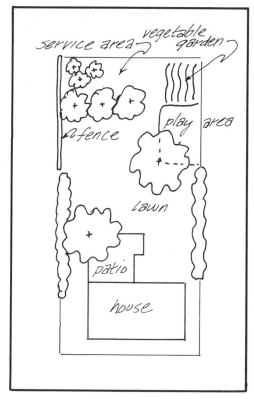

Lots that are considerably longer than wide present special problems in landscaping. Plantings made along the outline of the property only serve to accent the depth of the lot. Designs with plantings which protrude toward the center of the lot help reduce the illusion of depth. The landscape design illustrated divides a long lot into functional areas and reduces the feeling that the lot is excessively long.

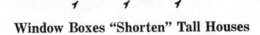

Window Boxes "Shorten" Tall Houses

Tall houses can be made to look shorter by using plants which draw the eye *away* from the full height of the house. One attractive way to do this is to construct flower boxes on the lower floor.

Plant Groups of Plants

A mistake commonly made by beginning gardeners is to scatter plants randomly over a large area. Single plants of any kind give a spotty effect in a garden. Plant in grouping of threes—even in the smallest of gardens.

Existing Plants Tell What Will Grow

It is often difficult to foretell what types of plants will grow well on your property. Existing plants can give some clues. For instance, a site with oak trees offers acid leaf mold and partial shade, conditions favorable for rhododendrons, mountain laurel, and other members of the heath family. If such water-loving trees as willows thrive on your site, conditions are probably moist. In this case, it would be wise to select plants adapted to moist conditions, or improve the drainage.

🌱   🌱   🌱

Don't Overplant

The most common error in landscaping is overplanting. Plants are often arranged so that they are attractive when planted, without considering how they will look several years later. As a rule, a planting that looks "right" the first year will soon be overcrowded. Remember that plants grow. To avoid a bare look in new landscapes, use annual flowers that can be phased out as the primary plants begin to mature.

🌱   🌱   🌱

Number of Trees Per Lot

The number of trees that should be planted depends on the size of one's lot and the mature size of the trees planted. About 5 small trees, such as flowering dogwood and white birch, are sufficient for a 50-foot x 100-foot lot. Two large trees, such as oak, maple, or linden, and two small trees could also be sustained on the same lot.

🌱   🌱   🌱

Relate Roof Line with Tree Shapes

Houses will tie in with a landscape better if the shape of the vegetation and the shape of the house correspond. Roof lines with pronounced pointed features should be repeated in the landscape with plant forms wherever possible. The little-leafed linden tree in the top drawing corresponds to the roof lines of the house. In the bottom drawing, pyramidal evergreens are used to repeat the shape of the gables of the house.

✓   ✓   ✓

Don't Plant Shade Trees Close to the House

Shade trees can become a nuisance if planted too close to the house. They will require pruning and can cause injury to the foundation. Shade trees should be planted a minimum of 15 feet from the house. You will also find that positioning shade trees off to the corners of the house will interfere least with views.

✓   ✓   ✓

Informal Gardens

Most of us want gardens that require little attention. If this is the case, plan an informal garden with plants that grow to their natural full shapes and do not require pruning. The beauty of natural growth patterns will be satisfying to the eye and the time saved in pruning can be used to good advantage elsewhere. Plants to avoid because of their formal appearance or the care they require are boxwoods, arborvitae, and columnar evergreens.

✓   ✓   ✓

Plants for Entranceways

Plants which flank the entranceway to a house should draw attention to the entrance yet not dominate it. Use small shrubs that grow under 5 feet tall. Plants to consider are cotoneaster, February daphne, dwarf cranberry-bush, glossy abelia, mugo pine, azaleas, and various species and varieties of yews.

✓   ✓   ✓

Softening the Sharp Corners of a House

Most houses have straight walls and sharp corners. Straight, sharp lines are not aesthetically pleasing and should be softened with plants. Large, informal plants set at the corners of houses will soften these lines. Dogwoods, crabapples, and white pines are good choices.

✓   ✓   ✓

Squat Evergreens for Foundation Plantings

A house is more effectively tied into its surroundings if squat, low-growing plants are placed around its foundation. Evergreens work well for this purpose. Tall-growing evergreens will block windows and require constant pruning. Some desirable low-growing evergreens are: Japanese hollies, azaleas, spreading yews, and mugo pines.

✁   ✁   ✁

Choose Accent Points for Foundation Planting

It is difficult to arrange plantings around the foundation so as to create a harmonious effect. Choose a few accent points and embellish the foundation planting around them. Such accents are best placed at corners, bay windows, porch pillars, and entrances. The largest and most conspicuous plants should be planted at these points. The space between them should be filled with smaller plants having softer textures.

✁   ✁   ✁

Avoid Coarse-Textured Plants in Small Areas

Coarse-textured plants should be used only in large areas because they make small areas appear even smaller. In contrast, plants with fine twigs, small or shiny leaves, and open growth habits visually increase the size of the area due to their fine texture.

✁   ✁   ✁

Planting under Wide Overhangs

Plants set under wide overhangs of buildings often die because of lack of water. If you must plant under an overhang, make sure that the plants receive sufficient water. Before making such plantings, remember the extra work that they will require. The overhang might also limit the amount of light available to plants. This can be either a positive or negative factor depending on whether the plant is sun-loving or shade-loving.

✁   ✁   ✁

Don't Frame Windows with Tall Shrubs

A common practice is to frame windows with tall shrubs on either side. Such an arrangement cuts the house into small sections and makes it appear smaller. To avoid this, use low-growing shrubs around windows.

✓   ✓   ✓

Consider the Sun

Many plants used in landscapes do not grow well because their light requirements were never considered. Sun-lovers are commonly placed in the shade. The following plants grow best in *full sun* and require at least 5 to 6 hours of full sun a day: most flowering annuals and perennials; most deciduous shrubs, vegetables, herbs; most fruits, tulips, gladioli, dahlias, roses; and all conifers except yews and hemlocks.

✓   ✓   ✓

Broad-Leaved Evergreens Not for Windy Corners

Winter winds, which dry out the leaves, are destructive to evergreen plants. Since the water in the soil is frozen during the winter, there is no way to replenish the moisture deficit in the leaves. For this reason, it is best to avoid planting broad-leaved evergreens on windy corners. Some better choices are the semi-evergreen spreading euonymus (*Euonymus patens*) or deciduous viburnums.

✓   ✓   ✓

Evergreen Shrubs for Winter Enjoyment

In northern climates, evergreen plants help keep the yard and garden "alive" during the winter. A wide array of foliage colors are available, from the deep green yews to the lighter green or grayish-green of shrub junipers. Disperse evergreen shrubs and trees throughout your planting groups rather than planting them in one area.

✓   ✓   ✓

Container Plants as Patio Accents

Often, porches and patios are enhanced by the softening effect of plants. Consider planting in containers, which will enable you to bring plants closer to the house and break the coldness of concrete and stone. Containers can be made out of plastic, wood, metal, or decorated concrete. This chapter contains a listing of plants that will thrive in containers.

✓   ✓   ✓

Nail Kegs as Containers

Unlikely containers stored around a house may make good receptacles for plants. Nail kegs are a good example. Remember to put holes in the

Container Plant Suggestions for Various Conditions

Plants for Low Temperature (50°–60° F. at Night)

Australian laurel	Citrus	Jerusalem-cherry
Azalea	Cyclamen	Kalanchoe
Babytears	Easter lily	Miniature holly
Black pepper	English ivy cultivars	Mother-of-thousands
Boxwood	Fatshedera	Oxalis
Bromeliads	Flowering maple	Primrose
Calceolaria	Fuchsia	Sensitive plant
Camellia	Geraniums	Spindle tree
Christmas begonia	German ivy	Vinca
Cineraria	Honeysuckle	White calla lily

Plants for Medium Temperature (60°–65° F. at Night)

Achimenes	Crown of thorns	Poinsettia
Amaryllis	Easter lily	Rose
Ardisia	English ivy cultivars	Shrimp plant
Avocado	Gardenia	Silk-oak
Bromeliads	Grape ivy	Ti Plant
Browallia	Hibiscus	Tuberous begonia
Chenille plant	Hydrangea	Velvet plant
Christmas cactus	Norfolk Island pine	Wax begonia
Chrysanthemum	Palms	Wax plant
Citrus	Peperomia	Yellow calla lily
Copperleaf	Pilea	

Plants for High Temperature (65°–75° F. at Night)

African-violet	Chinese evergreen	Golddust plant
Aphelandra	Croton	Philodendron
Arrowhead	Dracaena	Scindapsus (Pothos)
Australian umbrella tree	Episcia	Seersucker plant
Banded Maranta	Figs	Snake plant
Cacti and succulents	Gloxinia	Spathyphyllum
Caladium		Veitch screwpine

Plants That Will Withstand Abuse

Arrowhead	Fiddle-leaf fig	Pleomele
Australian umbrella tree	Grape ivy	Snake plant
Cast-iron plant	Heartleaf Philodendron	Spathyphyllum
Chinese evergreen	India-rubber plant	Trileaf Wonder
Crown of thorns	Jade plant	Tuftroot (*D. amoena*)
Devil's ivy	Ovalleaf Peperomia	Veitch screwpine
		Zebra plant

Plants for Extremely Dry Conditions

Bromeliads	Crown of thorns	Snake plant
Cacti	Ovalleaf Peperomia	Scindapsus (Pothos)
		Wandering-Jew

Vines and Trailing Plants for Totem Poles

Arrowhead	Grape ivy	Philodendron
Black pepper	Kangaroo vine	Scindapsus (Pothos)
Creeping fig	Pellionia	Syngonium
English ivy cultivars		Wax Plant

Plants for Hanging Baskets

African-violet	Fuchsia (some cultivars)	Philodendron (some species)
Anthericum	German ivy	Saxifraga
(Spider plant)	Goldfish plant	Scindapsus (pothos)
Asparagus fern	Grape ivy	Syngonium
Begonias (some types)	Honeysuckle	Trailing-coleus

Container Plant Suggestions for Various Conditions—Continued

Black pepper	Italian bellflower	Wandering-Jew
English ivy cultivars	Ivy geranium	Wax plant
Episcia	Peperomia (some species)	

Suggestions for Large Tubbed Specimens

Australian umbrella tree	Fiddle-leaf fig	Philodendrons
Dracaenas	India-rubber plant	Silk-oak
False-aralia	and cultivars	Tuftroot
Fatshedera	Palms	Veitch screwpine

For Special Exposures
SOUTH OR WEST WINDOWS

Amaryllis	Coleus	Oxalis
Azalea	Cyclamen	Poinsettia
Begonia (in winter)	Easter lily	Rose
Bloodleaf	Gardenia	Sweetflag
Cacti and succulents	Geranium	Tulip
Calla lily	Lily	Velvet plant

NORTH WINDOW

African-violet	Dracaena	Philodendron
(in summer)	Dumbcane	Piggyback plant
Anthericum	Fern	Pleomele
Arrowhead	Ivy	Rubber plant
Australian umbrella tree	Mother-of-thousands	Scindapsus (Pothos)
Babytears	Norfolk Island pine	Snake plant
Cast-iron plant	Peperomia	Tuftroot
Chinese evergreen		Wandering-Jew

EAST WINDOW

African-violet	Gloxinia	Serissa
Banded maranta	Ivy	Silk-oak
Caladium	Peperomia	Tuftroot
Dracaena	Philodendron	Veitch screwpine
Fatshedera	Rubber plant	Wandering-Jew
Fern	Scindapsus (Pothos)	Wax Plant

bottom for drainage. Dwarf mugo pines, cotoneasters, and flowering sedums are attractive in nail kegs.

Flue Tiles as Containers

Flue tiles, which come in a variety of colors and shapes, present intriguing possibilities as containers. Stand them directly on the soil and fill them with a good planting mix. Use ordinary round drain tile or square chimney flue tile. Both are available at lumber yards and building supply centers.

✔   ✔   ✔

Trees Compete with Garden Plants

If garden sites are too close to large trees, the plants will suffer by having to compete with the trees for sunlight and nutrients. The best rule of thumb is to not locate a garden in any area shaded by trees.

✔   ✔   ✔

Poisonous Plants in the Landscape

If children visit your home, it is a good idea not to include poisonous plants in your landscape. Fortunately, most poisonous plants are bitter to the taste and thereby discourage nibblers. Plants with milky juices, such as milkweeds and spurges, are potentially dangerous; they often cause severe irritation of the skin or alimentary canal if taken internally. The following plants may be harmful if eaten: *Datura* (all parts, seeds deadly); *Delphinium* (foliage); *Digitalis*-foxglove (foliage); *Euphorbia* (juice); *Lantana* (berries); *Nicotiana* (leaves); *Ricinus communis*—castor bean plant (all parts, seeds deadly).

Section Five

CONSTRUCTION IDEAS FOR LANDSCAPES

Mowing Bands

Bands of tile or brick placed along grassy edges and next to trees makes mowing much easier. Along grass edges, set the brick or tile flush with the lawn surface so that the mower can roll smoothly. A mowing band around trees eliminates time-consuming hand trimming and protects trees from mower damage.

✓   ✓   ✓

Sand-Filled Trenches for Easier Maintenance

Sand-filled trenches around trees, grass edges, and other plants make mowing and weed pulling easier. When trenches are used, you will avoid having to mow close to the plants, thereby reducing the chance of injury. When weeds develop in the trenched area, they can be pulled easily from the sand. To make trenches around trees, remove all sod and soil within a 2-foot ring around the base of the tree. The trench should be 4 to 6 inches deep and replaced with sand. The edge of the lawn along sidewalks and flower beds is also maintained more easily by creating sand-filled trenches.

✓   ✓   ✓

Apply Edging for a Neater Lawn

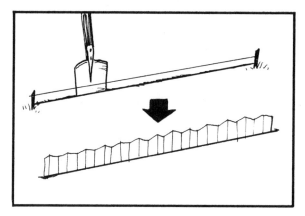

An edging of metal, wood, or brick to separate walks from grass, and flower beds from the rest of the yard makes for neater landscaping. To apply edging, place stakes along the line where it is needed and stretch a string between the stakes. Cut a furrow along the line with a spade. Then, neatly burrow the edging in the furrow. Brick or wood edging should be set in sand and buried to the top of the surface. Wood should be treated with a preservative before using.

✓   ✓   ✓

Avoid Saw-toothed Brick Edgings

Saw-toothed brick edgings are sometimes used to encircle or separate grass from flower beds. This type of arrangement should be avoided. A saw-toothed pattern is hard to lay, falls out of alignment, and is easy to trip over. Saw-toothed edgings also make mowing difficult.

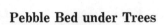

Pebble Bed under Trees

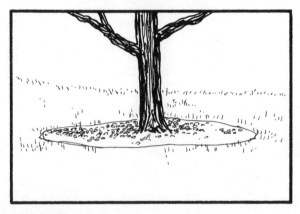

The shade and the root competition under trees is sometimes so severe that even ground cover plants do not grow well. Consider creating a pebble bed under such trees. Place edging material in a circle around the tree at the furthest extension of the branches (or, if the tree has a large spread, at a radius of 2 to 4 feet). Fill the enclosed area 2 inches deep with pebbles that blend with the landscape.

Construction of a Gravel Path

If gravel paths are not constructed properly, they require constant repair and attention. The diagram shows the proper way to construct a gravel path. Dig out the soil to a depth of 15 inches and replace it with rocks and course gravel. Elevate the middle slightly to improve surface drainage. The sides of the path are contained by concrete slabs or boards treated with a wood preservative.

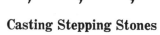

Casting Stepping Stones

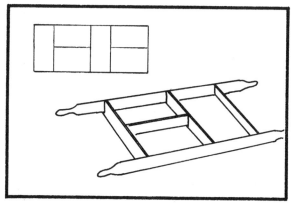

Attractive stepping stones for the garden area can be cast out of concrete. Build a form as illustrated. Grease the inside of the form with axle grease and position it where you want to lay the tiles. Fill the form with ready-mix concrete prepared according to directions. Lift off the form when the concrete is dry. Sand or gravel can be used to fill the crevices vacated by the form.

Brick Patterns for Walks and Patios

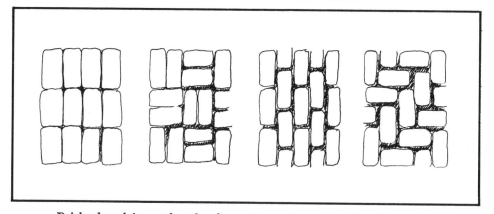

Bricks layed in sand make decorative walks and patios. Prepare a bed with 2 inches of gravel. Cover the gravel with 2 inches of sand. Embed the bricks in the sand and fill the cracks between bricks with additional sand. Some of the most popular patterns are shown in the diagram.

Picking Quality Flagstones

The color of flagstones indicates the quality. Poor quality stone is light gray in color and comes from near the surface of a shallow quarry. Its lack of density will result in chipping. High quality flagstone is a deep blue-gray color and its high density yields a chip-resistant and maintenance-free surface.

✓   ✓   ✓

Hard-Burned Bricks for Main Walks

If bricks are not hard-burned, they take up moisture and become hazardous to walk on. In the winter, the moisture freezes and makes them slick. Moss, which is slippery, grows on them in the warmer months, also making walking dangerous. Therefore, use less porous hard-burned bricks, rather than the cheaper more porous ones, for main walks.

✓   ✓   ✓

Use Brushed Concrete for Walkways

Brushed concrete is safer for walkways than smooth concrete. After pouring a normal mixture of concrete containing pebbles, and before it hardens, brush it with a stiff brush. Then hose it off. Repeat the procedure until some of the pebbles in the concrete are exposed.

✓   ✓   ✓

Curved Hedges

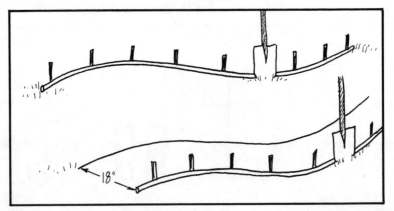

Hedges are often most attractive when planted in curved trenches along the border of a yard or garden. To help you design and lay out appealing curves, use a section of garden hose. After laying out a pleasing line, position the hose in place with wooden stakes. Cut along the hose line with a spade. By measuring 18 inches from the hose line at close intervals, a duplicate of the original curve will be achieved. The 18-inch swath will form the planting trench area. The chapter on shrubs and hedges will give specific information on what and how to plant.

❧   ❧   ❧

Tree Bench for Garden Visitors

A bench constructed around a tree can be an inviting garden feature. Construct the bench to stand on its own base. *Don't* attach it to the tree; it will have to be moved as the tree grows. Treat any part of the wood making contact with the soil with creosote.

❧   ❧   ❧

A Hinged Trellis

Trellises placed along the sides of buildings often create obstructions which make painting difficult. In order to avoid this problem, construct trellises that are hinged at the bottom so that they can be pulled away from the building for painting and then replaced. Plants can usually withstand the slight bending needed.

❧   ❧   ❧

Fencing the Garden

When fencing a garden to keep out animals, remember that some animals are diggers and can go under normal fencing. Bury garden fencing at least 6 inches to keep the diggers out.

Avoid Chain Link Fences

Chain link fences do not blend well into garden landscapes. Avoid chain link or wire fencing when privacy or screening is desired. Redwood and red cedar last as long as metal, cost less to install, and offer a greater variety of design.

Rock Gardens on Level Ground

Completely flat lots are usually not aesthetically pleasing. One way to add more interest to the landscape is to create rocky areas which appear natural. Place large rocks on a base of smaller stones or rubble for drainage. Rocky areas make attractive planting sites.

Rocks on a Slope

Rocks can be buried on slopes to prevent erosion and form planting pockets. More of the rock should be buried than is exposed. Each rock should be slanted so that the end *outside* of the soil is *a bit* higher than the end buried in the soil.

✓   ✓   ✓

Existing Rocks for Rock Gardens

Existing rocks can sometimes be incorporated into rock gardens. Before spending time and money removing rocks from your property, consider making them part of a rock garden.

✓   ✓   ✓

Retaining Walls that Promote Plant Growth

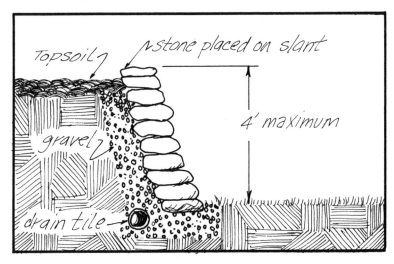

Border plants, grass, and shrubs sometimes do not grow well near excavated areas held by retaining walls. Often this is caused by poor construction of the retaining wall without regard to the requirements for plant growth. Plants are not provided with fertile soil and good drainage. The illustration shows the right way to construct retaining walls in relation to plant growth.

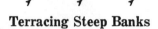

Terracing Steep Banks

It is sometimes impractical or too costly to build a wall to contain a steep bank. One solution is to terrace steep banks with 2 or 3 low walls. This kind of terracing creates a number of flat beds which are ideal for flowers.

Durable Wood for Fence Posts

If you plan to use untreated wood for fence posts, choose wood that will not rot. The following are the expected durabilities of various untreated woods when set into soil.

Over 20 years	*10 to 20 years*
redwood	white oak
red cedar	swamp white oak
black locust	honey locust
red mulberry	white cedar
osage orange	black walnut
catalpa	

Reducing Maintenance on Dry Walls

Dry walls (stone walls without mortar) are not recommended for low-maintenance grounds. Freezing, thawing, and water runoff can cause shifting of the stones. To minimize the care of dry walls, make sure that the base stones are at least 1 foot below ground level, avoid using small stones, and avoid making the wall too narrow or too high (over 5 feet).

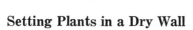

Setting Plants in a Dry Wall

Dry walls can often be made more attractive by planting in the cracks. To set plants in crevices in a dry wall, first soak or shake the soil off the roots and wrap the roots in moist sphagnum moss. Slide the roots and moss into crevices using a spatula to guide the way. Then, tamp as much soil around the roots as the opening will allow. Perennials that are useful in wall cracks include: spurge, baby's breath, coralbells, purple wallcress, maiden pink, candytuft, and cinquefoil.

Slant Fence Post Tops

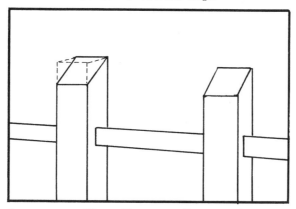

Wooden fence posts will rot if water collects on the tops and soaks in. To avoid this problem, slant the tops of wooden fence posts.

Bracing High Retainer Walls

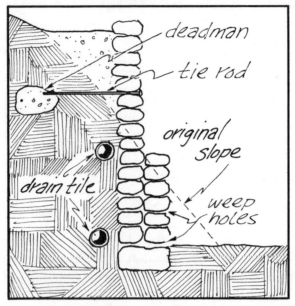

High retainer walls will collapse unless properly constructed. If it is necessary to construct a retainer wall more than 4 feet high, provide frequent weep holes for water to drain through the wall, an iron tie rod ⅜ inches in diameter anchored to a concrete deadman of poured concrete every 3 feet, and drainage tile at the base. By doing this, you will give the wall the added strength it needs and reduce the chance of collapse.

✔   ✔   ✔

Variety in Post-and-Rail Fencing

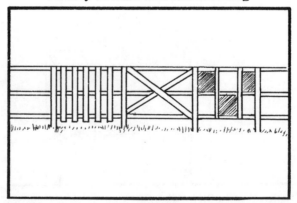

Post-and-rail fencing has many variations. Consider the designs shown here when planning your landscape. To save effort and money in installation, consider renting a power-driven post hole digger from a tool rental store. It generally takes two people to operate these diggers, but the work itself is not overly taxing.

✓   ✓   ✓

Fences on a Slope

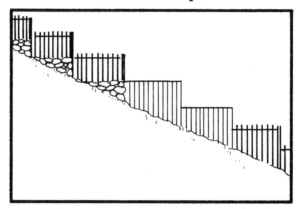

Constructing fencing on a slope can be difficult because of the need to vary the height of the fence according to the slope so that all rungs are vertical. As an attractive alternative to a conventional fence, consider the stair-step arrangement pictured. Rectangular sections can be placed horizontally with stones used to build up the higher end as shown at the left, or the bottom of the fence can be truncated to conform to the slope. To add interest, the pattern of each fence section can be varied. The fence sections at the left are supported on terraces anchored by a stone wall.

✓   ✓   ✓

Leveling Sand with a Screed

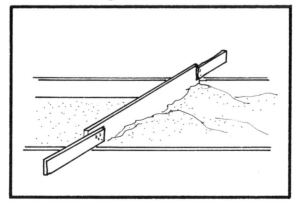

When sand is used as a base for walks, it is difficult to prepare a level bed to receive the brick or flagstone. To solve this problem, a gauge (screed)

can be constructed by attaching two arms on a board at equal distances, as illustrated. The screed can then be moved along the form to level the sand.

✔   ✔   ✔

Steepness of Outdoor Steps

Outdoor steps should be less steep than indoor steps. A rule of thumb for exterior step construction is a maximum riser height of 6 inches and a tread depth of 14 inches.

✔   ✔   ✔

Ramps for Grade Changes

It is often difficult to move heavy gardening equipment over terraces or up steps in your yard. To eliminate this problem, consider building ramps where there are abrupt changes in grade. They can be constructed out of either concrete or wood that has been treated to withstand weather.

✔   ✔   ✔

Wrecking Companies for Landscape Materials

Wrecking companies often collect and sell many interesting items. It is sometimes possible to find just what you need to highlight a garden area. Such items as handcut blocks from an old Victorian house can add real elegance to a garden.

✔   ✔   ✔

Railroad Ties for Outdoor Construction

Railroad ties are excellent for raised flower beds and retaining walls. Sometimes, they can be obtained free for the hauling. Check with your local railroad company. Railroad ties are saturated with wood preservative and will stand up for years in contact with soil. Their rustic appearance makes them especially suitable for country or woodland sites. Make sure to obtain *old* ties, since the creosote preservative with which the new ties are treated will work their way into the soil and inhibit plant growth.

✓   ✓   ✓

Large Pools for Gardens

For large, permanent ornamental garden pools, there is only one material to use—reinforced concrete. Don't use concrete blocks or bricks; they tend

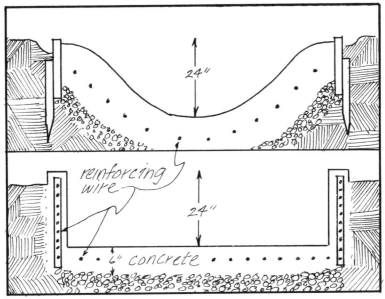

to crack and leak. Make the corners and edges of the pool level so that the water won't seem higher in one part than in the other. The diagram shows how to construct a sloping and straight-sided pool.

✓   ✓   ✓

Constructing Above-Ground Planters

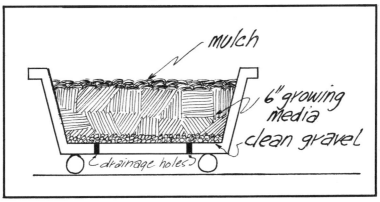

The success or failure of plants in above-ground planters depends on how the planter is constructed and what kind of growth medium is used. A growth medium containing ⅓ organic matter (such as peat) and ⅔ topsoil is recommended. The most common problems that develop in containers result from poor drainage. In order to ensure adequate drainage construct your container like the one illustrated. The drainage holes in the bottom are imperative.

CHAPTER TWO

Planting and Maintaining a Lawn

Overview

Grasses for lawns can be divided into two basic groups: *southern, warm-season grasses,* which begin growing in early spring and become brown and dormant with frost (examples are Bermudas, zoysias, and St. Augustine); and *northern, cool-season grasses,* which grow best during the cool season of the year (examples are bluegrass, bents, fescues, and ryegrass).

Certain strains of grass, such as bluegrass, **grow well in the shade; others,** such as Bermuda grass, **require full sunlight.** Some, such as rye, are vigorous growers; others, such as bluegrass, grow more slowly.

Grasses vary in their fertilizer requirements. Merion Kentucky bluegrass demands heavy fertilization; Bermuda grass requires little.

Select grasses that are adapted to the shade, moisture, and soil in **your yard.** Be aware of the amount of work required to maintain the lawn *before* planting it.

Proper soil preparation is the key to establishing good lawns. During any construction around the house, make sure topsoil is replaced on top and not covered with the excavated subsoil. If the soil is too sandy, add 2 to 3 inches of clay soil. If the soil is mostly clay, add 2 to 3 inches of sharp, course sand or cinders.

Get a soil test to see whether your soil is too acid or too alkaline. Acidity can be remedied by the addition of limestone, alkalinity by adding gypsum.

Lawns should not be perfectly flat. They should slope gently away from the house. A drop of 1 foot in 100 feet is sufficient. Avoid sharp changes in grade so that the grass won't be scalped when mowed.

Before planting, **prepare a fine seed bed** by cultivating to a depth of 12 inches, and raking the soil to remove rocks and large clumps of soil. Add a mixed fertilizer and lime if tests show that it is needed. Mix the lime and fertilizer into the top several inches of soil.

Lawns can be planted by seeding or by vegetative propagation with sod, plugs (small sections of sod), or sprigs (grass plant divisions). Use fresh, clean seed and broadcast it uniformly on the seed bed during a calm day with a mechanical spreader. Do not use more seed than is recommended on the package. In the North, seeding and sodding from mid-August to mid-September is best. In the South, lawns should be

73

planted as soon as the soil begins to warm up in the spring.

To plant vegetatively, prepare the soil as described above. Use fresh sod, plugs, or sprigs, planting sprigs or plugs 6 to 12 inches apart. Lay strips of sod so that joints in parallel rows are uneven (see the hint section for diagram). Roll newly planted sod so that the roots are pressed into the soil. **Newly planted sod should be watered every day for the first month.** After the roots become established, watering can be reduced to once a week.

Prior to planting grass seed, the soil should be thoroughly moistened throughout the area where the grass root system will develop. Germination of some grass seed is facilitated by soaking the seed in water 12 hours before sowing and drying it on paper toweling. After grass is planted, it should be watered immediately.

After seeding, **it is extremely important that the surface soil be kept continuously moist until the seed has germinated and the seedlings have become well established.** If the weather is warm and windy, it may be necessary to sprinkle lightly several times each day. After the grass is established, water deeply when needed to promote root development.

An average soil loses 50 gallons (a barrel) of water per 1,000 square feet each day. In 6 days, this amounts to 300 gallons or ½ inch of rain. It takes 3 hours of steady sprinkling to replace this amount of water on each 1,000 square feet. Keep track of the rainfall and apply additional water as needed on a weekly basis.

Lawn fertilizers should be applied several times during the growing season: early spring, late May, early July, mid-August, and mid-September. Liquid fertilizers, such as 30-10-15, applied at a rate sufficient to supply 1 pound actual nitrogen per 1,000 square feet are most desirable. Liquid fertilizers can be applied with a hose-proportioner set-up or with a watering can. If dry fertilizers are used, apply them evenly at the same intervals and rate. **Dry fertilizers must be watered in thoroughly after they are applied.**

Lawn weeds should be removed before they spread. They can be pulled up by hand, using tools, or if need be, chemicals can be applied. Weed control chemicals can be purchased at garden centers. They are sold under such names as Silvex, 2,4-D, Trizine, and Dicamba.

Some fertilizers have weed control chemicals mixed in with them. Use these mixtures strictly as directed, or the grass and other plants nearby may be damaged. Most weeds can be controlled by proper planting, fertilization, and mowing.

In general, fine-leaved grasses should be mowed closer than coarse-leaved grasses. **When mowing, never remove more than 50% of the height of the grass blade.** Grasses allowed only to grow to a specific height between clippings develop a balance between roots and leaf growth. Varying the cutting height during the growing season upsets this balance.

It is best to remove clippings. If they are allowed to accumulate on top of the lawn, they will present poor growing conditions for the grass

LAWN CARE CALENDAR

MARCH

SEEDING: Seed sown any time between Thanksgiving and spring will germinate as soil warms up.

FERTILIZING: Use a fertilizer high in nitrogen, low in phosphorous and medium in potassium. Apply at a rate of 1 lb. actual N per 1,000 sq. ft. (more if slow release). Fertilize in early spring, in early summer, and again in early fall. Granules can be spread over dry turf, but water in if area is heavily used.

HEAVED CROWNS, BARE SPOTS: Overseed the lawn as early as possible since 1 lb. seed per 1,000 sq. ft. Roll the lawn in early March to keep crowns from drying out. Rolling before spring rains is better than after.

CRABGRASS PREVENTION: Better to apply crabgrass preventer after desired grass starts active growth. See April recommendations.

WILD ONION CONTROL: Use liquid 2,4-D plus Dicamba, or waxbar of 2,4-D. Apply in early March to kill growing stems and soft bulbs. Repeat the following year for complete eradication.

BROWN LEAFTIPS: Due to winter drying. Set mower lower than normal and mow off brown tips, thus exposing the green grass earlier. For Zoysia grass, thatch and brown tips may be burned off, but keep a broom ready to prevent unwanted spread of fire.

APRIL

FERTILIZING: As needed. See March recommendations.

MOWING: For bluegrass and fescue, set mower at 2-inch cutting height. Mow often enough to remove less than ½ the leaf. Remove clippings if desired. For Zoysia, bent and bermudagrass, set mower at less than 1-inch.

HEAVED CROWNS: If a problem, see March.

CRABGRASS PREVENTION: Spreading uniformly and following label directions, use either Betasan, Balan, Azak, Tupersan, Dacthal, Bandane or Chlordane on established turf. On new lawns Tupersan can be applied at time of seeding. It is selective.

WILD ONION: Getting rather late. See March.

LEAFSPOT: If it develops, an application of turf fungicide, used according to label, will reduce severity.

SOIL INSECTS AND MOLES: Insecticides will kill grubs in soil, thus starving

MAY

FERTILIZING: Make second fertilizer application any time between May and July. See March.

CRABGRASS PREVENTION: Can still apply crabgrass preventers in some areas of Indiana. See April.

BROADLEAF WEEDS: Control dandelions, plantain, buckhorn, shepherd's purse and others with 2,4-D sprays, granulars, or waxbars. Standard application rate is 1 lb. active ingredient per acre.

KNOTWEED, CLOVER, CHICKWEED: Use Dicamba. Standard rate is ¼ to ½ lb. active ingredient per acre. If Dicamba and 2,4-D are formulated together, use less of each.

LEAFSPOT: May develop into "fading out" with severe loss. Common bluegrass more susceptible. Changes in weather to dry, clear periods often reduce damage. Use turf fungicide according to label directions. Repeat in 10 to 14 days.

JUNE AND JULY

SOD WEBWORM: Kill larvae of the first brood in mid-May with insecticides such as Dylox, Dieldrin or Spectracide. Read the label!

WATERING: Be ready to water if dry weather comes. Traveling sprinklers with automatic cutoffs save time and water.

CLIPPINGS: May be removed if excessive, but replace removed nutrients by extra fertilizing.

CRABGRASS, FOXTAIL, BARNYARDGRASS, SEDGE, GOOSEGRASS: Can be killed with 2 or 3 treatments of organic arsenicals (DSMA or AMA) at 5-day intervals. Keep soil moist during treatment period. If weather is hot, reduce application rate, but stay on the 5-day spray schedule. Carefully read and follow label directions.

CHIGGERS: Spray or dust with Malathion. Can re-treat for other insects, including sod webworm at the same time.

AUGUST

WATERING: Supplement early fall rains to keep existing leaves.

SEEDING NEW LAWNS: Early fall is best time. If possible, seed and keep moist until established. If necessary, seed into dust and wait for rains to bring germination later in the fall.

RUST: With Merion, Windsor and some varieties, rust pustules on leaves can severely weaken turf. Fertilize and water to force new growth. If severe, treat with a fungicide such as Dithane as directed on label.

SEPTEMBER

FERTILIZING: Fertilize to force fall recovery. See March. Water in for prompt response.

WATERING: As needed to force grass recovery during fall.

VERTICAL THINNING: Machine removal of thatch and matted grass provides room for new growth and reduces competition for space.

RESEEDING: Where needed use a blend of seed of improved varieties. Spread seed, than rake and water to get seed into the soil surface.

DANDELION: Use 2,4-D sprays, granules or waxbars at suggested medium rates in warm weather periods for best-time-of-year treatment.

MILDEW: Most likely to show up in shade, especially on Merion. Use Karathane if damage is serious.

SOIL INSECTS: If a problem, see April-July recommendations. Control now to ward off trouble next year.

OCTOBER AND NOVEMBER

FERTILIZING: A late fall feeding can maintain green color long into winter and promote early spring recovery. See March.

LEAVES: Rake tree leaves to keep them from matting turf and smothering grass.

CHICKWEED: May germinate in thin turf. See May.

WILD ONION: If present, spot-treat with liquid 2,4-D.

LEAFSPOT: Can become serious on weak susceptible varieties. See May.

beneath. If it is not possible to gather clippings, make sure that the clippings left are not so thick as to clog the existing lawn and prevent sunlight from reaching the blades.

Section One

GENERAL ADVICE

Guarantees by Landscape Contractors

You have a right to ask landscape contractors or nurserymen to give written guarantees on their landscaping. Guarantees on seeding should specify a minimum of 30% grass coverage 2 to 3 weeks after sowing, and 100% coverage at the end of the season. Sodded or sprigged lawn guarantees should ensure continuous growth until the first or second cutting.

✓   ✓   ✓

Subsoil Should Settle before Replacing Topsoil

A newly established lawn on a new site which has settled unevenly is difficult to maintain and unattractive. To prevent this, allow several rains to penetrate and settle the subsoil before the topsoil is added. If rainfall is slight, heavy watering can accomplish the same result. Loamy soils settle 20% of their original depth.

✓   ✓   ✓

Avoid Square-Cornered Lawns

Lawns with square corners are difficult to mow: the mower has to be repeatedly stopped and lined up again. To avoid this problem, design your yard with free-flowing curves as illustrated.

✔   ✔   ✔

Lawns Too High above Sidewalks

Sometimes, lawns are graded above sidewalks, and water drains off the property rather than onto the lawn. This can result in the loss of much needed water for your lawn, particularly during dry periods. Grade lawns even with sidewalks and driveways so that the runoff will be evenly distributed on the lawn.

✔   ✔   ✔

Avoid Temporary Lawns

Temporary grasses, such as annual rye, are often planted merely because they grow quickly. It takes as much labor to establish a temporary lawn as a permanent one. Therefore, avoid planting temporary grasses which later have to be eliminated in order to allow permanent grass to flourish.

Section Two

SELECTING GRASSES

The Best Bluegrass

Fylking bluegrass (U.S. 0217) is rated by many turf experts as the best bluegrass seed available at this time. Fylking is resistant to the three most important diseases common to bluegrass: *Helminthosporium* leaf spot, striped smut, and melting-out. It has more resistance to rust and powdery mildew than Merion bluegrass. Bluegrass can be planted in most parts of the country.

✔   ✔   ✔

Bahia Grass for Florida and the Gulf Coast

Because of the sandy, dry soils in Florida and the Gulf Coast states, a turf is needed with roots that can penetrate the soil deeply enough to reach moisture. Bahia grass is the answer. Bahia has a deep, vigorous root system that will penetrate as far as 2 feet to reach water. Bahia grass flourishes where other grasses do not. The only limiting factor is that Bahia requires a pH of between 6.5 and 7.5. This will necessitate adding lime to the soil in those areas with a low pH.

✔   ✔   ✔

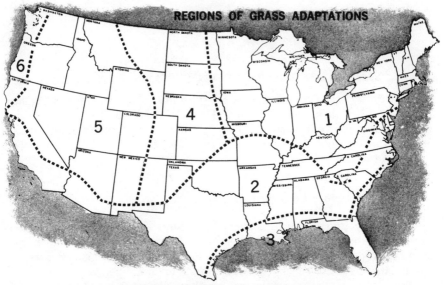

REGIONS OF GRASS ADAPTATIONS

CLIMATIC REGIONS, IN WHICH THE
FOLLOWING GRASSES ARE SUITABLE FOR LAWNS:

1. Kentucky bluegrass, red fescue, and Colonial bentgrass. Tall fescue, bermuda, and zoysiagrasses in the southern part.

2. Bermuda and zoysiagrasses. Centipede, carpet, and St. Augustinegrasses in the southern part; tall fescue and Kentucky bluegrass in some northern areas.

3. St. Augustine, bermuda, zoysia, carpet, and bahiagrasses.

4. Nonirrigated areas: Crested wheat, buffalo, and blue gramagrasses. Irrigated areas: Kentucky bluegrass and red fescue.

5. Nonirrigated areas: Crested wheatgrass. Irrigated areas: Kentucky bluegrass and red fescue.

6. Colonial bent, Kentucky bluegrass, and red fescue.

Best Grass for Dry Soils

It is often difficult to establish grass on dry soils—particularly in shady areas. If this is your problem, select red fescue, Pennlawn, Illahee fescue, and chewing fescue—all of which are drought-resistant and shade-tolerant. They take longer to start growing in the spring, but retain their color longer in the summer.

A Grass for the "Twilight Zone"

There is an area of the United States which is too "northern" for southern grasses and too "southern" for northern grasses. This area is bounded by Philadelphia, Pennsylvania; Omaha, Nebraska; St. Louis, Missouri; and Richmond, Virginia. If you have been having trouble establishing a lawn in this area, consider planting Meyer Zoysia. Though

Meyer will turn brown during the winter months, it will produce a thick, green lawn during the growing season.

✓   ✓   ✓

Grass on Northern Shaded Areas with Poor Drainage

Grass is difficult to establish in shaded areas with poor drainage. A mixture of 30% Kentucky bluegrass, 30% rough bluegrass, and 40% red fescue is recommended for such problem areas in northern climates. Apply at a rate of 4 pounds per 1,000 square feet.

✓   ✓   ✓

Grasses to Avoid

Some "grasses" will eventually become very much like weeds. Although they establish themselves well, their growth habits, toughness, or some other characteristics may make them undesirable for your lawn. Check the seed package label to make sure you are planting only those grasses desired. Avoid orchard grass, timothy, and tall fescue seed.

✓   ✓   ✓

Merion Kentucky Bluegrass Has Its Troubles

Merion Kentucky bluegrass has been on the market for over 20 years and is planted extensively. In recent years, it has been attacked severely by a disease called "striped smut." This disease kills the blades and produces a black powder. Avoid Merion Kentucky bluegrass in southern areas where the disease is more prevalent. If your lawn does contract striped smut, plant varieties of bluegrass that are resistant, such as Fylking bluegrass (U.S. 0217).

✓   ✓   ✓

Grass Surrounding Swimming Pools

Because zoysias are salt- and chlorine-tolerant, they make excellent grasses to plant around swimming pools, provided that they are adapted to your area. Grasses such as Bermuda, fescue, and bluegrass will be damaged if they come into contact with chlorine.

✓   ✓   ✓

Check Labels on Lawn Seed Packages

If you accidentally plant an undesirable grass strain, it is both expensive and time consuming to correct the mistake. Check the labels on lawn seed packages. Make sure they contain at least 80% permanent, fine-textured lawn grass, such as Kentucky bluegrass, red fescue, colonial bentgrass, or rough bluegrass. Do not choose packages that contain more than 20% of such temporary "hay" grass as tall fescue, meadow fescue, timothy, redtop, and the rye grasses. The purpose of these hay grasses, which generally take hold in 7 to 10 days, is to prevent erosion. The finer seeds of a proper mixture will eventually crowd out the weed grasses.

✔   ✔   ✔

Grasses under Trees

It is often difficult to establish and maintain grasses under trees. To solve this problem, use such shade-tolerant grasses as Pennlawn, creeping red fescue, chewing fescue, alta, or Kentucky 31 tall fescue.

Section Three

SEEDING, SODDING AND SPRIGGING

Don't Seed on Snow

Recommendations are sometimes made that grass seed be sown on top of snow. This method has its shortcomings. When the snow melts during a warm spell and the soil becomes dry, some of the seed washes away. Birds eat the rest. It is more reliable to sow seed in spring or fall.

✔   ✔   ✔

Don't Waste Seed on a Thin Lawn

After a lawn has been seeded and established, it often develops thin areas and bare spots. If the thin areas have been seeded before, do not waste grass seed by reseeding it. The thin grass is a result of either lack of food or improper mowing. Fertilization and intelligent cutting will do much more to restore thin areas than seed. Do not reseed bare areas unless they are at least 1 foot in diameter.

✔   ✔   ✔

Fall Seeding in the North

Fall is the best time to seed grasses in the North. Fall-seeded plants tend to be more "bunchy" and thus produce a thicker sod. Fall-grown plants also develop more extensive root systems, enabling them to better withstand dry, hot summer weather. Plants seeded in early fall will become well established before the coming of winter freezes.

✔   ✔   ✔

Lawn Grasses: Planting Time, Propagation, Fertilization, and Mowing Height

Grass	Best planting time	Seed (lbs. per 1,000 sq. ft.)	Sod (sq. ft.)[1]	Fertilizer (lbs. of nitrogen 1,000 sq. ft.)	Height of mowing (in.)
Bahia	Spring	2–3		4	2
Bentgrass, Colonial	Fall	1–2		4–6	½–1
Bermuda (hulled)	Spring	1–1½	5–10	5–10	¾–1
Blue grama	"	1–1½		[2]	1–2
Buffalo (treated)	"	½–1½	25–30	[2]	1–2
Carpet	"	3–4	8–10	2–3	2–2½
Centipede	"	¼–½	8–10	2–3	1–1½
Crested wheat	Fall	1–2		0–1	2
Ky. bluegrass	"	1½–2		3–6	1½–2
Red fescue	"	3–4		2–3	1½–2
Rough bluegrass	"	1½–2		2–4	1½–2
Ryegrass	"	3–4		3–4	1½–2
St. Augustine	Spring	None	8–10	4–5	2–2½
Tall fescue	Fall	5–6		3–5	2
Zoysia	Spring	None	8–10	4–6	¾–1½

[1] Needed to sprig 1,000 sq. ft.   [2] Seldom required on most soils.

Seeding Grass by Hand

Seed can be sown quite satisfactorily by hand. While walking, slowly move the arm in a wide arc and let the seed slip through the fingers as the arm is in motion. The wider the arm is swung, the better.

Cover Grass Seed Lightly

If grass seed is covered with too much soil, a spotty, uneven stand results. Seed should be covered slightly to facilitate germination and prevent it from blowing or washing away. Use a steel-toothed rake to cover grass seed. The teeth should be spaced far enough apart so that soil flows through the rake easily with no buildup of soil. Cover seed to a depth of about ¼ inch. It is of no consequence if 5% to 10% of the seed remains on the surface.

Save on Seed Mixtures

Grass seed mixtures are expensive. After deciding on the grass seed mixture needed, buy the strains of seed separately and mix your own. You will save substantially.

Using Mulches

Grass is difficult to establish on slopes because the seed often washes away. One solution is to apply a straw mulch on top of the seed. One bale of straw per 1,000 square feet of lawn is sufficient. Remove the straw when the grass seedlings are established. If the mulch is not removed, it will eventually be decomposed by microorganisms, depriving the grass of needed nutrients.

Another alternative is to cover the area with cheesecloth or a commercial mulching cloth. Either cloth will soon disintegrate.

✓   ✓   ✓

When to Plant Plugs and Sprigs

Plant *plugs* and *sprigs* between May 1 and August 1. This allows the new plants to take maximum advantage of favorable summer growing conditions. Fall plantings often do not survive the first winter. Plants whose roots have not yet become established may be heaved out of the ground by alternate freezing and thawing. Fall-sown *seeds* establish better contact with the soil and are not as susceptible to heaving.

✓   ✓   ✓

Producing Your Own Zoysia Plants

Once a zoysia sod is established, it can be used as a "nursery." Simply remove plugs from the established sod and transplant them into other areas. It should take a month or so for the plug hole to become filled in with new growth.

✓   ✓   ✓

Planting Zoysia in Established Lawns

It is best to use plugs when attempting to establish zoysia in old lawns. Plugs are better able than seeds to compete with existing grass. To transplant, remove a plug of old sod the same size as the one to be planted. Then, put sufficient compost or leaf mold in the hole, so that when the plug is inserted, it will be level with the existing lawn. Inexpensive plugging tools are available.

Plugs for Bare Spots

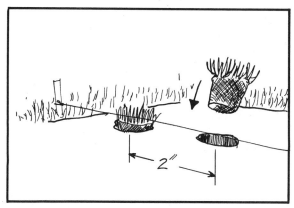

It is sometimes difficult to establish grass in bare spots in the yard. Don't just sprinkle some seed in these areas and expect seedlings to become established. Grass seedlings have little chance in old sod. First, improve the fertility and drainage of the spot. Then, transplant plugs of sod from remote areas of your yard into the spots. Space the plugs about 2 inches apart. Plugs 1½ to 2 inches in diameter dug to a depth of about 1½ inches should begin to take root in about 2 weeks. It is important to keep the plugs moist while they are taking root.

Stagger Sod Joints

If sod is improperly laid, it will not become well rooted, and bare spots will develop. If sod is laid so that joints in adjacent rows meet (to form a cross), it is possible that the area around the joints will dry out or become uneven. Lay sod as illustrated so joints are staggered (like the pattern for running base brick). Four corners should never meet. After the sod is down, roll it to press roots into the soil firmly.

✓   ✓   ✓

Temporary Fencing for Grassed Areas

Grass is often destroyed by passersby who inadvertently trample it. Pieces of rag hung on a string barrier, as illustrated, will remind passersby that seed is sprouting. Keep the fence in place about 3 months or until grass is well established. The blowing rags might also discourage birds from eating newly-sown seed.

Section Four

WATERING, FERTILIZING AND AERATING

The Best Time to Water

There is no best time of day to water. Less water evaporation occurs when water is applied in the evening, but grass that is wet all night runs a greater risk of contracting disease. The advantages of watering in the morning are that the low temperatures, high humidities, and absence of winds reduce evaporation. Midday is the best time to water to prevent disease, but the worst time to water to prevent evaporation. Conclusion: water when it is most convenient.

✓   ✓   ✓

Judging Distribution and Amount of Sprinklers

Is your sprinkler delivering even coverage of water? To test the distribution of a sprinkler, place 4 or 5 coffee cans evenly over the spray pattern of the sprinkler. After the sprinkler has run for ½ hour, compare the amounts of water in each can. The next time you water, station the sprinkler so as to compensate for areas that did not receive adequate amounts of water. This method will also tell you the average depth of water delivered in a given period of time.

✓   ✓   ✓

Timers for Sprinklers

Sprinklers demand constant attention to prevent over- or underwatering. Prevent overwatering by attaching a timer to the outside faucet. Timers can be set to deliver a given number of gallons or to run for a given period of time. Timers are inexpensive and eliminate clockwatching.

✓   ✓   ✓

Inside Diameter Important in Garden Hose

The output of a garden hose is related to its inside diameter. A 50-foot length of hose with a ½-inch inside diameter can deliver more than one gallon in 15 seconds. A ⅝-inch inside diameter can deliver 50% more water. Needless to say, pay attention to the inside diameters of garden hoses when you buy them.

✓   ✓   ✓

Avoid Light Watering

Light sprinkling of water on grass should be avoided because it produces a shallow, weak root system. Such root systems die easily during dry periods. When watering, soak the ground to a depth of 5 to 6 inches. Until you are experienced, you may have to dig a hole and examine the soil to

Fertilizers for Lawn Use and Application Rate

Fertilizer	Type	Amount per 1,000 square feet when amount of nitrogen desired is—		
		1 pound	2 pounds	3 pounds

For establishment and maintenance

		Pounds	Pounds	Pounds
5–10–5 _____	Complete,[1] inorganic [2] ___	20	40	60
____ do _____	____ do _____	25	50	75
5–10–10 _____	____ do _____	20	40	60
10–10–10 _____	____ do _____	10	20	30
8–8–8 _____	____ do _____	13	25	38
10–6–4 _____	____ do _____	10	20	30
7–40–6 _____	____ do _____	14	28	42
10–20–10 _____	____ do _____	10	20	30
6–12–4 _____	____ do _____	17	34	50

For maintenance

		Pounds	Pounds	Pounds
Processed sewage sludge [3] _____	Nitrogen, organic [4] _____	17	34	51
Ammonium nitrate ___	Nitrogen, inorganic ____	3	6	9
Ammonium sulfate ___	____ do _____	5	10	15
Nitrate of soda _____	____ do _____	7	13	20
Steamed bonemeal ____	Nitrogen, phosphorus, organic.	50	100	150
Cottonseed meal _____	Nitrogen, organic _____	17	34	51
Peanut hull meal _____	____ do _____	50	100	150
Cocoa shell meal _____	____ do _____	50	100	150
Castor pomace _____	____ do _____	20	40	60
Dried cattle manure __	Complete, organic _____	50	100	150
Dried sheep manure __	____ do _____	70	140	210
Sewage sludge _____	Nitrogen, organic _____	50	100	150
Animal tankage _____	Nitrogen, phosphorus, organic.	15	30	45
Tobacco stems _____	Nitrogen, potash, organic	50	100	150
Urea _____	Nitrogen, inorganic ____	3	5	7
Processed tankage [5] __	Nitrogen, organic _____	13	26	39
Soybean meal _____	____ do _____	17	34	51
Urea-form _____	Nitrogen, synthetic ____	3	6	9

[1] A complete fertilizer contains nitrogen, phosphorus, and potash.
[2] An inorganic fertilizer is a chemical fertilizer that is easily soluble and quickly available to plants.
[3] Milorganite and Huo-actinite are processed sewage-sludge materials.
[4] An organic fertilizer is slowly available to plants over a period of time.
[5] Agrinite is processed tankage material.

determine the depth the water has penetrated.

✓   ✓   ✓

Keep New Grass Seedlings Moist

More young grass is lost because it is allowed to dry out than for any other reason. New seedlings should be kept moist until they are well established. Make light applications of water several times daily, if necessary, to ensure that the top half-inch of soil remains moist at all times.

✓   ✓   ✓

Position Sprinklers before Sowing

Set your hose and sprinklers on your lawn before you finish sowing the seed. This avoids uprooting seedlings by dragging the hose over them.

✓   ✓   ✓

Starter Fertilizers for Seedbeds

Grass seedlihgs get off to a better start if a fertilizer is incorporated into the seedbed. Broadcast a complete fertilizer, such as 5-10-5, over the seedbed at the rate of 20 pounds per 1,000 square feet, and rake it into the soil lightly. To most benefit the young seedlings, the fertilizer should be worked into the top 1 to 2 inches of soil.

✓   ✓   ✓

Recognizing Nitrogen Deficiency

Grasses are starved more for nitrogen than for any other element. Nitrogen deficiency can be recognized by the sickly, yellowish-green color of the grass blades. Slow and dwarfed growth and a browning of the leaves which starts at the bottom and proceeds upward will also be apparent. Nitrogen deficiency should be remedied immediately with a nitrogen-rich fertilizer.

✓   ✓   ✓

Fertilize Sparingly during Hot Weather

Fertilizers promote weed growth—as well as grass growth—under some conditions. For this reason, don't fertilize any more than is recommended during the summer months. Some weedy plants, such as crabgrass, are better adapted to high temperatures than turf grasses and are thus given the edge by heavy fertilization.

✓   ✓   ✓

Preventing Fertilizer Burn

The best way to handle lawn problems is to prevent them. This is particularly true of fertilizer burn, which results from using the wrong type of fertilizer or from using excessive amounts. The following practices will reduce the chances of fertilizer burn: (1) Do not apply more than 2 pounds of nitrogen per 1,000 feet at any one time. (2) Spread fertilizer evenly. (3) Only apply fertilizer when the foliage is dry. (4) Use granulated rather than pulverized formulations; the latter are more apt to stick to the foliage and burn. (5) Water immediately after application.

✓   ✓   ✓

Better Pattern for Spreaders and Seeders

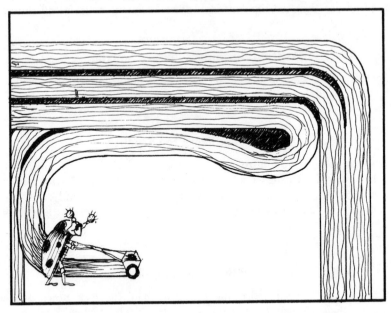

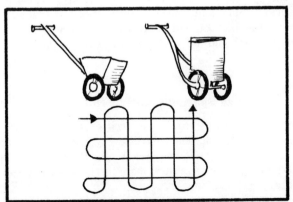

Often, uneven lawns develop because of the poor distribution of seed and fertilizer, as shown in the top illustration. To avoid poor distribution, follow the pattern in the bottom illustration. If it is necessary to turn the spreader around, close it, realign it, and open it again at the spot where you left off.

Iron Deficiency Chlorosis

If your grass is generally yellow, and nitrogen fertilizer doesn't seem to help, it may be suffering from an iron deficiency. Several turf grasses display iron deficiency symptoms. Centipede is the most sensitive to short-ages of iron. The factors most commonly contributing to iron deficiency are: (1) overfertilization, (2) extended dry periods during the previous fall, and (3) too much lime. To cure iron deficiency, have your soil tested and treat according to recommendation.

✦   ✦   ✦

Treating Fertilizer Burn

It is possible to completely burn out grass tops and roots by applying too much fertilizer. Fertilizer burn, which usually shows up within a few days after excessive applications, can cause a general yellowing of the blade and a browning and dieback of the blade tips. The effects will correspond with the distribution pattern of your fertilizer application. If lawns are only partially damaged by fertilizer, the excess fertilizer should be flushed away with water. Apply at least 1 inch of water per week until the effect is no longer noticeable.

✦   ✦   ✦

Test Soil before Liming

Many gardeners add lime to their soil whether or not it is needed. Excessive amounts of lime can cause as poor a turf as insufficient amounts. Therefore, before adding lime to your soil, get a soil test and follow the recommendations of the soil testing laboratory.

✦   ✦   ✦

Feeding New Bluegrass

Newly-planted bluegrass can be easily burned by fertilizers. The best way to avoid this eventuality is to cut the recommended rate of fertiliza-tion in half. Rather than making 1 concentrated application, make 2 light applications about 2 weeks apart. This reduces the chance of fertilization burn.

✦   ✦   ✦

Aerate Compacted Lawns

Grass roots require good air and water movement. Heavily traversed lawns are often compacted to a point where sufficient air and water does not reach the roots. Soil aeration is the solution to this problem. Com-mercial aeration equipment, which punches many small holes into the lawn to a depth of 3 to 4 inches, is available. Professionals can be con-tracted to perform the service, or the equipment can be rented.

Section Five

WEEDING

Reducing Introduced Weed Seed

Many of the weeds in your yard originate from seeds from other areas that are washed or blown in by the wind. If there is a nearby lot or field in which weeds are abundant, chances are that many of the weed seeds originate there. You can reduce the weed population in your yard by mowing the weeds on that lot at least twice a year to prevent its seed from maturing.

✓   ✓   ✓

How to Dig Out a Dandelion

Dandelions that are not properly removed will not only continue to live but will produce additional plants, thus compounding the problem. Cutting in the fall does not kill a large percentage of dandelions, even when cut 5 inches below the soil, because the fall offers ideal conditions for the root to regenerate itself. The best time to cut dandelions is early spring. Make your cut at least 3 inches below the soil surface. A dandelion cut out in the early spring will find itself without enough root area to support itself during its most vigorous growth period and will thereby starve itself as it attempts to grow.

✓   ✓   ✓

Removing Dandelion Seed Heads

Gardeners are often unable to dig out dandelions before the heads set seed. The seeds soon blow around and multiply the dandelion problem many times over. To solve this problem, attach a vacuum cleaner to a long extension cord and sweep up the seed heads.

✓   ✓   ✓

Common Lawn Weeds

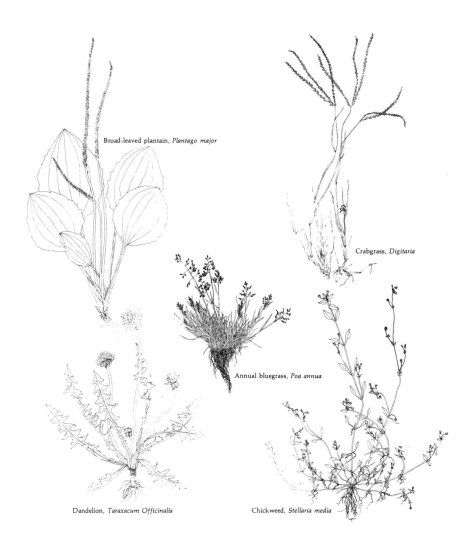

Broad-leaved plantain, *Plantago major*

Crabgrass, *Digitaria*

Annual bluegrass, *Poa annua*

Dandelion, *Taraxacum Officinalis*

Chickweed, *Stellaria media*

Hand Weeding Important

Although much attention is given to chemical control of weeds, hand weeding is still a helpful means of controlling weeds in the yard. When weeds first appear, hand weeding is particularly effective. Patches of perennial weedy grasses—such as tall fescue, nimberwill, quackgrass, and bents —are best removed by hand hoeing, as are weeds near trees and between shrubs.

Broadleaf Weeds

Some Common Turf Weeds and Suggested Chemical Control.

Weed	Life Cycle[1]	Recommended[2] Chemical	Time of Application	Degree of Control
Black medic	A	silvex or dicamba[4]	early spring	good
Carrot, wild	B	2,4-D	spring	good
Chickweed, common	A	silvex, MCPP, or dicamba[4]	spring or fall	good
Chickweed, mouse-ear	P	silvex, MCPP, or dicamba[4]	fall or spring	good
Chickory	P	2,4-D	spring	good
Cinquefoil	P	2,4-D	fall or spring	good
Dandelion	P	2,4-D or MCPP	fall or spring	good
Dock, curly	P	2,4-D or dicamba[4]	fall or spring	good
Garlic or onion	P	2,4-D ester	late fall, early spring	fair
Ground Ivy	P	silvex or MCPP	summer, fall or spring	fair to good
Heal-all	P	2,4-D	spring	good
Henbit	A	silvex	spring	good
Knotweed	A	2,4-D or MCPP	spring or early summer	fair
		dicamba[4]	spring to mid-summer	good
Mallow roundleaf	A	silvex	spring	fair
Pigweed	A	2,4-D or MCPP	summer	good
Plantain, buckhorn	P	2,4-D or MCPP	fall or sprng	good
Plantain, common	P	2,4-D or MCPP	fall or spring	good
Poison Ivy	P	silvex	spring or summer	good
Red sorrel	P	dicamba[4]	spring, summer or fall	good
Speedwell, thyme-leaved	P	silvex	fall or spring	poor
Speedwell, annual	A	silvex	spring or fall	fair
Spurge, spotted	A	dicamba[4] or MCPP	spring	good
Sow thistle	A	2,4-D or dicamba[4]	fall	good
Thistle[3]	P or B	dicamba[4] or 2,4-D	spring	fair
Violet	P	silvex or dicamba[4]	spring	good
White clover	P	silvex, MCPP or dicamba[4]	spring, summer or fall	good
Wild carrot	B	2,4-D or dicamba[4]	fall	good
Woodsorrel	A	silvex	spring	fair
Yarrow	P	silvex	spring	fair

[1] A = Annual, B = Biennial, P = Perennial.
[2] Do not use silvex on bentgrass turf. Silvex may also cause injury on fine fescues. Do not use 2,4-D on golf course greens and use with caution on other bentgrass turf.
[3] Three or more applications may be necessary to eradicate this
[4] Dicamba may accumulate in the soil with frequent or exten which may result in damage to trees, shrubs, or other ornam

Killing Crabgrass without Herbicides

Crabgrass does not compete successfully with taller-growing lawn grasses. If a lawn is fertilized, watered well, and not cut lower than 3 inches, the taller lawn grass will soon shade and crowd out the crabgrass.

Avoid Herbicide/Fertilizer Combinations

Fertilizer/herbicide mixtures are sold on the market with the claim that one application both feeds the lawn and kills the weeds. The practicability of these mixtures is questionable. Often, you will be paying for a chemical that is not needed. What also makes these mixtures undesirable is that the best time for weed control is generally not the best time for fertilization.

Use 2,4-D with Caution

The herbicide 2,4-D is a common ingredient of weed killers. Use it with caution. A slight amount of spray blown by the wind can cause damage to nearby vegetation. Fine spray may blow 50 feet or more and kill plants in neighboring yards. Dry granular formulations of 2,4-D are safer than sprays. Apply as directed on the label.

Lawn Weeds Controlled By —
2,4-D

Buckhorn plantain _____	*Plantago lanceolata*
Carpetweed _____	*Mollugo verticillata*
Cinquefoils _____	*Potentilla* species
Daisies _____	*Chrysanthemum* species
Dandelion _____	*Taraxacum officinale*
Dichondra _____	*Dichondra repens*
Docks _____	*Rumex* species
Hawkweed _____	*Hieracium* species
Healall _____	*Prunella vulgaris*
Lambsquarters _____	*Chenopodium album*
Mayweed _____	*Anthemis cotula*
Moneywort _____	*Lysimachia numularia*
Mustards _____	*Brassica* species
Pennycress _____	*Thlaspi arvense*
Pepperweed _____	*Lepidium* species
Plantains _____	*Plantago* species
Puncture vine _____	*Tribulus* terrestris
Shepherdspurse _____	*Capsella Bursa-pastoris*
Speedwell _____	*Veronica* species
Velvetleaf _____	*Abutilon theophrasti*
Vervains _____	*Verbena* species
Wild carrot _____	*Daucus carota*
Wild garlic _____	*Allium vineale*
Wild onion _____	*Allium canadense*
Yarrow _____	*Achillea millefolium*
Yellow rocket _____	*Barbarea vulgaris*

Silvex

Black medic (yellow trefoil)	*Medicago lupulina*
Buttercups _____	*Ranunculus* species
Catsear _____	*Hypochaeris radicata*
Chickweed (common) _____	*Stellaria media*
Chickweed (mouse-ear) ____	*Cerastium vulgatum*
Ground ivy _____	*Glechoma hederacea*
Knotweed _____	*Polygonum* species
Lespedeza _____	*Lespedeza* species
Pearlwort _____	*Sagina procumbens*
Pennywort _____	*Hydrocotyle sibthorpioides*
Purslane _____	*Portulaca oleracea*
Sorrels _____	*Rumex* species
Spurges _____	*Euphorbia* species
White clover _____	*Trifolium repens*

Herbicides for Winter Weeds

Weeds that grow during the winter are generally easy to kill with a variety of herbicides. When dormant, grasses are relatively tolerant to most herbicides. Thus, winter weeds can be controlled with chemicals that the grass would not tolerate during the growing period. Because St. Augustine and centipede grasses are very sensitive to most herbicides, it is best to use herbicides only when these grasses are dormant.

Best Time to Apply Herbicides

The effectiveness of herbicides is influenced by the time of application. Herbicides are most effective if applied when turf grasses are growing well. In the North, fall treatments are best because lawn grasses fill in after fall treatments, whereas crabgrass is more apt to fill in after spring treatments.

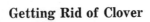

Getting Rid of Clover

Clover can become a nuisance in yards where superior types of grasses are desired. Clover can easily be controlled by spring or fall applications of Silvex, according to the directions on the package.

A Leaf Dip for Poison Ivy

Poison ivy in the lawn is often very difficult to kill with herbicides. Because plants absorb weed killer through the leaves, one technique certain to kill individual vines is to dip an end of a growing vine in concentrated weed killer (Silvex is recommended). This technique is especially useful where spraying may endanger nearby plants. Be sure to wear gloves when handling poison ivy. After handling it, wash your hands thoroughly with soap and water to remove any of its toxic oil.

✓   ✓   ✓

Pesticides May Injure Young Grass

Young grass is highly sensitive to weed killers and insecticides. These chemicals should not be used on lawns less than 1 year old. If too much of the grass is killed by these chemicals, weeds will take over, defeating the purpose of the herbicide.

✓   ✓   ✓

Chickweed Control in Lawns

Chickweed is a common problem in lawns. It can be controlled with Silvex by following the directions on the container. Apply in late fall or in the spring before air temperatures reach 80 degrees F. At high temperatures, Silvex injures grasses. The inset in the upper right corner of the illustration shows the chickweed flower.

Section Six

MOWING, RAKING, ROLLING AND DETHATCHING

Mowers Can Damage Grass

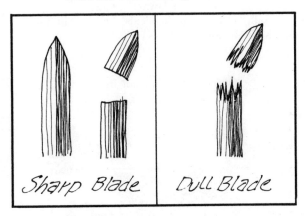

Sharp Blade | Dull Blade

Mowers in poor condition can cause browning of lawn grass. A reel-type mower that is dull or the reel of which is too far from the bed plate, may crimp the grass instead of cutting it. The leaf tips are killed and turn brown. A rotary mower that is dull or the blade of which turns too slowly will cause grass to fray. The grass will show a white cast, and its tips will eventually turn brown. So, keep mowers sharp and properly adjusted.

✓   ✓   ✓

Greening up the Yard Early

An easy way to make your lawn green 2 or 3 weeks earlier than that of your neighbor is to give the lawn an extra early mowing—just as soon as the ground is free of frost. The dormant top ½ inch of grass prevents lawns from greening. An early mowing solves the problem.

✓   ✓   ✓

Starved Grass Still Needs Mowing

Many people don't fertilize their lawns, thinking that they won't have to mow as often. This is poor reasoning: although fertilization increases the clippings per mowing, it does not increase the frequency of mowing. So, why not fertilize and mow a healthy lawn?

✓   ✓   ✓

Inspect Lawns before Mowing

Before mowing, walk around the lawn and clear it of stones and other objects that might obstruct the blades of the mower. Such objects are ejected at great speed by rotary mowers and can cause severe damage to people, structures and the mower blade.

✓   ✓   ✓

Mow Shaded Grass Less Frequently

Grass in shady areas should be mowed less frequently and at a greater height than is recommended for sunny areas. The reduced light available to shaded grasses makes it difficult for plants to produce enough food for healthy growth. Higher and less frequent mowings permit grass to produce food and to survive in those areas where it would die if cut more frequently.

✓   ✓   ✓

Don't Cut Extra Tall Grass All at Once

When grass is allowed to go for a long period between cuttings, the appearance and health of the grass can be preserved if the excess growth is cut off gradually, in successive mowings, rather than all at once. Removal of too much of the growth at once shocks the roots, which are dependent on the food manufactured by the leaves.

✓   ✓   ✓

Don't Mow Wet Grass

Wet grass is difficult to mow. It sticks to the blades and clogs the mower. The result is a sloppy job. Wait for the water-laden grass to dry out before mowing.

✓   ✓   ✓

When to Mow New Lawns

After new grass starts to grow, there is the perpetual question: when should it first be mowed? As a rule of thumb, mow new grass when it reaches a height of 2½ inches, cutting it to approximately 1½ inches. Mowing to heights less than 1½ inches will weaken the grass and encourage weeds.

✓   ✓   ✓

Cut Higher during Dry Summers

Close mowing during hot weather weakens cool season grasses—bluegrass, bents, fescues—which need a high top-to-root ratio during this period. It is advisable to increase cutting height during the hot and dry part of the summer. An additional advantage is that longer grass smothers weed seedlings and makes the lawn more attractive.

✓   ✓   ✓

Remove Clippings Only When Necessary

Clippings are not a problem if they are small enough to work between the remaining blades and fall to the ground. Long clippings, however, form mats on the surface of the grass and smother it. In these cases, clippings should be removed with a rake or grass catcher.

✓   ✓   ✓

Utilize Grass Clippings

Grass clippings are an excellent source of nitrogen. Don't discard them. Use them as mulch around trees and bushes. Place them under turned-over garden soil to rot over the winter and serve as green manure. Use them in compost heaps.

✓   ✓   ✓

Avoid Summer Raking

The summer is a tempting time to get out in the yard and do some raking. Resist the temptation. Young grass seedlings develop during the summer, and raking the yard can uproot and kill them. Lawns are best raked in the early spring or the late fall (provided that no seed has been sown that fall).

✓   ✓   ✓

Rake Leaves for the Sake of the Grass

Air and light are necessary for the growth of grass. Fallen leaves can prevent both from reaching the grass in your lawn. Since autumn is an important growing season for many grasses. be sure to rake leaves when they fall off of the trees in autumn.

✓   ✓   ✓

Avoid Rigid Garden Rakes for Leaves

Use a broom-type rake to gather the leaves in the yard. Rigid, steel garden rakes will pull up grass plants and destroy them.

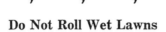

Do Not Roll Wet Lawns

Heavy rollers are sometimes used to level out bumpy lawns. However, rolling a wet lawn may do more harm than good. Rollers can force needed air out of wet soil and compact it to the extent that it will not spring back. To be safe, avoid rolling soil that water can be forced out of when pressed hard with your foot. Soils containing large percentages of clay should never be rolled.

Dethatching Grass

Thatch is a dried-out, undecomposed layer of grass clippings trapped at the base of grass plants. If not removed, it can cause poor growth and promote disease and insect problems. Dethatching is best done after the heat of midsummer. The grass recovers quickly from tearing in the fall. Don't dethatch in spring because too many young grass plants will be destroyed. Special dethatching tools equipped with metal rakes should be used. A drawing of such a rake is provided in Chapter Twelve.

Section Seven

INSECTS, DISEASES AND OTHER PESTS

Sampling Sod for Disease and Insects

If you are unable to diagnose your grass problem, you may want to have a grass sample examined. Most states have plant disease clinics (in conjunction with their Agricultural Experiment Stations) that can make pest diagnoses. To take a grass sample, cut a 6-inch diameter plug from the margin of a diseased patch so that both diseased and healthy plants are included. Wrap the plug tightly in a polyethylene bag. Do not add extra water. Label clearly, and mail it *promptly* in a cardboard box. Do not expose the box to too much heat, or it may be impossible to make an accurate diagnosis of the contents. Your county agricultural agent should be able to tell you where to send the sample.

✦   ✦   ✦

Sod Webworm Control

The sod webworm is extremely destructive to bluegrass. The pests cause areas of grass to be killed, resulting in bare spots in the yard. Damage is caused by the larvae that feed on grass roots. Adult webworms are small, cigar-shaped moths which fly up when you are mowing or walking through the grass. Chemicals are needed to control them. The time for treatment is about 2 weeks after a sharp decline in the number of moths is seen. The insecticide Sevin will work. Read the instructions on the label.

✦   ✦   ✦

Japanese Beetle Control

Japanese beetles are very destructive because the adults feed on the foliage of many different plants and the immature beetles (grubs) eat at root systems. To control grub damage to grass, encourage the development of "milky white disease" which will kill the beetles. Spores of the bacterium that cause this disease of Japanese beetle grubs are available at garden centers. Follow the directions on the label.

✓   ✓   ✓

Stop Digging Skunks

Skunks in search of grubs for food dig up lawns and gardens. To solve this problem, establish milky white disease (previous hint) in your lawn to kill the grubs. The skunks will soon disappear.

✓   ✓   ✓

Burrowing Insects Kill Grass

Burrowing insects can destroy the roots of grass and kill it. To determine whether such insects are present, cut out the bottom of a coffee can. Push the can into the turf and fill it with water. Keep it full for 2 or 3 minutes. Any insects underneath will pop to the surface to avoid drowning. This is a particularly good way to spot chinch bugs that feed on grass roots. See the next hint to learn how to eliminate them.

✓   ✓   ✓

GUIDE FOR SELECTING FUNGICIDES

Application Per 1,000 Square Feet—Follow Directions On Label

Disease and Casual Organism	Fungicide	Directions
Leafspot (Blight, Going-out, Melting-out) *Helminthosporium*	Acti-dione-thiram Captan Daconil 2787 Dyrene Fore Zineb	Disease can appear from April to August, depending on kind of grass and species of fungus. Treat your lawn every 7 to 14 days three times consecutively or until the disease has been controlled.
Brown Patch *Rhizoctonia solani*	Dyrene Fore PCNB	Disease can appear from June to August. Treat your lawn every 5 to 10 days until the disease has been controlled.
Rust *Puccinia*	Acti-dione-thiram Daconil 2787 Zineb	Disease can appear from June to September. Treat your lawn every 7 to 14 days until rust disappears.
Grease Spot and Cottony Blight *Pythium*	Dexon Zineb	Disease can appear from July to September and in fall and winter during warm, humid periods in the South. Treat your lawn every 5 to 14 days until the disease has been controlled.
Dollar Spot *Sclerotinia homeocarpa*	Acti-dione-thiram Daconil 2787 Dyrene Fore	Disease can appear from June to October. Treat your lawn at 7 to 14 day intervals until the disease has been controlled.
Stripe Smut Ustilago striiformis	Tersan 1991	Apply in October or early spring before grass begins growing. Water lawn well.
Snow Mold *Typhula* Fusarium Patch *Fusarium*	Dyrene Tersan 1991	Disease can appear from fall to spring. Treat your lawn at intervals of 2 to 6 weeks as needed.
Mushrooms Fairy Rings *Marasmius, Psalliota campestris, Lepiota*	Captan Methyl Bromide	Disease can appear throughout the growing season. Pour double or triple strength concentrate of captan into 1-inch holes punched 4 to 6 inches deep and 6 to 8 inches apart both inside and outside the affected area. Alternative method: fumigate infected area with methyl bromide; reseed or resod.
Slime Molds *Physarum cinereum*	Fore Zineb	Disease can appear throughout the growing season and can be controlled without fungicides.

[1] Acti-dione-thiram formulations containing more than one active ingredient. Methyl bromide is applied as a vapor or gas. For all applications, read the manufacturer's directions.

CAUTION: Do not graze treated areas or feed clippings to livestock or poultry.

Chinch Bug Control the Organic Way

Actual Size

Chinch bugs are little black sucking insects that can cause large brown patches in your lawn. They thrive on nitrogen-deficient plants. Applications of a compost top dressing will remove the deficiency and avoid the problem. The top dressing should be scattered over the grass and gently raked until it falls between the grass blades. Making compost is discussed elsewhere in this book.

✓   ✓   ✓

Dollar Spot Control

Sclerotinia dollar spot disease is characterized by small circular dying areas about 2 inches in diameter. In the final stages of this fungus disease, the blades turn straw-colored. Susceptible grasses include bentgrass, the bluegrasses, Bermudas, ryegrasses, and fescues. Turf deficient in nitrogen tends to develop more dollar spot than adequately fertilized lawns. For control: (1) Keep thatch at a minimum. (2) Water only when needed to a depth of 8 to 12 inches. (3) Apply adequate nitrogen. (4) Mow high and rake vigorously. (5) If all else fails, treat the affected areas with Daconil 2787 as recommended on the label.

✓   ✓   ✓

Powdery Mildew Disease Control

Powdery mildew is a grass disease caused by the fungus *Erysiphe graminis*. It can be recognized by the gray-white cobwebby growth that occurs mainly on the upper surface of the leaf. The leaves have the appearance of having been dusted with flour. To eliminate the problem: (1) Use resistant varieties. Common Kentucky bluegrass is more resistant than Merion bluegrass. (2) Provide better air circulation and more light. Pruning trees and shrubs should be considered. (3) If these measures fail, apply Actidione fungicide as directed on the label.

✓   ✓   ✓

How to diagnose problems on lawns

PROBLEMS	CAUSES
NEW LAWNS:	
Seed doesn't come up.	Lack of moisture, old seed, too cold, sown too deep.
Lawn is spotty.	Lack of moisture, washing, variable soil types or soil depths, variable nutrition, especially lack of nitrogen.
Grass is yellow.	Lack of nitrogen due to: lack of fertilizer, excess moisture, low temperature. Nematodes.
Dead patches.	Damping-off.
ESTABLISHED LAWNS:	
Browning of lawn.	Lack of moisture, improper cutting, white grubs, fertilizer burn, herbicide burn, disease.
Circular brown areas in bents and bluegrass.	Brown patch (warm, humid weather). Dollar spot (usually cool weather).
Large areas of lawn are dead in the spring.	Smothering from leaves. Ice areas for skating, especially if soil is not frozen. Foot traffic across frozen turf.
Rusty brown appearance.	Rust disease, can be severe on Merion bluegrass, low nitrogen, dull mower blades.
Dusted with flour appearance.	Powdery mildew, slime mold.
Blades of grass have small yellow spots.	Leaf-spot disease.
Clover in excess.	Low nitrogen.

PROBLEMS	CAUSES
Green circular spots—(may turn brown).	Dog urine.
Mushroom, toadstools or fairy rings in the lawn.	Due to decaying organic matter; (many kinds are poisonous).
Mold or webby growth (in spring).	Snow mold (near-freezing temperatures and excess moisture).
Turf is thin.	Low nutrition, especially nitrogen, shallow topsoil, excess moisture (poor drainage), improper mowing height.
Yellow-brown color.	Lack of nitrogen.
Streaking of lawn (long narrow yellow strips in a dark green turf).	Uneven distribution of fertilizer.
Moss (or algae) in the lawn.	Low fertility, poor drainage, excess shade.
Lawn is bumpy, small circular spots, tunnels.	Earthworm casts, ants, moles, improperly graded.
Bees in the lawn (sting bare feet).	Bees associated with clover in the lawn, wasps.
Bluegrass lawn, infested with bent grass.	Caused by small amount of bent grass seed in seed mixture, soil, sod.
Mower cuts with difficulty.	Mower needs to be sharpened, turf not cut frequently enough.
Lawn is weedy.	Turf in poor vigor, turf cut too close, high weed population in area.

General Practices to Reduce Grass Diseases

Grass diseases have a number of causes and, therefore, a number of different treatments for control. However, there are general practices that will reduce the incidence of most grass diseases. These include: (1) Do not fertilize to promote fast lush growth in hot, humid weather. (2) Collect clippings to reduce thatch in which certain disease-causing organisms thrive. (3) Maintain adequate soil moisture with infrequent but deep waterings. Light, daily watering favors disease-causing organisms. (4) Keep the lawn clipped at the proper height for the grass you select. Too short a cut will weaken the grass and make it susceptible to disease; too high a cut will trap moisture so that the grass fails to dry rapidly. (5) Mow the lawn through the fall until the grass stops growing.

✦   ✦   ✦

Fusarium Blight Control

Fusarium blight is a serious disease that afflicts bluegrass. Infected areas of grass become tan and eventually straw-colored, and form either streaks or circular spots of dead grass. The dead areas may have centers of green, producing a "frog-eye" appearance. The following practice will help reduce disease incidence: (1) Maintain grass in optimum growing condition, and avoid excessive nitrogen fertilization during hot periods of summer when disease attack occurs. (2) Apply enough water to avoid water stress. (3) Avoid thatch buildup. (4) If these practices don't work, apply Tersan 1991 to infected areas as recommended on the label.

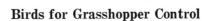

Birds for Grasshopper Control

Grasshoppers can often become a problem in lawns and gardens by eating the grass and other vegetation. If your lawn is plagued by grasshoppers, encourage the local bird population to frequent your area. Virtually every kind of bird has a craving for grasshoppers. Construct birdhouses and establish plants that make good bird cover and food.

Stripe and Flag Smut Disease Control

Stripe and flag smut diseases are caused by two fungi. They occur most commonly on bluegrass, bentgrass, fescue, and ryegrass. The disease can be first recognized by the long yellow-green streaks that develop on the leaves. Later, the streaked areas rupture and release black sooty spores. The following practices will help you deal with this problem: (1) Use resistant varieties. Merion bluegrass is very susceptible to smut. Common and Troy Kentucky bluegrass are moderately susceptible. Park, Newport, Fylking, Delta, Pennstar, A-20, A-24, and Ken-blue are most resistant.

(2) Use smut-free clean seed that has been bought from a certified grower. (3) Apply the fungicide Tersan 1991 in late fall or early spring as directed on the label.

✓   ✓   ✓

Controlling Snow Mold

Patches of grass can be killed during the winter by snow molds which operate under a snow cover. The patches will have a whitish, bleached appearance. A whitish-pink or dirty gray to black mold growth can often be seen on the diseased grass in the spring. For control: (1) Avoid bent-grasses, which are highly susceptible. (2) Prevent heavy thatch buildup and dense grass in late fall. (3) Reduce nitrogen fertilization in late summer and fall to prevent a heavy mat of grass. (4) Use snow fences or other barriers to reduce snow drifting on the lawn.

✓   ✓   ✓

Brown Patch Control

Many grasses are susceptible to brown patch, a disease caused by the fungus *Rhizoctonia solani*. Irregularly-shaped brown spots, 1 inch to several feet in diameter, develop in the yard. If this becomes a problem in your yard, the following measures are recommended: (1) Use resistant varieties. Bentgrasses are very susceptible; meadow fescue, redtop, and Merion Kentucky bluegrasses are more susceptible than common Kentucky bluegrass or Illahee fescue. (2) Avoid overwatering and high nitrogen fertilization. (3) Increase air circulation by pruning trees and shrubs. (4) Remove clippings.

✓   ✓   ✓

"Fading Out" Disease of Bluegrass

The most important bluegrass disease is caused by species of the fungus *Helminthosporium*, and is commonly called "fading out," "melting out," or "dying out." A variety of symptoms may become apparent, including a general browning of the leaves. If the grass is examined closely, brown or purple spots about $\frac{1}{4}$ to $\frac{3}{8}$-inch long and 1/16 to $\frac{1}{8}$-inch wide can be seen on individual grass blades. For control: (1) Grow the more resistant varieties, such as Campus, Fylking, Pennstar, Baron, Nugget, and A-20. (2) Avoid continuous watering. Soak the soil to a depth of 6 inches once a week. (3) Do not overfertilize, which will promote thatch formation. (4) Mow bluegrass $1\frac{3}{4}$ to 2 inches high.

✓   ✓   ✓

Controlling Fairy Rings

Fairy rings in the lawn can be produced by one of over 50 different species of mushrooms, toadstools, and puffballs. Fairy rings are continuous bands or rings of dark green grass surrounded by a band or ring of dead grass. Mushrooms may pop up within the green band. Lawns with this problem generally have excessive amounts of organic material in the soil that promote the growth of the fungi. This problem can be attacked in a number of ways: (1) Mow off the mushrooms and leave the stems to shrivel up; little damage will result. (2) Even out the fertility of the lawn to mask the dark green rings. (3) Dig out the rotting wood that is the source of the excessive organic material. (4) Dig up the rings, break up the soil, and water copiously.

Controlling Algae

Green patches of growth, called algae, may develop in bare spots on a lawn. Poor drainage is the main cause of this condition. Piercing and loosening the soil with a hand aerifier or tined fork will help. It may be necessary to install drain tiles if water-logged soil is a constant problem. Reduce foot traffic in the area.

Discouraging Moles with Thorns

The blood of moles does not clot. If they are scratched, they will bleed to death. For this reason, they are very wary of thorns and sticky objects. Moles can be discouraged from entering their burrows by pushing twigs with thorns from rose, hawthorn, blackberry, or mesquite plants into the burrows. The moles tend to abandon such places.

Soda Bottles to Scare Moles

Moles can become bothersome pests where their burrows create mounds in the turf. One way to control moles is to place empty soda bottles in their burrows. Leave 2 or 3 inches of the neck exposed. The wind blowing in the empty bottles will cause a vibration that scares the moles away.

Chasing Away Groundhogs

Groundhogs dig up lawns and can become a nuisance. To eliminate them, soak rags in gasoline and poke the rags down the burrows. Cover up all their entrances with rocks and soil. It may be necessary to repeat this treatment several times, but the groundhogs will eventually disappear.

Dogs Can Damage Grass

The urine of female dogs may cause green or brown spots on the lawn.

The larger the dog, the drier the soil, and the higher the temperature, the greater the damage will be. Grass not killed will turn greener in and around the affected spots because of nitrogen in the urine. The only sure way to deter dogs is with fencing.

CHAPTER THREE

Ground Cover and Vines

Overview

Ground cover are low-growing plants that can substitute for grass. They require less maintenance, feeding, and watering than grass but do not hold up under heavy traffic. Ground cover spread along the surface of the ground. As a result, there is little vertical growth.

Vines behave like ground cover, except that their stems twine or develop attachments (tendrils, adhesive disks, or holdfasts) which allow them to cling to objects and grow vertically as well as horizontally. Many vines can serve well as ground cover. Ivy is a prime example.

Consider ground cover where grass is difficult to establish or maintain. They function well on steep slopes to prevent erosion or eliminate mowing. They are also an advantage in moist soil, shaded areas, woodland and rock gardens, and crevices between stones or blocks on patios. Tree stumps and roots that are impractical to remove can also be covered with ground cover.

Because of the variety of plants available, ground cover are very useful in landscaping. Use them in rough or rocky areas where a different texture is needed. Consider them for narrow strips between buildings, along walks, and as under-plantings for trees and shrubs. Properly selected plants soften the edges of steps and paths to make them blend with the surrounding landscape. Stems of "leggy" plants can be concealed with ground cover.

Some ground cover produce flowers and/or fruit. Among the flowering selections are candytuft, phlox, daphne, myrtle, and St. Johnswort. The brightly colored fruit of cotoneasters add interest to a planting. For year-round beauty, try such evergreens as pachysandra, myrtle, English ivy, pachistima, and sedum.

Select plants that are adapted to your area of the country and to the site where they will be planted. Plants differ in their tolerance to dry soils, shade, open sun, and acid conditions.

Most ground cover plants can be planted successfully anytime during the growing season, though spring and fall plantings survive best. Plants should be spaced according to their growth habit, rate of growth, and the effect desired. Plants such as English ivy, pachysandra, and myrtle are usually planted 1 foot apart. If an immediate cover is needed, space plants closer.

A selection of ground cover.

When planting, remove all sod and till 6 inches deep in the planting area. Using a trowel, dig a hole larger than the root system and place the plant in the hole at the same depth it was growing. Tamp fertile or enriched soil around the roots.

Using a lawn sprinkler or soaker hose, **water plants at least once a week until they are established.** Once they are established, water only when they show signs of wilting.

A commercial fertilizer, such as 4-12-12 or 5-10-10, **should be applied annually** at the rate of 2 to 4 pounds per 100 square feet.

Weeds in ground cover **can be reduced by mulching** the soil around the plants with peat, wood chips, bark, etc. Herbicides such as Simazine and Dacthal can be used to control weeds in established plantings. Read labels for directions.

Ground cover may require pruning to keep them in bounds, to remove old or diseased growth, and to rejuvenate the plants. Evergreen ground cover such as English ivy, pachysandra, vinca, and euonymus wintercreeper benefit from periodic shearing to promote new growth. Rotary mowers with high wheels can be used to trim certain ground cover. If winter damage occurs, prune out injured parts and remove dead plants. **Ground cover can be pruned at any time of the year.** As long as one-half to one-third of the plant's leaves are retained, there is little danger of injury.

New plantings of ground cover **can be established from old ones.** Some ground cover plants can be transplanted from divisions or cuttings. Examples of easily divided plants are ajuga, duchesnea, and thymus (*T.*

sersphyllum). Cuttings from ivy *(Hedra)*, honeysuckle *(Lonicera)*, and the vincas root easily.

Vines can be a welcome addition to gardens as well. They provide a way to cover such eyesores as unsightly wires, poles, down spouts, and tree stumps. Many vines produce flowers. They are, therefore, both utilitarian and aesthetically pleasing.

Vines may require support for their growth. Select a vine that will climb and twine naturally. This will eliminate the labor of tying them.

Spring is the best time to plant vines. Loosen the soil in the planting area to a depth of 10 inches. Work in 2 inches of peat or other organic matter. Annual vines should be started at location from seed. Perennial vines should be started from young plants.

One warning about vines: Do not let them grow up living trees. The vines will shade the tree's leaves (its food-manufacturing apparatus) and reduce its capacity to nourish itself. Vines also serve as a trap for dead leaves and other debris.

Section One

USES FOR GROUND COVER

Ground Cover to Unify the Landscape

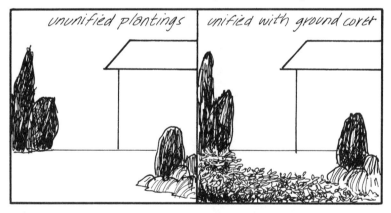

Garden plantings often lack a unified appearance, and ground cover is an excellent way to unify various plants and plantings. Plants can be given a common setting by surrounding them with the same bed of ground cover. Beds with curved, natural lines are most appealing.

Ground Cover to Cover UP

Debris that falls from trees requires a constant cleanup operation.

Ground cover can be used to assist in keeping the yard neat. Loosely-textured plants, such as *Vinca minor,* Algerian ivy, and St. Johnswort, can be planted under shedding trees and shrubs to absorb buds, seeds, blossoms, and leaves. The debris in turn acts as a mulch for the ground cover. Periodically, the ground cover will, of course, have to be cleaned. See Section III of this chapter.

❧   ❧   ❧

Ground Cover to Replace a Flower Bed

Flower beds can become burdensome. To convert them to areas requiring less care, replace the flower bed with a ground cover. Since the soil is already prepared and the bed has been designed to fit into the landscape, little bother is involved.

❧   ❧   ❧

Cover at the Base of Ornaments

Garden ornaments, such as small pools, figures, and benches, do not blend naturally into the landscape. Ground cover at the base of ornaments help soften their lines and make them look natural in their surroundings. English ivy, periwinkle, and Christmas fern will all help break the sharp outline of a shady pool.

❧   ❧   ❧

Cover "Leggy" Perennials with Ground Cover

candytuft

Tall-growing perennials often have long awkward-looking stems. Conceal these with such ground cover as candytuft, pachistima, coral bells, or lady's-mantle. The soil must be rich enough to support both the perennials and the ground cover.

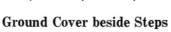

Flower Cover for Country Fences

It is often desirable to establish ground cover along fences in rural landscapes to eliminate mowing and soften the lines of the fence. Naturalized day lilies make an ideal ground cover for these situations. These tall perennials, with their graceful leaves, are showy and form a continuous and functional ground cover. They can be increased by root division at almost any time during the year.

Ground Cover beside Steps

The lawn area beside steps is often difficult to mow. A simple solution to this problem is to plant a ground cover beside the steps.

Reducing Weeds in Perennials with Ground Cover

Ground cover can be functional as well as attractive. One way to use ground cover is to plant it with perennials so that it smothers out weeds. This practice is especially useful with such large perennials as peonies, hardy asters, chrysanthemums, poppies, iris, and day lilies.

Ground Cover in Flower Arrangements

Ground cover plants have a variety of leaves, flowers, and fruit. Many of these plants make excellent accents in flower arrangements. Try sprays of cotoneaster, branches of dwarf yew, and pieces of ivy, myrtle, and pachysandra.

Section Two

SELECTION OF GROUND COVER

Ground Cover for a Variety of Conditions

The following ground cover will survive and prosper under a wide range of environmental conditions and are recommended for general use: *Ajuga* (Bugleweed), especially good under trees and shrubs; *Cotoneaster,* good for hot, dry conditions; *Euonymus fortunei* (Wintercreeper), holds slopes well because of its deep-rooting habit; *Hedra helix* (English ivy), one of the choicest of ground cover; *Liriope spicata* (Lily turf), does well under shrubs and trees; *Pachysandra terminalis,* use in any shaded area; *Sedum* (Stonecrop), good for walls and rock gardens; *Vinca minor* (myrtle, periwinkle). hardy and fast growing.

✓   ✓   ✓

Ground Cover for Wet Soils

Some soils remain wet because of poor drainage or a clay texture. Ground cover that will grow under these conditions include: bog-rosemary, creeping snowberry, red-osier dogwood, bluets, Labrador tea, moneywort, true forget-me-not, and yellow root.

✓   ✓   ✓

Ground Cover for Seashore Plantings

Seashore plants must be especially adapted to sand, salt, and windy conditions. Recommended ground cover for these conditions are: common thrift, beach wormwood, bearberry, bellflower, sweet-fern, broom, aronsbeard, St. Johnswort, gold flower, shore juniper, creeping juniper, Japanese honeysuckle, bayberry, and Virginia rose.

✓   ✓   ✓

Ground Cover between Stepping Stones

Ground cover can be grown between stepping stones to soften the harsh-

Ground Cover for Special Locations

Common name	Latin name	Height	Spacing
SUNNY AREAS			
Scotch Heather [1,2]	*Calluna vulgaris*	1'+	1'
Rockspray [5]	*Cotoneaster horizontalis*	3'	4'
Candytuft	*Iberis sempervirens*	1'	1'
Sargent Juniper	*Juniperus chinensis* var. *sargentii*	1'	4'
Creeping Juniper	*Juniperus horizontalis* and variants	1'	4'
Moss Pink	*Phlox subulata*	6"	8"
Stonecrop [4]	*Sedum* species	3-6"	6"
Creeping Thyme	*Thymus serpyllum*	3"	6"
SHADED AREAS			
Bugle Plant [3]	*Ajuga reptans*	3"	8"
Lily-of-the-Valley [3,5]	*Convallaria majalis*	6"	6-8"
Ferns	*Dennstaedtia (Dicksonia)* sp.	2'	8-10"
	Dryopteris goldiana	3'	3'
	Polypodium sp.	6"	1'
Epimedium [5]	*Epimedium* sp.	1'	1'
English Ivy [7]	*Hedera helix* and variants	1'	1'
Canby Pachistima	*Pachistima canbyi*	1'	1'
Japanese Spurge	*Pachysandra terminalis*	8"	1'
Chamaedrys Germander	*Teucrium chamaedrys*	10"	1'
Periwinkle or Myrtle [3]	*Vinca minor*	6"	1'
GROUND COVERS FOR SEASHORE			
(A) For Exposed Conditions			
Bearberry [1,2,6]	*Arctostaphylos uva-ursi*	1'	3'
Hall's Honeysuckle [4,7]	*Lonicera japonica 'Halliana'*	1'	3'
Virginia Creeper [5,7]	*Parthenocissus quinquefolia*	1'	5'
(B) For More Sheltered Areas			
Rockspray [5]	*Cotoneaster horizontalis*	3'	4'
Wintercreeper [7]	*Euonymus fortunei*	6"	3'
English Ivy [7]	*Hedera helix* and variants	1'	1'
Creeping Juniper	*Juniperus procumbens*	1'	4'
Shore Juniper	*Juniperus conferta*	1'	3'
Creeping Juniper	*Juniperus horizontalis* and variants	1'	4'
Memorial Rose [4,5]	*Rosa wichuraiana*	1'	3'
Common Periwinkle	*Vinca minor*	6"	1'
CITY CONDITIONS			
Goutweed	*Aegopodium podograria*	1'	1'
Bugle Plant [3]	*Ajuga reptans*	3"	8"
Rock-cress	*Arabis caucasica*	8"	1'
Snow-in-Summer	*Cerastium tomentosum*	6"	1'
Lily-of-the-Valley [5]	*Convallaria majalis*	6"	6-8"
English Ivy [7]	*Hedera helix* and variants	1'	1'
Japanese Spurge	*Pachysandra terminalis*	8"	1'

[1] Well-drained soil important
[2] Acid soil site best
[3] Good in sun or shade
[4] Confine, may grow out-of-bounds
[5] Deciduous
[6] Difficult to transplant
[7] Climbs as a vine where it has support. Spacing given is approximate for use as a ground cover

ness of concrete. Plants that will perform this function are: Corsican sand-wort, moss sandwart, common thrift, baby winter creeper, moneywort, ground ivy, pearlwort, goldmoss stonecrop, wollystem thyme, mother-of-thyme, and violets.

✓   ✓   ✓

Ground Cover Where Soil Is Sparse

Both in a wall and in a rock garden where soil is sparse, species of *Sedum* are the most adaptable plants. They are low growing, flower abun-dantly, and require little care. Flower colors range from white to pink, red and purple, and the blooming season extends from spring until autumn.

✓   ✓   ✓

Ground Cover for Hot, Dry Climates

Cotoneasters are woody shrubs that serve well as ground cover in hot, dry climates. They are particularly decorative along the bases of walls and as underplantings to trees and shrubs. Occasional light pruning helps keep the plants dense and attractive. Other plants adapted to these conditions include: goutweed, bearberry, broom, matrimony-vine, ribbon-grass, fleece-flower, rose acacia, and fragrant sumac.

✓   ✓   ✓

Cover for Steep Banks

Ground cover on steep banks can reduce erosion and eliminate the need to mow. Ground cover suited to steep banks should establish itself rapidly and hold to the soil well. Recommended are: sweet-fern, rock spray, dwarf bush honeysuckle, matrimony-vine, and coral berry.

✓   ✓   ✓

Plants for a Rapid Ground Cover

Some ground cover plants grow more rapidly than others. If a ground cover is needed immediately, the following plants are recommended: *Akebia quinata, Aegopodium podograria, Campanula carpatica, Hedra helix, Loni-cera henryi, Lycium halimifolium, Sasa pumila,* and *Vinca minor.*

✓   ✓   ✓

Ground Cover with Colored Fruit

Some ground cover bears attractively colored fruit. Recommended are: bearberry (red), black chokeberry (black), bunchberry (red), cotoneaster (red), wintergreen (red), Oregon holly grape (blue), bayberry (gray), and coralberry (red).

✓   ✓   ✓

Ferns for Shaded Northern Exposures

If you find it difficult to establish cover in northern exposures along the sides of buildings, try ferns. They often prove successful where other plants fail for lack of light. The evergreen varieties are more desirable because they make permanent cover. The Christmas fern is the most desirable and adaptable of the evergreen ferns.

✓   ✓   ✓

Annuals for Temporary Cover

It is sometimes desirable to provide a temporary ground cover before permanent plantings are made. Annuals such as sweet alyssum, portulaca, verbenas, and California poppies can provide an attractive ground cover within a month.

✓   ✓   ✓

Cover That Cascades over Banks

It is sometimes difficult to establish plants on the sides of rock walls and banks, and yet plants are needed. Consider planting a cover with a weeping habit on top of the bank. The growth will cascade over the side. An ideal choice for this is weeping forsythia (*Forsythia suspensa*). It has showy, yellow flowers and a graceful, weeping habit.

✓   ✓   ✓

Native Plants as Ground Cover

There are a number of native plants that will work well in your landscape as ground cover. If you have access to such plants, they make a cost-free addition to your landscape. Among the more useful plants are: anemone, bellwort, blue bead clintonia, bluebells, butterfly-weed, Canada mayflower, dogtooth violet, rattlesnake plantain, toadflax, and wild geranium. Abandoned farms and rural roadside areas are likely places to find these plants.

✓   ✓   ✓

Strawberry Plants for Ground Cover

Strawberry plants make excellent ground cover. Their leaves create a thick cover with an appealing texture. And, you get the bonus of juicy strawberries! Select an everbearing variety so that berries can be yours throughout the growing season.

✓   ✓   ✓

Dwarf Shrubs as Ground Cover

Evergreens and other shrubs that do not exceed 3 feet in height can be planted together to form a ground cover for a contemporary landscaping.

Dwarfs to consider are: bayberry, bog rosemary, box-huckleberry, broom, carmel creeper, coralberry, drooping *Leucothoe,* dwarf Japanese quince, dwarf yew, English lavender, mugo pine, and sweet fern.

✓   ✓   ✓

Numerous Shapes of English Ivy

The most popular ground cover is English ivy (*Hedra helix*). Many people don't realize the great variety of English ivy leaf shapes that are extant. Some varieties have leaves so deeply cut that they give a fine, fern-like texture to the ground cover. The leaves of the variety "Heron" resemble a bird's foot. If you choose English ivy for a cover, study the various leaf shapes that are available before buying.

✓   ✓   ✓

Air Pollution-Resistant English Ivy

English ivy and other plants have difficulty surviving in large cities because of damage from air pollution. Dr. T. H. Everett, of the New York Botanical Garden, has discovered a strain of English ivy called "238th Street" that withstands urban air pollution as well as adverse winter conditions. Ask your nurseryman for this selection if you live in densely populated areas.

✓   ✓   ✓

The Hardiest Evergreen Ground Cover

Creeping myrtle (*Vinca minor*) has earned a reputation as the hardiest evergreen ground cover. It has a trailing habit and produces a woody vine that grows prostrate along the ground. Creeping myrtle is hardy in frigid Minnesota and does equally well in Florida and California. If you want a ground cover that will survive in your particular area, *Vinca minor* is a good bet.

✓   ✓   ✓

Roses for Ground Cover

Roses are generally not thought of as ground cover. But, there are selections that work well under special circumstances. Roses are especially adapted to use on banks, where fast growing shoots will root and aid in erosion control. Roses also have their place in rocky areas. Among the many types of roses that can serve as ground cover are: "Max Graf rose," "memorial rose," and "crimson shower."

✓   ✓   ✓

Caution: Beware of Rapidly Growing Ground Cover

Some ground cover grow so rapidly that they extend out of their boundaries and become pests. Hall's Japanese honeysuckle is an example.

Such ground cover should be used only in remote areas of the landscape where they won't pose a problem.

Section Three

GROWING AND MAINTAINING GROUND COVER

Propagate Your Own Ground Cover

One major drawback to the use of ground cover is cost per plant. Plants currently cost as much as 50¢ each. You can save money by purchasing plants and propagating other plants from them by cuttings or division. A bed of sand or vermiculite, protected from the sun by snow fencing or burlap shade, can be used to root such cuttings as Boston ivy. Some plants—lily-of-the-valley, for example—can be multiplied by dividing the clumps.

✓   ✓   ✓

Inexpensive Ivy Transplants

Many of the ivies, such as English ivy, will naturally develop roots where their stems come into contact with the soil. By separating the terminal growth with its new roots intact, you in effect have a new plant. Such plants make excellent and inexpensive transplants.

✓   ✓   ✓

Ground Cover That Needs a Lean Diet

Fertilization of some ground cover plants actually does more harm than good. Root systems of plants that are adapted to poor soils can be burned by fertilization. Plants that grow naturally in poor soils, particularly the alpine types (e.g. Alpine bugle), should not be fertilized. Check with your nurseryman as to the fertilization requirements of the ground cover you purchase.

✓   ✓   ✓

Protecting against Winter Damage

Ground cover, like other plants, can be damaged by severe winter temperatures. In the North, ground cover is often damaged by "winter heaving" caused by alternate freezing and thawing. Small plants are thrust out of the ground, roots are exposed, and the plants die. Small areas of ground cover can be protected against this type of damage by covering it with burlap sacks or evergreen boughs.

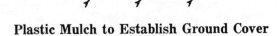

Plastic Mulch to Establish Ground Cover

Weeds can become a real problem before ground cover plants are established. Plastic mulch will help overcome this problem. Place black plastic over well-prepared soil. Cut an X slit in the plastic over each planting hole. Make each hole 3 inches in diameter and set a plant through it. A mulch of pine bark or wood chips can be used to obscure the plastic. The plastic can be left on permanently to reduce weed growth between the ground cover plants.

Cleaning Ground Cover

Ground cover eventually becomes littered with leaves, dust, and other debris. Using a rake to clean the cover may destroy plants, so use a broom to sweep off the large debris and hose off the rest with water.

Feeding Ground Cover through the Leaves

The way to get the quickest fertilization response with ground cover is to spray liquid fertilizer directly on the leaves (foliar feeding). That fertilizer which is not absorbed by the leaves falls to the ground and is taken up by the roots. Special fertilizer formulations are available at garden centers for this purpose. Follow label directions as to concentration and method of application.

Wait before Discarding Frost-Damaged Plants

Damage from cold cannot be clearly determined until plants resume growth in the spring. Plants that appear to be killed by winter's cold temperatures often make a remarkable recovery in the spring. No pruning should be done until growth has begun, at which time the damaged parts may be removed.

Separate Ground Cover from Grass

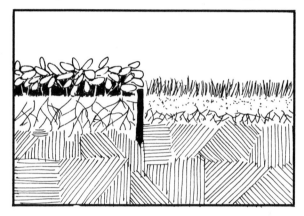

Ground cover can spread out of its bounds and make a ragged-looking yard. To separate ground cover from grass, use a metal or redwood mowing strip between the grass and the ground cover. Whenever the cover reaches the mowing strip, trim it back.

Section Four

SELECTION OF VINES

Choose Long-Lived Vines

When planning to use vines to permanently conceal or landscape an area, be sure to select plants that are long-lived. Vines such as campsis, jasminum and mandevilla sometimes only live for 2 or 3 years, while lace vine, English ivy, clematis, and climbing hydrangea will live for many years.

The Best Hardy Vine

Among hardy vines, clematis is the choice for small gardens. The better varieties of clematis can be confined to a trellis and make a colorful display on a terrace or patio. Clematis vines can use the same supports set out for climbing or rambling roses. They do not harm the rose plants when they climb over them.

✓   ✓   ✓

Grape Vines to Shade Terraces

Grape vines on an overhead trellis make an attractive way to shade terraces and patios. The loss of leaves in the fall allows needed sunlight to enter during the winter months. Concord grape vines provide sufficient shade *and* tasty fruit.

✓   ✓   ✓

Coordinate Vines with Their Surroundings

Color and texture values of areas where you plant a vine should be considered. A small-leaved vine should not be used in an area where most of the plants have large leaves. Flower color of the vine should blend in with the surrounding plants and structures.

✓   ✓   ✓

Combining Annual and Perennial Vines

Some annual vines are attractive when grown with permanent woody vines. The permanent vine can act as a support for the annual. Morning glories will climb up an *Anemone clematis* and precede it in bloom. Other annual vines that can be combined with perennials are cardinal climber, canary-bird vine, nasturitium, and cathedral bells (*Cobaea scandes*).

✓   ✓   ✓

Vines for the Great Plains

Because of cold and wind, only a select number of plants are adaptable to the Great Plains area. The following vines are recommended for these conditions: *Aristolochia durior, Celastrus arbiculatus, Clematis paniculata, Lonicera sempervirens, Partheonocissus quinquefolia, Vitis amurensis,* and *Vitis labrusca.*

✓   ✓   ✓

Vines Not Suitable as Screens

A number of vines are open-growing and not suitable as screens but are attractive and useful for other purposes. If you plant open-growing vines as screens, you will be disappointed to find that they don't perform their job. Among the open-growing vines are: *Ampelopsis aconitifolia, Clematis*

ANNUAL VINES

Botanical Name	Common Name	Manner of Growth	Flowers	Height
Bryonopsis laciniosa	Marble Vine	Climbs by tendrils	Yellow	10 ft.
Calonyction aculeatum	Moonflower	Twining stems	White to violet	30 ft.
Cardiospermum halicacabum	Ballon Vine	Climbs by tendrils	Inconspicuous	10 ft.
Cobaea scadens	Cup-and-Saucer Vine	Climbs by tendrils	Violet or purple	10-25 ft
Cucurbita pepo ovifera	Small-fruited gourd	Twines and tendrils	Yellow or white	20-40 ft.
Dolichos lablab	Hyacinth Bean	Twining stems	Purple to white	15 ft.
Ipomoea purpurea	Sweet Pea	Climbs by tendrils	Wide range	5-8 ft.
Phaseolus coccineus	Scarlet Runner Bean	Climbs by tendrils with suction disks	Deep scarlet	30-40 ft.
Tropaeolum majus	Nasturtium	Twining	Color varies	3-7 ft.

PERENNIAL (WOODY) VINES

Botanical Name	Common Name	Manner of Growth	Flowers	Height
Actinidia arguta	Bower actinidia	Twining	Not showy	50 ft.
Akebia quinata	Five-leaf Akebia	Twining	Lavender	15-30 ft.
Ampelopsis brevipedunculata	Porcelain Ivy Porcelain Berry	Twines and tendrils	Inconspicuous	25 ft.
Aristolochia durior	Dutchman's Pipe	Twining	Yellow-green to brown	30 ft.
Campsis radicans	Trumpet Creeper	Twining stems and rootlike holdfasts	Orange scarlet	30 ft.
Campsis tagliabuana 'Mme. Galen'	Mme. Galen Trumpet Creeper	Twining stems and root-like holdfasts	Brown pod	30 ft.+
Celastrus orbiculatus	Oriental Bitter-sweet	Twining	Inconspicuous	30 ft.
Celastrus scandens	American Bitter-sweet	Twining	Inconspicuous	30 ft.
Clematis crispa	Curly Clematis	Twining of leaf petioles	Lavender-blue	10 ft.
Clematis jackmani	Jackman Clematis	Twining stems and leaf petioles	Violet-purple	12 ft.
Clematis montana rubens	Pink Anemone Clematis	Twining by leaf petioles	Soft Pink	25 ft.
Clematis paniculata	Sweet Autumn Clematis	Twining by leaf petioles	White	30 ft.
Clematis tongutica	Golden Clematis	Twining by leaf petioles	Yellow	10 ft.
Clematis texensis	Scarlet Clematis	Twining by leaf petioles	Bright scarlet	8 ft.
Euonymus fortunei 'Carrierei'	Glossy Winter-creeper	Aerial rootlets	Inconspicuous	20 ft.+
Euonymus fortunei coloratus	Purple leaf Winter-creeper	Aerial rootlets	Inconspicuous	20 ft.+
Euonymus fortunei vegetus	Bigleaf Winter-creeper	Aerial rootlets	Inconspicuous	20 ft.+
Euonymus fortunei minimus	Baby Wintercreeper	Aerial rootlets	Inconspicuous	5 ft.
Hedera helix	English Ivy	Aerial rootlets	Inconspicuous	30 ft.+

Botanical Name	Common Name	Manner of Growth	Flowers	Height
Hydrangea petiolaris	Climbing Hydrangea	Aerial rootlets	White	75 ft.
Lonicera henryri	Henry Honeysuckle	Twining stems	Purplish-red	15 ft.
Lonicera japonica halliana	Hall's Honeysuckle	Twining stems	White to Yellow	20 ft.+
Lonicera sempervirens	Trumpet Honeysuckle	Twining stem	Scarlet and yellow	50 ft.
Parthenocissus quinquefolia	Virginia Creeper	Tendrils and suction disks	Inconspicuous	30 ft.+
Parthenocissus tricuspidata	Boston Ivy	Tendrils and suction disks	Inconspicuous	30 ft.+
Polygonum auberti	Silver Lace Vine	Twining stems	White	25 ft.
Wisteria floribunda	Japanese Wisteria	Twining stems	Violet-blue	25 ft.+
Wisteria sinensis	Chinese Wisteria	Twining stems	Violet-blue	25 ft.+

(large flowering hybrids and their parents), *Lonicera, Mandevilla sauveolens,* and *Parthenocissus quinquefolia.*

✔   ✔   ✔

Vines with Colorful Fruits

Some vines have colorful fruits which add much to their attractiveness. Among the most outstanding are: *Ampelopsis aconitifolia, Celastrus, Clematis, Euonymus fortunei* 'Vegetus,' *Kadsura japonica, Lycium halimifolium, Parthenocissus, Schisandra propinqua,* and *Smilax.*

✔   ✔   ✔

Vines That Withstand Wet Soil Conditions

Most plants are not adapted to wet soil conditions. Vines are no exception. Among the vines which have the best chance of surviving moist to wet soil conditions are: *Boussingaultia baselloides, Campsis radicans, Cissus incisa, Clematis virginiana, Menispermum canadense, Smilax rotundifolia,* and *Trachelospermum.*

✔   ✔   ✔

Evergreen Vines

Evergreen vines are most effective for screening undesirable parts of the landscape since vines which lose their leaves in the fall also lose part of their screening ability. The following evergreen vines are recommended for the South: *Boussingaultia baselloides, Cobaea scandens, Euonymus fortunei, Passifolia caerulea, Smilax megalantha,* and *Trachelospermum asiaticum.* For the North, try *Euonymus fortunei* and *Hedra helix.*

✔   ✔   ✔

Vines That Withstand Shade

Vines are often needed for shady places, particularly when they are used next to buildings. The following are recommended: *Akebia quinata,*

Clematis, Hedra, Hydrangea anomala petiolaris, Lonicera, Parthenocissus, and *Vitis.*

✔   ✔   ✔

Vines That Withstand Dry Soils

Some planting sites for vines are dry and receive inadequate rainfall. Under these conditions, choose a vine that is adapted to dry soils. Consider: *Ampelopsis arborea, Boussingaultia baselloides, Campsis radicans, Cissus texensis, Ficus pumila, Lonicera sempervirens, Parthenocissus, Polygonum aubertii,* and *Pueraria lobata.*

✔   ✔   ✔

Flowering Vines

Flowering vines make spectacular displays in the landscape. Some of the best flowering vines include: *Bignonia capreolata, Boussingaultia baselloides, Campsis,* and *Clematis.*

Section Five

MAINTENANCE OF VINES

Making Wisterias Bloom

Wisterias are sometimes "reluctant" to bloom. One remedy is to dig a trench all around the plant about 3 feet from the stem. Dig deep enough to sever the root system and then fill the trench with rich soil. The shock from the root pruning plus the added nutrients will generally cause blooming.

Be Aware of Rampant Vines

Some vines grow so rapidly that they overgrow structures and cover nearby plants. The red trumpet vine is a good example. It has lovely flowers, but be ready to trim it before it gets out of control. *Jasminum officinale* is an example of a more self-contained vine.

Preventing Bird Nesting in Ivy

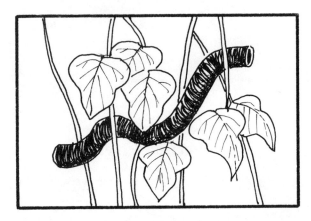

When allowed to climb up the sides of houses, ivy attracts birds and provides cover for them. If the bird population has settled in your ivy, it is difficult to discourage them without damaging the ivy. A simple solution is to take a length of black rubber hose about 3 or 4 feet long. Insert a piece of heavy wire and weave the hose through the ivy to simulate a snake. No more birds!

Pruning Vines

Many fast-growing vines require pruning. How and when you prune them is important. Always prune back to a lateral branch, twig, or bud. Prune all dead, weak, and thin wood back to healthy wood. Do not leave any stubs. The best time to prune most vines is in the dormant season just before new growth begins. Because new growth which develops after pruning produces buds for the following year, early spring flowering vines should be pruned *after* they flower.

Vines on the Sides of Buildings

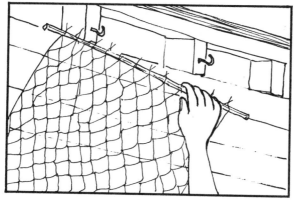

Many vines attach themselves to wooden walls, causing deterioration of the wood. If you wish to grow a vine on the side of a building, make a support out of chicken wire. Thread a pole through one end of the wire and hang it from hooks that are set in eaves. Vines will grow on the chicken wire without becoming attached to the building.

✓   ✓   ✓

Vines from Eaves

The eaves of houses can sometimes be decorated by training plants to grow under them. One approach is to suspend a dowel from the eaves of a house and grow a vine along the dowel. The dowel can be suspended by attaching an eye hook to each eave and a hook to the dowel at each corresponding point. The top and bottom hooks can be joined by light chain or wire.

✓   ✓   ✓

Support for Annual Vines

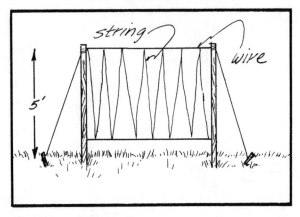

Annual vines such as sweet pea can be grown on strings threaded between two parallel wires. Make sure that the wooden or metal poles which hold the wire are driven into the ground to a minimum depth of 18 inches.

✓   ✓   ✓

Easy-to-Make Trellis for Lightweight Vines

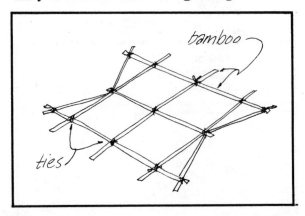

Vines are attractive when grown on a trellis. The trellis can be supported by a building or used as fencing. Trellises for lightweight vines can be made from bamboo sticks that are lashed together. Fasten the sticks together with plant ties, covered wire, or plastic clothesline, as illustrated.

✓   ✓   ✓

Vines for Masonry Walls

Some vines produce adhesive disks or rootlike holdfasts that allow them to cling to masonry walls. Because they destroy wooden siding, these

Adhesive Disks   Rootlike holdfasts

vines should only be used on masonry walls. Vines producing adhesive disks are: Boston ivy, cross-vine, silver-vine creeper, and Virginia creeper. Some rootlike holdfast producers are: climbing hydrangea, euonymus, trumpet-creeper, and Baltic ivy. Wall-clinging vines should be set close (6 to 12 inches) to the brick or stone wall.

CHAPTER FOUR

Shade and Ornamental Trees

Overview

The secret to good tree landscaping lies in placing the right tree in the right place. Always ask yourself why you have chosen to plant a particular tree. Besides providing shade and beauty, trees can perform various useful functions: they can reduce noise and dust levels, screen out unsightly views, protect against snowdrifts, and serve as windbreaks. **Select the tree best suited to the job**—one that fits your landscape and is readily adapted to the site where it will be planted.

Before choosing a trée, **learn what is available to choose from.** Walks through a botanical garden, a well-stocked nursery, or even your own neighborhood will give you an idea of the range of choice that exists. If you have several acres to plant on, choosing the wrong tree isn't crucial; if you have room for only one tree, a wrong choice can affect your entire property.

The ultimate size and shape of the tree is important. **Little seedlings become big trees.** If you are planting around a one-story house on a small lot, choose trees that will remain relatively small. A spreading tree, such as a weeping willow, will overwhelm a small area in a short period, likely cracking sidewalks and drainage pipes in the process.

Know the nature, or habit, of the tree you are about to plant. If you are planning to prune a shade tree to keep it within your lot, make sure that the tree is prunable. A hemlock tree can be contained at just about any size. A maple tree looks awkward when pruned.

Be aware of the seeds and fruits which some trees produce. Some fruits mess up lawns and emit unpleasant orders.

Consider the planting site. For wet soils, plant only species that are adapted to such conditions. Select only trees that will be hardy enough to survive summer heat and winter cold. U.S. Department of Agriculture Handbook 425 gives much of the information needed in choosing a tree.

Once a shade or ornamental tree has been selected, **dig a good hole.** The planting hole should be at least one foot wider and deeper than the spread of the roots, or the ball of earth holding the roots. If your roots spread 8 inches, the hole should be 20 inches wide and 20 inches deep.

Set the tree no lower than the level at which it was formerly grown (slightly higher in poorly drained soil). You will usually find a soil mark on the tree to use as a guide. After the tree is positioned, fill the hole with a mix containing 2/3 good top-soil and 1/3 peat moss or other organic material. If your soil is heavy, add some sand and gravel to the mix. If the tree is planted in fertile soil, there is no need to add fertilizer.

The most frequent cause of death to newly established shade trees is lack of water. In digging the tree for transplanting, a good part of the old root system is destroyed. Following transplanting, a critical period exists before an adequate root system sufficient to maintain the tree can be reestablished. During this period, ample water *must* be provided to allow maximum use of those few roots that are functional. The soil around each tree should be saturated deeply but not flooded. For the first two months following planting, it may be necessary to water twice weekly. Remember also that proper pruning of newly transplanted trees reduces the water needs of the tree in its new site.

Young trees should be fenced to a minimum height of 8 inches if rodents are likely to eat the bark. Plastic tree guards are available for this purpose. Hardware cloth (a wire mesh) is better, though.

Nitrogen fertilizers can be applied at the rate of 1 pound of actual nitrogen per inch of tree trunk diameter. A lawn fertilizer spreader can be used and application made on the ground over which the branches extend. **Fertilizers are most effective when applied in the spring.**

Established trees may or may not require watering. If the leaves appear wilted during drought periods, trees should be watered daily until wilting disappears or the rains resume.

Trees may show such symptoms of decline as dieback, wilting, yellowing, streaking, and spotting. These symptoms can result from insect or disease attacks, or from adverse environmental conditions. Diagnosis of such problems and their proper treatment generally requires an expert. Don't use chemical sprays for insects or disease control until you are certain you are using the right compound and are able to apply it properly. Some chemicals can severely injure plants and people.

Section One

SELECTION

Start a Home Nursery

Landscaping is an ongoing operation that involves continual addition, replacement, and removal of plants. You can save considerable money if you set aside a corner of your yard as a nursery. Small, inexpensive trees and shrubs can be planted in rows or appealing groupings. After several years, attractive plants will be at your disposal to redesign the landscape at considerable savings.

✔   ✔   ✔

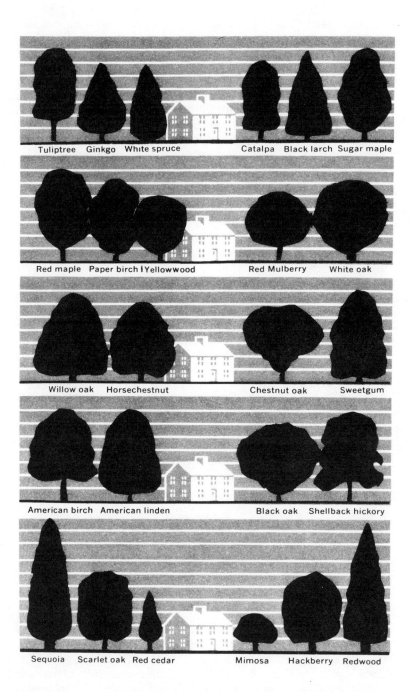

Size of mature shade trees in relation to the height of a 2-story house. Each horizontal line represents 10 feet.

Trunk Single,
Branches Horizontal
White Pine

Trunk Dividing,
Branches Spreading
Elm

Branches Pendulant
Willow

Branches Ascending
White Oak

Branching habits of trees.

Regional Map

To use the following chart, first locate your hardiness zone from the chart at the beginning of Chapter One. Next, locate your region from the chart above. If your zone number is no lower than that listed, the plant stands a good chance of living. In the event that a plant is not listed for your area, it might nevertheless grow there with special attention. Consult your Extension agent.

Name	Zone/Region	Notes
African Tuliptree (Bell Flambeau) *Spathodea campanulata*	10/3	broadleaf evergreen, rapid-growing, to 75 ft
Ailanthus (Tree of Heaven) *Ailanthus altissima*	5/7	deciduous, rapid-growing, to 60-80 ft.
Arborvitae, Eastern *Thuja occidentalis*	2/1,2,4	evergreen, slow-growing, to 60 ft.
Arborvitae, Giant *Thuja plicata*	6/6,9	evergreen, moderate-growing, to 100 ft.
Arborvitae, Japanese *Thuja standishii*	6/1	conical evergreen, slow-growing, to 40 ft.
Arborvitae, Oriental *Thuja orientalis*	3/2,4-6,8,9	conical evergreen, moderate-growing, to 60
Ash, European *Fraxinus excelsior*	3/6,9	deciduous, moderate-growing, to 100 ft.
Ash, Green *Fraxinus pennsylvanica*	2/1,4-7,9	deciduous, moderate-growing, to 40-60 ft.
Ash, Modesto (Arizona Ash) *Fraxinus velutina*	7/6-8	deciduous, moderate-growing, to 45 ft.
Ash, White *Fraxinus americana*	3/1,2,4,9	deciduous, rapid-growing, to 75-100 ft.
Aspen, Quaking *Populus tremuloides*	2/1	deciduous, rapid-growing, to 50-75 ft.

Name	Zone/Region	Notes
Baldcypress *Taxodium distichum*	5/1-3,5	deciduous conifer, moderate-growing, to 100 ft.
Beech, American *Fagus grandifolia*	3/1,2	deciduous, moderate-growing, to 100 ft.
Beech, European *Fagus sylvatica*	5/1,2,5,6,9	deciduous, moderate-growing, to 80-100 ft.
Birch, Paper *Betula payrifera*	2/1,4	deciduous, rapid-growing, to 90 ft.
Birch, White *Betula alba*	2/1,4,9	deciduous, moderate-growing, to 35-50 ft.
Buckeye *Aesculus glabra*	4/1,2,5,6	deciduous, rapid-growing, to 50 ft.
Camphor Tree *Cinnamomum camphoram*	9/2,8	broadleaf evergreen, slow-growing, to 50-60 ft.
Carob *Ceratonia siliqua*	9/7,8	broadleaf evergreen, slow-growing, to 50 ft.
Catalpa, Northern *Catalpa speciosa*	3/1,2,4-6	deciduous, rapid-growing, to 75 ft.
Catalpa, Southern *Catalpa bignonioides*	5/1,2,5	deciduous, moderate-growing, to 50 ft.
Cedar, Atlas *Cedrus atlantica*	6/2,5-9	needle-leaf evergreen, moderate- growing, to 50-100 ft.
Cedar, Eastern Red (Juniper) *Juniperus virginiana*	2/1-7	needle-leaf evergreen, moderate- growing, to 50-75 ft.
Cedar, Incense *Libocedrus decurrens*	6/2,4,6,8,9	needle-leaf evergreen, moderate- growing, to 100 ft.
Cedar of Lebanon *Cedrus libani*	6/1,2,8	needle-leaf evergreen, moderate- growing, to 100 ft.
Cherry, Black *Prunus serotina*	3/2,4	deciduous, moderate-growing, to 75 ft.
Chinaberry (Umbrella Tree) *Melia azedarach*	7/2,5,7,8	deciduous, rapid-growing, to 25-50 ft.
Chinese Tallow Tree *Sepium sebiferum*	7/2	deciduous, slow-growing, to 30 ft.
Cork Tree, Amur *Phellodendron amurense*	4/1,9	deciduous, moderate-growing, to 50 ft.
Cottonwood, Fremont *Populus fremontii*	5/7,8	deciduous, rapid-growing, to 75-90 ft.
Cucumber Tree (Cucumber Magnolia) *Magnolia acuminata*	5/1-3	deciduous, moderate-to-fast-growing, to 50-75 ft.
Cypress, Arizona *Cupressus arizonica*	7/5,7,8	needle-leaf evergreen, rapid-growing, to 50-70 ft.
Dogwood, Pacific *Cornus nuttallii*	7/9	deciduous, slow-growing, to 50 ft.
Douglas Fir *Pseudotsuga menziesii*	3/4,6,7	needle-leaf evergreen, moderate- growing, to 50-100 ft.
Elm, American *Ulmus americana*	3/1,2,4-6,8,9	deciduous, fast-growing, to 100 ft.
Elm, Chinese *Ulmus parvifolia*	5/5-9	deciduous, rapid-growing, to 50-60 ft.
Elm, English *Ulmus procera*	6/1,2,5,9	deciduous, moderate-growing, to 100 ft.
Elm, Scotch *Ulmus glabra*	5/1,9	deciduous, moderate-growing, to 100 ft.
Elm, Siberian *Ulmus pumila*	3/4-9	deciduous, rapid-growing, to 50-75 ft.

Name	Zone/Region	Notes
Eucalyptus (Gum) *Eucalyptus*	10/7,8	mostly broadleaf evergreen, fast-growing
Fir, Silver *Abies alba*	5/7	needle-leaf evergreen, slow-growing, to 80 ft.
Fir, White *Abies concolor*	5/1,6	needle-leaf evergreen, moderate-growing, to 100 ft.
Ginkgo *Ginkgo biloba*	5/1,2,6-9	deciduous, moderate-growing, to 50-100 ft.
Golden Chain Tree *Laburnum anagyroides*	7/9	deciduous, moderate-growing, to 30 ft.
Goldenrain Tree *Koelreuteria paniculata*	5/1-3, 5-9	deciduous, moderate-growing, to 40 ft.
Hackberry, Eastern *Celtis occidentalis*	3/1,2,4-8	deciduous, moderate-growing, to 100 ft.
Hemlock, Canadian *Tsuga canadensis*	3/1,4	needle-leaf evergreen, slow-growing, to 90 ft.
Hemlock, Carolina *Tsuga caroliniana*	7/2	needle-leaf evergreen, slow-to-fast-growing, to 75 ft.
Hickory, Bitternut *Carya cordiformis*	5/1,2	deciduous, moderate-growing, to 75 ft.
Hickory, Shagbark *Carya ovata*	5/1,2	deciduous, moderate-growing, to 100 ft.
Holly, American *Ilex opaca*	6/1-3	broadleaf evergreen, slow-growing, to 75 ft.
Holly, Chinese *Ilex cornuta*	7/2,3	broadleaf evergreen, slow-growing, to 60 ft.
Holly, English *Ilex aquifolium*	7/2,9	broadleaf evergreen, moderate-growing, to 70 ft.
Honeylocust, Thornless *Gleditsia triacanthos inermis*	3/1,2,4-8	deciduous, moderate-to-fast-growing, · to 40-70 ft.
Hornbeam, *American* *Carpinus caroliniana*	3/1,2,9	deciduous, slow-to-moderate-growing, to 50 ft.
Hornbeam, European *Carpinus betulus*	6/1	deciduous, slow-growing, to 60 ft.
Hornbeam, Hop *Ostrya virginiana*	5/1,2	deciduous, slow-growing, to 60 ft.
Horsechestnut *Aesculus hippocastanum*	3/1,6,9	deciduous, moderate-growing, to 75 ft.
Indian Rubber Tree *Ficus elastica*	10/3	broadleaf evergreen, fast-growing, to 100 ft.
Japanese Pagoda Tree *Sophora japonica*	5/1,2,5,6,8,9	deciduous, moderate-growing, to 75 ft.
Juniper, Rocky Mountain *Juniperus scopulorum*	3/4-7	needle-leaf evergreen, moderate-growing, to 20-30 ft.
Katsura *Cercidiphyllum japonicum*	5/1,2,4-6	deciduous, rapid-growing, to 75 ft.
Kentucky Coffeetree *Gymnocladus dioica*	5/1,2,5,6,9	deciduous, moderate-growing, to 90 ft.
Larch, European *Larix decidua*	3/1	needle-leaf deciduous, moderate-growing, to 75 ft.
Larch, Siberian *Larix sibirica*	3/4	needle-leaf deciduous, rapid-growing, to 60 ft.
Laurel, California *Umbellularia californica*	7/8	broadleaf evergreen, moderate-growing, to 75 ft.
Linden, American *Tilia americana*	3/1-4,6,9	deciduous, fast-growing, to 75 ft.

Name	Zone/Region	Notes
Linden, Littleleaf *Tilia cordata*	3/1,2,4,6,7,9	deciduous, moderate-growing, to 50-75 ft.
Locust, Black *Robinia pseudoacacia*	3/1,7,8	deciduous, rapid-growing, to 75 ft.
London Plane *Platanus acerifolia*	6/1,2,6-9	deciduous, rapid-growing, to 75 ft.
Magnolia, Southern *Magnolia grandiflora*	7/1-3,8,9	broadleaf evergreen, moderate-growing, to 75-100 ft.
Mahogany, West Indies *Swietenia mahagonii*	10/3	broadleaf evergreen, rapid-growing, to 75 ft.
Maple, Norway *Acer platanoides*	4/1,2,6,8,9	deciduous, moderate-growing, to 75 ft.
Maple, Red *Acer rubrum*	3/1-3,8,9	deciduous, moderate-growing, to 75-100 ft.
Maple, Silver *Acer saccharinum*	3/2,4,5,7	deciduous, rapid-growing, to 75-100 ft.
Maple, Sugar *Acer saccharum*	3/1,6,9	deciduous, moderate-growing, to 100 ft.
Maple, Sycamore *Acer pseudoplatanus*	6/1,2,5	deciduous, moderate-growing, to 75-90 ft.
Mimosa *Albizia julibrissin*	7/1-3,8,9	deciduous, rapid-growing, to 25-40 ft.
Mulberry, Russian *Morus alba forma tatarica*	5/5-8	deciduous, rapid-growing, to 40 ft.
Norfolk Island Pine *Araucaria excelsa*	10/8	needle-leaf evergreen, moderate- growing, to 100 ft.
Oak, Black *Quercus velutina*	5/1,2	deciduous, moderate-growing, to 100 ft.
Oak, Chestnut *Quercus prinus*	5/1,2,5	deciduous, moderate-growing, to 75-100 ft.
Oak, English *Quercus robur*	5/8	deciduous, slow-growing, to 100 ft.
Oak, Live *Quercus virginiana*	8/2,3,5,8	broadleaf evergreen, moderate-growing, to 75 ft.
Oak, Northern Red *Quercus borealis*	4/1,4,6,8,9	deciduous, moderate-growing, to 75 ft.
Oak, Pin *Quercus palustris*	4/1,2,4-9	deciduous, rapid-growing, to 75 ft.
Oak, Post *Quercus stellata*	7/2,5	deciduous, moderate-growing, to 100 ft.
Oak, Scarlet *Quercus coccinea*	4/1,2,4,5,8,9	deciduous, moderate-growing, to 75 ft.
Oak, Southern Red *Quercus rubra*	7/2,7	deciduous, moderate-growing, to 75-100 ft.
Oak, Texas (Shumard Oak) *Quercus shumardii*	5/5	deciduous, moderate-growing, to 75 ft.
Oak, Turkey *Quercus falcata*	6/1	deciduous, moderate-growing, to 75 ft.
Oak, Water *Quercus nigra*	8/2,3	deciduous, fast-growing, to 75-100 ft.
Oak, White *Quercus alba*	5/1,2,6,9	deciduous, moderate-growing, to 90-150 ft.
Oak, Willow *Quercus phellos*	6/1,2	deciduous, fast-growing, to 75-100 ft.
Olive, Common *Olea europaea*	9/6,7	broadleaf evergreen, slow-growing, to 75 ft.

Name	Zone/Region	Notes
Olive, Russian *Elaeagnus augustifolia*	5/6,7	broadleaf evergreen, moderate-growing, to 25-40 ft.
Palm, Canary Date *Phoenix canariensis*	9/7,8	palm, rapid-growing, to 50-75 ft.
Palm, Coconut *Cocos nucifera*	10/3	palm, rapid-growing, to 90-100 ft.
Palm, Florida Royal *Roystonea elata*	10/3	palm, moderate-to-rapid-growing, to 90-100 ft.
Palmetto, Cabbage *Sabal palmetto*	8/2,3	palm, moderate-growing, to 80 ft.
Pear, Bradford *Pyrus calleryana* 'Bradford'	5/1,2	deciduous, rapid-growing, to 40-50 ft.
Pecan *Carya illinoinensis*	7/2,3,5,7	deciduous, rapid-growing, to 75-100 ft.
Pine, Austrian *Pinus nigra var. austriaca*	3/4-7,9	needle-leaf evergreen, moderate-growing, to 50-60 ft.
Pine, Eastern White *Pinus strobus*	3/1,2	needle-leaf evergreen, moderate-growing, to 100 ft.
Pine, Loblolly *Pinus taeda*	7/2,5	needle-leaf evergreen, rapid-growing, to 50-75 ft.
Pine, Ponderosa *Pinus ponderosa*	3/4-6,9	needle-leaf ·ergreen, moderate-growing, to 60-100 ft.
Pine, Red *Pinus resinosa*	2/1	needle-leaf evergreen, moderate-growing, to 75 ft.
Pine, Scotch *Pinus sylvestris*	3/4	needle-leaf evergreen, moderate-growing, to 50 ft.
Poplar, Carolina *Populus canadensis*	5/7	deciduous, rapid-growing, to 50 ft.
Redbud, Eastern *Cercis canadensis*	6/2,3,5	deciduous, moderate-growing, to 35 ft.
Sassafras *Sassafras albidum*	5/1,2,5	deciduous, moderate-growing, to 75 ft.
Sourgum *Nyssa sylvatica*	5/1,2	deciduous, moderate-growing, to 75 ft.
Sourwood *Oxydendrum arboreum*	7/2,9	deciduous, slow-to-moderate-growing, to 75 ft.
Spruce, Colorado Blue *Picea pungens*	2/1,2,4-6,8,9	needle-leaf evergreen, slow-growing, to 75-100 ft.
Spruce, White *Picea glauca*	2/1,4	needle-leaf evergreen, slow-growing, to 40 ft.
Sweetgum *Liquidamber styraciflua*	5/1-3,6-9	deciduous, rapid-growing, to 75 ft.
Sycamore *Platanus occidentalis*	5/1,2,5	deciduous, rapid-growing, to 75-100 ft.
Tamarack *Larix laricina*	2/1	deciduous needle-leaf, moderate-growing, to 100 ft.
Tulip Poplar *Liriodendron tulipifera*	5/1,2,8,9	deciduous, fast-growing, to 100 ft.
Willow, Weeping *Salix*	6/1	deciduous, fast-growing, to 50 ft.

Buy a Good Root System

When shopping for a shade tree, bear in mind that it is more important to buy a good root system than a large top. A three-foot tree with good roots is a far better buy than a six-foot tree with roots in mediocre or poor condition. The size of the ball or can in which the roots sit will give you some indication of the extent of the root system. Poking a stick into the ball or can will give you a further indication.

✦   ✦   ✦

Avoid Extremely Rapid-Growing Trees

Some trees are advertised and sold as "rapid-growing." Avoid them. Rapid-growing trees have brittle branches and are short-lived. Examples are poplars and silver maples.

✦   ✦   ✦

Trees with Character

Individual specimen trees that have character add much to the landscape. Much of the character of a tree lies in the sculptural quality of its trunk and branches. The branching habit of some trees give them "built-in" character; such trees only require light pruning to maintain their appearance. Examples are: hazelnut, willow, mimosa, pine, Japanese maple, and beach plum.

✦   ✦   ✦

Evergreens Can Care for Broadleaf Plants

If plants are properly located, they can have beneficial effects on each other. Evergreens are very hardy. If tender broadleaf shrubs are planted near hardy evergreens they will benefit from their shade and wind protection. The needles that fall will provide mulch.

✦   ✦   ✦

Plant Deciduous Trees South of House

Before purchasing trees, remember that deciduous trees (trees that lose their leaves in the fall) should be planted on the south side of the house. They will provide shade in the summer and let the sun in during the winter.

✦   ✦   ✦

Flowering Dogwoods Like Shade

Although they sometimes survive in full sunlight, flowering dogwoods do much better if planted in partial shade. The reason: dogwoods are accustomed to living in the shaded understory of forests.

✦   ✦   ✦

Windbreaks for Exposed Sites

Windbreaks are advisable to protect exposed property against heavy winds. A windbreak should consist of several rows (3 or more) of tall shrubs and trees, both evergreens and deciduous, with the tallest row in the center. In the Northeast, a windbreak should be placed north to northwest of the house or driveway. In other sections of the country, winds may sweep from other directions. For an effective windbreak, trees should be spaced as shown in the diagram.

Trees That Make You Sneeze

When choosing tree species for your yard, it may be wise to consider the allergenic properties of their pollen. Tree pollen is responsible for some cases of spring hayfever. The fact that tree pollen is responsible for only a small proportion of all hayfever and asthma cases is of no comfort to those who are afflicted.

Among the most important hayfever-causing trees are: juniper, cypress, birch, alder, planetree, beech, oak, elm, paper mulberry, walnut, hickory, poplar, willow, maple, and ash.

Avoid Tree Debris

When shopping for trees to shade a patio, choose a "clean" one. Some trees produce messy seeds, fruits, or leaves, and keep you busy cleaning up after them. These include ash and locust trees. In certain cases, clean varieties of messy trees are available. Both seedless ash and podless locust trees are available. Ask for them.

Trees for Wet Areas

It is difficult to establish trees in wet areas, but some do better than others. The following trees have the best chance of surviving in a wet environment: red maple, silver maple, alder, service berry, river birch, honeylocust, European larch, American sweetgum, sweetbay magnolia, black tupelo, London planetree, poplar, swamp white oak, willow, and common bald cypress.

✓   ✓   ✓

Choose a Male Ginkgo Tree

Ginkgo trees are desirable as shade trees because they are attractive and free of insect and disease problems. However, when buying a ginkgo, choose a male tree. The fruits from female trees will litter the ground and have a vile odor. Reliable nurseries can often guarantee the sex of their ginkgo trees. Most trees produce both sexual flowers on the same tree rather than on different trees as is the case with the ginkgo.

✓   ✓   ✓

Avoid Trees That Clog Sewers

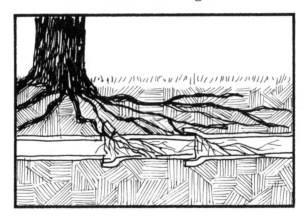

Some trees have extensive root systems that penetrate underground sewer lines and clog them, as illustrated. The best way to avoid this costly problem is not to plant trees with this characteristic close to sewer or drainage lines. Trees most notorious for clogging sewers are poplars, willows, sycamores, and silver maples. On larger plots, these trees should be judiciously placed; on smaller plots, they should not be planted at all.

✓   ✓   ✓

Plant Small Trees under Power Lines

The branches from large trees grow into power lines and require continual pruning. To solve this problem, plant only small trees under power lines. The following trees are suitable for planting directly under power lines: Lavalle hawthorn, upright European hornbeam, *Acer platanoides* *'Globorum,'* purple-leaved plum, and Washington hawthorn.

✓   ✓   ✓

Trees That Attract Birds

Trees provide nesting sites, cover, and food for birds. Some trees are more attractive to birds than others. The following are particularly attractive: Mimosa, alder, birch, dogwood, hawthorn, apple, mulberry, sycamore, oak, and European mountain ash. If the presence of birds proves more a problem than a pleasure, avoid these trees.

Section Two

PLANTING

Locating Trees

The positioning of trees in your yard is an important consideration which often receives little attention. Place large trees to the south or southwest of outdoor living areas, where they will not cast excess shade. If space is limited, grow small flowering trees in the shade of large ones (dogwoods and redbuds can be planted in the shade of elms or oaks). Trees planted off of the corners of a house will block window views the least.

✓   ✓   ✓

Carrying Balled and Burlapped Plants

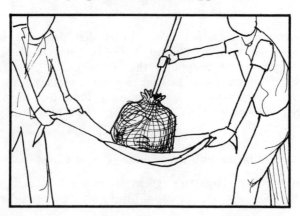

Balled and burlapped plants are sometimes so heavy that one person cannot lift them. A helpful way to carry heavy plants is to roll them in a piece of canvas. Two people will then be able to transport the plant by lifting the corners of the canvas.

✔   ✔   ✔

When to Plant Landscape Plants

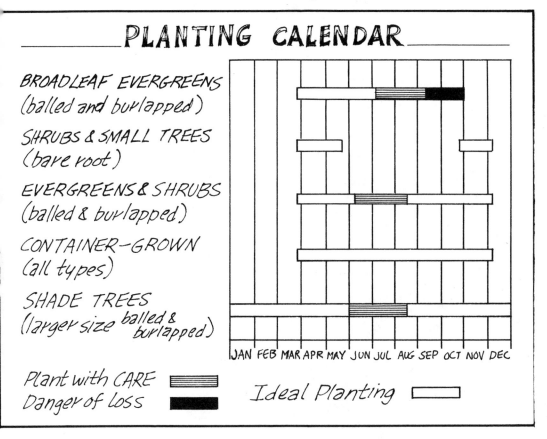

PLANTING CALENDAR

BROADLEAF EVERGREENS (balled and burlapped)

SHRUBS & SMALL TREES (bare root)

EVERGREENS & SHRUBS (balled & burlapped)

CONTAINER-GROWN (all types)

SHADE TREES (larger size balled & burlapped)

JAN FEB MAR APR MAY JUN JUL AUG SEP OCT NOV DEC

Plant with CARE
Danger of loss

Ideal Planting

The survival of transplanted landscape plants depends on when and how they are planted. The chart can serve as a guide to the best time to transplant. Broadleaf evergreens include rhododendrons and azaleas.

✔   ✔   ✔

Trees That Break Sidewalks and Driveways

When tall-growing trees are planted in small spaces near sidewalks and driveways, their roots will eventually lift and crack the concrete. To avoid

this problem, allow at least a 6-foot-square planting area for a tree that will be 20 to 35 feet tall at maturity.

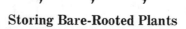

Beware: Wire-Attached Labels Kill

Plants bought from nurseries often have labels attached to them with wire. If the wire is too tight, it may constrict and kill branches. Remove the wire and labels at planting time.

Storing Bare-Rooted Plants

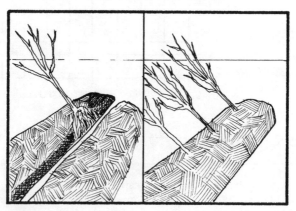

Often, bare-rooted trees and shrubs need to be stored between the time they are received and planted. The best way to provide temporary storage is to "heal in" the plants. Follow this procedure: Dig a trench large enough to accommodate the root systems. Place the roots in the trench. Cover them with a mound of soil. Individual plants can be easily removed when needed.

Making Planting Hole Drain

If water can stand in a hole for more than 12 hours, it is inadvisable to use that hole for planting. Standing water excludes oxygen, and when roots are deprived of oxygen, they die. A technique that is used to create adequate drainage in planting holes with inadequate drainage is to con-

struct a chimney. Using a post hole digger, dig through the tight clay soil into more porous soil below. This will not be possible if the layer of tight soil is too thick, but it is worth a try. Test the drainage properties of the reconstructed planting hole by filling it with water. If, after building a drain of this type, all the water still doesn't disappear in 12 hours, find a new planting site.

Planting Container-Grown Trees

Many container-grown trees are raised in a light, loose, fast-draining mix that favors quick root development. If roots grown in this environment are transplanted into dense soil, they will grow neither outward nor downward. To avoid this problem, dig holes for container-grown trees twice the size of the container. If the roots are crowded or coiled after the container is removed, straighten them out, place them into the planting hole, and fill the remainder of the hole with a 1 to 1 mixture of good soil and peat.

Remove Strings and Wires around Balled Trees

When trees are balled in burlap, the ball is often anchored to the stem with a string or wire. Although it is not harmful to leave the burlap on the ball when you plant (it will rot), be sure to remove any string or wire wrapped around the trunk. String and wire will constrict the tree as it grows and, possibly, kill it.

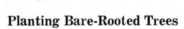

Planting Bare-Rooted Trees

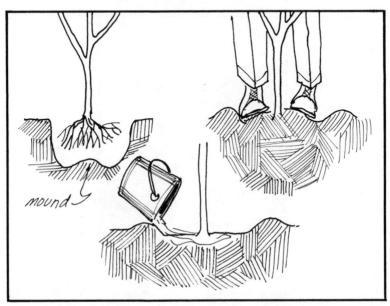

Bare-rooted trees need special attention to create conditions for the establishment of new roots. As illustrated, dig the planting hole twice as wide and 12 inches deeper than the roots. Set the plant on a mound of fertile soil at the depth that it grew previously. Fill the hole slowly with ⅔ fertile soil and ⅓ peat moss, tamping as you fill. Allow the refilled area to remain an inch or two below the level of the surrounding ground. Slowly add a bucket of water. The earth in the hole will sink somewhat, creating a water catch. Check the next day to see if any air pockets have developed.

Prune Bare-Rooted Trees

Considerable root loss of bare-rooted trees is to be expected when they are dug out of a nursery. In order to compensate for this loss and increase the tree's chance of survival, the tree's top must be pruned to reduce the leaf burden on the roots. How the tree is pruned depends on its shape. If the tree is unbranched, cut off the top ⅓. If the tree is branched, and has a good root system, all side branches should be pruned back at least halfway.

Prune the branches just above a bud directed *away* from the trunk. The leader may or may not be pruned depending upon its shape.

Prune Roots of Bare-Rooted Trees

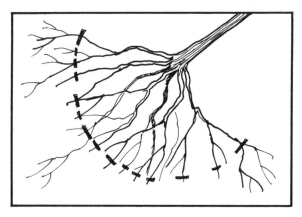

In order to give bare-rooted trees a good start, their roots should be pruned. Inspect the root system thoroughly and prune out any straggly, unhealthy, or broken roots. Remove ½ to 1 inch from the ends of all main roots.

Mud Bath for Bare-Rooted Trees

When planting a number of bare-rooted trees at the same time, do not allow the roots of some of the trees to remain exposed to the air while others are being planted. Even short periods of exposure can cause the roots to dry out and die. As a precaution, soak the root systems of un-planted trees in buckets of water until planting. Before transporting, dip the root systems in a mud bath. The mud will form a moisture-preserving protective coating.

✔   ✔   ✔

Late Planting of Bare-Rooted Trees

It is sometimes necessary to plant bare-rooted trees during the summer, later than the accepted deadline for transplanting. Enhance the chances of survival of late transplants by spraying the tree tops with Wilt Pruf to prevent drying. Mulch deeply over the roots after planting.

✔   ✔   ✔

Staking Newly Planted Trees

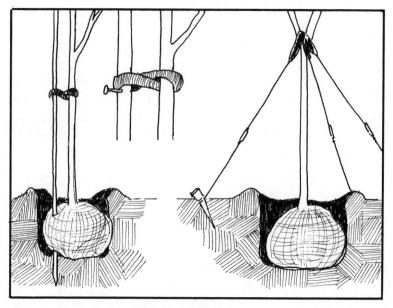

Trees will develop stronger trunks if they are not staked when they are planted. However, if a newly planted tree cannot stand firmly alone without being staked, the tree must be anchored. Thread wire through old garden hose, wrap it around the tree trunk, and attach it to stakes or posts. The diagram shows two ways that this can be done. Be sure not to constrict the growth of the tree with the attached wire.

✔   ✔   ✔

Don't Add Chemical Fertilizers to the Planting Hole

If granular chemical fertilizers come into direct contact with roots, they may burn and kill them. For this reason, it is advisable *not* to add chemical fertilizers to the planting hole when transplanting. Organic fertilizers, such as well-rotted manure, are harmless. Mix them well with the soil used to refill the hole.

Controlled-Release Fertilizers

Fertilizers are now being manufactured with a coating over the fertilizer particles that slows down their release to the plant. Such fertilizers, which last longer in the soil and reduce the frequency that fertilization is necessary, can be placed in the planting hole at the time of planting without danger of injuring the plant. They are available at garden centers as "Agriform" tablets. Follow the directions on the label.

Balling and Burlapping Trees

One way to assure the survival of a tree which you plan to transplant from one area of the landscape to another is to "ball and burlap" the root system of the tree with a spade. Slip a piece of burlap under the roots and surrounding soil, and lift the plant out of the hole. The ball of soil and roots should then be wrapped with burlap, and the burlap secured with string or nails (used as pins). Balling and burlapping is particularly recommended for evergreen trees and shrubs. Dig no closer than 10 inches from the trunk of the tree. The larger the ball of earth, the less the roots will be disturbed, thus improving the tree's chances of survival in its new location.

Labeling of Landscape Plants

The exact variety of a plant is often hard to determine once the identification label has been removed. Make it a practice to label landscape plants on stakes placed next to the plants. Put the labelled stakes in the same position relative to each plant. This will eliminate confusion when you want to identify a given plant. An alternative is to attach tags to the tree. When attaching tags, take care not to constrict any branches.

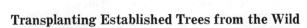

Transplanting Established Trees from the Wild

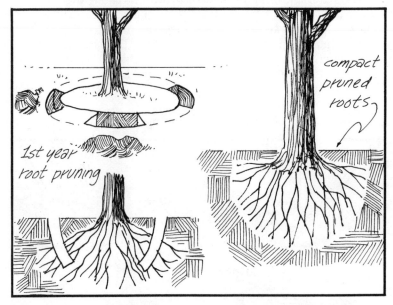

compact
pruned
roots

1st year
root pruning

It is difficult to transplant trees from the wild because their rambling root systems are difficult to dig. If trees are root pruned one to two years before they are removed, a denser and easier-to-dig root system will develop that will enhance the chances of the tree's survival. The first year, tree trenches one-spade-wide are dug, as illustrated. Fertile soil is placed in the trenches. The second year, the remaining trenches are dug around the tree. The trenching will encourage the tree to develop a more compact root system which will enable it to withstand transplanting. The tree can be dug and moved in the spring or fall of the third year.

Section Three

PRUNING AND FELLING

How a Branch Grows

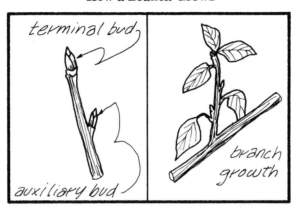

Before pruning a tree or shrub, it is important to understand how different kinds of buds develop. A terminal bud—located at the end of a shoot—will form next year's stem growth. A side, or auxiliary, bud will make new branches. The vertical branch in the right of the diagram has emerged from a side bud. In turn, it has developed both side buds and a terminal bud for next year's growth.

✦   ✦   ✦

Fertilize before Major Pruning

The ability of a tree to heal wounds following pruning is dependent on its general vitality. If you plan to perform "major surgery" on a tree, fertilize it adequately the year prior to the surgery. This will allow the tree to heal more rapidly following pruning.

✦   ✦   ✦

Don't Prune Main Leaders

Trees grow taller through the extension of a dominant, main leader. Though many of them will establish a new leader if the current one is removed, some have difficulty doing so. Examples are pines, oaks, and nut trees. When pruning, be extremely careful not to remove the main leader. If the leader is destroyed, the tree may become misshapen for life. When in doubt, it is always best to discuss your plans with a good nurseryman before taking knife in hand.

✦   ✦   ✦

Avoid Double Leaders on Trees

Unless your tree is a spreading type (dogwoods, fruit trees, and flowering crab), train it to have a main leader (in other words, *one* dominant stem). A tree with a double leader is subject to splitting when the branches get heavier. Prune off all branches that compete with the main leader, as illustrated.

✓   ✓   ✓

Tree Crotch Angles Are Important

The angle that is formed at the intersection of a tree branch and the main stem is important. Eliminate those branches that form acute angles with the stem. They tend to split away from the stem. Leave crotches that make wide angles (approaching 90 degrees) with the stem.

✓   ✓   ✓

Preventing Pruned Maples from Bleeding

Maples often bleed at cut surfaces after they are pruned. The slime that runs down the tree is both unsightly and detrimental to the tree. To prevent this, maples should be pruned during subfreezing periods in the winter. Freezing temperatures prevent bleeding of maple sap.

✓   ✓   ✓

Pruning Dogwoods and other Flowering Trees

When dogwoods and other flowering trees are pruned can affect their flowering. Prune them immediately *after* they bloom. Earlier pruning will delay flower bud development for a year or more.

✓   ✓   ✓

Radical Pruning Can Cause Sunscald

It is sometimes necessary to prune out large portions of a tree to improve a window view or remove damaged wood. In doing this, you may suddenly expose to the sun large areas of the tree that have grown accustomed to the shade. Damage (sunscald) to tree bark and branches may result. Thin-barked trees are particularly susceptible to sunscald. If this problem is anticipated, exposed areas of bark can be wrapped with porous cloth strips or tree wrap for several months prior to pruning, or temporary shading can be provided with snow fence until the tissues have become accustomed to the new exposure.

✓   ✓   ✓

Pruning Large Branches from Trees

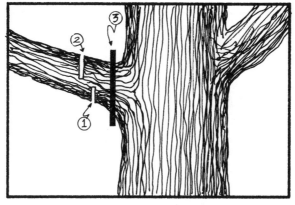

When a large, heavy branch is pruned from a tree, it often strips the bark off the main stem as it falls. Avoid this by making a series of three cuts into the branch. First, make a cut ¼ of the way through the bottom of the branch, 8 to 24 inches away from the main stem. Next, cut ¾ through the width of the branch, from the top side, about 2 to 4 inches further out on the branch than the first cut. The branch will crack and break at (2). When the main part of the branch is severed, a small stub will be left attached to the tree. With a third cut, the small stem can then be removed by making a single cut flush with the main stem without stripping bark from the main stem.

✔   ✔   ✔

Pruning Evergreens

In general, evergreens should be pruned during the winter, when they are dormant. Prune evergreens according to their growth habit. In pruning, don't shear off portions of *all the branches;* remove instead individual stems, leaving those that give the plant a pleasing shape. Shearing ruins the natural habit of growth and prevents light from penetrating the center of the plant, resulting in foliage drop. A plant should only be sheared when it is young and dense growth is being encouraged to prevent a sparse plant.

✔   ✔   ✔

Remove All Stubs

If branches are not cut flush with the main stem or a connecting branch, dead stubs remain on trees. These stubs are not only unsightly, but also provide an entranceway for rot fungi to enter the heartwood of the tree. Therefore, make all pruning cuts flush.

✔   ✔   ✔

Treating Bark Wounds on Trees

The bark of trees is continually wounded by storms, vandals, gardening equipment, etc. If these wounds are not properly treated, they can cause rot to develop in the tree itself. It is imperative that all dead and damaged bark be removed and the wound shaped to promote rapid healing.

With a chisel and mallet, trace out an elliptical outline around the wounded area (as illustrated), making sure the dead area is inside the ellipse. A tree wound dressing is not necessary, but can be applied to the wounded surface for cosmetic purposes. A properly treated wound will soon form new growth to replace the old.

✤   ✤   ✤

Remove Girdling Roots

POSSIBLE UNDERGROUND GIRDLE

Sometimes, a tree's own roots will girdle it, choking off the movement of food through the trunk. This can be easily observed when the roots at the base of the trunk are intertwined. Girdling roots are suspected when the trunk of a tree is perpendicular to the ground line, rather than flaring out as trunks usually do. Girdling roots should be pruned out and removed. If underground girdling is suspected, it will be necessary to excavate around the base of the tree.

✤   ✤   ✤

Pruning Palm Trees

Because their growth patterns differ from other shade trees, palms must be pruned in a special way. To enhance the overall appearance of palms, cut out old, withering fronds as soon as new ones have emerged. Cut palm leaves from the underside to avoid tearing the fibers of the tree trunk. Never prune the terminal (top) bud of a palm, which would be deadly.

✤   ✤   ✤

Felling Trees in Your Yard

When shade trees die, they should be removed. If dead trees are not removed, falling branches can become a hazard. When felling a tree, cut it so that it falls into a clear area. By using a proper cutting technique, trees can usually be directed to fall where you wish. With a power chain saw, handsaw, or ax make a level cut at waist height, $\frac{1}{3}$ the way into the tree on the side where you want the tree to fall (1). Next, make a diagonal cut at a 45-degree angle above the first cut and remove the V-shaped wedge

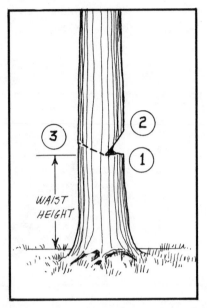

of wood (2). Fell the tree by making a slightly downward cut on the opposite side of the tree toward the point of the V-cut (3). Unless you feel you have the expertise, call in a tree specialist to remove large trees that have branches overhanging your house and other structures.

Section Four

CULTURAL PRACTICES

Getting Tree Seeds to Germinate

Many tree seeds—acorns, nuts, pits, etc.—will not germinate in the spring unless they have undergone a special cold treatment during the winter. Seed that is collected in the fall and stored in a dry, warm place over winter may lose its viability. To ensure tree germination store seeds in a moist 1 to 1 mixture of peat and sand. Place the seeds in a refrigerator for 2 months before planting in the spring.

Heavy Snow and Evergreens

Evergreen branches can catch and hold large quantities of snow. But the snow accumulated during heavy snowfalls can cause branches to break. To prevent this, brush the snow from evergreens before large quantities accumulate.

✓   ✓   ✓

Preventing Trees from Fruiting

If you want to enjoy fruit trees only for their foliage and shade, it is possible to prevent them from fruiting. Synthetic hormone sprays containing naphthaleneacetic acid (sold as App-L-Set, or Parmone) can be applied during bloom to prevent fruit set. Apply according to the directions on the label. Eliminating the fruit from trees will eliminate the insects which it attracts.

✓   ✓   ✓

Water Evergreens in the Fall

During the winter months, evergreens lose water through their needles. This occurs predominantly during periods when soil moisture is frozen and, as a result, not available to the trees. To ensure that evergreens have sufficient water throughout the winter season, do not allow them to pass the winter under "water stress." If there has not been ample autumn rainfall, water your evergreens in the fall. The erection of windbreaks around evergreen trees will further lessen the drying effect of winter winds.

✓   ✓   ✓

Aluminum Foil as a Trunk Wrap

Aluminum foil can serve as a tree trunk wrap to prevent winter sun from scalding the bark. It also works to "foil" rabbits, mice, and other pests which nibble at tree trunks.

✓   ✓   ✓

Keep Salt away from Tree Root Zones

In northern regions of the United States, salt is commonly used on driveways and walks to remove snow and ice. Be careful not to allow salt to accumulate around the root zones of trees and other plants. Salt will severely damage or, possibly, kill them. Be careful also not to pile salt-laden snow around trees and vegetation.

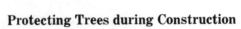

Outdoor Barbecue Pits and Fireplaces
Can Injure Trees

Most of us are aware that air pollution can injure trees. The same is true of "local" air pollution created in our own backyards. Be careful to position outdoor barbecue pits and fireplaces so that the smoke emanating from them does not reach surrounding shade trees.

Protecting Trees during Construction

Established shade trees can be irreversibly damaged during the construction of homes. Most damage is caused by heavy equipment, which compacts the soil around trees and severs roots. Tree trunks are also often bruised by bulldozers and the like. Before beginning construction, surround all trees with temporary fences. Snow fencing attached to posts driven into the ground works well. Scrap lumber and crates can also be used. Construct each fence 4 to 5 feet away from the trunk so as to protect part of the root system.

Changing the Grade around Trees

If special precautions are not taken when fill dirt is placed around trees to raise the grade, the tree roots will be killed for lack of oxygen.

When making changes in the grading of land which will affect existing trees, construct masonry wells around the stem of each tree. The well formed around the tree can be left open or filled with gravel. Areas shaded by the trees should be filled with only 6 inches of topsoil and supported by large crushed gravel. The gravel allows oxygen to reach the roots and carbon dioxide to be expelled. Tiles should be run vertically from the soil surface to the gravel area to further facilitate gas exchange. Space the tiles about 4 feet apart in the area filled with gravel.

Section Five

PEST CONTROL

Check Credentials of Tree "Experts"

Fly-by-night tree "experts" are easy to find. These people can damage your trees, while charging you for useless services. Before contracting to have work done, check with your county agent or Better Business Bureau as to the competence and reliability of the individual or company you are considering hiring.

Spraying Trees Properly

Occasionally, it is necessary to spray shade trees to control insects or disease. Even when the proper pesticide is used, the success or failure of a treatment is dependent on the spraying method used. The spray material should be applied in a mist form that drifts onto the tree. First, spray beneath the tree, moving the spray nozzle very slowly in an arc (1). Then,

encircle the outside of the tree with a slow arc allowing the spray mist to penetrate the leaves (2). It is important that both sides of the leaves be coated with the pesticide. Do not spray so heavily that the spray material coalesces and runs off the leaves.

✔   ✔   ✔

Don't Spray during Hot Weather

Some spray materials can severely damage trees if applied during very hot weather by chemically burning the leaves. Sulfur is such a substance. Spray only when temperatures range between 40 and 79 degrees F., and when it is expected that temperatures will not radically change for at least 24 hours.

✔   ✔   ✔

Organic Gypsy Moth Control

The gypsy moth is an important defoliator of trees in the Eastern United States. This pest can be combatted without the use of insecticides. *Bacillus thuringiensis* is a bacterium which, when sprayed on foliage, will kill the gypsy moth larvae. Apply as directed on the label. A sticky substance known as "tanglefoot" can also be applied to tree trunks in circular bands about 3 to 6 feet above the ground. The band should be about 4 inches wide and thick enough to be very sticky. This prevents the larvae from crawling up the tree and attacking the foliage. "Tanglefoot" is available at garden centers.

✔   ✔   ✔

How to diagnose problems of trees and shrubs

INJURY	CAUSES

WHOLE PLANT

Plant makes poor growth first or second year after planting.

Pot bound if container grown. Insufficient root system to supply shrub. Planted too deep or too shallow. Poor drainage. Dried-out. Root competition from nearby trees.

Twisted terminal growth of stems and leaves.

2,4-D injury.

TRUNK or BRANCHES

Gray or brown shell-like areas.

Scald.

Partial die-back.

Winter injury, borer, basal mechanical injury, fungus.

Young stems with dark stripes.

Bacterial blight.

Swelling of stems, irregular branching.

Nematodes.

Round abnormal growths (usually at node).

Galls.

LEAVES

Curled and distorted.

Aphids, 2,4-D injury.

Brown irregular areas.

Spray injury, fungus.

Lines or tunnels.

Leaf miner.

White or powdery appearance.

Powdery mildew.

Grayish or yellowish fine specks, sometimes accompanied with web.

Spider mite.

Leaves gray, then become black.

Bacterial blight, dog urine.

Poor green or yellowish green.

Mineral deficiency, excessive soil salts in soil.

Wilting of young growth, eventual death of plant.

Gas leak, lack of water, poor drainage, anthracnose.

Brown to black circular spots.

Fungus or bacteria.

Chewed leaf margins.

Taxus vine weevil.

Greenish young insects crowded near tips of stems and under leaves.

Aphids.

Leaves skeletonized.

Webworm.

Leaves rolled.

Leaf roller, dry weather, extreme cold.

FLOWERS

Shrub never flowered.

Too much shade, flower buds frozen, excessive vegetative growth.

Flowers only partially develop, some turn brown.

Winter damage, spray injury, bacterial blight.

Short flowering period.

Temperatures unusually high, extreme dryness, borer.

Flowers suppressed.

Nematodes, too much shade.

Weak color.

Nutrient deficiency.

FRUIT

No fruit.

Male or female plant, poor pollinating, spring freeze, too much shade, insufficient light.

Few fruit.

Poor pollination, excessive vegetative growth.

How to diagnose problems of evergreens

INJURY	CAUSES
WHOLE YOUNG PLANT Seeds fail to come up.	Lack of moisture, collar rot.
ROOTS Mechanical injury to roots.	Lack of moisture, mechanical injury from cultivating or transplanting, freezing, too much moisture, nematodes.
TRUNK or BRANCHES Pitch on stem below soil line.	Pine root weevil.
Bark injury.	Mechanical, sunscald, bark beetle, Red Cedar aphid.
Dying of lower branches.	Lack of moisture or sunlight, spruce canker.
Swelling on stems. Orange pustules on bark.	Spruce gall aphid, blister rust, other rust.
White cottony masses or foamy matter on trunk and limbs.	Bark louse aphid, mealy bug, spittle insects.
Holes or tunnels in trunk or branches.	Borers.
Terminal leader girdled, wilting new branches, distortion of branches ruin shape of tree.	Mechanical injury, European pine shoot moth, tip moth, pine weevil.
NEEDLES Wilting, ragged areas and tunnels on young needles and flower buds.	Frost, lack of moisture, gall mite, black vine weevil, saw fly, leaf-miner.
Discoloration, drying, browning.	Frost, lack of moisture, too much fertilizer, drying wind, sunscald, cedar nursery blight, leaf blight.
Needles curl.	Lack of moisture.
Needles fall.	Natural every year.
Lifeless gray tinge to foliage.	Red spider (hand lens).
Needles become yellowish green.	Lack of moisture and fertilizer, nematodes on roots, grubs in soil.
Hard green galls or long yellow tongue-like growths in warm, rainy weather.	Cedar apple rust.

Scale Control

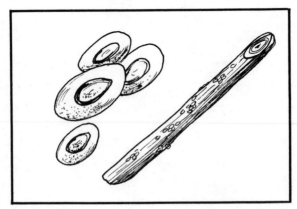

Scale insects, which suck out plant juices, form scablike crusts on trees and shrubs. They can best be controlled by spraying infested plants with a dormant oil emulsion. Follow directions on the label for concentration and timing.

✓   ✓   ✓

Don't Use Oil Sprays during the Summer

Oil sprays are used to control scale insects on trees. Do not apply these sprays during the hot summer months. Burning of the foliage and bark can result. Oil sprays should be applied during the dormant season before the tree develops foliage.

✓   ✓   ✓

Trees That Can't Take Oil Sprays

Although dormant oil sprays are an effective means of controlling scale insects, some trees are injured by the treatment. Don't use oil sprays on hemlocks or firs. Also, avoid application of these sprays on thin-barked deciduous trees. Japanese maple, beech, butternut, and walnut trees are particularly susceptible to injury.

✓   ✓   ✓

Controlling Dogwood Borers

Dogwood borers are very harmful to dogwoods. They penetrate the bark and can enter a tree only through its wounds. Therefore, taking measures to reduce wounding of a tree will at the same time prevent borers. Newly planted trees should be braced to prevent wind damage; wrap their trunks with burlap or tree wrap paper.

✓   ✓   ✓

Preventing Dogwood Crown Canker

Dogwood crown canker is the most serious disease that afflicts dogwoods. Once crown canker has struck, little can be done to control its spread. The infection enters the dogwood through wounds at the base of the trunk. First symptom of the disease is the unhealthy appearance of smaller leaves that turn red early in the fall. The telltale sign is a dead area (canker) at the base of the trunk. Sometimes, the dead area encircles and kills the tree. As a preventive measure, take extreme care not to wound dogwoods with lawnmowers and other types of machinery.

✓   ✓   ✓

Curing Yellowing (Chlorosis) of Trees

Leaves of trees often turn yellow (chlorotic) during the growing season. This condition may be the result of nitrogen starvation. But a common cause of yellowing of leaves of the pin oak, sweetgum, and maple is iron deficiency. Whether the cause is nitrogen starvation or iron deficiency, the following mixture is recommended to cure chlorotic trees: 5 pounds aluminum sulfate, 7 pounds finely ground sulfur, 3 pounds chelated iron, 85 pounds of a complete fertilizer (10-6-4). Apply 3 pounds of this mixture per inch diameter of the tree. Spread the fertilizer mixture evenly on the ground in the root zone of the tree and water it in. Make applications in early spring. In highly alkaline soils, repeated applications may be necessary every year. A capsule fertilizer, called "medicap," that can be implanted in the stem of the tree is also available. Apply according to the directions for treatment of iron chlorosis.

Tent Caterpillar Control with a Bacterium

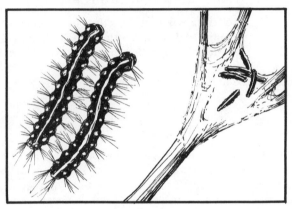

Tent caterpillars cast a webbing over leaves, and the larvae devour them. Wild cherries are particularly susceptible. When a bacterium called *Bacillus thuringiensis* is eaten by the tent caterpillar, it will kill the insect within 24 hours. This bacterium is not harmful to man and can be purchased at some garden centers and applied as a spray.

Don't Place "Tanglefoot" Directly on Bark

"Tanglefoot" prevents crawling insects from ascending trees and eating the leaves. If "tanglefoot" is placed directly on the bark, it will do the job adequately, but it will leave a messy residue. To prevent this, apply the "tanglefoot" to a band of cotton that is wrapped around the tree. When the treatment has served its purpose, the cotton and tanglefoot can be removed easily and without leaving an unsightly mess.

Cankerworm Control

Cankerworms are green, brown, or black worms that do extensive damage to tree leaves—particularly maple, oak, and elm. They can be controlled

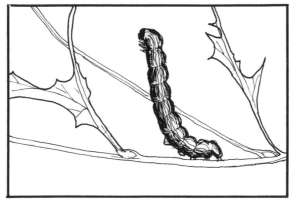

by placing a sticky band of "tanglefoot" material around the base of a tree. In order to prevent infestation by egg-laying females, make applications before the first of November.

🗸   🗸   🗸

Controlling Bagworms

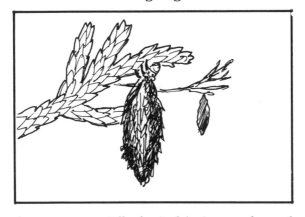

Bagworm insects are especially fond of junipers, cedars, arborvitae, and white pine. They cause severe defoliation of plants and are recognized by the carrot-shaped bags that hang from branches. The best way to eliminate bagworms is to handpick and destroy the bags in which the worms hide. For best results, do this in the fall, winter, or before the eggs hatch in the spring. Be thorough: just one female can lay enough eggs to start a new infestation.

🗸   🗸   🗸

Leaf Scorch of Shade Trees

Most shade trees are subject to leaf scorch, a condition in which the leaves turn brown around the edges and, sometimes, between the veins.

Leaf scorch is due to lack of a water balance in the tree, which may be caused by high temperatures, root injury, fill dirt, and grade changes. To reduce damage, supply water during dry periods, and fertilize trees in low vigor. Top pruning may help trees with severe root damage.

✔   ✔   ✔

Fire Blight Control on Crabapple

Sometimes, the new shoots of Crabapple trees suddenly wilt, turn either brown or black, and die. The remaining branches look as if they had been burned; in fact, they have been invaded by a bacterial disease called fire blight. For control, remove infected branches by breaking them off 8 to 12 inches below the diseased areas. Avoid excess nitrogen fertilization, which favors the disease. A streptomycin spray applied during flower bloom is also effective. Follow the directions on the label. Above all, check with your nurseryman for fire blight-resistant crabapples before purchasing new trees.

✔   ✔   ✔

Wet Wood Disease of Shade Trees

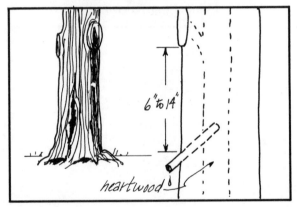

When sap is seen seeping out of cracks, wounds, and pruning cuts in shade trees and flowing down their trunks, chances are that the trees have been afflicted by a condition called wet wood. This condition, most prevalent on maple, birch, elm, oak, poplar, sycamore, and willow trees, results from gas produced by bacteria that live in the heartwood of trees. To prevent this "bleeding," drill ½-inch holes into the heartwood 6 to 14 inches below affected areas. Drill the holes on a slightly upward slant and insert a piece of pipe in the end of the hole to carry the sap away from the tree where it will fall to the ground.

✔   ✔   ✔

Dutch Elm Disease Control

Dutch elm disease, now prevalent throughout the United States, causes leaves to turn yellow and whole branches to wilt and die. All of our native elms are susceptible and once infected, a tree is usually killed within a year. If you suspect that your elm has the disease, cut into a branch with a knife. If brown or green streaks are evident in the wood, your suspicions have been confirmed.

A chemical injection treatment can be used to save trees if they are treated when symptoms first appear. Check with a reputable tree expert company or your county agent. When buying new elm trees, remember that the Siberian elm is resistant to the disease. Other resistant varieties are being developed.

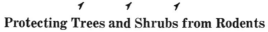

Controlling Leaf Spots on Shade Trees

Although a variety of tree diseases cause leaf spotting, fungi are most often responsible. Because many leaf-spotting fungi live over winter in diseased leaves on the ground, these leaves should be gathered and destroyed or composted. It is difficult to completely cover leaves with a fungicide on large trees and many applications may be necessary. Therefore, fungicide sprays for the control of leaf spots are not recommended. If trees are severely defoliated by leaf-spotting diseases, fertilize them to compensate for the loss and keep them vigorous.

Protecting Trees and Shrubs from Rodents

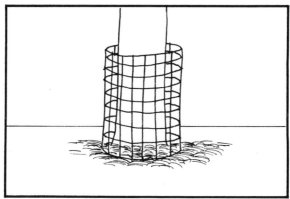

Rabbits and mice gnaw at the bark of such woody plants as crabapple, mountain ash, hawthorn, and winged euonymus. The bark can become completely girdled and the tree killed. These injuries also serve as entrance-ways for borers and disease-causing organisms. Protect the trunks or main stems of young trees with a collar of ½-inch mesh wire from the soil line up to a height of 2 or 3 feet. Plastic wraparound protectors are also available. As an alternative to fencing, the trunks can be sprayed with a rodent repellent, such as Arasan 425 or Improved ZIP.

Beware of Choking Vines

Vines which grow up onto large trees can be quite picturesque. Although you may be tempted to leave such vines because of their aesthetic appeal, they can literally choke the life out of your tree. Poison ivy is one of the most common "chokers." To remove poison ivy, first protect yourself with a pair of gloves. Then, cut the vines at the base of the tree with a saw. A year later it will be easy to remove the dead, dried, brittle vines from the top of the tree. Always wash your hands and arms throroughly with soap and water after having possibly made contact with poison ivy.

✓   ✓   ✓

Controlling Sooty Mold on Trees

A black and unsightly growth, called "black" mold, or "sooty" mold, occasionally develops on leaves of trees and shrubs. The black growth is a fungus that does not attack leaves directly but lives off the sugary secretions of such creatures as aphids, white flies, and scale insects. To control the sooty mold, it is necessary to control the insects. Malathion is the insecticide of choice. Apply according to the directions on the label.

✓   ✓   ✓

Deer Repellent for Trees

If you live in a rural area or near a forest, deer can become pests. They feed on the bark of young trees during the winter and rub them with their antlers. To make a deer repellent, mix 7 pounds of powdered rosin in a gallon of denatured alcohol. Set it in a warm place for a day or so until the rosin is dissolved. Then, spray or paint this mixture onto the bark of trees or shrubs from ground level to safely above the browsing level (5 to 6 feet). The rosin mixture will turn white and will protect the trees through the winter.

CHAPTER FIVE

Shrubs and Hedges

Overview

Although the distinction is not absolute, a shrub differs from a tree in that it has several stems protruding from its base, while a tree has only one. When shrubs (or trees) are growing in close proximity, they can be shaped into a continuous hedge. Flowering and evergreen shrubs can be incorporated into the landscape as individuals or in groups. As hedges, they can function as fences or screens. Many shrubs flower or have distinctive leaf coloration that is desirable. Evergreen shrubs are generally planted at the bases of houses and other structures to visually "tie them into the landscape."

The best way to buy shrubs is to **visit a reputable nursery and pick your plants** from its selection. A poorly shaped shrub is harder to rectify than a poorly shaped tree, and plants ordered through the mail may not live up to their picture. The containerized plants which most nurseries now offer are particularly good. An advantage of containerized plants is that you can see them with a full set of leaves.

Select shrubs that have the growth habit you want. Some are bushy; others may be column-shaped. Low-spreading shrubs can be used as ground cover and weeping shrubs create special effects.

Choose shrubs that are adapted to your geographic region and soil type. It is important to know whether your soil is acid, alkaline, or neutral. If it is acid or neutral (pH less than 7.0), you can grow most shrubs that will survive in your climate. If it is alkaline, you cannot grow rhododendrons, azaleas, camellias, and other acid-loving plants, without altering the soil. **Don't disregard the acidity factor; it is crucial.**

In arranging shrubs, **consider the type of foliage** you have chosen. A *gradual* transition from coarse to fine foliage is more restful than an abrupt one. Grouping 3 or more similar shrubs together gives a more pleasing effect than planting distinct individuals in a row.

A well-drained area is as **essential for shrubs** as for other plants. If water stands on the surface for prolonged periods, drainage is a problem, and it will be necessary to install underground drainage gravel and tile.

Shrubs are normally planted in the autumn or spring, while they are still dormant. **Autumn is the best time to plant most shrubs. Container-grown plants can be planted at any time** if they are planted properly and watered adequately.

If you anticipate   planting a large area with shrubs, it is better to prepare the whole area than to dig individual holes. An average hole for an *individual* specimen shrub should be a circle not less than 2 feet in diameter and 18 inches deep. Incorporate well-rotted manure or a mixture of peat and a small amount of fertilizer in the bottom of the hole to give the plant a good start. **Remember, plants grow!** As a rule, plant large-growing shrubs 6 feet apart, middle-sized shrubs 3 feet apart, and small shrubs 18 inches to 2 feet apart.

When used as a hedge, shrubs are planted closer together. Common deciduous shrubs, such as privet, are usually planted 9 inches apart to form a hedge. Finer-leaved deciduous plants and most evergreens are set at least 18 inches apart, while some of the larger evergreens do best at 24 inches. To insure dense growth, deciduous plants are usually cut back to within a few inches of the ground when planted to form a hedge.

Do not disturb the root system of shrubs after they have been planted. Mulch around the base to prevent weed growth and to conserve moisture. It will be necessary to water at least once a week until the plants are established.

Pruning is an important part of shrub maintenance. Pruning should involve sufficient thinning out of old wood to promote vigorous new growth. Pruning also enables large trees, such as hemlocks, to be contained as shrubs.

In general, **shrubs that flower before midsummer should receive their pruning immediately after flowering.** This will consist of the removal of old growth from the center and a little trimming of the ends of the branches. **Those that flower later need pruning before growth starts** in the spring since the flowers are borne on wood of the current season's growth.

Hedges can be pruned or left to grow freely. Free-growing hedges require more room. Evergreens are first choice for clipped hedges.

A properly shaped hedge is narrower at the top than at the bottom, and the top should be rounded rather than flat. Annual clipping of deciduous hedges should be done just as the first growth of the season is slowing down—in May or June—and again in late summer.

Evergreens grow more slowly and usually do not need clipping until well past midsummer. They **should never be severely pruned** or shaped.

Shrubs may or may not need supplemental watering. In extremely dry climates, a soaking once a week for two or three hours should prove sufficient. In many gardens, however, this will be accomplished by the runoff from lawn watering.

Fertilization of shrubs is a touchy business. Since fertilizer encourages growth, and most people prefer that their shrubs do not get out of hand, fertilization in most cases should be done sparingly at best. A good practice is to mulch your shrubs. The mulch will eventually break down and provide the shrubs with a moderate dose of additional nitrogen. Work the old mulch into the top two inches of soil once a year and apply additional mulch.

Section One

SELECTION

Plant Some Early Flowering Shrubs

Early flowering shrubs help announce spring. The first shrubs to bloom —as early as January in some areas—are the witch hazels (*Hamamelis*). The Cornelian cherry (*Cornus mos*) produces blossoms in late March. The first forsythia to bloom in the spring is the Dorean forsythia (*Forsythia orata*), which blooms in late March. Among those shrubs that will bloom even earlier if espaliered on a south wall are forsythias, fragrant viburnum, winter witch hazels, fragrant honeysuckle, and flowering quince.

✔   ✔   ✔

Low-Growing Yews

Low-growing evergreens, which will not grow uncontrollably and obstruct windows and other plants, are often desirable for foundation plantings. A variety of yews is ideal for this purpose. Yews that usually do not grow more than 4 feet tall and can easily be kept in bounds include the English yew, prostrate Anglojap yew, prostrate Japanese yew, Ward yew, dwarf Japanese yew, cushion Japanese yew, and Hill Anglojap yew.

✔   ✔   ✔

Aromatic Shrubs for the Garden

A garden is meant to be smelled as well as to be seen and felt. Besides the wide variety of aromatic flowers and herbs, there are also aromatic shrubs. The swamp azalea grows well in slightly moist places and has an unusual cinnamon-scented flower. Young leaves of the sweetbrier rose (*Rosa eglanteria*) are as fragrant as its bloom. The chaste tree (*Vitex agrus-castus*) has aromatic gray-green leaves and produces spikes of lavender flowers in August.

✔   ✔   ✔

An Ornamental and Practical Hedge

Gooseberry plants can be used to form both an ornamental and practical hedge. They make good low shrubs for marking boundaries, and their thorns deter dogs and cats. Expect a few gooseberry pies in the spring.

✔   ✔   ✔

Group Acid-Loving Plants

When purchasing shrubs and hedges, remember that acid-loving plants generally require special soil preparation to create the right conditions for

Shrubs for Various Purposes

Shrubs Withstanding City Conditions

Five-leaved Aralia, *Acanthopanax siebaldianus*
Amur Maple, *Acer ginnala*
Apple Serviceberry, *Amelanchier laevis*
Japanese Barberry, *Berberis thumbergii*
Siberian Peatree, *Caragana arborescens*
Siberian Dogwood, *Cornus alba*
Snow-flake Deutzia, *Deutzia scarbra*
Russian Olive, *Elaeagnus angustifolius*
Japanese Fatsia, *Fatsia japonica*
Forsythia, *Forsythia* species
Shrub Althea, *Hibiscus syriacus*
Sea-Buckthorn, *Hippophae rhamnoides*
Hydrangea, *Hydrangea* species
Japanese Holly, *Ilex crenata*
Chinese Juniper, *Juniperus chinesis 'Pfitzeriana'*
Kerria, *Kerria japonica*
Crape-myrtle, *Lagerstroemia indica*
Privet, *Ligustrum* species
Spicebush, *Lindera benzoin*
Honeysuckle, *Lonicera* species
Oregon Holly-grape, *Mahonia aquifolium*
Bayberry, *Myrica pensylvanica*
Sweet Mock-Orange, *Philodelphus coronarius*
Andromeda, *Pieris* species
Burk Cinquefoil, *Potentialla fruticosa*
Scarlet Firethorn, *Pyracantha coccinea* 'Lalandei'
Azalea, *Rhododendron*
Sumac, *Rhus* species
Alpine Currant, *Ribes alpinum*
Japanese Rose, *Rosa multiflora*
American Elder, *Sambucus canadensis*
False Spirea, *Sorbaria* species
Spirea, *Spiraea bumalda*
Yews, *Taxus* species

Dwarf Shrubs 3 Feet or Less at Maturity

Bog Rosemary, *Adromeda palifolia*
Black Chokeberry, *Aronia melancarpa*
Fringed Sagebrush, *Artemisia frigida*
Dwarf Magellan Barberry, *Berberis buxrifolianana*
Spike Heath, *Bruchenthalia spiculifolia*
Littleleaf Box, *Buxus microphylla*
Heather, *Calluna vulgaris*
New Jersey Tea, *Ceamothus americanus*
Japanese Quince, *Chaenomeles japonica*
Cotoneaster, *Cotoneaster* species
Irish Heath, *Daboecia cantabrica*
Alexandrian Laurel, *Danae racemosa*
Rose Daphne, *Daphne cneorum*
Heath, *Erica* species
Dwarf Euonymus, *Euonymus nanus*
Forsythia, *Forsythia* 'Arnold Dwarf'
Dwarf Fothergilla, *Fothergilla gardenii*
Magellan Fuchsia, *Fuchsia magellanica*

Miquel Wintergreen, *Gaultheria miqueliana*
St. Johnswort, *Hypericum* species
Japanese Holly, *Ilex crenata*
White Chinese Indigo, *Indigofera incarnata alba*
Sargent Juniper, *Juniperus chinesis sargentii*
Sheep-laurel, *Kalmia angustifolia*
Kalmiopsis, *Kalmiopsis leachiana*
True Lavender, *Lavendula officinalis*
Box Sandmyrtle, *Leiophyllum buxifolium*
Alpine-azalea, *Loiseleuria procumbens*
Creeping Mahonia, *Mahonia repens*
Chilean Pernettya, *Pernettya mucronata*
Magellan Box-lily, *Philesia magellanica*
Mugo Pine, *Pinus mugo pumilio*
Azaleas, *Rhododendron* species
Fragrant Sumac, *Rhus aromatica*
Rose-Acacia, *Robinia hispida*
Carolina Rose, *Rosa carolina*
Butcher's Broom, *Ruscus aculeatus*
Dwarf Palmetto, *Sabal minor*
Creeping Willow, *Salix repons*
Autumn Sage, *Salvia greggii*
Lavender-cotton, *Santolina chamaecyparissus*
Saw Palmetto, *Serenoa repens*
Reeves Skimmia, *Skimmia reevesiana*
Spirea, *Spiraea* species
Chenault Coralberry, *Symphoricarpus chenarttii*
Dwarf Taxus, *Taxus baccata* 'Nana'
American Arborvitae, *Thuja occidentalis* 'Globosa'
Coontie, *Zamia integrifolia*

Shrubs 4 to 5 Feet Tall at Maturity

'Edward Goucher' Abelia, *Abelia* 'Edward Goucher'
Leadleaf, *Amorpha canescens*
Southernwood, *Artemisia abrotanum*
Wormwood, *Artemisia absinthium*
Saltbush, *Atriplex* species
Threespine Barberry, *Berberis triacanthophora*
Japanese Beautyberry, *Callicarpa japonica*
Greenplume Rabbitbrush, *Chrysothamnus graveolens*
Sweet Fern, *Comptonia peregrina*
Broom, *Cytisus* hybrids
Winter Daphne, *Daphne odora*
Slender Deutzia, *Deutzia gracilis*
Southern Bush-honeysuckle, *Diervilla sessilifolia*
Mediterranean Heath, *Erica mediterranea*
Apache Plume, *Fallugia paradoxa*
Cape-jasmine Gardenia, *Gardenia jasminoides*
Boxleaf Hebe, *Hebe buxifolia*
Kerria, *Kerria japonica*
Keisk's Leucothoe, *Leucothoe keiskei*
Oregon Holly-grape, *Mahonia aquifolium*
Tree Peony, *Paeonia suffruticosa*
Bush Cinquefoil, *Potentilla fruticosa*
Dwarf Flowering Almond, *Prunus glandulosa*
Azalea, *Rhododendron* species
Japanese Skimmia, *Skimmia japonica*

Garland Spirea, *Spiraea arguta*
Thunberg Spirea, *Spiraea thunbergii*
Coralberry, *Symphoricarpus orbiculatus*
Kashgar Tamarix, *Tamarix hispida*
Canada Yew, *Taxus canadensis*
Korean Spice Viburnum, *Viburnum carlesii*

Shrubs 6 to 9 Feet Tall at Maturity

Mexican Abelia, *Abelia floribunda*
Red Chokeberry, *Aronia arbutifolia*
Sagebrush, *Artemisia tridentata*
Barberry, *Berberis* species
Carolina Allspice, *Calycanthus floridus*
Evergreen Mock-Orange, *Carpenteria californica*
Delisle Ceanathus, *Ceanothus delibianus*
Flowering Quince, *Chaenomeles speciosa*
Wintersweet, *Chimonanthus praecox*
Mexican Orange, *Choisya ternata*
Whiteleaf Rock-Rose, *Cistus albidus*
Summersweet, *Clethra alnifolia*
Winter-hazel, *Corylopsis spicata*
Cotoneaster, *Cotoneaster* species
White Spanish Broom, *Cytisus multiflorus*
Burkwood Daphne, *Daphne burkwoodii*
Cherry Elaeagnus, *Elaeagnus multiflorus*
Southern-plume, *Elliottia racemosa*
White Enkianthus, *Enkianthus perulatus*
Burningbush, *Euonymus altus*
Fatshedera, *Fatshedera lizei*
Cliff Fenderbush, *Fendlera rupicola*
Large Fothergilla, *Fothergilla major*
Franklinia, *Franklinia alatamaha*
Silk-tassel, *Garrya elliptica*
Salt Tree, *Halimodendron halodendron*
Christmasberry, *Heteromeles arbutifolia*
Oak-leaved Hydrangea, *Hydrangea quercifolia*
Black-alder, *Ilex verticillata*
Florida Anise Tree, *Illicium floridanum*
Pink Indigo, *Indigofera amblyantha*
Drooping Leucothoe, *Leucothoe fontanesiana*
Formosa Honeysuckle, *Leycesteria formosa*
Honeysuckles, *Lonicera* species
Bayberry, *Myrica pensylvanica*
Myrtle, *Myrtus communis*
Nandina, *Nandina domestica*
New Zealand Daisy-bush, *Olearia haastii*
Japanese Orixa, *Orixa japonica*
Mock-Orange, *Philadelphus* species
Eastern Ninebark, *Physocarpus opulifolius*
Mountain Andromeda, *Pieris floribunda*
Mugo Pine, *Pinus mugo mugo*
Rhododendron, *Rhododendron* species
Roses, *Rosa* species
Rosemary, *Rosamrinus officinalis*
Boulder Raspberry, *Rubus deliciosus*
Rose-gold Pussy Willow, *Salix gràcilistyla*
Chinese Box-Orange, *Severinia buxifolia*

Russet Buffalo-berry, *Shepherdia canadensis*
Vetch Sophora, *Sophora davidii*
Kashmir False Spirea, *Sorbaria aitchisonii*
Billiard Spirea, *Spiraea billiardii*
Hoary Spirea, *Spiraea canescens*
Wilson Spirea, *Spiraea wilsonii*
Cutleaf Stephanandra, *Stephanandra incisa*
Snowberry, *Symphoricarpos albus*
Lilac, *Syringa* species
Odessa Tamarix, *Tamarix odessana*
Vilburnum, *Vilburnum* species
Chaste-tree, *Vitex agnus-castus*

Shrubs 10 to 15 Feet Tall at Maturity

Opopanax, *Acacia farnesiana*
Japanese Aucuba, *Aucuba japonica*
Groundsel Bush, *Baccharis halimifolia*
Darwin Barberry, *Berberis darwinii*
Fountain Buddleia, *Buddleia alternifolia*
Flowery Senna, *Cassia cornybosa*
Bladder-senna, *Colutea arborescens*
Gray Dogwood, *Cornus racemosa*
Griffith Winter-hazel, *Corylopsis griffithii*
Franchet Cotoneaster, *Cotoneaster franchetii*
Henry Cotoneaster, *Cotoneaster henryana*
Simon's Cotoneaster, *Cotoneaster simonsii*
Sago Cycus, *Cycas revoluta*
Thorny Elaeagnus, *Elaeagnus pungens*
Japanese Fatsia, *Fatsia japonica*
House Hydrangea, *Hydrangea macrophylla*
Yunnan Holly, *Ilex yunnanensis*
Beauty-bush, *Kolkwitzia amabilis*
Sweet Bells, *Leucothoe racemosa*
Privat, *Ligustrum* species
Spicebush, *Lindera benzoin*
Leatherleaf Mahonia, *Mahonia bealei*
Banashrub, *Michelia figo*
Fortune's Osmanthus, *Osmanthus fortunei*
Purplecup Mock-Orange, *Philadelphus pur-purascens*
Himalayan Andromeda, *Pieris formosa*
Japanese Pittosporum, *Pittosporum tobira*
Cherry Prinsepia, *Prinsepia sinesis*
Flowering Almond, *Prunus triboba*
Pomegranate, *Punica granatum*
Formosa Firethorn, *Pyracantha koidzumii*
American Elder, *Sambucus canadensis*
Spanish Broom, *Spartium junceum*
Veitch Broom, *Spiraea veitchii*
Wilson Snowbell, *Styrax wilsonii*
Flower Tamarix, *Tamarix parviflora*
Highbush Blueberry, *Vaccinium corymbosum*
Viburnum, *Viburnum* species
Cut-leaved Chaste-tree, *Vitex negundo*

their growth. To facilitate care, group acid soil-requiring plants—such as rhododendrons, azaleas, hollies, and pieris—together in a planting. Add a mixture of 1 part acid peat to 1 part soil to the planting soil. This mixture should produce the pH of between 4.5 and 5.2 which most acid-loving plants prefer. Fertilize acid-loving plants with a mixture of 1 part nitrate to 2 parts acid phosphate (Superphosphate) applied at the rate of one handful per 3 foot plant.

✓   ✓   ✓

Hydrangeas with Varicolored Blooms

Hydrangeas can be induced to produce varicolored blooms by treating the soil. *Hydrangea macrophylla* is the best plant to use. Its flower color is controlled by the acidity of the soil. Additions of aluminum or iron to acid soil will make blue flowers bluer, and turn pink flowers blue. Alkaline soil encourages pink flowers.

✓   ✓   ✓

Distinguishing Male and Female Hollies

If you want a holly shrub that produces berries, be sure to choose a female plant. Male and female hollies can be distinguished by their flowers. The male flowers (see diagram, right) have plump yellow anthers (which release pollen when the flowers are fully open) and undeveloped pistils. Male flowers are usually borne three on a stalk. Female flowers (diagram, left) are borne one to a stalk and have a well-developed pistil (small green knob in the center of the flower) and undeveloped anthers. Male and female hollies should be planted within 200 feet of each other to ensure pollination.

✓   ✓   ✓

A Fruiting Shrub for Foundation Planting

A beautiful fruiting shrub that also fits well into foundation plantings is the blueberry. Blueberry plants will provide pretty white flowers in May, berries a little later, good foliage all season along, and fine fall color.

❧   ❧   ❧

Selecting Harmonious Azaleas and Rhododendrons

Sometimes after a number of azaleas and rhododendrons have been planted, it is discovered that the colors of their flowers clash. In order to be sure that flower colors are harmonious, select your plants while they are in bloom. It is perfectly fine to plant container plants while they are in full blossom.

❧   ❧   ❧

Shrubs to Plant for Berries

Some shrubs have berries that are even showier than their flowers or leaves. The following are good examples:

Beauty berry	*Callicarpa japonica*
Bush honeysuckle	*Lonicera tatarica*
Cranberry cotoneaster	*Cotoneaster apiculata*
Deciduous holly	*Ilex serrata*
Golden cranberry	*Viburnum zanthocarpum*
Jetbead	*Rhodatypos scandens*

❧   ❧   ❧

The Hardiest Rhododendrons

In northern regions, many rhododendrons do not survive the winter. Catawba rhododendron (*Rhododendron catawbiense*) and its hybrids are the hardiest. They have large handsome leaves and flower in early to mid-June. A medium amount of sun is required for bloom.

❧   ❧   ❧

Camellias for Northerners

Camellias are typically a southern plant, but selections exist that can be grown in northern climates. Among the selections that will survive temperatures of 0 to 7 degrees F. for short periods are the pink varieties of Kumasako and Lady Clare, variegated Elegans (Chandler), red-flowered Blood of China, and Purity (a white variety). Even if varieties tolerant to low temperatures are selected, it is important that they be planted in sites protected from wind and exposure by buildings and other plantings. If planted in eastern and southern exposures, they should be protected from the sun during the winter months.

❧   ❧   ❧

Forty Shrubs for Minimum Care

Abelia grandiflora .... Glossy abelia—Z 6b–10a, M, 1, 3
Acanthopanax sieboldianus ...... Aralia—Z 5b–8a, T, 3, 5
Arbutus unedo .... Strawberry tree—Z 8–10, T, 2, 3
Aronia arbutifolia .... Red chokeberry—Z 4–9a, T, 1, 2, 4
Berberis thunbergii .... Japanese barberry—Z 3–10a, M, 2, 4
Buxus microphylla japonica ..... Japanese boxwood—Z 6–10a, M, 3, 5
Camellia japonica (in variety) .. Camellia—Z 7–10a, T, 1, 3, 5
Chionanthus virginicus .... Fringe tree—Z 5–10a, T, 1, 2, 4
Clethra alnifolia .... Summersweet—Z 3b–9, T, 1, 4
Deutzia gracilis .... Slender deutzia—Z 5–8, D, 1
Elaeagnus angustifolia .... Russian olive—Z 3–9, T, 2, 3
Euonymus alatus .... Burningbush—Z 3b–10a, T, 2, 3, 4
Forsythia intermedia .... Forsythia—Z 5b–8, T, 1
Fothergilla monticola .... Alabama fothergilla—Z 5–9, M, 1, 4
Hamamelis mollis .... Chinese witch-hazel—Z 6–9, T, 1, 4
Hibiscus rosa-sinensis .... Chinese hibiscus—Z 9–10, T, 1, 3
Hibiscus syriacus .... Shrub althea—Z 5b–10a, T, 1
Hypericum patulum henryi ..... Henry St. Johnswort—Z 7b–10, D, 1, 3
Ilex crenata .... Japanese holly—Z 6b–9, T, 3, 5
Juniperus chinensis 'Pfitzeriana' . Pfitzer juniper—Z 4–10, M, 3
Kalmia latifolia .... Mountain-laurel—Z 5–9a, 1, 3, 5
Kolkwitzia amabilis .... Beautybush—Z 5–9, T, 1, 2
Lagerstroemia indica .... Crapemyrtle—Z 7–9, T or M, 1, 3, 4
Lonicera tatarica .... Tatarian honeysuckle—Z 3–8, T, 1, 2
Nerium oleander .... Oleander—Z 8b–10, T, 1, 3
Philadelphus coronarius .... Mock-orange—Z 4b–9a, T, 1
Pieris japonica .... Japanese andromeda—Z 6–9, M, 1, 3
Pittosporum tobira .... Japanese pittosporum—Z 8–10, T, 1, 3
Potentilla fruticosa .... Bush cinquefoil—Z 2b–9, M, 1, 3
Raphiolepis indica .... India hawthorn—Z 8–10, M, 1, 2, 3
Rhododendron (in variety) ..... Rhododendron and azalea—Z 4–9, T, M, D, 1, 3, 4, 5
Rhodotypos scandens .... Jetbead—Z 5–9a, M, 1, 2, 3
Rhus copallina .... Shining sumac—Z 5–9, T, 2, 3, 4
Rosa rugosa .... Rugosa rose—Z 3–8, M, 1, 2, 3, 4
Spiraea bumalda .... Bumalda spirea—Z 4–9a, D, 1, 3
Spiraea vanhouttei .... Vanhoutte spirea—Z 4–10a, M, 1, 4
Taxus cuspidata .... Japanese yew—Z 5–8, T or M, 2, 3, 5
Viburnum carcephalum .... Fragrant snowball—Z 5b–10a, T, 1, 2, 3
Viburnum plicatum 'Mariesii' .... Maries doublefile viburnum—Z 5b–8, T, 1, 2, 3, 4
Xanthorhiza simplicissima ...... Yellowroot—Z 5–9, D, 3, 5

Key to Symbols

Hardiness

Z—Zone range adaptability

Height at Maturity

T—Tall, above 6 ft.
M—Medium, 3–6 ft.
D—Dwarf, below 3 ft.

Decorative or Other Values

1—Showy flowers
2—Ornamental fruits
3—Evergreen or interesting foliage
4—Fall foliage color
5—Suitable for light shade

Landscaping with Shrub Roses

When choosing shrubs, don't forget shrub roses. Roses don't have to be grown in a rose garden; they also make excellent boundary plantings, privacy screens, and background shrubs. The best choices for hedge roses are the hybrid rigoros, hybrid musks, and modern shrub roses. The flowers of these roses are comparable to many of the hybrid tea or floribunda types.

✔   ✔   ✔

Mixing Junipers and Apples

Cedar apple rust is a disease that requires cedars and apples to complete its life cycle and do its damage. If you decide to plant both junipers (cedar family) and apples, make sure one or the other is resistant to the disease. When planting a juniper hedge near apple trees, choose the resistant keteleer juniper rather than the susceptible canaert. You will be protecting both the junipers and apples from disfigurement.

✔   ✔   ✔

Honeysuckle for Songbirds

Easy-to-grow tatarian honeysuckle is one of the best shrubs to attract songbirds. Birds feast on the berries in early summer and nest in the branches.

✔   ✔   ✔

Euonymus Shrubs Are Useful

Euonymus shrubs are valued chiefly for their attractive fruit and fall color. A few species have evergreen foliage. *Euonymus altus* (burning bush or winged euonymus) has brilliant scarlet autumn color. *Euonymus bungeanus semipersispens* is desirable because abundant fruit remains on the plant long after its leaves have fallen. *Euonymus japonicus* (evergreen euonymus) is a lustrous-leaved evergreen grown throughout the south. It requires special care in the north. *Euonymus kiautschovius* (spreading euonymus) is an evergreen suitable for northern climates. The habits of euonymus vary from upright shrubs to low-creeping vines.

In addition to the standard euonymus varieties, various cultivars with special traits are available. Among the most interesting are those having variegated leaves.

The only shortcoming of euonymus is its susceptibility to euonymus scale. Euonymus scale can be prevented by applying dormant oil before growth has begun or malathion in June.

Section Two

PLANTING AND CARE

Newspapers for Supplemental Mulch

Some weeds will grow through wood chip and gravel mulches placed around landscape plants. A simple way to prevent this is to make a newspaper underlay beneath the mulches. Lay a newspaper covering (8 to 12 layers thick) over the area to be mulched. Add a decorative mulch 3 to 6 inches thick over the newspaper.

✓ ✓ ✓

Computing Distance between Shrubs

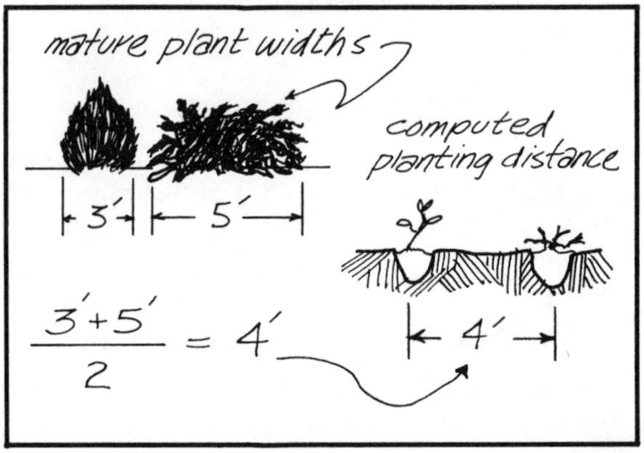

How far apart should shrubs be spaced? For two different kinds of shrubs, estimate the mature spread of each, add them together, and divide by 2. Your answer is the suggested distance between the centers of the planting holes for each.

✓ ✓ ✓

Don't Plant after Foliage Develops

It is wise not to plant or transplant shrubs after the leaves have appeared (or, in the case of evergreens, once the buds have started to swell). The chances of survival of such plants is greatly reduced over plants that are dormant. The best time to plant shrubs is in the fall after they have become dormant or in early spring before they have leafed out. Container-grown shrubs are an exception and may be planted almost anytime, though the summer is best avoided.

✓ ✓ ✓

Arranging an Informal Hedge

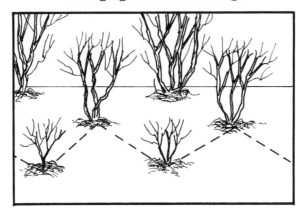

When arranging shrubs as informal hedge borders, place large shrubs in the rear, medium-sized shrubs in the center, and low-growing shrubs in front. Stagger the plants rather than setting them in a straight line.

✔   ✔   ✔

Trenches for Hedges

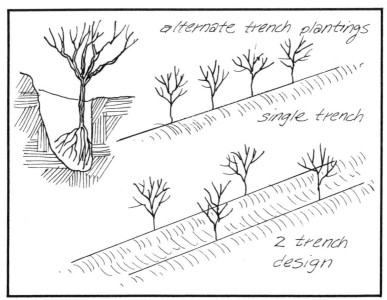

alternate trench plantings

single trench

2 trench design

When preparing to plant an extensive hedge, dig trenches rather than individual holes for the plants. This procedure takes less time for the total planting process and creates better growing conditions for the roots. Make the trench about twice as deep as the roots require and about 2 feet wide.

✔   ✔   ✔

Set Hedge Plants Deep to Increase Branching

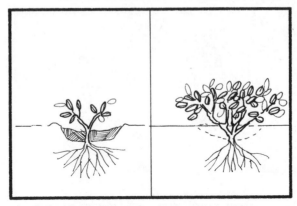

Branching at the base of hedges can be increased by a single planting procedure. When you plant a hedge such as privet or euonymus, set the plants slightly deeper than the previous planting line and leave about ⅓ of the planting hole unfilled. New branches will develop on the uncovered parts of the stem, making the hedge bushier at the base. Gradually fill in the depression as the hedge grows.

✓   ✓   ✓

Soak Root Balls before Planting

Balled and burlapped shrubs dry out very rapidly. To make sure the plant gets off to a good start, soak the root ball thoroughly, with the burlap intact, in a tub of water before planting.

✓   ✓   ✓

Dividing Hedges and Shrubs

It is sometimes worthwhile to revive old shrubbery that has outgrown

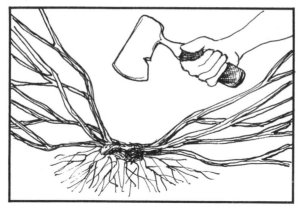

its location by dividing and replanting it. This operation should be performed in the fall or spring. Use an ax to divide the plant. Old wood and roots should be discarded and the tops pruned before replanting. This practice will work on most multistem shrubs and hedges.

✓   ✓   ✓

Tie Thorny Shrubs before Handling

Shrubs with thorns are difficult to dig up without tearing your clothing or skin. Suggestion: tie branches together with strong twine before handling.

✓   ✓   ✓

Don't Plant Rhododendrons Deep

Rhododendrons are very shallow rooted. Don't set them too deep in the planting hole. In poorly drained soil, it is good to plant above the soil line and then mound up the soil to the previous growing height.

✓   ✓   ✓

Don't Overshade Rhododendrons

Rhododendrons live and grow in rather dense shade in their natural state. However, they will bloom more profusely if the shade is not too dense. A "dappled" shade suits them well. The north side of a building, where they will receive some sun but not the direct rays of a midday sun, is suitable.

✠   ✠   ✠

Don't Cultivate around Rhododendrons and Azaleas

Rhododendrons and azaleas have very shallow root systems. Cultivation with hoes and rakes can, therefore, cause considerable damage to their roots. It is most advisable to control weed growth around these plants with mulches.

✠   ✠   ✠

Shading New Shrubs

Newly planted shrubs benefit from protection from the wind and sun until they have become well established. A number of devices can be used to provide this protection, as illustrated.

✠   ✠   ✠

Don't Fertilize Shrubs in the Fall

Shrubs and other plants can be damaged if fertilized in the fall. New, tender growth that can't harden off enough to withstand winter temperatures will be stimulated. Such growth will be killed back, thus weakening and disfiguring the shrub. Fertilizers should not be applied after September in cold regions.

Soak Ground before Digging Evergreens

When digging evergreens, it is important that a large portion of the root system be dug out with the plant. To ease the job of digging, using a crow bar punch holes in the area of the roots. Then, soak the area around the bush once a day for a week. The punched holes will facilitate penetration of the water into the soil. After the soaking process, the roots will be much easier to dig.

Coniferous Evergreens Need Sun

Except for hemlock and yew, which will survive in partial shade, most coniferous evergreens—fir, spruce, cedar, etc.—need lots of sunshine. Don't make the mistake of planting them in the shade.

Protect Evergreens from Winter

Narrow and broadleaved evergreens lose moisture through their leaves even in the winter. Because the water in the soil is frozen, plants are unable to replace lost moisture. As a result, leaves and needles turn brown and may fall off. This is a serious problem with hollies, rhododendrons, and azaleas. To reduce water loss, spray the plants in early December and again in early

February with an antidesiccant such as Foli-Gard, Wilt-Pruf, or Vapor-Gard. These sprays form a film over the leaves and prevent water loss.

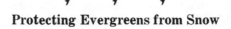

Protecting Evergreens from Snow

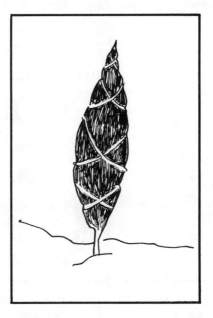

Multiple-stemmed evergreens, such as juniper and arborvitae, can collect heavy loads of snow which may break their branches. To prevent such breakage, fasten heavy twine to the base of the trunk, wind it spirally upward to the top, and back down in a reverse spiral. This will give the branches extra support and help reduce the snow load carried by the branches.

Hollies Can Injure Themselves

If hollies are not properly pruned or cared for, they are capable of injuring themselves. The spines on holly leaves sometimes puncture adjacent leaves, making small, gray spots with purple haloes. To prevent this, prune plants so that branches don't rub and cause injury. Use windbreaks in the winter to prevent branches from being blown against each other.

Watering Container Plants

Shrubs are often planted in containers and placed outdoors. How such plants are watered can affect their growth and survival. Don't use a strong

jet of water from a hose which can wash away the soil and expose the roots. Special soaker heads can be attached to a hose. They will add water without disturbing the soil around the roots. A soaker head releases the water through numerous small openings rather than with one forceful stream.

✔   ✔   ✔

Extracting Plants from Containers

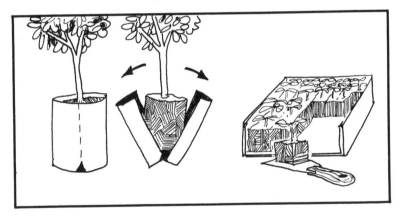

Landscape plants grown in containers are often difficult to extract before planting. Tin snips can be used to cut the sides of metal cans vertically, making them easier to open. Be careful with the cut edges. Corrugated cans and smooth plastic cans need no cutting. Tap the bottom, lay the container on its side, and pull the stem gently. Be careful not to injure the roots when extracting plants from cans. To remove plants from flats, use a spatula and cut out the plants as you would a cake.

Section Three

PRUNING

Prune Transplanted Bare-Rooted Shrubs

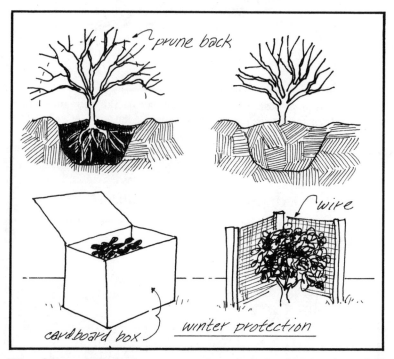

When bare-rooted shrubs are transplanted, their chances of survival are improved if some pruning is done. Remove any dead or damaged roots. The branches of bare-rooted shrubs should be pruned back about 50% to offset the loss of roots in transplanting. Leave some terminal buds. It is also advisable to provide protection for newly planted shrubs in exposed areas during the first winter.

Remove Lilac Suckers

Lilacs commonly develop suckers which grow up from the base of the stem. At least 80% of these suckers, which drain the rest of the plant of nourishment, should be removed as soon as they appear. The rest can be left to replace old branches that may need to be pruned out.

Spring Flowering Trees and Shrubs Which Should Be Pruned after Flowering

Scientific name	Common name
Amelanchier	Shadblow
Azalea	Azalea
Berberis	Barberry
Calycanthus	Sweetshrub
Carangana	Peashrub
Celastrus orbiculatus	Bittersweet
Cersis	Redbud
Chaenomeles	Flowering quince
Cotinus coggygria	Smoketree
Cornus florida	Flowering dogwood
Cornus kousa	Kousa dogwood
Cornus mas	Cornelian cherry
Crataegus	Hawthorn
Deutzia	Deutzia
Forsythia	Forsythia
Kalmia latifolia	Mountain laurel
Kolkwitzia amabilis	Beautybush
Ligustrum	Privet
Lonicera	Honeysuckle
Magnolia	Magnolia
Malus	Crabapple
Philadelphus	Mock orange
Pieris	Andromeda
Pyracantha	Firethorn
Prunus	Flowering cherry and plum
Rhododendron	Rhododendron
Rhodotypus scandens	Black jetbead
Rosa	Climbers and shrub roses
Sorbus	Mountain ash
Spiraea thunbergii	Thunberg spirea
Spiraea vanhouttei	Vanhoutte spirea
Styrax japonica	Japanese snowball
Syringa	Common, Chinese, and French lilacs
Viburnum burkwoodii	Burkwood Viburnum
Viburnum carlesii	Korean spice Viburnum
Viburnum lantana	Wayfaring tree
Viburnum opulus	European cranberrybush
Viburnum plicatum tomentosum	Doublefile Viburnum

What to Do with "Leggy" Hedges

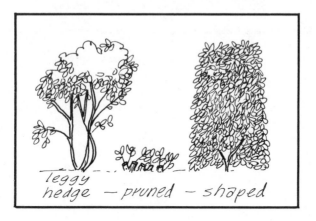

Hedges often lose their lower leaves and become "leggy." If you wish to restore a fuller growth at the base, cut the plant almost to the ground and shape the new growth as it develops. To achieve a properly shaped hedge, you must begin pruning when the plants are small and continue this procedure throughout the life of the plants. Before planting a hedge, realize that it requires more pruning than other plants. In general, a hedge should be pruned so that it is broader at the base than at the top.

Don't Prune Off Branch Ends

Attractive shrubs can be ruined by improper pruning. A common mistake is to cut off the ends of branches, causing the remaining wood to send out numerous side branches. The result is a stubby, unattractive plant. Instead, remove longer shoots at the ground line or at the juncture

Summer Flowering Trees and Shrubs Which Should Be Pruned before Spring Growth Begins

Scientific name	Common name
Acanthopanax	Aralia
Abelia grandiflora	Glossy Abelia
Albizia	Silk tree
Buddleia	Butterflybush
Callicarpa	Beautyberry
Clematis	Clematis
Hibiscus syriacus	Shrub-althea
Hydrangea paniculata 'Grandiflora'	P. G. Hydrangea
Hydrangea quercifolia	Oakleaf Hydrangea
Koelreuteria paniculata	Goldenrain tree
Rosa	Hybrid tea

of larger branches. This type of pruning will not disturb the plant's natural form and grace.

✔   ✔   ✔

Don't Prune Shrubs in the Fall

Shrubs can be severely damaged by winter temperatures if they are pruned in the fall. The fall pruning stimulates summer formed buds into growth that is tender and will be killed back by the first frost. Wait until a hard frost has ended growth for the season before undertaking any pruning.

✔   ✔   ✔

Pruning Junipers

Junipers can be pruned into a wide range of shapes and sizes. The best time to prune is in early spring—March 1 to April 15—before growth has begun. There is no objection to shearing juniper in the winter for use as Christmas greenery. The only objectionable time to prune junipers is when new growth is soft—from May 1 to June 15. When pruning, pay attention to the overall shape of the shrub or tree.

✔   ✔   ✔

Pruning Overgrown Rhododendrons

Rhododendrons sometimes overgrow their bounds and drastic pruning is necessary. April is the best time of the year to prune radically. When you prune, you must be prepared to accept the loss of bloom for one year.

Pruning cuts should be made ¼ inch above dormant lateral buds on old wood. Buds will be found all along the stem and the cuts should be made so that the desired shape is achieved. Rhododendrons should not be fertilized immediately after pruning. Wait until new growth has begun the following year.

✓   ✓   ✓

Remove Rhododendron, Azalea, and Lilac Blooms

If blooms are not removed from plants, they produce seed. Seed production requires considerable nutrition and energy that could be used by other parts of the plant. After rhododendrons, azaleas, and lilacs flower, remove the spent blooms. The plants will be stronger and bloom more fully the following year.

✓   ✓   ✓

Pruning Shrubs

If shrubs aren't pruned at the right time and in the right manner, some of the branches may die back, thereby reducing flowering. For most shrubs, the ideal time to prune is during the dormant season immediately prior to the beginning of new growth. In order to retain flower buds, shrubs which flower prior to June (such as forsythia, lilac, and mockorange) should be pruned shortly after flowering. The buds for these plants are produced during the preceding growing season. Shrubs which bloom after the end of June and which flower on buds developed during the spring should be pruned in the winter or spring before new growth starts. Examples include *Abelia*, butterflybush, shrub altlea, and oakleaf hydrangea. Where you prune is important. Make pruning cuts about ¼ inch above a bud and slightly angled away from the bud.

✓   ✓   ✓

Pruning Older Lilacs

Lilacs that have become overgrown should be pruned back to promote new growth and improve their shape. Use the "gradual renewal method." Cut out 10% of the oldest branches each year; cut them close to the ground. In this way, an older lilac will constantly be renewed without losing its natural appearance.

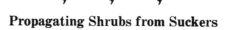

Propagating Shrubs from Suckers

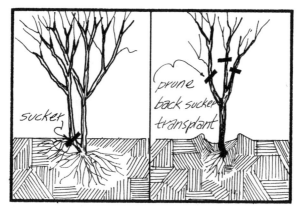

Shrubs commonly form shoots (suckers) beneath the soil. These suckers, which have separate root systems of their own, can be pruned from the parent plant and can be replanted. Suckers formed by grafted plants *below* the soil level will not produce individuals like the tops of the parent and should be removed even if they are not to be transplanted.

Use Pruning Tools Properly

The condition of pruning tools and how they are used will affect the health and appearance of your shrubs and hedges. Keep pruning tools sharp so that cuts will be "clean." Jagged cuts do not heal properly. Make branch pruning cuts flush with the stem. Do not leave stubs.

Shrubs for Espalier Training

Many kinds of shrubs and small trees can be trained as two-dimensional or espaliered plants against fences or other supports. The shrub most often used for this purpose is forsythia. Flowering quince, winter jasmine, fragrant honeysuckle, and other blooming shrubs do particularly well when planted on the south side of a house or other structure.

Section Four

PEST CONTROL

Rhododendron Wilt Control

Rhododendrons can contract a serious disease known as *wilt,* which causes its terminal leaves to turn yellow, wilt, and droop. Eventually, the entire plant wilts and dies. The disease is worse under high moisture and temperature conditions. No cure for the disease exists as yet. To prevent the spread of the disease, remove and destroy dead plants. When planting new rhododendrons, do not plant in wet areas and be sure to buy clean, uninfected plants from a reliable nursery.

✔   ✔   ✔

Powdery Mildew Control on Shrubs

Almost all shrubs are susceptible to one species or another of a powdery mildew fungus. These organisms form a white or gray growth on leaves and twigs and can cause considerable plant damage. Avoid shady locations for susceptible species. High nitrogen fertilization favors mildew development. Cut fertilizer applications if you think this is a factor. If all else fails, spray with Karathane as directed on the label.

✔   ✔   ✔

Controlling Fire Blight of Cotoneaster

Fire blight of cotoneaster is a bacterial disease that causes the ends of twigs and branches to crook and die, with the appearance of having been burned. To avoid further infection, prune out and destroy infected parts and avoid heavy nitrogen fertilization, which favors disease development.

✔   ✔   ✔

Controlling Azalea Leaf and Flower Gall

If the leaves of your azalea thicken, become fleshy, and turn pale green or white, they have a fungus disease called leaf and flower gall. This disease is most prevalent in the southern United States. To control, pick off the galled parts and spray with Zineb just before the leaves unfurl, as directed on the label.

✔   ✔   ✔

Scab on Pyracantha

If your pyracantha berries turn black instead of orange, it is probably due to a disease called scab. Scab can be prevented by spraying with ferbam, benomyl, or captan before buds open. Repeat the spray procedure every 10 days until leaves are well formed. Follow directions on the label of the fungicide.

✓   ✓   ✓

Cat-and-Dog-Proof Hedges

Hedges are sometimes effective in keeping neighborhood animals out of the yard. Two hedges that make good cat and dog barriers are Japanese barberry and floribunda rose. Japanese barberry is available in green, red, and golden-leaved varieties.

✓   ✓   ✓

Dog and Cat Repellent

Dogs and cats do damage to shrubs and become pests with their restroom habits. They cause particular problems with evergreens. To repel dogs and cats, spray shrubs with nicotine sulfate. Mix 1 teaspoon of nicotine sulfate to 2 quarts of soapy water. Spray once a week those plants that you want to protect.

CHAPTER SIX

Flower Gardening

Overview

Flower gardening is perhaps the most rewarding type of gardening. In addition to gracing a yard, flowers and their foliage provide materials for indoor arrangements.

Flowering plants are divided into four categories: annuals, biennals, perennials, and bulb plants.

Annuals are grown from seeds or cuttings that **bloom, set seed, and die in one growing season.** Examples are petunias, marigolds, pansies, and violas. Annuals, as their name indicates, have to be replanted each year.

Where winters are mild, spring-blooming annuals should be planted in the fall; in colder climates, plant them in early spring. Summer-blooming annuals should be planted in spring, after the last frost.

Annuals should be cultivated frequently but not too deeply. Deep cultivation will injure roots. **Spent blossoms should be removed** before they go to seed. Shear back annuals after each flowering to renew growth.

Biennials are plants grown from seeds or cuttings that **form clumps the first year and flower the second years.** Examples are Canterbury bells, money plants, and sweet Williams. After the second growing season, the plants die.

Most biennials are somewhat temperamental—unless environmental conditions are ideal. In harsh climates, where the temperature drops 10 degrees F. below freezing, they often succumb to winter. Where July to September temperatures seldom exceed 85 degrees F., biennial flowers should be sown in the garden in July. Where summer heat is extreme, it is better to sow seed in August or September in a cold frame (an outdoor propagation box).

Perennials are comparatively long-lived plants grown from seeds, cuttings, or vegetative divisions. Examples are roses, delphiniums, phlox, and snow-in-summer.

The woody plants most often grown in flower gardens are roses. Roses require a sunny, well-drained area. Sprays are necessary throughout the growing season to control disease and insect pests. Roses may need winter protection in northern climates.

Perennials should form the backbone of your flower garden.

Choose perennials that will bloom through most of the season. Dianthuses, some primroses, and candytufts will flower in March or early April and will continue to bloom until frost. In most climates, the greatest show of perennials comes from May to July. Autumn provides the climax with displays of chrysanthemums, Michaelmas daisies, artemisias, and Japanese anemones.

Perennials require care to keep them healthy and flourishing. Some may need dividing or transplanting when they start to become crowded. **Cut back** or remove woody or **dying parts of plants,** and **remove dead flowers** after they bloom.

Bulbs (including corms, tubers, and rhizomes) **are dried underground remnants of a mother plant.** They come from a food-swollen bud, stem, or other part of the mother plant and are capable of resuming growth and producing new plants. Examples of bulb flowers are tulips, irises, hyacinths, and lilies.

Some bulbs, such as tulips and hyacinths, **require a period of cold weather** to break their dormancy **before the growing season.** Where winters are mild, this may be difficult to accomplish naturally. In such cases, purchase bulbs in early fall and store them in a refrigerator for 1 month before planting.

Once the bulbs have flowered, remove the dead blooms, but leave the foliage untouched. The foliage is needed to produce food for the next year's growth and bloom.

Most flowering plants prefer full sunlight, or at least direct sunlight, **for 5 to 6 hours daily.** Some plants, such as coleus, are adapted to shade and will not survive in full sunlight.

Annuals, biennials, perennials, or bulbs cannot compete with grass or the roots of trees. Don't plant them under trees.

Plan flower gardens during the winter. Seeds and bulbs should be ordered during this period. Sketch out your house, garage, and yard on a sheet of paper and sketch in flower beds that fit the overall landscape. Don't design beds with straight edges; free-form beds are generally more graceful than geometric designs. Beds on the edges of the yard are generally more appealing than those in the center.

In planning the bed, **don't put tall flowers in front of short ones.** Arrange them in stair-step fashion with the shorter flowers in front. Choose flowers for the same bed that are harmonious in color and texture.

Prior to the growing season, **seedlings can be started in the house** from seed and transplanted to flower beds in the spring. Plants should be started 2 to 3 months prior to the usual date of the last killing frost. Seeds will sprout in any shallow container such as a pot or foil cake pan. The container should be filled with at least 2 inches of growing medium suitable for starting plants. Once they have sprouted, plants can be grown in a sunny window or under artificial light.

Prior to planting, prepare a fertile, well-drained, and cultivated seed bed. Remove rocks and clods. Always transplant in the morning or early evening to reduce losses from strong sunlight or wind. Water the plants thoroughly the night before transplanting them.

Prepare a hole for transplants 2 to 3 times **larger than the roots require.** Fill the hole with water and allow it to soak into the soil 2 times. **Set the plants the same depth as in the original container.** Water plants daily for the first week, weekly for the next two weeks, and thereafter when they show signs of wilting.

When seeding a flower garden directly, soak the seed bed thoroughly a day or two prior to seeding. Sow seeds according to the recommended dates and rates on the package. Cover seed with soil to a depth equal to 2½ times their diameter. Keep the area moist until the seeds sprout.

Most weeding in flower beds **can be done by hand or with a hoe.** Natural or plastic mulches can be used to reduce weed growth. If an extensive formal garden is planned, an all-purpose herbicide can lessen the need for cultivation and weeding.

Section One

GENERAL ADVICE

Raised Flower Beds

Raised flower beds are useful where the soil is poor or where another dimension is needed to improve a flat landscape. By and large, they are neat and easy to maintain. To build one, prepare a good soil mix and pile it up where you would like to form a bed. Consider bordering the bed with rocks.

Gray as a Color Blender

Flowers of different colors are often difficult to harmonize in a flower bed. Interspersing plants with gray foliage among the flowers is an excellent way to blend them. White, which some people consider a blender, actually separates the colors and makes them more distinct.

Contrasts in Foliage Colors

Often, dramatic effects can be created in flower gardens by contrasting foliage colors. Silver-leaved artemisias and veronicas contrast well with the very dark green foliage of aconitum. The gray-green, bearded iris foliage is well set off against the shiny dark leaves of dictamanus. The almost-white leaves of *Stachys olympica* or *Lynchnis coronaria* contrasts interestingly with most other plants.

Foliage Annuals

Some annuals are grown primarily because of their attractive foliage. Summer cypress is a neat and showy foliage annual with burning red autumn leaves. Foliage plants such as amaranthus, argemone, and the Mexican fire plant are large and coarse and can be used as a substitute for shrubbery. The beefsteak plant, with its red-purple leaves and variety of colors, is useful as a foliar plant in mixed borders.

❦   ❦   ❦

Evergreen Perennials

Some grasslike perennials retain their leaves the year 'round. They make excellent edging plants and ground covers. Among the most useful are: *Dianthus barbatus*, *Heuchera sanguinea*, *Iberis semperiurens*, *Sedum*, *Thymus serpyllum*, and *Yucca smalliana*.

❦   ❦   ❦

Flowers among Ferns

Flowers mixed in among ferns add color and variety to a garden. Plant ferns and Virginia bluebells (*Mertensia*) together. As the bluebells finish blooming and its foliage yellows, the fern fronds unfurl.

❦   ❦   ❦

Early Color in Window Boxes

Early flowers in a window box are a nice way to usher in the spring. To get early color, pot bulbs of tulips or hyacinths in the fall and store them for the winter in a cool basement. Place the pots with bulbs in the window box in March. Because of the early start they receive in their pots, and the warmer spring soil in the window box, they will grow and bloom earlier than bulbs planted in the yard.

❦   ❦   ❦

Outdoor Plants in Pots

When flowering plants are grown in pots outdoors, it is easier to store them for winter. Caladiums and tuberous begonias can be grown more easily in pots than directly in the ground. Sink such pots in soil up to the rims. Since these plants will freeze if left outdoors in the winter in the North, just lift pot and plant as one and store indoors.

❦   ❦   ❦

Bridging the Blooming Gap

If you choose flowering plants which only bloom for short periods, combine them with plants that bloom between seasons or that have an extended blooming period. Daffodils are good for this purpose in the spring. Roses are useful in bridging the June slump. True lilies are nice additions in early July before annuals reach their peak.

✓   ✓   ✓

Low-Maintenance Flowers

Flowers require more maintenance per square foot of garden than other garden plants. If your time is limited, and you still want to enjoy flower gardening, choose low-maintenance flowers requiring no pinching, spraying, or other special treatment. Flowers that require little maintenance but that are still effective are: daffodils, iris, peonies, day lilies, tall summer phlox, and hardy chrysanthemums.

✓   ✓   ✓

Annuals to Fill the Gap

Ground cover generally spreads slowly. To fill gaps until there is a complete cover, plant annuals in between the ground cover plants. In addition to adding color, weeds are crowded out. Summer impatiens can be interspersed with English ivy in the shade. Spring flowering bulbs can be planted in sunny areas with ground cover.

✓   ✓   ✓

Foam for Flower Arrangements

New foam materials available at florists and garden centers are excellent for holding cut flowers and foliage in flower arrangements. The foam can be cut to fit any shape container. Place the foam in the container, allowing enough room for water to be added. Saturate the foam well with water before inserting the cut ends of the stems. Insert the stems *into* the foam, not through it. Do not partially withdraw the stem after you have inserted it. This will allow air pockets to develop which disturb water uptake.

✓   ✓   ✓

Wiring and Taping Leaves and Flowers

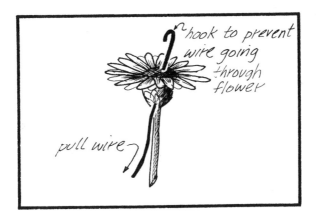

Cut flowers and leaves can be wired and taped to make them stand more upright in flower arrangements. To wire leaves, use a hairpin (as illustrated) and then wrap with tape. Special tape is available at florists or garden centers. When taping flowers, start under the head of the flower and wind the tape spirally, tightening it as you go.

Bottomless Container Boxes for Gardening

Both vegetable and flower gardening can be done effectively in container boxes. If you have poor soil, container boxes can be constructed and filled with good soil. Construct bottomless boxes out of 2- by 12-inch lumber. The fact that the boxes have no bottoms will enable the roots of the plant to

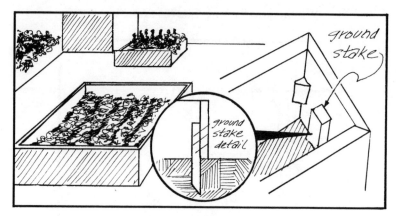

grow into the soil. The basic construction of the boxes is shown in the diagram.

Section Two

SEEDING AND TRANSPLANTING

Swap with Your Neighbor

Plants and seeds are expensive. A cost-free way to achieve a beautiful garden is to swap plant material with your neighbors. Many perennials can be started from divisions or seeds from your neighbors' plants.

"All-American" Seed Selections

A program was started in 1932 by several seedsmen organizations to test and evaluate varieties of flowers and vegetables being introduced onto the market. Under this program, which still exists, seeds are sown and evaluated in various climates throughout the United States before they are placed on sale to the public. If a seed packet contains the phrasing "All-American Selection," the variety of seeds contained therein was a winner in these test trials and has outstanding merit.

Sowing Small Annual Seeds

Some annual seeds are so fine that they are difficult to sow. To achieve best results, mix the seed well with five times its bulk of fine, dry sand.

Planting and Culture of Selected Garden Annuals

Plant	When to plant seed	Exposure	Germina-tion time	Plant spacing	Remarks
			Days	*Inches*	
Ageratum..........	After last frost..........	Semishade or full sun.	5	10 to 12	Pinch tips of plants to encourage branching. Remove dead flowers.
Babysbreath.......	Early spring or in summer.	Sun..........	10	10 to 12	Make successive sowings for prolonged blooming period. Shade summer plantings.
Balsam............	After last frost..........	.....do........	10	12 to 14	
Calendula.........	Early spring or late fall...	Shade or sun..	10	8 to 10	
Calliopsis.........	After last frost..........	.....do........	8	10 to 14	
Candytuft.........	Early spring or late fall...	.....do........	20	8 to 12	
China-aster........	After last frost..........	.....do........	8	10 to 12	For best plants start early, grow in coldframe. Make successive sowings for prolonged bloom.
Cockscomb........	.....do.........	.....do........	10	10 to 12	
Coleus.............	Sow indoors anytime; outdoors after last frost.	Sun or partial shade.	10	10 to 12	
Cornflower........	Early spring.............	Partial shade...	5	12 to 14	
Cosmos...........	After last frost..........	Sun...........	5	10 to 12	
Dahlia.............	.....do.................	.....do........	5	12 to 14	For maximum bloom, sow several weeks before other annuals.
Forget-me-not.......	Spring or summer; shade in summer.	Partial shade...	10	10 to 12	
Four-o'clock.......	After last frost..........	Sun...........	5	12 to 14	Store roots, plant next year.
Gaillardia.........	Early spring through summer; shade in summer.	.....do........	20	10 to 12	
Globe-amaranth.....	Early spring.............	.....do........	15	10 to 12	
Impatiens..........	Indoors anytime. Set out after last frost.	Partial shade or deep shade.	15	10 to 12	
Larkspur...........	Late fall in South, early spring in North.	Sun...........	20	6 to 8	Difficult to transplant; grow in peat pots.
Lupine.............	Early spring or late fall...	.....do........	20	6 to 8	Soak seed before planting. Guard against damping-off.
Marigold..........	After last frost..........	.....do........	5	10 to 14	High fertility delays bloom.
Morning-glory......	.....do.................	.....do........	5	24 to 36	Reseeds itself.
Nasturtium.........	.....do.................	.....do........	8	8 to 12	For best flowers, grow in soil of low fertility.
Pansy.............	Spring or summer; shade in summer.	Sun or shade...	10	6 to 8	Does best in cool season.
Petunia...........	Late fall (in South).......	Sun...........	10	12 to 14	Start early in spring indoors. Keep cool.
Phlox.............	Early spring.............	.....do........	10	6 to 8	Make successive plantings for prolonged bloom.
Pink..............	Early spring, spring or summer; shade in summer.	.....do........	5	8 to 12	Start early in spring indoors. Keep cool. Remove dead flowers.
Poppy.............	Early spring through summer; shade in summer.	.....do........	10	6 to 10	Difficult to transplant; start in peat pots. Make successive plantings.
Portulaca..........	After last frost or in late fall.	.....do........	10	10 to 12	
Rudbeckia.........	Spring or summer; shade in summer.	Sun or partial shade.	20	10 to 14	Perennial grown as annual. Blooms first year.
Salpiglossis........	Early spring.............	Sun...........	15	10 to 12	Needs supports. Avoid cold, heavy soil.
Scabiosa...........	Spring or summer; shade in summer.	.....do........	10	12 to 14	Keep old flowers removed.
Scarlet sage........	.....do.................	.....do........	15	8 to 12	
Snapdragon........	Spring or late fall........	.....do........	15	6 to 10	Start cool, pinch tips to encourage branching.
Spider plant........	Early spring; spring, or fall.	.....do........	10	12 to 14	Reseeds freely. Pinch to keep plant short. Water and fertilize freely.
Stock.............		.....do........	5	6 to 10	
Strawflower........	Early spring.............	.....do........	5	10 to 12	
Summer-cypress.....	.....do.................	.....do........	15	18 to 24	
Sunflower..........	After last frost..........	.....do........	5	12 to 14	
Sweet alyssum......	Early spring.............	.....do........	5	10 to 12	Damps off easily. Sow in hills, do not thin.
Sweetpea	Early spring or late summer through late fall.	.....do........	15	6 to 8	Select heat-resistant types.
Verbena...........	After last frost..........	.....do........	20	18 to 24	Pinch tips often to encourage branching.
Vinca.............	.....do.................	.....do........	15	10 to 12	Avoid overwatering.
Zinnia.............	.....do.................	.....do........	5	8 to 12	Thin after plants begin to bloom; remove poor-flowering plants.

Planting and Culture Guide of Selected Perennials and Biennials

Common Name	Approximate Height	Range of Colors	Peak Bloom Season	Sun or Shade
Aster, Cushion	9"-15"	Most except yellow	fall	sun
Aster, New England	36"-60"	Blue, violet, pink, white	fall	sun
Basket of Gold	8"-12"	golden-yellow, tinged with chartreuse	early spring	sun
Blanket-Flower	24"-36"	yellow or bicolor with deep red	summer-fall	sun
Bleeding Heart	24"-36"	pink, rose, white	spring	light shade
Bugle or Bugle Weed	4"-8"	bronze-green leaves, violet flowers	summer	sun or shade
Candytuft, Perennial	8"-12"	white	early summer	sun
Chives	10"-12"	lavender-pink; cloverlike	summer-fall	sun
Columbine, Long-Spurred	24"-48"	mostly mixed bicolors	early summer	sun or light shade
Coral Bells	12"-18"	red, pink, white	early summer	sun or light
Day-lily	12"-72"	most colors except blue, green, violet, true red	midsummer to fall	sun or light
Delphinium, 'Connecticut Yankees'	24"-36"	blue, violet, white	early summer	sun
Hens and Chickens	2"-4"	gray-green rosettes, orange-pink flower spikes	summer-fall	light shade or full sun
Hollyhock	48"-108"	most colors except true blue and green	summer	sun
Iris, Bearded or German	Mostly 24"-48" Dwarfs 3"-12"	most except scarlet and true green	early summer; spring where mild	sun
Japanese Spurge	6"-8"	inconspicuous	clean green foliage year-round	light to deep shade
Lily	12"-84"	white, pink, yellow, mahogany, orange, gold with bicolors	early summer	full sun to light shade
Peony	18"-48"	white, pink, crimson, lavender, cream	early summer	light shade or sun
Phlox, Creeping	To 6"	lavender-blue, scarlet, cerise, white	late spring	sun
Phlox, Perennial or Summer Phlox	24"-48"	pink, purple, rose, white, orange, scarlet	late summer-fall	sun
Plantain-Lily, Frangrant or Funkia	24"-36"	white with light, yellow-green leaves	late summer	light to heavy shade
Primrose, English	10"-14"	mixed with bicolors; spectacular blues, yellows, reds	late spring; winter where mild	light shade
Shasta Daisy	24"-30"	white	summer-fall	sun
Snow-in-Summer	6"-12"	white, with gray foliage	early summer	sun
Sweet Violet	6"-12"	white, blue, lavender, pink	spring	moderate shade
Tickseed	18"-30"	golden yellow	summer	sun
Virginia Bluebells	Up to 18"	bicolor blue-pink	early spring	light shade

The sand will separate the seed and make it easier to dispense when you plant. It is not harmful to sow the sand with the seed.

✓   ✓   ✓

Pre-Soaked Seed Germinates Faster

Hard-coated seeds, such as sweet peas and morning glories, germinate faster if soaked overnight in water. Dry them on a paper towel before planting for easier handling.

✓   ✓   ✓

Choose Hybrid Seed When Available

Hybrid seed results from the controlled crossing of two separate plants to produce a superior individual. Hybrid seed produces plants that are larger, more uniform, more vigorous, more productive, and more disease-resistant than standard varieties. They are worth the higher cost. Hybrids need large amounts of fertilizer and water.

✓   ✓   ✓

Don't Collect Seed from Hybrid Plants

If you collect and plant seed from hybrid plants, don't expect the new plants to look like their parents. Hybrid flowers and vegetables are produced by crossing two related but different parent lines. Each time the hybrid mix is desired, it is necessary to start with the original two parent lines: seeds from hybrids tend to produce plants that look like one of the parents, not like the desired mix.

✓   ✓   ✓

An Easy Flower to Grow from Seed

One of the easiest flowers to grow from seed is the moss rose, commonly called "portulaca." Scatter portulaca seeds over a carefully prepared seedbed. When they start to sprout, water them until established. They will require little care and provide a beautiful mass of growth for very little money.

✓   ✓   ✓

Annuals to Plant in the Fall

Most people don't realize that all annuals do not have to be planted in the spring. Hardy annuals can be planted in the fall for an early start in the spring. Examples are alyssum, calliopsis, cosmos, gypsophila, larkspur, nigella, annual pinks, snapdragons, and sweet pea.

✓   ✓   ✓

Plant Some Annuals That Will Reseed

Some annuals reseed themselves and reappear each year without replanting. Among the more reliable ones are: alyssum, cornflower, larkspur, petunia, and portulaca. Include some of these among your annuals, and part of your work for next year will already be done this year.

✓   ✓   ✓

Paper Cups for Annual Transplants

When annual transplants are first set out, they often wilt and die because of the shock of transplanting. Paper cups provide ideal shade and prevent transplant shock when placed over young seedlings. Cups will deflect the sun and keep plants cool. Paper cups also prevent cutworms from attacking the plants. Once the plants are well established—after a week or so—the cups can be removed.

✓   ✓   ✓

Umbrella Hot Caps

Hotcaps are transparent covers that can be placed over plants to protect them from frost or heat and to reduce moisture loss. A clever way to make a giant hotcap is to convert a large clear plastic umbrella into a hothouse. The handle can be removed and placed on top. The shaft can be poked into the soil as an anchor.

✓   ✓   ✓

Cuttings to Replace Petunias

Gaps will often appear in beds or boxes of petunias in midseason due to the loss of plants. A simple way to fill these gaps is to start new plants from cuttings of established plants. Break off a 6-inch stem, insert the lower half—stripped of leaves—in soil, and keep watered until it roots. A new plant will soon become established.

✓   ✓   ✓

Enrich Soil around Flower Transplants

Transplants will get off to a much better start if the soil placed around them is enriched. Topsoil alone is usually insufficient. Add some form of organic matter at the rate of one-third of the volume of soil replaced in the hole. There are many sources of organic matter, including sphagnum peat moss, leaf mold, and compost. Peat moss is the most readily available and works well.

✗   ✗   ✗

Root Cuttings in the Garden

A cutting bed can be created right in the garden. Choose a small area containing a 1 to 1 mixture of soil and sand. Take a cutting from a suitable plant, press it into the mixture, and cover it with a glass jar. This miniature greenhouse makes an excellent environment for the cutting to root. The best time to root cuttings is in the spring. Houseplants, roses, and other shrubs make good prospective cuttings.

✗   ✗   ✗

Protecting Stored Seed

Seed, when stored, must be protected from mice and other animals. Therefore, store seed in a metal container. Add mothballs to repel weevils and other insects. Not all seeds will remain viable for longer than a year. It usually does not pay to save small packets of flower seed. If you are left with a large amount of seed, it is best to test-germinate some of it to see if it will still sprout.

✗   ✗   ✗

Don't Allow Plants to Go to Seed

Don't allow flowering plants to go to seed. When plants go to seed, energy which could be used to produce a healthier plant and more flowers is sapped from the mother plant. Clip off spent flowers as soon as they begin to wither or droop.

Section Three

CARING FOR FLOWERING BULBS AND ROOTS

Stimulating Bulb Growth

Bulbs can be stimulated to grow faster and produce bigger blooms. Soak bulbs in a liquid plant food, such as RA-PID-GRO, for 1 hour before planting. Use a strength of 1 tablespoon per gallon of water.

✔   ✔   ✔

Planting Depth for Flower Bulbs

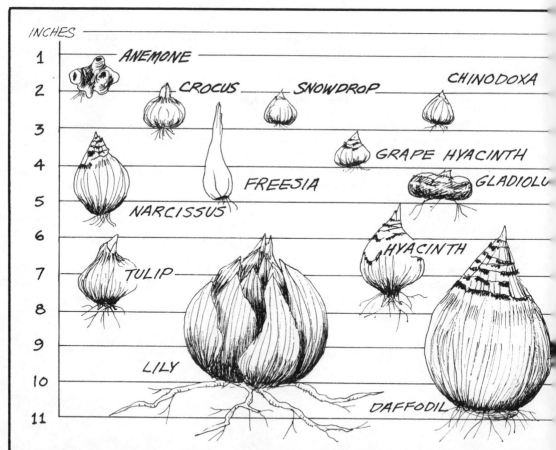

The depth at which flower bulbs are planted has much to do with their success. Recommended depths for most popular bulbs are illustrated.

✔   ✔   ✔

A Selection of Bulbs
(* Indicates not hardy and must be stored over winter)

PLANT NAME	FLOWER COLORS	TIME OF BLOOM	HEIGHT (INCHES)	REMARKS
Anemone (windflower)	purple, red, blue, white	March-April	5-12	Mulch in winter to reduce freeze-thaw action.
*Begonia (tuberous)	red, pink, orange, white, yellow	summer	12-18	Use rich soil in shade.
*Caladium	foliage green or white, variegated	summer (foliage)	9-18	Pot plant. Shade
Hyacinth	white, cream, yellow, pink, blue	April	6-12	Good filler between early and late spring bulbs.
Lily (hardy)	various	June-Aug.	24-48	Many varieties available.
Ornamental Onion (Flowering Onion) (Allium)	white, yellow	June-July	9-60	Many varieties available.
Snowdrop (Galanthus)	variable	Feb.-March	6	Countless varieties available.
Squill (Scilla):				
Siberian	blue, pink, white	March-April	3-6	Tolerates shade. Good for edging.
Spanish	blue, pink, white	May-June	12	Tolerates shade.
Tulips (Tulipa):				
Botanicals	various	April	3-6	Excellent for rockeries.
Cottage	various	May-June	12-36	Plant several tulip varieties
Darwin	various	May-June	12-36	for bloom succession. Use groups

PLANT NAME	FLOWER COLORS	TIME OF BLOOM	HEIGHT (INCHES)	REMARKS
Lily-flowered	various	May-June	12-30	of one color for best effect.
Winter Aconite	yellow	March (often Feb.)	2-6	Mulching is necessary to reduce frost heave. Often overlooked due to early bloom.

Correct Way to Set Bulbs

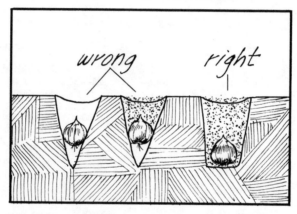

How a bulb is set into the planting hole can affect its survival. The planting hole should have straight sides and the bulbs planted so that their rooted bases are down. Make sure good contact is made between the bulb and the soil. If air space is left around the bulb, it may die before roots are established.

Don't Plant Bulbs in Outdoor Planters

Because outdoor planters are exposed, in colder climates most plants contained in them will freeze during the winter. For this reason, don't leave bulbs in planters outside throughout the winter.

Fertilizing Bulbs

Many gardeners don't realize that bulbs grow better if fertilized. Bulbs profit from fertilization just before they are ready to flower and, again, after they have bloomed, at which time they prepare next year's food.

The easiest way to fertilize is to scatter a quarter-handful of mixed fertilizer (5-10-5) around each bulb at the appropriate time.

✓   ✓   ✓

Mulching Bulb Beds

It may be necessary to mulch bulb beds. In cold, northern climates, it is advisable to mulch with straw, evergreen boughs, or similar material to prevent the ground from "heaving" during the winter. In those areas of the South subject to alternate thaws and cold stretches, it is good practice to mulch bulb beds during the winter to prevent premature growth during warm winter spells.

✓   ✓   ✓

When to Mulch Bulbs

Bulbs need a period of low soil temperature to ensure root and bulb development. Mulching too early keeps the frost *out* of the ground and can cause leaves to develop prematurely—to the detriment of the bulb. The function of mulching is primarily to keep the frost *in the ground,* thereby preventing premature leafing. For this reason, mulch after the ground is frozen.

✓   ✓   ✓

Don't Move Spring-Flowering Bulbs Too Late

Moving bulbs after roots start to develop interferes with blooming and may be fatal. Established daffodils and narcissi should not be moved after August 15; tulips after September 1; and early bulbs, such as crocuses, never later than July 30. Newly purchased bulbs can be planted as late as December because they are kept in a dormant state until delivered.

✓   ✓   ✓

Naturalizing Crocuses

Croscuses are easy to establish as permanent residents (naturalized) around shrubs, rocks, and the bases of trees. The soil needs no preparation. Just lift a slab of sod with a trowel, slip in the bulb, and replace the sod. The plant will grow through the sod.

✓   ✓   ✓

Don't Store Ismene Bulbs Right Side Up

If ismene bulbs are stored right side up, a rot will develop in the embryo. To prevent this, leave dried foliage on the bulbs and hang them from the ceiling of a storage cellar, stems down, at a temperature of approximately 45 to 50 degrees F.

✓   ✓   ✓

Dividing Daffodils

Daffodils and other members of the narcissus family do not need to be divided as often as other bulb flowers. Eventually, however, they will gradu-

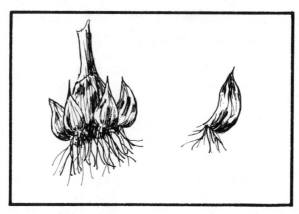

ally become crowded to the point where they cease to bloom. If this occurs, dig up the plants when the foliage dries in late spring. You will notice that the mother bulb will be surrounded by several bulblets. Remove *only* those bulblets that break away easily and store and replant them in the fall. Discard the mother bulb.

Daffodils Can Be Toxic

Leaves and flowers of daffodils may cause skin irritation. If you suspect that you are sensitive to daffodil toxin, wear rubber gloves while handling leaves and blossoms.

Bulbs That Don't Flower

If hardy bulbs fail to bloom, it is probably because they are over-crowded. Most hardy bulbs should be dug from the ground, separated, and replanted every 2 or 3 years.

Naturalizing Bulbs near Shrubbery

Shrubbery is often surrounded by naked areas where grass does not grow. Such areas make excellent places to plant bulbs. Plant little bulbs such as scillas and glory-of-the-morn at the southern edge of shrubbery where grass doesn't grow and where you are not tempted to grade or hoe. These bulbs will multiply, form colonies, and bloom very early because of the protection of the shrubbery.

Planting Dahlias

Dahlia bulbs are difficult for some people to grow. One trick is to fill the planting hole *as* the sprouts grow, rather than filling it completely at first. After the last frost, dig a 10-inch hole and fill the bottom 3 inches with fertilized soil. Then, add 1 inch of fresh soil. Put the dahlia tuber in the hole and cover it with 2 inches of fresh soil. Add additional soil as the sprout develops. A supporting stake will be necessary for large blooms.

🌶 🌶 🌶

Producing Large Dahlia Flowers

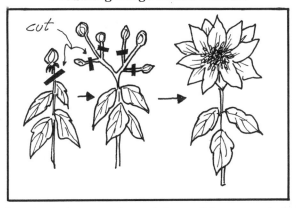

By a series of pruning procedures, it is possible to practically double the size of dahlia flowers: (1) When the plants are a foot high, pinch back the terminal bud causing side branches to develop. Buds on the side branches come in clusters of three, the middle bud being the strongest. (2) Remove the two outer buds, thereby inducing the central bud to produce a larger flower. (3) If desired, remove the 2 or 3 branches below the original terminal bud, increasing blossom size even more.

🌶 🌶 🌶

Digging Up Dahlia Bulbs

Digging up dahlia bulbs without causing injury requires a degree of skill. After frost has killed the tops, cut them off about 3 inches above the ground. The roots should then be left in the ground for a week to 10 days to allow for better separation of the bulb from the soil. Dig with a long-tined spading fork about 12 to 20 inches from the plants. As the soil is being loosened around the circumference of the root system, a light gradual pull on the old stump will release the entire clump.

✓   ✓   ✓

Prolonging the Life of Cut Dahlias

To prolong the life of dahlia flowers which have been cut for the house: (1) Cut the flowers early in the morning. (2) Use a sharp knife so the vessels will not be crushed and so unable to "take in" water. (3) Place stems in cool water and cut 1 to 2 inches of the base off the stem under water. This removes trapped air in the stem, which slows down water intake.

✓   ✓   ✓

Dividing and Storing Dahlia Tubers

Dahlia tubers should be unearthed and stored each year and replanted in the spring. The tubers should be dug up after frost has turned the foliage brown. Divide the tubers before storing. Cut apart the new tubers so each has part of the crown (the center upright stalk in the illustration) attached to it and at least one dormant eye. Tubers should be stored over winter in dry sand or peat moss in a dry, cool cellar.

✓   ✓   ✓

Tuberous Begonias for the Shade

Most flowering plants need full sunlight. For flowers adapted to shade, consider tuberous begonias. In areas where midday temperatures go much over 75 degrees F., tuberous begonias *must* be shaded. They supply beautiful and colorful flowers.

↗   ↗   ↗

Picking Tuberous Begonia Flowers

Begonia flowers can be used effectively in low table decorations as well as in corsages. However, they will not last long unless handled properly. Pick the blossoms in the morning, before the temperature gets too high. Spray them with a fine mist of water and place them in the refrigerator for 2 hours to harden the flowers. This treatment will prolong the life of the cut flower as much as threefold.

↗   ↗   ↗

Digging Up Tuberous Begonias

Although many people wait until frost has killed the foliage before digging up tuberous begonias, it is better that the bulbs be dug up and potted before frost. After digging, set the pots in the garage or basement, letting the tops gradually dry. This causes nutrients to enter the bulbs, giving them a better chance of lasting over the winter.

↗   ↗   ↗

Increasing Tuberous Begonias

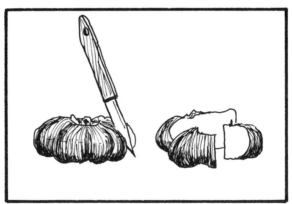

Tuberous begonia bulbs are expensive. The number of plants yielded by a bulb can be increased by dividing the bulb as soon as new shoots appear after planting. Dig up only good-sized tubers with 3 or more shoots and cut pie-shaped pieces out of the tuber, making sure each piece has a growing shoot. Dip cut surfaces in powdered sulfur and allow them to dry 3 or 4 days before replanting. This procedure may reduce the size of your plants slightly.

↗   ↗   ↗

Forcing Hyacinth Bulbs

Hyacinth bulbs can be potted in a basic potting soil and forced to bloom in the house. Keep the soil moist and place the pot in a dark place for 3 weeks for the roots to develop. Then, bring the plant to a warm, sunny window or place it under fluorescent lights for blooming. A cone-shaped transparent paper cover placed over forced hyacinth plants promotes tall growth and fuller blooms. Place the cone over the plants when shoots first emerge and remove it when blooms start to develop.

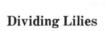

Dividing Lilies

When lilies become crowded, bloom size is reduced. If small flowers are noticed, it is time to divide the bulbs. Dig up the bulbs in the fall and remove a few outer scales. Plant the scales to a depth of 2 inches in a loose, well-drained soil. Both the old and new bulbs can be replanted.

Some Lilies Are Poisonous

The leaves, flowers, and roots of the lily-of-the-valley are toxic. Ingestion of these parts will cause nausea, severe vomiting, and diarrhea, and will be accompanied by irregular heartbeat, slow pulse, and low blood pressure.

Planting Water Lilies

Water lilies are categorized in two ways: tropical or hardy. Tropical varieties are planted 6 to 8 inches below the water's surface in the spring and are grown for only one season in colder climates. Hardy varieties should be planted deep enough to prevent roots from freezing in the water. Generally, 10 to 12 inches will be deep enough. Plant the lilies in containers

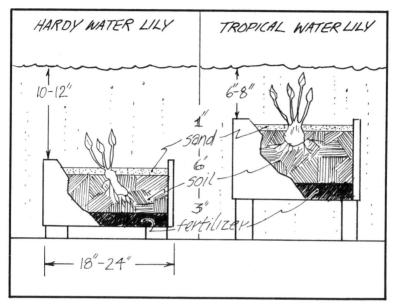

filled with heavy loam soil and lined with well-rotted cow manure or the like on the bottom.

✓   ✓   ✓

Dividing a Gladiolus

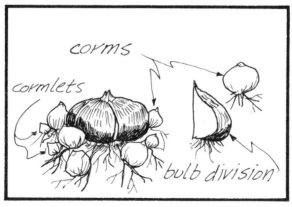

For better gladioli, the corms (bulbs) should be dug up in the fall, stored during winter, and replanted in the spring. If this is not done, the plants will deteriorate. If large corms have developed on the sides of the main corm, break them off. The main corm can be divided by cutting it in halves or thirds. Furthermore, small cormlets at the base of the corms can be grown to full-sized plants in 2 or 3 years.

✓   ✓   ✓

When to Dig Gladiolus Bulbs

When bulbs are dug up can determine their chances of survival in storage. Gladiolus corms (bulbs) are ready to be unearthed 3 or 4 weeks after they finish flowering. Cut off the foliage close to the ground and lift the plants with a pitchfork. It is best to dig on a warm, dry day so that the corms will be dry. Cure the corms for a few days in the sun before storing.

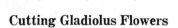

Cutting Gladiolus Flowers

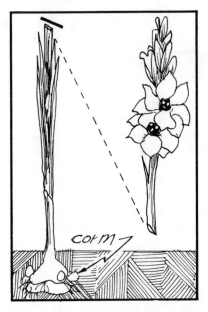

How flowers are cut can affect the health of the plant. When cutting gladiolus flowers for the house, leave at least 4 of the large lower leaves on the plant to ensure the maturity of good corms (bulbs) for the next year. Cut the spikes (stems) after 1 or 2 flowers have opened; others will open in the house.

Gladioli Bloom the Season Long

Gladioli can bloom in the garden throughout the entire growing season. Plant the corms (bulbs) 4 to 6 inches apart and about 4 inches below ground level as soon as the soil can be worked in the spring. Planting at 10- to 14-day intervals from early spring until late June will give a flowering season of approximately 100 days.

Self-Supporting Gladioli

Gladioli plants will often fall over if not staked. To make gladioli self-supporting, plant 18 to 24 bulbs in a 36-inch circle. The plants will support each other.

✓   ✓   ✓

Digging Up and Dividing Peonies

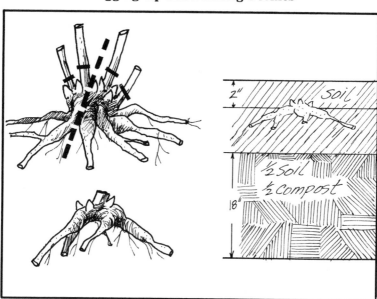

When peonies start to produce smaller than normal blooms, the roots should be dug up and divided. Division can also be used to produce additional plants. Digging is best done in September. First, cut off the foliage 6 inches above the ground. Next, cut a circle about 6 inches from the stems to a depth of 2 feet. Then, cut under the plant as much as possible before prying up the whole clump. Wash off the soil with a weak stream of water so as not to damage the new growth ("eyes"). The clump can now be divided. Be sure each division has a greenish bud, or "eye." When planting divisions, be sure the bud is covered with at least 2 inches of soil.

✓   ✓   ✓

Pinching Mums

Mums that are not pinched grow very tall and spindly. When plants are about 6 inches tall, pinch off the top 2 inches of new growth. This stimulates new growth: the stem will soon have many stalks. Pinch again when new shoots are 6 inches long, but don't pinch after late July. That may prevent blooming before frost.

✓   ✓   ✓

Dividing Day Lily Roots

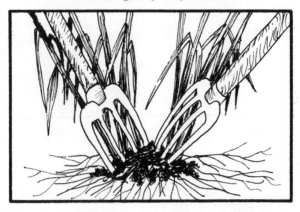

Intertwined day lily roots are very difficult to divide without injuring the plant. A simple method involves inserting two spade forks together at the point of division. The roots are divided by pulling the spade handles apart (as illustrated). The same method can be used for acanthus, asparagus, agapanthus, Siberian iris, and poker plant.

✓   ✓   ✓

Dunk Roots When Dividing Flowers

It is difficult to see what you are doing when dividing the roots of such plants as chrysanthemums, shasta daisies, or asters because their root systems hold the soil in a dense ball. This problem can be overcome by dunking the root clump in a tub full of water, causing the soil to fall away. This procedure is easier on tender new growth than washing off the soil with a hose.

✓   ✓   ✓

Correct Way to Divide Irises

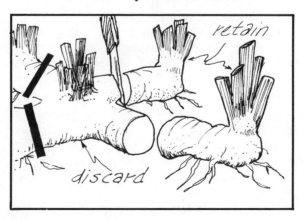

Irises show signs of becoming crowded every 3 years or so; when they do, divide them in late summer or early fall. Lift out the root mass with a spading fork. Cut off and plant the new rhizomes growing on the edge of the clump and discard the rest. Plant rhizomes on the sides of mounds to ensure good drainage.

✔   ✔   ✔

Irises Can Be Toxic

The underground stems and bulbs of irises contain a toxic agent. The toxin is an acrid resin which, if ingested, causes nausea, violent diarrhea, and abdominal burning.

✔   ✔   ✔

Divide Chrysanthemum Plants Each Spring

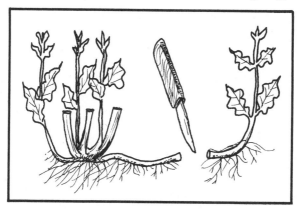

For best results with chrysanthemums in the fall, they should be divided each spring. Dig the plants out of the ground and cut off and save the vigorous new growth from the edges of clumps. Discard weak growth from old woody stems. Plant the strong, new divisions 12 inches apart in well-prepared soil.

✔   ✔   ✔

Caring for Gift Mums

Mums sold by florists are a popular gift, and the receiver often wonders how to care for them. Potted mums need much water and bright light. After bloom, cut the plant back halfway and store it in the basement until spring. The plant will remain dormant during this period. In warm weather, set the plant out, or divide it and grow the divisions in separate pots. In the fall, bring the plants indoors; they will flower again. If you can determine that the mum you have is a hardy selection, it can be left outdoors during the winter.

Section Four

ROSES

Roses for Special Geographic Areas

Most roses can be grown in any part of the United States. People living in the extreme North, Southwest, and at high altitudes should, however, select roses especially adapted for their special conditions.

Roses for the North

Floribunda varieties—Pinocchio, Vogue, and Goldilocks.

Sub-zero hybrid teas—Queen o' the Lakes (red), Red Duchess, Cedric Adams (scarlet), Henry Field (rose-red), Anne Vanderbilt (two-tone red), Country Doctor (pink), Curly Pink (pink), Dolly Darling (rose-pink), King Boreas (yellow), V for Victory (yellow), and Lily Pons (white).

Roses for the Arid Southwest

Climbers—Paul's Scarlet, Blaze, and Fran Karl Druschki.

Hybrid teas—Peace, Eclipse, Buccaneer, Golden Masterpiece, Fred Howard, Comtesse Amstrong, Helen Traubel, Jojave, Mme. Henri Guillot, Tallyho, Mrs. Sam McGredy, Etoile de Hollande, Texas Centennial, New Yorker, Bravo, Poinsettia, McGredy's Ivory, K. A. Viktoria, and Rex Anderson.

Grandifloras—Queen Elizabeth, Roundelay, Carrousel, and Buccaneer.

Floribundas—Fashion, Else Paulsen, Donald Prior, Eutin, Circus, Valentine, and Summer Snow.

Roses for High Altitudes (4,000 to 7,000 feet)

Most roses will grow well at high altitudes *if* given proper winter protection and *if* grown on such *California* root stocks as Mr. Huey (Shafter Robin), Ragged Robin, and *Rosa multiflora*.

✔   ✔   ✔

Narrow Beds for Roses

When planting roses, keep in mind that they have thorns. Plant them in narrow beds, not more than 4 feet wide so that all bushes can be reached from both sides.

✔   ✔   ✔

Guide to Planting Depth for Roses

Most commercially-grown roses are produced by budding the part of the plant above the ground to a root stock. The bud union produces a knob at the base of the plant that should be used as a guide when planting. The

The Best Modern Roses

HYBRID TEAS	COLOR
American Heritage	Yellow Blend
Apollo	Medium Yellow
Big Ben	Dark Red
Charlotte Armstrong	Deep Pink
Chicago Peace	Pink Blend
Chrysler Imperial	Dark Red
City of Hereford	Medium Pink
Confidence	Pink Blend
Crimson Glory	Dark Red
Dainty Bess	Light Pink
Electron	Deep Pink
First Love	Light Pink
First Prize	Pink Blend
Garden Party	White
Gypsy	Orange Red
Hawaii	Orange Red
Helen Traubel	Pink Blend
Innocence	White
Isabel de Ortiz	Pink Blend
John F. Kennedy	White
Karl Herbst	Medium Red
Kings Ransom	Dark Yellow
Kordes' Perfecta	Pink Blend
Matterhorn	White
Medallion	Apricot Yellow
Miss All-American Beauty	Medium Pink
Mister Lincoln	Dark Red
Mojave	Orange-Orange Blend
Oklahoma	Dark Red
Pascali	White
Peace	Yellow Blend
Perfume Delight	Clear Pink
Prima Ballerina	Dark Pink
Portrait	Pink Blend
Proud Land	Dark Red
Rex Anderson	White
Royal Highness	Light Pink
Rubaiyat	Dark Pink
Swarthmore	Pink Blend
Tiffany	Pink Blend
Tropicana	Orange Red

GRANDIFLORA	
Aida	Medium Red
Apricot Nectar	Apricot Blend
Aquarius	Pink Blend
Camelot	Medium Pink
Carrousel	Dark Red
Duet	Medium Pink
El Capitan	Medium Red
Granada	Red Blend
John S. Armstrong	Dark Red
Montezuma	Orange Red
Mount Shasta	White
Pink Parfait	Pink Blend
Queen Elizabeth	Medium Pink
Roundelay	Dark Red
Scarlet Knight	Dark Red

FLORIBUNDA	
Angel Face	Mauve
Anna Wheatcroft	Orange Red
Bahia	Orange-Pink
Betty Prior	Medium Pink
Bon Bon	Pink-White
Border Gem	Yellow Blend
Circus	Yellow Blend
City of Belfast	Orange Red
Cocorico	Orange Red
Crimson Rosette	Dark Red
Cupids Charm	Pink Blend

FLORIBUNDA (continued)	COLOR
Dearest	Pink Blend
Europeana	Dark Red
Fashion	Pink Blend
Frensham	Dark Red
Gene Boerner	Medium Pink
Gertrude Raffel	Dark Pink
Ginger	Orange Red
Iceberg	White
Ice White	White
Ivory Fashion	White
Little Darling	Yellow Blend
Red Glory	Medium Red
Redgold	Yellow Blend
Saratoga	White
Spartan	Orange Red
Vogue	Pink Blend
White Bouquet	White

CLIMBERS	
Blaze	Medium Red
Blossomtime	Medium Pink
Casa Blanca	White
City of York	White
Climbing Dainty Bess	Light Pink
Climbing Mrs. Sam McGredy	Orange Blend
Climbing Tropicana	Orange Blend
Don Juan	Dark Red
Golden Showers	Medium Yellow
Gallway	Medium Pink
Iceland Queen	White
Mme. Gregoire Staechelin	Red Blend
New Dawn	Light Pink
Paul's Scarlet Climber	Medium Red
Royal Sunset	Apricot Blend
Sombreuil	White
Sunday Best	Red Blend

MINIATURE	
Baby Darling	Orange Blend
Baby Masquerade	Red Blend
Baby Ophelia	Pink Blend
Beauty Secret	Medium Red
Bo-Peep	Medium Pink
Candy Cane	Red Blend
Chipper	Light Pink
Cinderella	White
Cricri	Medium Pink
Debbie	Yellow Blend
Dian	Dark Pink
Dwarfking	Medium Red
Gold Coin	Deep Yellow
Granate	Dark Red
Hi Ho	Deep Pink
Jet Trail	White
Judy Fischer	Medium Pink
Lavendar Lace	Mauve
Little Buckaroo	Medium Red
Marilyn	Light Pink
Mary Adair	Apricot Blend
Mary Marshall	Orange and Orange Blend
Mon Petit	Dark Pink
Pink Cameo	Medium Pink
Pixie	White
Pixie Rose	Dark Pink
Primila	Dark Pink
Red Improved	Dark Red
Scarlet Gem	Orange-Red
Simplex	White
Sweet Vivid	Medium Pink
Tinker Bell	Medium Pink
Toy Clown	Red Blend

For a complete rating of many more roses, consult the *Handbook for Selecting Roses,* available at a nominal charge from: The American Rose Society, P.O. Box 30,000, Shreveport, Louisiana 71130.

rose should be placed in a hole so that the bud union or knob is a little above the soil level. If growth develops below the bud union, it should be pruned back to the main steam.

✔   ✔   ✔

Don't Combine Bush-Type and Hybrid Tea Roses

If bush-type and hybrid tea roses are planted together, the strong growth of the bush-type will tend to overrun and crowd out the more delicate hybrid tea varieties. It is more desirable that each class of roses be planted in separate locations.

✔   ✔   ✔

Form a Soil Depression around Roses

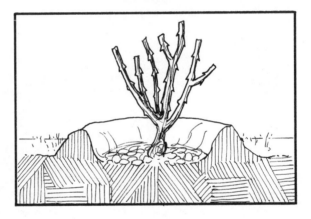

When newly planted roses are watered, the water often runs off and does not sink down to the roots of the plant. For roses and other woody plants, make a soil depression around the planting hole. The water will be contained in the depressed area until it seeps down to the roots.

✔   ✔   ✔

Pruning Roses

Roses need periodic pruning to remain attractive and healthy. At the end of the growing season, and after the first frost, cut off those branches that have broken, as well as any tall thin branches which are likely to break in winter wind. Final pruning for shape should be done in the spring before growth begins. Make all pruning cuts directly above a bud that points *away* from the center of the bush.

Roses bear on the current year's growth. Except for support, there is no point in keeping growth that is more than 2 years old. The top set of drawings shows how to prune shrub and tree roses. The bottom drawing

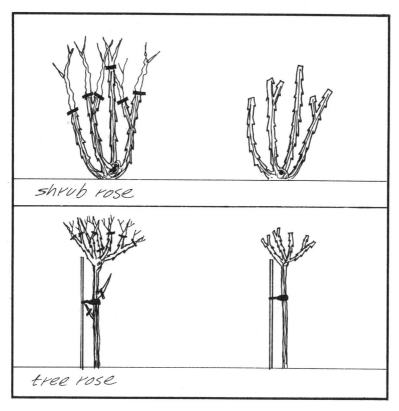

shrub rose

tree rose

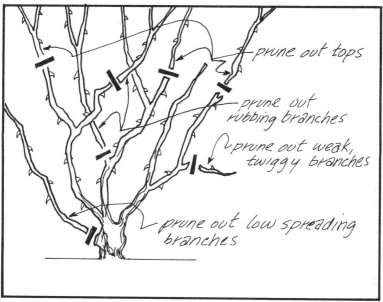

prune out tops

prune out
rubbing branches

prune out weak,
twiggy branches

prune out low spreading
branches

gives more specific pruning information for shrub roses.

Remember the following points in pruning shrub roses: (1) Remove any canes which are broken or damaged by insects or disease. (2) Remove canes which rub. (3) Remove spindly canes that are less than ¼-inch thick. (4) After doing all of this, the main stems should be pruned to a height of 18 to 24 inches. The same rules apply to tree roses with the exception that branches are generally pruned at a length of 12 inches.

🗸   🗸   🗸

Pruning Rose Crowns

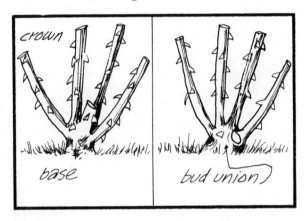

When pruning roses, it is often necessary to remove old canes at the crown, or base, of the plant. Cut old canes flush with the bud union, as illustrated on the right of the diagram. If a stub is left, rot organisms may enter the plant and damage it throughout.

🗸   🗸   🗸

Spraying Roses for Disease and Insect Control

Roses are subject to attack by a number of insects and diseases. Most pest problems can be solved by spraying rose plants at 10-day intervals during the growing season with a commercially-available, all-purpose rose pesticide containing both insecticide and fungicide. Some good pesticides to look for in these mixes are malathion, karathane, maneb, captan, and benomyl. Follow the directions on the label.

If you are tending only a few roses, aerosol cans with these preparations are available; they work well. A garden sprayer is required for sizable plaintings. If you are spraying other plants at the same time that you are spraying roses, it is possible to use the same formulation if extreme care is taken that the materials used are suited to all plants involved.

🗸   🗸   🗸

Rose Black Spot Control without Spray

The main reason roses are sprayed is to control a fungus disease called rose black spot. Disease losses can be reduced considerably without spraying if you: (1) select resistant varieties, (2) remove all diseased leaves in early spring, (3) rake away leaves on the ground that may serve to overwinter spores, (4) plant in an area that receives full sunlight, and (5) provide adequate air movement around the plants.

Powdery Mildew-Resistant Roses

If your roses are covered by a white powdery growth on the leaves, they are probably suffering from powdery mildew. If so, look for hardier, less susceptible roses. Hybrid teas, climbers, and ramblers are more susceptible than Wichuraina, Welch multiflora, and Rugosa types. The fungicide karathane can be used to control powdery mildew on susceptible varieties. Follow the directions on the label.

Preventing Winter Rose Damage

Roses are often damaged and sometimes killed by cold temperatures in areas where winters are severe. Roses can be protected from the cold in a number of ways: (1) Soil or mulch can be built up around the base of the plant to a height of 8 to 10 inches. This insulates the plant from cold temperature, and lessens the possibility of damage to the crown and roots. (2) Tepee-like structures can be built out of asphalt paper and placed around the base of the plant. (3) The plant base can be encircled with collars or cones made out of asphalt paper, styrofoam, fiberglass, or cardboard and filled with mulch or soil. If soil is used for protection, it should be removed in the spring. The illustration on the left is of mounded soil; the one on the right shows a collar of fiberglass filled with mulch.

🌱   🌱   🌱

Making "Blind" Rose Shoots Set Buds

Occasionally, you will notice new rose canes that have no buds at their tip. Treat them as though they had finished blooming. Cut the shoot back to a vigorous group of leaves and a new bud-bearing shoot will appear.

🌱   🌱   🌱

Watering Roses

Many roses die during the first year after planting because of inadequate water. The way the soil is prepared for a rose planting has a bearing on how often the rose bed needs watering. If much peat moss, stable manure, humus, or other organic material has been incorporated into the soil, the need for watering will be reduced because of the water-holding capacity of these materials. Mulching will also reduce the need for watering. Even with these procedures, roses require considerable watering—particularly during dry periods. To test whether a bed needs water, scoop into the soil to a depth of 3 inches with a trowel. If the soil is dry at 3 inches, more watering is required.

Section Five

GENERAL MAINTENANCE SUGGESTIONS

Water Deep for Hardy Plants

The depth to which flowers are watered influences their hardiness and beauty. Light watering makes plants develop shallow root systems. Such plants are often damaged during hot spells. Deep watering causes plants to send roots deep into cool soil. These plants are larger and more able to withstand stress. Infrequent but deep waterings are more desirable than frequent sprinkling. Frequent but shallow waterings also encourage growth of weed seed and fungus disease organisms.

✓   ✓   ✓

Fertilize Flowers as They Grow

Flowers should be fertilized during the growing season in order that they may realize their maximum beauty. About 14 days after growth commences, feed the plants with a liquid fertilizer that is high in nitrogen (e.g., 10-5-5) in amounts suggested on the label. Continue to feed every 2 to 3 weeks until flower buds begin to form, then use a food that is low in nitrogen and high in phosphorus and potassium (e.g., 5-10-10) until midsummer. Sprinkle the plants with water after feeding to wash all fertilizer from the leaves.

✓   ✓   ✓

Flowers in Containers Need More Fertilizer and Water

When a plant is grown in a container, the soil and roots are exposed to drying air on all sides, and water draining through the soil flushes out some of the nutrients through the drainage holes. For this reason, flowers in containers require more fertilizer and water than those growing in beds. Both the nature of the plant and the growing conditions should determine how often container plants should be fed and watered. Apply water when the top inch of soil becomes dry. Fertilize with a liquid fertilizer, such as 10-10-10, every two weeks during the growing season in the amount recommended on the label.

✓   ✓   ✓

Producing Extra Large Flowers

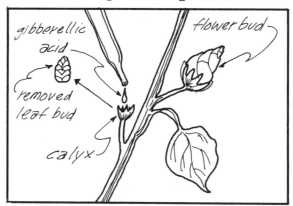

It is sometimes desirable to produce exceptionally large flowers for show. Some flower buds, if treated with gibberellic acid, will develop flowers 2 or 3 times the normal size. Camellias respond particularly well. To treat plants,

remove the leaf bud that is nearest the largest flower bud and drop gibberellic acid into the calyx that remains after the bud has been removed.
Leaf buds are narrower and more pointed than the plumper flower buds.
The gibberellic acid, which can be purchased at some garden centers, acts
as a hormone in the plant and thus causes the flower enlargement.

Prune for Heavier Bloom Next Year

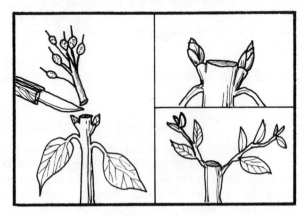

How a plant blooms the following year is affected by the care it receives
during the current year. One way to promote blooms on perennial flower
plants is to prune spent flower heads off of all plants following bloom. This
will force the development of new buds for a heavier bloom next year.

Bigger Blooms by Pinching

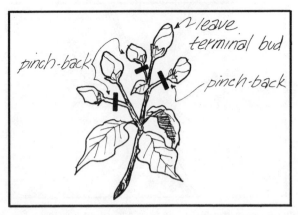

Flowering plants will sometimes develop a cluster of abundant but relatively small blooms. If you selectively pinch out some of the flower buds,

the size of the remaining flowers will be considerably larger. Side buds are removed to encourage the greater development of the larger terminal buds to produce one large central flower.

✔   ✔   ✔

Rejuvenating Annuals after Hot Weather

Plants that bloom throughout the season—such as cosmos, bachelor's-buttons, calendulas, and marigolds—tend to fade out after hot weather. They can be stimulated to continue blooming by removing dead seed heads. The best tools for the job are a kitchen knife or garden shears.

✔   ✔   ✔

Protecting Camellias

Camellias are a southern plant. If they are grown on the edge of their area of adaptability, winter protection should be provided. Spray plants in late fall with an antitranspirant, such as Wilt-Pruf. It will prevent bloom and foliage damage during light, cold periods in which the temperature dips just below freezing. Follow directions on the label.

✔   ✔   ✔

Keeping Geraniums over Winter

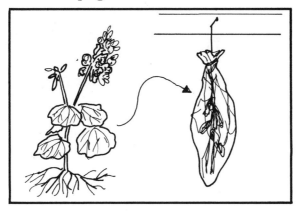

Geranium plants can be stored very easily during the winter, and re-planted in the spring. In late fall, pull up geraniums, wash the soil from their roots, and place each plant in an individual plastic bag. Hang plants upside down in plastic bags. Store the plants in the basement, keeping the roots slightly moist throughout the winter. In the spring, cut the tops back and pot what is left of the plant. The plant will soon revive and should be blooming by Memorial Day if placed in a warm, sunny spot.

✔   ✔   ✔

Preventing Injury to Gardenia Flowers

Gardenia flowers are easily bruised by handling. To prevent bruising, moisten your fingers when working with gardenias.

✓   ✓   ✓

Preventing Columbines from Fading

Columbines tend to fade away after 2 or 3 years. This "fading" is partially caused by the sapping of strength needed for the production of seed. To prolong their lifespan, pinch off the seed heads of the columbines *before* they start to enlarge.

✓   ✓   ✓

Mulches Reduce Labor

Mulches can reduce labor in every type of gardening by preventing weed growth. Use a permanent mulch, such as gravel or large wood chips, in areas of the garden that are not replanted each year. For flower beds in which annual replanting is done, use finer organic mulches, such as peat that will ultimately decay and work into the soil.

Section Six

FLOWER PESTS

Damping-Off Control for Annual Bedding Plants

When weather conditions are cool and moist, annual bedding plants may be attacked by damping-off fungi. These fungi either prevent the seed from germinating or kill the plants at the ground line after they have germinated. Affected plants fall to the ground and die. To control, drench the soil with Captan 50 as directed on the label.

✓   ✓   ✓

Fungicides for Disease Control of Perennials

Perennial plants will remain relatively free of disease if planted in well-drained soils in areas where there is adequate air circulation. Leaf spot of irises or phlox, leaf blotch of peonies, black spot and powdery mildrew of roses, and *Botrytis* flower blight are the most common diseases encountered. Maneb 80% WP or folpet 75% WP will give adequate protection against most of these diseases if applied as directed. Folpet, karathane, and sulfur are effective against powdery mildew of rose.

✓   ✓   ✓

Control of Botrytis Blight of Peonies

Sometimes, peony flower buds will not open and bloom because they have been attacked by the *Botrytis* fungus. To control, spray the peonies with either ferbam or zineb fungicide every 10 days from mid-May until the buds are fully developed. In the fall, cut back old foliage and stalks.

✓   ✓   ✓

Powdery Mildew on Zinnias

If your zinnias have a white powdery growth on them, they have probably been attacked by the powdery mildew fungus which most often affects roses. To prevent this, grow the zenith, big tetra, and ruffled jumbo zinnias— all of which show some resistance to this disease. In addition, space the plants wider so that there is adequate air movement between them.

✓   ✓   ✓

Reducing Fusarium Rot of Lilies

Perennial lilies often develop a root and bulb rot caused by the *Fusarium* fungus. Symptoms are a gradual yellowing and wilting of the plant during warm weather. Removal of infected plants is the best control.

✓   ✓   ✓

Leaf Spot Diseases on Flowers

Leaf spot diseases are common on the foliage of flowering plants. Most of these are caused by fungi and are favored by cool, wet weather. Most leaf spots can be prevented by a protective spray program when the disease first appears by using maneb 80% WP. Apply as directed on the label.

✓   ✓   ✓

Control of Botrytis Blight of Tulips

The most common disease of bulb flowers is *Botrytis* blight of the tulip. The fungus that causes this disease can blight the leaves and grow down to the bulb, causing it to rot. It is important that you control the leaf infection phase to prevent subsequent spread to he bulb. To control, improve air circulation around the plants and use maneb 80% WP or ferbam 76% WP as directed on the label.

✓   ✓   ✓

Control of Gladiolus Thrips

Thrips are seedlike insects that overwinter on gladiolus bulbs, and when the foliage develops, feed on it, causing white streaks. To control, dust the bulbs with malathion before storing. Some control is also possible by hanging Vapona strips in the storage area.

✓   ✓   ✓

Treating Iris Borer-Infested Plants

One of the most common pests you will find when dividing iris rhizomes is the iris borer. This pest can be recognized by its caterpillarlike larvae with rows of black spots along their sides. To control this pest, remove the larvae and destroy them. Then, cut off the rotted section of the rhizome and discard. If the entire rhizome is affected, destroy it, too. Plant only unaffected rhizomes or rhizome pieces. Borer attack can be prevented by spraying with Cygon (dimethoate) as directed on the label.

Aphid Control on Water Lilies

Aphids can build up on water lilies and cause damage. They can be controlled simply by knocking them off the plants with a blast of water from a hose. If there are goldfish in the pond, they will devour them. You may have to stage a number of anti-aphid attacks.

Aphid Control without Insecticides

Aphids can become a pest on a variety of flowers. If you prefer not to use an insecticide, try the following concoction: Put a small onion or garlic clove in the blender and puree it with 2 cups of water. Strain and spray over the plants. Do it 2 or 3 times a season.

How to "Foil" Aphids

Aphids are repelled by direct sunlight and thus tend to congregate on the underside of the leaf. Trick them by placing shiny aluminum foil around the base of each plant so that sunlight is reflected upward onto the underside of the plant. When the aphid finds sunlight on both the top and bottom of the leaves, he will abandon the plant.

Protect Tulip Bulbs from Rodents

Rodents commonly dig up and destroy tulip bulbs. Hot pepper and mothballs scattered on the ground above the bulbs discourage rodents.

CHAPTER SEVEN

Home Vegetable Gardening

Overview

Proper **advance planning** in the selection **of** vegetable **seeds and transplants, and careful choice of a planting site are the secrets to good vegetable gardening.** Select varieties of vegetables which suit your taste and climate. Select a garden site that receives a minimum of 6 hours of full sunlight a day.

If your objective is to grow an appreciable amount of the family's food, a garden plot of 30 feet x 50 feet minimum will be needed. However, large amounts of specific crops can be grown in much smaller areas. If possible, select a well-drained area with fertile soil. It may be necessary to lay underground tiles and add rotted manure, chemical fertilizer, and lime to enhance fertility. **Before planting, test your soil.** Your county agent can do it, and it is worth the cost and effort.

If dogs, rabbits, or children are a problem, fence in the garden area with 2-inch mesh chicken wire at least 2 feet high. The lower edge of the wire should be buried 2 or 3 inches deep to check burrowing animals.

Soil in the garden is best turned over the preceding fall to get the benefit of the pulverizing and sterilizing action of winter freezing and thawing. Renting a roto-tiller is one of the easiest ways to work your soil. If you have a large plot and your neighbor is a farmer, he might be willing to plow your soil in the fall and disk it (cut it up) in the spring.

A garden plan should be drawn out on paper and the seed ordered during the winter months. **Buy top quality seed.** In choosing seed, consider the time needed for the plant to fruit, the local climate, disease resistance, insect resistance, and yield potential.

Crops such as beans, beets, broccoli, cabbage, carrots, Swiss chard, lettuce, onions, spinach, peppers, radishes, staked tomatoes, and turnips **can produce large amoungs of food in a relatively small amount of space.** Sweet corn and vine crops, such as melons, cucumbers, pumpkins, and vining type squash, require large areas for growing. Growing vine crops in a small area does not make for the most productive use of space. However, they can be included in a small garden by practicing certain cultivation techniques discussed in the hint section of this chapter.

Plant perennial crops, such as asparagus and rhubarb, **along one side of the garden,** where they will not interfere with soil preparation

233

and cultural practices used for growing annual vegetables. Perennial crops can remain in the garden for from 5 to 20 years.

In early spring, the garden site shoud be finely cultivated as deeply as is practical (to a depth of at least 6 inches). Fine cultivation entails removing rocks, breaking up clumps of earth and sod, and raking the soil into a fine seed bed. Do not cultivate when the soil is wet. Small gardens can be cultivated by hand. Larger ones require power tillers.

Add a complete fertilizer, such as 5-10-5, or well-rotted manure with either bone meal or superphosphate **and work it into the top 3 inches of soil.** Your soil test results will tell you how much to add.

Lay out rows by stretching a string and making a straight line with the edges of a hoe. Make sure the rows are straight and far enough apart to allow for cultivation after the vegetables are fully grown.

Small seeds, such as lettuce, carrots and onions, should be sown thinly and lightly covered with soil. Larger seeds, such as peas, beans and corn, should be placed 2 to 3 inches apart and covered with 2 to 3 inches of soil. Some seeds, such as cucumbers, can be sown in "hills" made by digging a hole 5 to 6 inches deep into which manure or compost is thrown. The soil is then mounded to form a 6-inch hill and the seed planted on top. The seed packet will instruct you how deep to plant and how to space individual seeds and rows.

The planting period stretches from very early spring, when such hardy, frost-resistant vegetables as beets, carrots, turnips, lettuce, and onions are planted, **until mid-summer,** when late fall and winter crops such as beans are planted.

Some vegetable seeds can be given a "head start" by growing them in flats of soil or an artificial medium—such as peat-lite—in a greenhouse or in the house near a south window. In general, seeds are planted in flats in late February and early March to produce plants to be set out in April and May. If you do not want to grow your own, plants can be bought from nurserymen at planting time. Raising seedlings will not save you much, if any, money but *will* provide you with the exact varieties that you want.

Water transplants thoroughly several hours before planting. This will cause soil to stick to the roots when they are removed from the container, thereby reducing transplant shock. **Place plants in holes slightly deeper than those in which they were previously growing and firm the soil around them.**

After planting, the success of a garden depends on weed control, fertilization and watering. Weeds can be controlled by cultivation and pulling, chemicals, or mulches.

Mulches are one of the most effective ways to control weeds in the garden. Apply mulches after the warm-season crops become established in June. They should be applied around the plants 2 to 4 inches deep and may consist of weathered sawdust, peat, compost, or well-rotted manure. If straw or hay is used, add 2 to 3 pounds of 5-10-5 fertilizer per 100 square feet. If you decide to use cultivation as a means of weed control, be sure to cultivate shallowly so as not to injure vegetable roots.

One side dressing of **a nitrogen-carrying fertilizer should be applied to vegetables during the growing season.** Apply 2 pounds of 8-16-16 per 100 feet of row to leafy vegetables after they are well established, to corn when it is 12 to 15 inches high, and to tomatoes after the first fruits have set. Side dressing is applied by sprinkling fertilizer along the side of the row about 4 inches from the plants. Avoid direct contact with plants or burning will result.

Except during wet growing seasons, **most vegetable gardens need supplemental watering.** Vegetables require about 1 inch of water each week. A solid soaking for about 3 hours will do the trick. Watering during dry periods improves the yield and quality of vegetables.

Each vegetable has its own set of diseases and insect pests. The secret to pest control is to identify pests early and apply the proper control procedure. Your county agricultural extension agent can alert you to special disease and insect problems in your area and the appropriate means of their control.

After harvest, **store only those vegetables that are free from disease and insect injury.** Some vegetables, such as carrots, beets, turnips, and parsnips, should be stored before they reach full maturity. Most, however, should be stored after they are mature in a high-humidity environment at 32 to 34 degrees F. Exceptions are tomatoes, peppers, cucumbers, squash, and melons which should be stored at a higher temperature (45 degrees F.) to avoid chill damage.

Section One

GENERAL INFORMATION

Don't Cultivate Too Deeply

Although it is generally recommended that vegetable garden soil be cultivated deeply, be careful not to cultivate *too* deeply. Digging too deeply can bring up sterile subsoil. When spading or plowing garden soil, cultivate to a depth of no more than 8 inches.

✓   ✓   ✓

Trenching to Improve Soil

Soils need to be cultivated thoroughly to produce a structure that is beneficial to plants and that is easy to weed. Good soil cultivation is difficult to accomplish *in situ*. A procedure called "trenching" therefore works to good advantage. At one end of the area, dig a trench 1 foot wide and 20 inches deep. Transfer the soil from this trench to the other end of the area to be cultivated. Then, dig a second trench adjoining the first, 1 foot

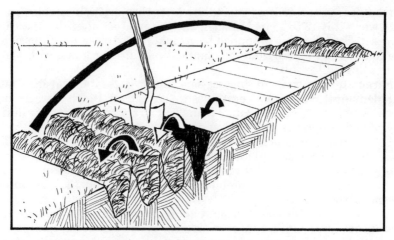

wide and 10 inches deep. Shovel this soil into the first trench and enrich with compost. Dig another 10 inches out of the trench and pile the soil into the first one. Continue until you reach the other end of the area to be cultivated. Into the last trench, place the soil that has been set aside from the first trench.

When Soil Is Too Wet to Cultivate

If soil is cultivated when it is too wet, large clods, which will impede plant growth and make future cultivation difficult, are produced. To determine whether or not the soil is too wet to cultivate, ball up a fist full of soil in your hand. If the compressed soil stays balled when you poke it with your finger, it is too wet. If it crumbles, consider it suitable for cultivation.

Place Seed Orders Early

Winter is the time to place orders for vegetable and flower seeds. Toward spring, many seed supply companies run out of the more popular varieties. Many catalogues contain valuable planting information, and studying them leisurely is a good way to get reacquainted with gardening practices after a winter rest.

Locate Your Garden near the House

If you are lucky enough to have a choice as to where your garden will be placed, consider the advantages of locating it near the house. The most obvious are the steps eliminated in carting supplies, implements, and produce to and from the garden. Equally important is the fact that activities around the house will discourage animals from entering the garden. Though rodents (and deer, if you live in a rural area) are quite brazen, they generally will stay away from an active house. A garden near a house might also reduce the need for a costly irrigation system.

✓   ✓   ✓

Rotate Your Gardening Areas

Vegetable crops differ in the relative amounts of nutrients that they extract from the soil. For instance, leaf crops such as lettuce remove nitrogen from the soil, and legumes such as peas replace it. Root crops require abundant potash, and seed crops demands a good supply of phosphorous. If the same crop is grown repeatedly in the same area, the soil will rapidly become depleted of those nutrients for which it has the most demand. For this reason, make it a practice not to plant the same crop in the same location for two consecutive years. It is also good practice to periodically relocate your entire garden area if at all possible.

✓   ✓   ✓

Watch the Space between Rows

Ample space is needed between garden rows to tend to your plants and allow them to grow. The amount of space you leave depends on the vegetables in the rows and the type of cultivation you intend to use. If you are using a roto-tiller or garden tractor, make sure enough room is provided for this equipment to pass through the row without injuring the plants. If you plan on hand cultivation, plant all small seed in rows spaced from 8 to 10 inches apart, peas in rows 30 inches apart, and corn in hills 30 inches apart in each direction. Most transplants can be placed in rows 24 inches apart. Place summer squash in hills 3 feet apart in all directions, and beans in rows 30 inches apart. Seed packets generally give spacing requirements. If in doubt, always allow extra room. Growing plants tend to reduce the space between what were originally ample rows.

✓   ✓   ✓

What Not to Plant in a Small Garden

If you are gardening in a small space, there are some plants which should *not* be considered because of their excessive space requirements. Potatoes, melons, winter squash, and pumpkins all require a great deal of surface space in relation to yield. Cucumbers should only be planted if a trellis is used. For corn to be able to cross-pollinate, they cannot be planted in small numbers; therefore, corn is not suitable for small gardens.

✓   ✓   ✓

Don't Start Transplants Too Early

It is good practice to start garden transplants indoors or in greenhouses before it is time to plant outdoors. However, if they are started too soon, you will end up with plants that will need transplanting before the proper time. The time to start transplants will vary with different regions of the country. In general, transplants should not be started before late March or early April. Given a choice, it is always better to set out plants that are somewhat small than those that are overgrown.

✦   ✦   ✦

Run Garden Rows Counter to Slope

If your garden has a slope that makes erosion of the soil a problem, run the garden rows counter to the slope. If the rows are run up and down the slope, they will act as channels for soil erosion. Rows set counter to the slope stop erosion and help capture rainfall before it runs off.

✦   ✦   ✦

Don't Use Fresh Manure in Gardens

Well-rotted manure makes an excellent fertilizer and soil conditioner for gardens. However, don't use *fresh* manure in your garden. It will burn the plants. Further, the micro-organisms needed to cause fresh manure to rot to the point where it is of use to plants tie up nutrients that would otherwise be available to the plants. Well-rotted manure is odorless, dark brown in color, and crumbly in texture.

✦   ✦   ✦

Trees Compete with Garden Plants

If gardens are set too close to large trees, the plants therein will suffer from the competition with the trees for sunlight and nutrients. In such competition, garden plants never win. The rule of thumb is never to locate a garden in an area shaded by trees.

✦   ✦   ✦

Treat Leaves and Grass before Composting

If leaves and grass clippings are placed fresh in a compost pile, they tend to decompose slower than the other ingredients, making the compost uneven. To prevent this problem, run leaves through a chopper or compost them separately and add the decomposed leafmold to the main compost pile afterwards. Green lawn clippings should be cured for several months before being introduced into the general compost pile.

✦   ✦   ✦

Making Compost

Compost is partially decomposed organic matter that can be used as fertilizer, mulch, and soil conditioner. Compost—which can be made inexpensively out of such material as leaves, grass clippings, stems and stalks of plants, corn husks, pea hulls, and fine twigs—can be substituted for peat moss.

To make compost, fill a bin with alternate layers of organic waste 6 to 12 inches thick and garden soil about 1 inch thick. To each layer of organic matter add 3 cups of fertilizer (5-10-5) per bushel. Add water until the mixture is moist. After 3 to 4 months of moderate to warm weather, mix the material thoroughly. The material can be used directly or allowed to compost further. To have a constant supply, start new compost heaps while the first one is still decomposing.

✦   ✦   ✦

Trash Bag Composting

Easy "anywhere" composting has been made possible through the advent of plastic bags. Place a couple of shovelfuls of plant wastes in a 32-gallon garbage can liner and sprinkle with fertilizer (5-10-5). Repeat until the bag is full, add about a quart of water, and tie the bag tightly. Store the bag in the cellar or a heated garage. Usable compost should be ready in about a month.

✦   ✦   ✦

Lime Not Necessary for Composting

Most recommendations for composting indicate that lime should be added to the compost pile. Recent research has proven this unnecessary. During the early stages of decomposition, a compost pile without lime will become more acid, but as decay progresses, acidity decreases; and by the time it is ready to be used, the compost is slightly alkaline.

✦   ✦   ✦

Seaweed for Composting

If you live near a seashore, don't underestimate the value of seaweed for composting. Composted seaweed compares favorably with barnyard manure as a fertilizer. Remove the surface salt from seaweed before composting. To remove the salt, spread the seaweed over wooden frames covered with chicken wire. One or 2 good rains will remove the salt.

✦   ✦   ✦

Removing Dirt from Under the Fingernails

It is often difficult to remove dirt from under your fingernails after a day in the garden. Here's a simple solution: Before working in soil, claw your nails into a bar of soft soap. You will be surprised to see how clean your nails emerge when washed following gardening.

Section Two

PLANT SELECTION AND LOCATION

Plant Pumpkins, Squash, and Corn Together

Garden space can be used more efficiently by planting some vegetable crops together. Plant pumpkins and vining squash in the sweet corn patch; the corn matures just in time to let the expanding squash and pumpkins take over.

Corn to Support Beans

Crops can sometimes be planted in partnership. Beans can be planted with late maturing corn; the corn stalks serve to support the beans.

Grow More in a Smaller Space

If your garden space is limited, consider growing two crops together (*companion cropping*), or grow one crop to maturity, harvest it, then plant another crop in the same row (*succession planting*).

An example of companion cropping is planting lettuce and cabbage alternately in the same row. The lettuce matures first and is harvested before it interferes with the growth of the cabbage. Radishes can be seeded between rows of cabbage, broccoli, and cauliflower; and early beans, lettuce, radishes, and spinach can be planted between tomato, eggplant, pepper, and late cabbage rows.

An example of succession planting is following an early sweet corn with a crop of turnips.

✓   ✓   ✓

Don't Plant Tall Vegetables to the South or East of Short Ones

Shade from tall-growing vegetables can reduce the growth of shorter vegetables. Corn, pole beans, and the like can reduce the growth of such low growers as bush beans and root crops. In order that they may receive maximum sunlight, plant low-growing vegetables on the south or east side of tall ones.

✓   ✓   ✓

Don't Locate Vegetable Gardens near Walnut Trees

The roots of walnut trees produce a toxic substance that inhibits the growth of some garden plants. Tomato plants are particularly susceptible. It is best practice not to plant a garden near a walnut tree.

✓   ✓   ✓

Support Cucumbers with a Trellis

Cucumbers have a tendency to climb. If they are grown on a trellis, straighter fruits are produced. Cucumbers climb best on 20-gauge poultry fencing wire. String the fencing (at least 6 feet tall) between two posts driven into the ground. Plant the cucumbers along one side of the fence. A trellis is also a great space saver.

✓   ✓   ✓

New Places for Tomatoes

Tomato plants don't have to be grown in the garden. You might consider other locations, such as against a building or in hanging baskets. All tomato plants require is some light and fertile soil. A single plant produces enough flowers to produce a healthy crop.

✓   ✓   ✓

The Best Potato Varieties

Different varieties of potatoes mature in different amounts of time. Irish cobbler is an excellent early maturing variety for the home garden. It should be planted early—late March to mid-May. Norland is an early red-skinned variety. Chippewa and Superior are white-skinned varieties; they mature later than Irish Cobbler. Katahdin, Kennebac, and Sebago varieties should be raised if you plan to store your potatoes. Always plant certified seed potatoes. Check with your County Agent to determine who handles certified seed potatoes in your area.

✔   ✔   ✔

Growing Giant Sunflowers

If you plan on growing giant sunflowers, be sure to select the right seed. The best selection is Mammoth Russian, the largest and most commonly grown variety, maturing in 80 days. The Manchurian is another tall, large-seeded strain; it matures in 83 days.

✔   ✔   ✔

Pumpkin Varieties to Show Off

Pumpkins are fun to grow for exhibit or just to brag about. If you wish to grow giant pumpkins, Big Max and Mammoth Chili both work well. Small Sugar and Turk's Turban varieties are exceptional for decorative purposes. Seed can be started indoors in early April; plant seedlings in hills 3 feet apart in the garden when danger of frost has passed. Mix well-rotted manure into the hill.

✔   ✔   ✔

Lettuce in the Summer

Lettuce is very difficult to grow in the summer because the heat drains water from the leaves. If you wish to have lettuce during the summer, provide it with shade. Winter lath-type fencing can be suspended 1 foot above the lettuce on a wooden frame. Some gardeners capitalize on shade protection from nearby plants and buildings to grow summer lettuce.

✔   ✔   ✔

Head Lettuce that Heads

Some varieties of head lettuce will not head during warm weather. To eliminate this problem, select such sure headers as Great Lakes, Pennlake, Iceburg, New York No. 12, and Imperial No. 44.

✔   ✔   ✔

Don't Plant Corn in Single Rows

In order for a corn ear to develop, the corn silks must receive pollen from another plant. To facilitate cross-pollination, corn should be planted in rows of two or more. Single rows of corn will result in many undeveloped kernels.

✔   ✔   ✔

A 15' X 25' VEGETABLE GARDEN

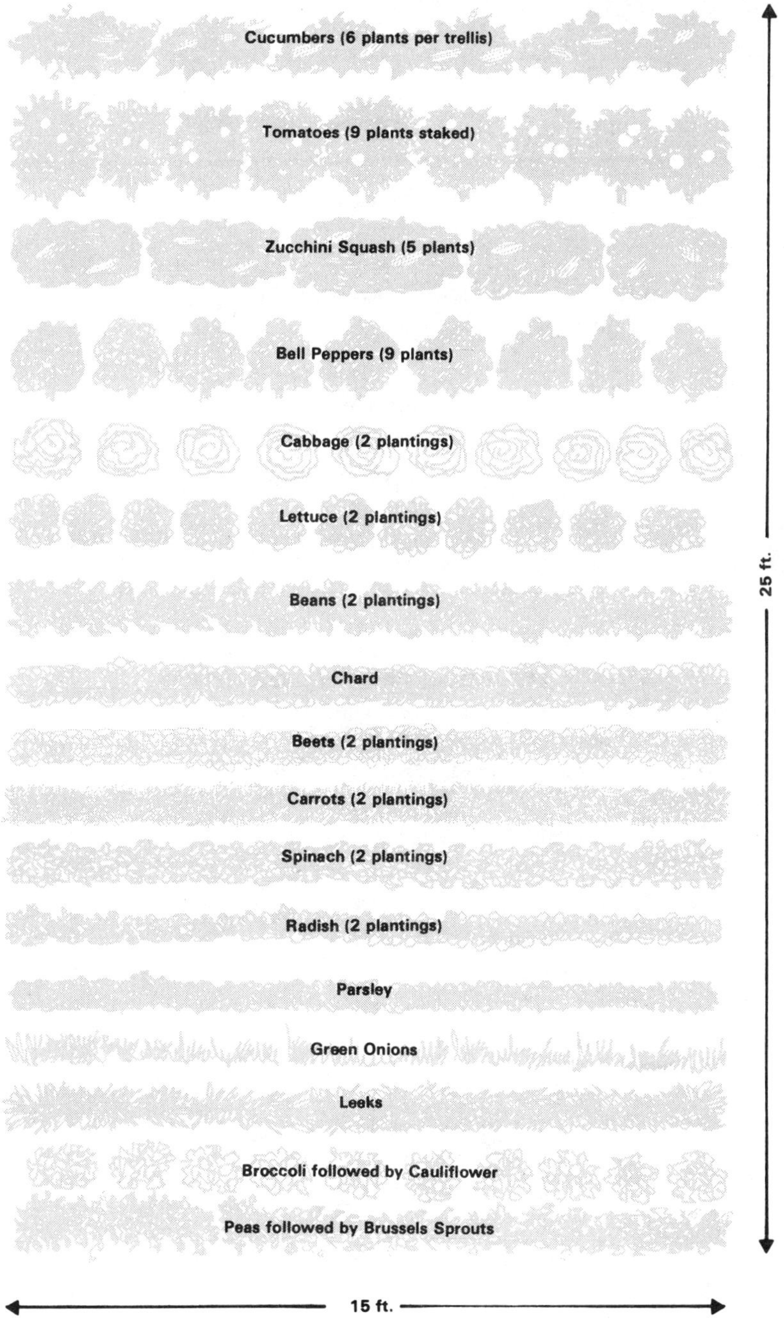

Cucumbers (6 plants per trellis)

Tomatoes (9 plants staked)

Zucchini Squash (5 plants)

Bell Peppers (9 plants)

Cabbage (2 plantings)

Lettuce (2 plantings)

Beans (2 plantings)

Chard

Beets (2 plantings)

Carrots (2 plantings)

Spinach (2 plantings)

Radish (2 plantings)

Parsley

Green Onions

Leeks

Broccoli followed by Cauliflower

Peas followed by Brussels Sprouts

25 ft.

15 ft.

A COMBINATION FLOWER-VEGETABLE GARDEN (10' X 10')

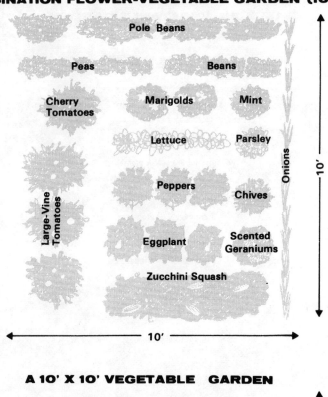

A 10' X 10' VEGETABLE GARDEN

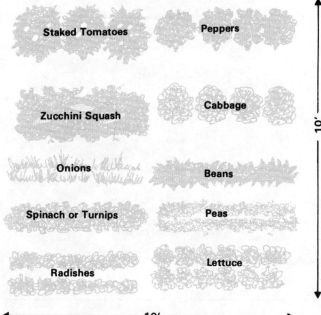

Don't Crowd Corn Plants

If corn plants are over-crowded, ear size and total yield will be reduced. In rows 30 inches apart, thin to 1 foot between plants. If the corn is planted in hills 36 inches apart, thin to 3 stalks to the hill.

Double-Row Pea Culture

Green peas are more efficiently grown if planted in double rows. One support can then be used for both rows. This method also makes fertilization and cultivation easier.

Avoiding Misshapen Carrots

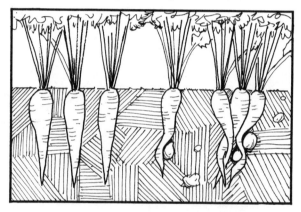

Stones or lumps of soil can cause forked or misshapen carrot roots. Failure to thin young carrots may cause root twisting as in the four carrots illustrated in the right of the diagram. To avoid these problems, choose deeply worked, well-drained soil for carrots, taking care to remove stones and lumps of soil. Thin carrot seedlings when they are 2 to 3 inches tall so that there are 1 or 2 inches between the plants. Carrot seed germinates slowly, so it may be necessary to thin more than once. If your soil tends to be heavy, consider using a short, stubby variety such as Short 'n Sweet.

Plants That Attract Birds

Birds can be very helpful in reducing the insect population of a garden. To attract birds, include plants that provide them with food and shelter. The best plants for this purpose are sunflowers, cosmos, marigolds, asters, and California poppies. A hedge of multiflora rose, bush honeysuckle, or Japanese barberry also offers good shelter and food for birds.

Plants That Attract Bees

Bees are the principal pollinators of garden plants, and many vegetables will not produce fruit unless properly pollinated. Therefore, it pays to attract bees to your garden area. Berganot, lemon balm, and thyme are especially good bee-attracting plants.

✓   ✓   ✓

Vegetables in Flower Beds

If you don't have a vegetable garden *per se,* consider growing vegetables in your flower garden. Vegetables in a flower bed can serve the double purpose of providing food and making an attractive display. Suggestions for vegetable edging plants are: parsley, leaf lettuce, bibb lettuce, purple and green kohlrabi, endive, and herbs of various kinds.

✓   ✓   ✓

A Herb Garden

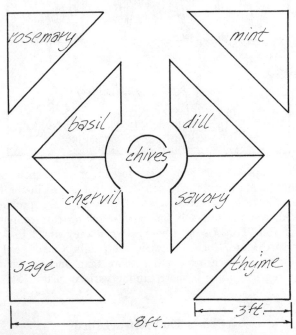

A separate herb garden can be an attractive part of your landscape. The diagram is a suggested design.

✓   ✓   ✓

Don't Grow Herbs in Rich Soil

Rich soil is recommended for most plants. Herbs, however, are not as fragrant if grown in extra rich soil. Most herbs perform best in a sandy soil that is not too fertile. Herbs need full sunlight for at least 6 hours each day.

Section Three

SEEDING AND TRANSPLANTING

Test Seed Germination

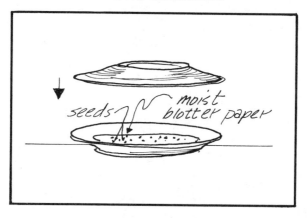

Sometimes, seeds do not germinate, and it is difficult to determine whether the cause is poor seed, disease, or poor growing conditions. To eliminate part of the mystery, test seed germination *before* planting. Place a counted number of seeds on a piece of moist blotter paper or paper toweling; keep them moist by enclosing with two plates. Do not allow the seeds to dry out throughout the test. Most seeds will germinate in 5 to 7 days. Expect at least 80% germination from good seed.

✓   ✓   ✓

Determining the Frost-Free Date

You will want to make the first planting of each vegetable as early as possible but without the danger of it being killed by frost. The development of plants *outside the garden* can be used to determine when to plant without risk. Many gardeners rely on the time that oak leaves appear as a safe time to plant frost-susceptible plants (e.g., tomatoes). Many vegetables (e.g. lettuce) are hardy enough to be planted a month or more before the average date of the last frost.

✓   ✓   ✓

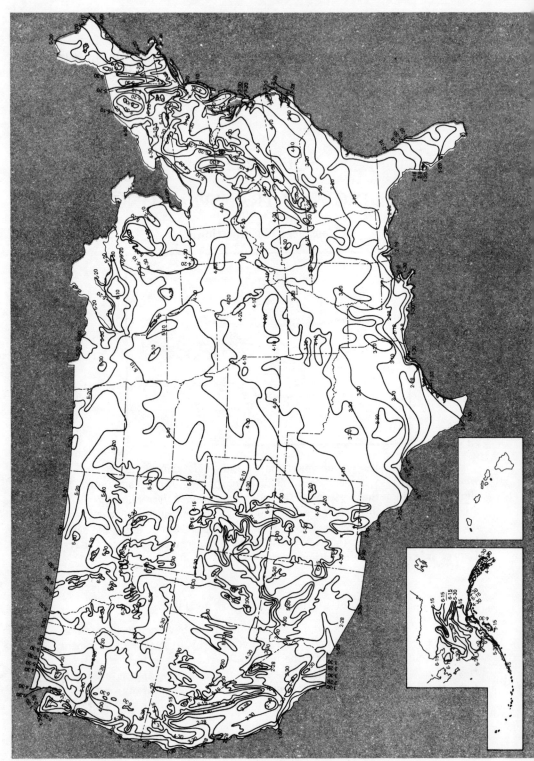

Average dates of the last killing frost in spring.

Earliest dates, and range of dates, for safe spring planting of vegetables in the open

Crop	Planting dates for localities in which average date of last freeze is—						
	Jan. 30	Feb. 8	Feb. 18	Feb. 28	Mar. 10	Mar. 20	Mar. 30
Asparagus[1]	Feb. 1-Apr. 15	Feb. 10-May 1	Mar. 1-May 1		Jan. 1-Mar. 1	Feb. 1-Mar. 10	Feb. 15-Mar. 20
Beans, lima	Feb. 1-Apr. 15	Feb. 1-May 1	Feb. 1-May 1	Mar. 15-June 1	Mar. 20-June 15	Apr. 1-June 15	Apr. 15-June 20
Beans, snap	Jan. 1-Mar. 15	Jan. 10-Mar. 15	Jan. 20-Apr. 1	Mar. 10-May 15	Mar. 15-May 15	Mar. 15-May 25	Apr. 1-June 1
Beet	Jan. 1-30	Jan. 1-30	Jan. 20-Apr. 1	Feb. 1-Mar. 1	Feb. 15-June 1	Mar. 15-May 15	Apr. 1-June 1
Broccoli, sprouting[1]	Jan. 1-30	Jan. 1-30	Jan. 15-Feb. 15	Feb. 1-Mar. 1	Feb. 15-Mar. 15	Feb. 15-Mar. 15	Mar. 1-20
Brussels sprouts[1]	Jan. 1-15	Jan. 1-Feb. 10	Jan. 1-Feb. 25	Feb. 1-Mar. 1	Feb. 15-Mar. 1	Feb. 15-Mar. 15	Mar. 1-20
Cabbage[1]	(2)	(2)	(2)	Jan. 15-Feb. 25	Jan. 25-Mar. 1	Feb. 1-Mar. 1	Feb. 15-Mar. 10
Cabbage, Chinese			(2)	(2)	(2)	(2)	(2)
Carrot	Jan. 1-Mar. 1	Jan. 1-Mar. 1	Jan. 15-Mar. 1	Feb. 1-Mar. 1	Feb. 10-Mar. 15	Feb. 15-Mar. 20	Mar. 1-Apr. 10
Cauliflower[1]	Jan. 1-Feb. 1	Jan. 1-Feb. 1	Jan. 10-Feb. 10	Jan. 20-Feb. 20	Feb. 1-Mar. 1	Feb. 10-Mar. 10	Feb. 20-Mar. 20
Celery and celeriac	Jan. 1-Feb. 1	Jan. 10-Feb. 10	Jan. 20-Feb. 20	Feb. 1-20	Feb. 20-Mar. 20	Mar. 1-Apr. 1	Apr. 1-Apr. 15
Chard	Jan. 1-Apr. 1	Jan. 1-Apr. 1	Jan. 20-Apr. 15	Feb. 1-May 1	Feb. 15-May 15	Feb. 20-May 20	Mar. 1-May 25
Chervil and chives	Jan. 1-Feb. 1	Jan. 1-Feb. 1	Jan. 1-Feb. 1	Jan. 1-Feb. 15	Feb. 1-Mar. 1	Feb. 1-Mar. 1	Feb. 15-Mar. 15
Chicory, witloof	(2)	(2)	(2)	(2)	June 1-July 1	June 1-July 1	June 1-July 1
Collards[1]	Jan. 1-Feb. 15	Jan. 1-Feb. 15	Jan. 1-Mar. 15	Jan. 15-Mar. 15	Jan. 15-Mar. 15	Feb. 1-Apr. 1	Mar. 1-June 1
Cornsalad	Jan. 1-Feb. 15	Jan. 1-Feb. 15	Jan. 1-Mar. 15	Jan. 1-Mar. 1	Jan. 1-Mar. 15	Jan. 15-Mar. 15	Jan. 15-Mar. 15
Corn, sweet	Feb. 1-Apr. 15	Feb. 1-Apr. 15	Feb. 20-Apr. 15	Mar. 1-Apr. 15	Mar. 10-Apr. 15	Mar. 15-May 15	Mar. 25-May 15
Cress, upland	Jan. 1-Feb. 15	Jan. 1-Feb. 15	Jan. 15-Feb. 15	Feb. 1-Mar. 1	Feb. 10-Mar. 15	Feb. 20-Mar. 15	Mar. 1-Apr. 1
Cucumber	Feb. 15-Mar. 15	Feb. 15-Apr. 1	Feb. 15-Apr. 15	Mar. 1-Apr. 15	Mar. 10-Apr. 15	Apr. 10-May 15	Apr. 10-May 15
Eggplant[1]	Feb. 15-Mar. 15	Feb. 10-Mar. 15	Feb. 20-Apr. 1	Mar. 10-Apr. 15	Mar. 15-Apr. 15	Apr. 1-May 1	Apr. 15-May 15
Endive	Jan. 1-Mar. 1	Jan. 1-Mar. 1	Jan. 1-Mar. 1	Feb. 15-Apr. 15	Feb. 15-Mar. 15	Mar. 1-Apr. 1	Mar. 10-Apr. 10
Fennel, Florence	Jan. 1-Mar. 1	Jan. 1-Mar. 1	Jan. 1-Mar. 1	Mar. 1-Apr. 1	Feb. 15-Apr. 15	Mar. 1-Apr. 1	Mar. 10-Apr. 10
Garlic	(2)	(2)	(2)	(2)	Feb. 1-Mar. 1	Feb. 1-Mar. 1	Mar. 1-Apr. 1
Horseradish[1]					(2)	(2)	(2)
Kale	Jan. 1-Feb. 1	Jan. 10-Feb. 1	Jan. 20-Feb. 10	Feb. 1-20	Feb. 10-Mar. 1	Feb. 20-Mar. 10	Mar. 1-20
Kohlrabi	Jan. 1-Feb. 1	Jan. 10-Feb. 1	Jan. 20-Feb. 10	Feb. 1-20	Feb. 10-Mar. 1	Feb. 20-Mar. 10	Mar. 1-Apr. 1
Leek	Jan. 1-Feb. 1	Jan. 1-Feb. 1	Jan. 1-Feb. 1	Jan. 15-Feb. 15	Jan. 25-Mar. 1	Feb. 1-Apr. 1	Feb. 15-Mar. 15
Lettuce, head[1]	Jan. 1-Feb. 1	Jan. 1-Feb. 1	Jan. 1-Feb. 1	Jan. 15-Feb. 15	Feb. 1-20	Feb. 15-Mar. 10	Mar. 1-20
Lettuce, leaf	Feb. 1-Apr. 1	Feb. 15-Apr. 1	Feb. 15-Apr. 15	Mar. 1-Apr. 1	Jan. 1-Apr. 1	Feb. 1-Apr. 1	Feb. 15-Apr. 15
Muskmelon	Feb. 15-Apr. 1	Feb. 15-Apr. 1	Mar. 1-June 1	Mar. 1-Apr. 1	Feb. 15-Apr. 1	Apr. 1-May 1	Apr. 10-May 15
Mustard	Jan. 1-Feb. 15	Jan. 1-Mar. 1	Jan. 1-15	Jan. 10-June 1	Mar. 20-June 1	Apr. 10-June 15	Apr. 10-June 15
Okra	Feb. 15-Apr. 1	Feb. 15-Apr. 15	Jan. 1-15	Jan. 1-Feb. 15	Jan. 1-Feb. 1	Jan. 1-Feb. 1	Apr. 10-June 15
Onion[1]	Jan. 1-15	Jan. 1-15	Jan. 1-15	Jan. 1-Feb. 15	Feb. 1-Mar. 1	Feb. 10-Mar. 10	Feb. 20-Mar. 15
Onion, seed	Jan. 1-15	Jan. 1-15	Jan. 1-30	Jan. 1-Feb. 1	Jan. 1-Mar. 1	Feb. 10-Mar. 10	Feb. 20-Mar. 15
Onion, sets	Jan. 1-15	Jan. 1-15			Jan. 15-Mar. 10	Feb. 15-Mar. 20	Feb. 15-Mar. 20
Parsley	Jan. 1-30	Jan. 1-30	Jan. 1-Mar. 1	Jan. 15-Mar. 1	Feb. 1-Mar. 10	Mar. 1-Apr. 1	Mar. 1-Apr. 1
Parsnip			Jan. 1-Feb. 1	Jan. 15-Mar. 1	Feb. 15-Mar. 15	Feb. 15-Mar. 15	Feb. 15-Mar. 15
Peas, garden	Jan. 1-Feb. 15	Jan. 1-Feb. 15	Feb. 1-Mar. 1	Jan. 15-Mar. 1	Jan. 15-Mar. 1	Feb. 10-Mar. 20	Feb. 10-Mar. 20
Peas, black-eye	Feb. 15-May 1	Feb. 15-May 15	Mar. 1-June 15	Mar. 10-June 20	Apr. 1-June 1	Apr. 1-July 1	Apr. 15-July 1
Pepper[1]	Feb. 15-Apr. 1	Feb. 15-Apr. 15	Mar. 1-May 1	Mar. 15-May 1	Apr. 1-June 1	Apr. 15-June 1	Apr. 15-June 1
Potato	Jan. 1-Feb. 1	Jan. 1-Feb. 15	Jan. 1-Feb. 15	Jan. 15-Mar. 1	Feb. 1-Mar. 1	Feb. 10-Mar. 15	Feb. 20-Mar. 20
Radish	Jan. 1-Apr. 1	Jan. 1-Apr. 1	Jan. 1-Apr. 1	Jan. 1-Apr. 1	Jan. 1-Apr. 15	Jan. 1-May 1	Feb. 15-May 1
Rhubarb[1]					(2)	(2)	(2)
Rutabaga							
Salsify	Jan. 1-Feb. 1	Jan. 1-Feb. 15	Jan. 15-Feb. 20	Jan. 1-Feb. 1	Jan. 15-Feb. 15	Jan. 15-Mar. 1	Feb. 1-Mar. 1
Shallot	Jan. 1-Feb. 1	Jan. 1-Feb. 10	Jan. 1-Feb. 20	Jan. 1-Feb. 1	Feb. 1-Feb. 15	Feb. 1-Mar. 10	Feb. 15-Mar. 15
Sorrel	Jan. 1-Mar. 1	Jan. 1-Mar. 1	Jan. 15-Mar. 15	Jan. 1-Mar. 1	Jan. 15-Mar. 15	Feb. 1-Mar. 10	Feb. 20-Apr. 1
Soybean	Mar. 1-June 30	Mar. 1-June 30	Mar. 10-June 30	Feb. 20-June 30	Apr. 10-June 30	Apr. 20-June 30	Feb. 20-June 30
Spinach	Jan. 1-Feb. 15	Jan. 1-Feb. 15	Jan. 1-Mar. 1	Jan. 1-Mar. 1	Jan. 1-Mar. 15	Jan. 15-Mar. 15	Feb. 1-Mar. 20
Spinach, New Zealand	Feb. 1-Apr. 15	Feb. 1-Apr. 15	Mar. 1-Apr. 15	Mar. 15-May 15	Mar. 20-May 15	Apr. 1-May 15	Apr. 10-June 1
Squash, summer	Feb. 1-Apr. 15	Feb. 15-Apr. 15	Mar. 1-Apr. 15	Mar. 15-May 1	Mar. 20-May 1	Apr. 1-May 15	Apr. 10-June 1
Sweetpotato	Mar. 15-May 15	Mar. 20-May 15	Mar. 20-June 1	Mar. 20-June 1	Mar. 20-June 10	Apr. 1-June 10	Apr. 20-June 1
Tomato	Feb. 1-Apr. 1	Feb. 20-Apr. 10	Mar. 1-Apr. 20	Mar. 10-May 1	Mar. 20-May 10	Apr. 1-June 1	Apr. 10-June 1
Turnip	Jan. 1-Mar. 1	Jan. 1-Mar. 1	Jan. 10-Mar. 1	Jan. 20-Mar. 1	Feb. 1-Mar. 1	Feb. 10-Mar. 10	Feb. 20-Mar. 20
Watermelon	Feb. 15-Mar. 15	Feb. 15-Apr. 1	Feb. 15-Apr. 15	Mar. 15-Apr. 15	Mar. 15-Apr. 15	Apr. 1-May 15	Apr. 10-May 15

[1] Plants.
[2] Generally fall-planted

Planting dates for localities in which average date of last freeze is—

Crop	Apr. 10	Apr. 20	Apr. 30	May 10	May 20	May 30	June 10
Asparagus [1]	Mar. 10-Apr. 10	Mar. 15-Apr. 15	Mar. 20-Apr. 15	Mar. 10-Apr. 30	Apr. 20-May 15	May 1-June 1	May 15-June 1.
Beans, lima	Apr. 1-June 30	May 1-June 20	May 15-June 15	May 25-June 15			
Beans, snap	Apr. 10-June 30	Apr. 25-June 30	May 10-June 30	May 15-June 15	Apr. 25-June 30	May 1-30	May 15-June 15.
Beet	Mar. 10-June 30	Mar. 20-June 1	May 10-June 30	May 10-June 15	May 1-June 15	May 1-30	May 20-June 10.
Broccoli, sprouting [1]	Mar. 15-Apr. 15	Mar. 25-Apr. 20	Apr. 1-May 1	Apr. 15-June 15	May 1-June 1	May 1-30	May 20-June 10.
Brussels sprouts [1]	Mar. 15-Apr. 15	Mar. 25-Apr. 20	Apr. 1-May 1	Apr. 15-June 15	May 1-June 1	May 1-30	May 20-June 1.
Cabbage [1]	Mar. 1-Apr. 1	Mar. 10-Apr. 1	Mar. 15-Apr. 10	Apr. 1-May 15	May 1-June 1	May 1-June 1	May 20-June 1.
Cabbage, Chinese	(²)	(²)	(²)	Apr. 1-May 15	Apr. 15-May 15	May 10-June 1	May 20-June 1.
Carrot	Mar. 10-Apr. 20	Apr. 1-May 15	Apr. 10-June 1	Apr. 20-June 15	May 10-June 1	May 20-June 1	June 1-June 15.
Cauliflower [1]	Mar. 1-Mar. 20	Mar. 15-Apr. 20	Apr. 10-May 10	Apr. 15-May 15	Apr. 15-June 1	May 10-June 15	June 1-June 15.
Celery and celeriac	Apr. 1-Apr. 20	Apr. 10-May 1	Apr. 15-May 1	Apr. 20-June 1	May 1-June 1	May 20-June 1	June 1-June 15.
Chard	Mar. 15-June 15	Apr. 1-June 15	Apr. 15-June 15	Apr. 20-June 15	May 1-June 1	May 1-June 1	May 15-June 1.
Chervil and chives	Mar. 1-Apr. 1	Mar. 15-June 1	Mar. 15-May 1	Apr. 1-May 1	Apr. 15-May 15	May 1-June 15	June 1-15.
Chicory, witloof	June 10-July 1	June 10-June 1	June 1-July 1	June 15-July 1	June 1-20	June 10-June 15	May 20-June 1.
Collards [1]	Mar. 1-June 1	Mar. 1-June 1	Mar. 1-June 1	Apr. 1-June 1	May 1-June 1	May 10-June 15	May 15-June 15.
Cornsalad	Feb. 1-Apr. 1	Feb. 15-Apr. 15	Mar. 1-Apr. 1	Apr. 15-June 1	May 15-June 1	May 15-June 15	
Corn, sweet	Apr. 10-June 1	Apr. 25-June 15	May 10-June 15	May 10-June 15	May 15-June 1	May 20-June 1	May 15-June 15.
Cress, upland	Mar. 10-Apr. 15	Mar. 20-May 1	Apr. 10-May 10	Apr. 20-June 20	May 15-June 1	June 1-June 15	May 15-June 1.
Cucumber	Apr. 20-May 1	May 10-June 15	May 15-June 15	May 20-June 15	June 1-15	June 1-15	May 15-June 1.
Eggplant [1]	May 1-June 1	May 10-June 1	May 15-June 10	May 20-June 15	June 1	June 1-15	May 15-June 1.
Endive	Mar. 15-Apr. 15	Mar. 25-Apr. 15	Apr. 1-May 1	Apr. 15-May 15	May 1-30	May 1-30	May 15-June 1.
Fennel, Florence	Mar. 15-Apr. 15	Mar. 25-Apr. 15	Apr. 1-May 1	Apr. 15-May 15	May 1-30	May 1-30	May 15-June 1.
Garlic	Feb. 20-Mar. 20	Mar. 10-Apr. 1	Mar. 15-Apr. 15	Apr. 1-May 1	Apr. 15-May 20	May 1-30	May 15-June 1.
Horseradish [1]	Mar. 10-Apr. 10	Mar. 20-Apr. 20	Apr. 1-30	Apr. 10-May 1	Apr. 20-May 20	May 1-30	May 1-15.
Kale	Mar. 10-Apr. 1	Mar. 20-Apr. 10	Apr. 1-May 1	Apr. 10-June 15	Apr. 20-May 20	May 1-30	May 20-June 30.
Kohlrabi	Mar. 10-Apr. 10	Mar. 20-May 1	Apr. 1-May 10	Apr. 10-May 15	Apr. 20-May 20	May 1-30	May 20-June 30.
Leek	Mar. 1-Apr. 1	Mar. 15-Apr. 15	Apr. 1-May 1	Apr. 1-May 1	Apr. 15-June 1	May 1-June 1	May 20-June 30.
Lettuce, head [1]	Mar. 10-Apr. 1	Mar. 20-Apr. 15	Apr. 1-May 1	Apr. 15-May 15	May 1-June 30	May 10-June 30	May 10-June 10.
Lettuce, leaf	Mar. 15-May 15	Mar. 20-May 15	Apr. 1-June 1	Apr. 15-June 15	May 1-June 30	May 10-June 30	May 10-June 10.
Muskmelon	Apr. 20-June 1	May 1-June 15	May 15-June 15	May 15-June 15	June 1-20		May 10-June 10.
Mustard	Mar. 10-Apr. 20	Mar. 20-May 1	Apr. 1-May 10	Apr. 15-June 1	May 1-June 30	May 1-30	May 20-June 10.
Okra	Apr. 20-June 15	May 1-June 1	May 10-June 1	May 20-June 10	June 1-20	June 1	May 20-June 10.
Onion [1]	Mar. 1-Apr. 1	Mar. 15-Apr. 10	Apr. 10-May 1	Apr. 20-May 15	Apr. 20-May 15	May 1-30	May 10-June 10.
Onion, seed	Mar. 1-Apr. 1	Mar. 15-Apr. 1	Apr. 1-May 1	Apr. 10-May 1	Apr. 20-May 15	May 1-30	May 10-June 10.
Onion, sets	Mar. 1-Apr. 1	Mar. 10-Apr. 1	Mar. 15-Apr. 15	Apr. 1-May 1	Apr. 15-May 15	May 1-30	May 10-June 10.
Parsley	Mar. 10-Apr. 10	Mar. 20-Apr. 20	Apr. 1-May 1	Apr. 15-May 15	May 1-20	May 10-June 1	May 20-June 15.
Parsnip	Mar. 10-Apr. 10	Mar. 20-May 1	Apr. 1-May 1	Apr. 15-June 1	May 1-June 1	May 1-June 1	May 10-June 10.
Peas, garden	Feb. 20-Mar. 20	Mar. 10-Apr. 1	Mar. 20-May 10	Apr. 1-May 15	Apr. 15-June 1	May 1-June 15	May 10-June 15.
Peas, black-eye	May 1-July 1	May 10-June 15	May 15-June 1	June 1-July 1	June 15-July 1		
Pepper [1]	May 1-June 1	May 10-June 1	May 15-June 10	May 20-June 1	June 1-15		May 15-June 1.
Potato	Mar. 10-Apr. 1	Mar. 20-May 10	Mar. 15-June 10	Apr. 1-June 1	Apr. 15-June 15	May 1-June 15	May 15-June 1.
Radish	Mar. 1-May 1	Mar. 10-May 10	Mar. 20-May 10	Apr. 1-June 1	Apr. 15-June 15	May 1-June 15	May 15-June 15.
Rhubarb [1]	Mar. 1-Apr. 1	Mar. 10-Apr. 10	Mar. 20-May 10	Apr. 1-May 1	Apr. 15-May 10	May 1-20	May 20-June 1.
Rutabaga	Mar. 10-Apr. 10	Mar. 10-Apr. 10	Mar. 10-May 1	Apr. 1-June 1	May 1-20	May 10-20	May 20-June 10.
Salsify	Mar. 10-Apr. 15	Mar. 20-May 1	Apr. 1-May 15	Apr. 15-June 1	May 1-June 1	May 10-June 1	May 15-June 1.
Shallot	Mar. 1-Apr. 1	Mar. 15-Apr. 15	Mar. 15-May 1	Apr. 1-May 1	Apr. 1-May 1	May 1-June 15	May 20-June 10.
Sorrel	Mar. 1-Apr. 15	Mar. 15-May 1	Mar. 15-June 1	Apr. 1-May 15	Apr. 15-June 1	May 1-June 15	May 10-June 1.
Soybean	May 1-June 30	May 15-June 20	May 15-June 15	May 25-June 10	June 1-20	June 1-June 10	May 10-June 10.
Spinach	Feb. 15-Apr. 1	Mar. 1-Apr. 15	Mar. 20-Apr. 20	Apr. 1-June 15	Apr. 20-June 15	May 1-June 1	May 1-June 15.
Spinach, New Zealand	Apr. 20-June 1	May 1-June 15	May 15-June 15	May 20-July 1	Apr. 10-June 15	Apr. 20-June 15	June 10-20.
Squash, summer	Apr. 20-June 1	May 1-June 15	May 1-June 15	May 20-June 15	1-15	June 1-15	
Sweetpotato	May 1-June 1	May 10-June 10	May 20-June 10	May 25-June 10	Apr. 20-June 1	June 1-15	
Tomato	Apr. 20-June 1	May 5-June 15	May 20-June 10	May 20-May 30	May 25-June 15	June 1-15	June 15-30.
Turnip	Mar. 1-Apr. 1	Mar. 10-Apr. 1	Mar. 20-May 1	Apr. 1-June 1	Apr. 15-June 1	May 1-June 15	
Watermelon	Apr. 20-June 1	May 1-June 15	May 15-June 15	May 1-June 15	June 15-July 1	May 15-June 1	May 15-June 15.

[1] Plants.

[2] Generally fall-planted

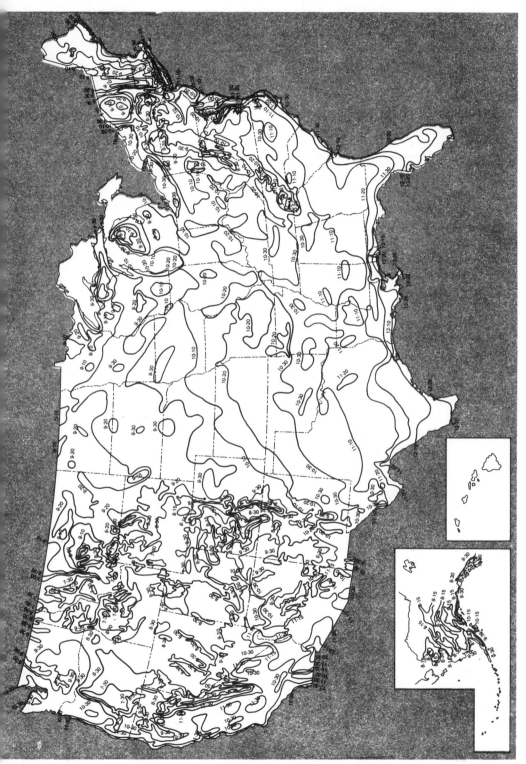

Average dates of the first killing frost in fall.

Latest dates, and range of dates, for safe fall planting of vegetables in the open

Crop	Planting dates for localities in which average dates of first freeze is—					
	Aug. 30	Sept. 10	Sept. 20	Sept. 30	Oct. 10	Oct. 20
Asparagus [1]					Oct. 20–Nov. 15	Nov. 1–Dec. 15.
Beans, lima				June 1–15	June 1–15	June 15–30.
Beans, snap		May 15–June 15	June 1–July 1	June 1–July 10	June 15–July 20	July 1–Aug. 1.
Beet	May 15–June 15	May 15–June 15	June 1–July 1	June 1–July 10	June 15–July 25	July 1–Aug. 5.
Broccoli, sprouting	May 1–June 1	May 1–June 1	May 1–June 15	June 1–30	June 15–July 15	July 1–Aug. 1.
Brussels sprouts	May 1–June 1	May 1–June 1	May 1–June 15	June 1–30	June 15–July 15	July 1–Aug. 1.
Cabbage [1]	May 1–June 1	May 1–June 1	May 1–June 15	June 1–July 10	June 15–July 15	July 1–20.
Cabbage, Chinese	May 15–June 15	May 15–June 15	June 1–July 1	June 1–July 15	June 15–Aug. 1	July 15–Aug. 15.
Carrot	May 15–June 15	May 15–June 15	June 1–July 1	June 1–July 10	June 1–July 20	June 15–Aug. 1.
Cauliflower [1]	May 1–June 1	May 1–July 1	May 1–July 1	May 10–July 15	June 1–July 25	July 1–Aug. 5.
Celery [1] and celeriac	May 1–June 1	May 15–June 15	May 15–July 1	June 1–July 5	June 1–July 15	June 1–Aug. 1.
Chard	May 15–July 1	May 15–July 1	June 1–July 1	June 1–July 5	June 1–July 20	June 1–Aug. 1.
Chervil and chives	May 10–June 10	May 1–June 15	May 15–June 15	(2)	(2)	(2)
Chicory, witloof	May 15–June 15	May 15–June 15	May 15–June 15	June 1–July 1	June 1–July 1	June 15–July 15.
Collards [1]	May 15–June 15	May 15–June 15	May 15–June 15	June 15–July 15	July 1–Aug. 1	July 15–Aug. 15.
Cornsalad	May 15–June 15	May 15–July 1	June 15–Aug. 1	July 15–Sept. 1	Aug. 15–Sept. 15	Sept. 1–Oct. 15.
Corn, sweet			June 1–July 1	June 1–July 1	June 1–July 10	June 1–July 20.
Cress, upland	May 15–June 15	May 15–July 1	June 15–Aug. 1	July 15–Sept. 1	Aug. 15–Sept. 15	Sept. 1–Oct. 15.
Cucumber			June 1–15	June 1–July 1	June 1–July 1	June 1–July 1.
Eggplant [1]				May 20–June 10	May 15–June 15	June 1–July 1.
Endive	June 1–July 1	June 1–July 1	June 15–July 15	June 15–Aug. 1	July 1–Aug. 15	July 15–Sept. 1.
Fennel, Florence	May 15–June 15	May 15–July 15	June 1–July 1	June 1–July 1	June 15–July 15	June 15–Aug. 1.
Garlic	(2)	(2)	(2)	(2)	(2)	(2)
Horseradish [1]	(2)	(2)	(2)	(2)	(2)	(2)
Kale	May 15–June 15	May 15–June 15	June 1–July 1	June 15–July 15	July 1–Aug. 1	July 15–Aug. 15.
Kohlrabi	May 15–June 15	June 1–July 1	June 1–July 15	June 15–July 15	July 1–Aug. 1	July 15–Aug. 15.
Leek	May 1–June 1	May 1–June 1	(2)	(2)	(2)	(2)
Lettuce, head [1]	May 15–July 1	May 15–July 1	June 1–July 15	June 15–Aug. 1	July 15–Aug. 15	Aug. 1–30.
Lettuce, leaf	May 15–July 15	May 15–July 15	June 1–Aug. 1	June 1–Aug. 1	July 15–Sept. 1	July 15–Sept. 1.
Muskmelon			May 1–June 15	May 15–June 1	June 15–June 15	June 15–July 20.
Mustard	May 15–July 15	May 15–July 15	June 1–Aug. 1	June 15–Aug. 1	July 15–Aug. 15	Aug. 1–Sept. 1.
Okra			June 1–20	June 1–July 1	June 1–July 15	June 1–Aug. 1.
Onion [1]	May 1–June 10	May 1–June 10	(2)	(2)	(2)	(2)
Onion, seed	May 1–June 1	May 1–June 10	(2)	(2)	(2)	(2)
Onion, sets	May 1–June 1	May 1–June 10	(2)	(2)	(2)	(2)
Parsley	May 15–June 15	May 1–June 15	June 1–July 1	June 1–July 15	June 15–Aug. 1	July 15–Aug. 15.
Parsnip	May 15–June 1	May 1–June 1	May 15–June 15	June 1–July 1	June 1–July 10	(2)
Peas, garden	May 10–June 15	May 1–July 1	June 1–July 15	June 1–Aug. 1	(2)	(2)
Peas, black-eye			June 1–June 20		June 1–July 1	June 1–July 1.
Pepper [1]			June 1–July 20	June 1–July 1	June 1–July 1	June 1–July 10.
Potato	May 15–June 1	May 1–June 15	May 1–June 15	May 1–June 15	May 15–June 15	June 15–July 15.
Radish	May 1–July 15	May 1–Aug. 1	June 1–Aug. 15	July 1–Sept. 1	July 15–Sept. 15	Aug. 1–Sept. 15.
Rhubarb [1]	Sept. 1–Oct. 1	Sept. 15–Oct. 15	Sept. 15–Nov. 1	Oct. 1–Nov. 1	Oct. 15–Nov. 15	Oct. 15–Dec. 1.
Rutabaga	May 15–June 15	May 1–June 15	June 1–July 1	June 1–July 1	June 15–July 15	July 10–20.
Salsify	May 15–June 1	May 10–June 10	May 20–June 20	June 1–20	June 1–July 1	June 1–July 1.
Shallot	(2)	(2)	(2)	(2)	(2)	(2)
Sorrel	May 15–June 15	May 1–June 15	June 1–July 1	June 1–July 15	July 1–Aug. 1	July 15–Aug. 15.
Soybean				May 25–June 10	June 1–25	June 1–July 5.
Spinach	May 15–July 1	June 1–July 15	June 1–Aug. 1	July 1–Aug. 15	Aug. 1–Sept. 1	Aug. 20–Sept. 10.
Spinach, New Zealand				May 15–July 1	June 1–July 15	June 1–Aug. 1.
Squash, summer	June 10–20	June 1–20	May 15–July 1	June 1–July 1	June 1–July 15	June 1–July 20.
Squash, winter			May 20–June 10	June 1–15	June 1–July 1	June 1–July 1.
Sweetpotato					May 20–June 10	June 1–15.
Tomato	June 20–30	June 10–20	June 1–20	June 1–20	June 1–20	June 1–July 1.
Turnip	May 15–June 15	June 1–July 1	June 1–July 15	June 1–Aug. 1	July 1–Aug. 1	July 15–Aug. 15.
Watermelon			May 1–June 15	May 15–June 1	June 1–June 15	June 15–July 20.

[1] Plants.
[2] Generally spring-planted

Latest dates, and range of dates, for safe fall planting of vegetables in the open

Crop	Planting dates for localities in which average date of first freeze is—					
	Oct. 30	Nov. 10	Nov. 20	Nov. 30	Dec. 10	Dec. 20
Asparagus [1]	Nov. 15–Jan. 1	Dec. 1–Jan. 1				
Beans, lima	July 1–Aug. 1	July 1–Aug. 15	July 15–Sept. 1	Aug. 1–Sept. 15	Sept. 1–30	Sept. 1–Oct. 1.
Beans, snap	July 1–Aug. 15	July 1–Sept. 1	July 1–Sept. 10	Aug. 15–Sept. 20	Sept. 1–30	Sept. 1–Nov. 1.
Beet	Aug. 1–Sept. 1	Aug. 1–Oct. 1	Sept. 1–Dec. 1	Sept. 1–Dec. 15	Sept. 1–Dec. 31	Sept. 1–Dec. 31.
Broccoli, sprouting	July 1–Aug. 15	Aug. 1–Sept. 1	Aug. 1–Sept. 15	Aug. 1–Oct. 1	Aug. 1–Nov. 1	Sept. 1–Dec. 31.
Brussels sprouts	July 1–Aug. 15	Aug. 1–Sept. 1	Aug. 1–Sept. 15	Aug. 1–Oct. 1	Aug. 1–Nov. 1	Sept. 1–Dec. 31.
Cabbage [1]	Aug. 1–Sept. 1	Sept. 1–15	Sept. 1–Dec. 1	Sept. 1–Dec. 31	Sept. 1–Dec. 31	Sept. 1–Dec. 31.
Cabbage, Chinese	Aug. 1–Sept. 15	Aug. 15–Oct. 1	Sept. 1–Oct. 15	Sept. 1–Nov. 1	Sept. 1–Nov. 15	Sept. 1–Dec. 1.
Carrot	July 1–Aug. 15	Aug. 1–Sept. 1	Sept. 1–Nov. 1	Sept. 15–Dec. 1	Sept. 15–Dec. 1	Sept. 15–Dec. 31.
Cauliflower [1]	July 15–Aug. 15	Aug. 1–Sept. 1	Aug. 1–Sept. 15	Aug. 15–Oct. 10	Sept. 1–Oct. 20	Sept. 15–Nov. 1.
Celery [1] and celeriac	June 15–Aug. 15	July 1–Aug. 15	July 15–Sept. 1	Aug. 1–Dec. 1	Sept. 1–Dec. 31	Oct. 1–Dec. 31.
Chard	June 1–Sept. 10	June 1–Sept. 15	June 1–Oct. 1	June 1–Nov. 1	June 1–Dec. 1	June 1–Dec. 31.
Chervil and chives	(2)	(2)	Nov. 1–Dec. 31	Nov. 1–Dec. 31	Nov. 1–Dec. 31	Nov. 1–Dec. 31.
Chicory, witloof	July 1–Aug. 10	July 10–Aug. 20	July 20–Sept. 1	Aug. 15–Sept. 30	Aug. 15–Oct. 15	Aug. 15–Oct. 15.
Collards [1]	Aug. 1–Sept. 15	Aug. 15–Oct. 1	Aug. 25–Nov. 1	Sept. 1–Dec. 1	Sept. 1–Dec. 31	Sept. 1–Dec. 31.
Cornsalad	Sept. 15–Nov. 1	Oct. 1–Dec. 1	Oct. 1–Dec. 1	Oct. 1–Dec. 31	Oct. 1–Dec. 31	Oct. 1–Dec. 31.
Corn, sweet	June 1–Aug. 1	June 1–Aug. 15	June 1–Sept. 1			
Cress, upland	Sept. 15–Nov. 1	Oct. 1–Dec. 1	Oct. 1–Dec. 1	Oct. 1–Dec. 31	Oct. 1–Dec. 31	Oct. 1–Dec. 31.
Cucumber	June 1–Aug. 1	June 1–Aug. 15	June 1–Aug. 15	July 15–Sept. 15	Aug. 15–Oct. 1	Aug. 15–Oct. 1.
Eggplant [1]	June 1–July 1	June 1–July 15	June 1–Aug. 1	July 1–Sept. 1	Aug. 1–Sept. 30	Aug. 1–Sept. 30.
Endive	July 15–Aug. 15	Aug. 1–Sept. 1	Sept. 1–Oct. 1	Sept. 1–Nov. 15	Sept. 1–Dec. 31	Sept. 1–Dec. 31.
Fennel, Florence	July 1–Aug. 1	July 15–Aug. 15	Aug. 15–Sept. 15	Sept. 1–Nov. 15	Sept. 1–Dec. 1	Sept. 1–Dec. 1.
Garlic	(2)	Aug. 1–Oct. 1	Aug. 15–Oct. 1	Sept. 1–Nov. 15	Sept. 15–Nov. 15	Sept. 15–Nov. 15.
Horseradish [1]	(2)	(2)	(2)	(2)	(2)	(2)
Kale	July 15–Sept. 1	Aug. 1–Sept. 15	Aug. 15–Oct. 15	Sept. 1–Dec. 1	Sept. 1–Dec. 31	Sept. 1–Dec. 31.
Kohlrabi	Aug. 1–Sept. 1	Aug. 15–Sept. 15	Sept. 1–Oct. 15	Sept. 1–Dec. 1	Sept. 15–Dec. 31	Sept. 1–Dec. 31.
Leek	(2)	(2)	Sept. 1–Nov. 1	Sept. 1–Nov. 1	Sept. 1–Nov. 1	Sept. 15–Nov. 1
Lettuce, head [1]	Aug. 1–Sept. 15	Aug. 15–Oct. 15	Sept. 1–Nov. 1	Sept. 1–Dec. 1	Sept. 15–Dec. 31	Sept. 15–Dec. 31.
Lettuce, leaf	Aug. 15–Oct. 1	Aug. 25–Oct. 1	Sept. 1–Nov. 1	Sept. 1–Dec. 1	Sept. 15–Dec. 31	Sept. 15–Dec. 31.
Muskmelon	July 1–July 15	July 15–July 30				
Mustard	Aug. 15–Oct. 15	Aug. 15–Nov. 1	Sept. 1–Dec. 1	Sept. 1–Dec. 1	Sept. 1–Dec. 1	Sept. 1–Dec. 1.
Okra	June 1–Aug. 10	June 1–Aug. 20	June 1–Sept. 10	June 1–Sept. 20	Aug. 1–Oct. 1	Aug. 1–Oct. 1.
Onion [1]		Sept. 1–Oct. 15	Oct. 1–Dec. 31	Oct. 1–Dec. 31	Oct. 1–Dec. 31	Oct. 1–Dec. 31.
Onion, seed			Sept. 1–Nov. 1	Sept. 1–Nov. 1	Sept. 1–Nov. 1	Sept. 15–Nov. 1.
Onion, sets		Oct. 1–Dec. 1	Nov. 1–Dec. 31	Nov. 1–Dec. 31	Nov. 1–Dec. 31	Nov. 1–Dec. 31.
Parsley	Aug. 1–Sept. 15	Sept. 1–Nov. 15	Sept. 1–Dec. 31	Sept. 1–Dec. 31	Sept. 1–Dec. 31	Sept. 1–Dec. 31.
Parsnip	(2)	(2)	Aug. 1–Sept. 1	Sept. 1–Nov. 15	Sept. 1–Dec. 1	Sept. 1–Dec. 1.
Peas, garden	Aug. 1–Sept. 15	Sept. 1–Nov. 1	Oct. 1–Dec. 1	Oct. 1–Dec. 31	Oct. 1–Dec. 31	Oct. 1–Dec. 31.
Peas, black-eye	June 1–Aug. 1	June 15–Aug. 15	July 1–Sept. 1	July 1–Sept. 10	July 1–Sept. 20	July 1–Sept. 20.
Pepper [1]	June 1–July 20	June 1–Aug. 1	June 1–Aug. 15	June 15–Sept. 1	Aug. 15–Oct. 1	Aug. 15–Oct. 1.
Potato	July 20–Aug. 10	July 25–Aug. 20	Aug. 10–Sept. 15	Aug. 1–Sept. 15	Aug. 1–Sept. 15	Aug. 1–Sept. 15.
Radish	Aug. 15–Oct. 15	Sept. 1–Nov. 15	Sept. 1–Dec. 1	Sept. 1–Dec. 31	Aug. 1–Sept. 15	Oct. 1–Dec. 31.
Rhubarb [1]	Nov. 1–Dec. 1					
Rutabaga	July 15–Aug. 15	Aug. 1–Sept. 1	Aug. 1–Sept. 15	Sept. 1–Nov. 15	Oct. 1–Nov. 15	Oct. 15–Nov. 15.
Salsify	June 1–July 10	June 15–July 20	July 15–Aug. 15	Aug. 15–Sept. 30	Aug. 15–Oct. 15	Sept. 1–Oct. 31.
Shallot	(2)	Aug. 1–Oct. 1	Aug. 15–Oct. 1	Aug. 15–Oct. 15	Sept. 15–Nov. 1	Sept. 15–Nov. 1.
Sorrel	Aug. 1–Sept. 15	Aug. 15–Oct. 1	Aug. 15–Oct. 15	Sept. 1–Nov. 15	Sept. 1–Dec. 15	Sept. 1–Dec. 31.
Soybean	June 1–July 15	June 1–July 25	June 1–July 30	June 1–July 30	June 1–July 30	June 1–July 30.
Spinach	Sept. 1–Oct. 1	Sept. 15–Nov. 1	Oct. 1–Dec. 1	Oct. 1–Dec. 31	Oct. 1–Dec. 31	Oct. 1–Dec. 31.
Spinach, New Zealand	June 1–Aug. 1	June 1–Aug. 15	June 1–Aug. 15			
Squash, summer	June 1–Aug. 1	June 1–Aug. 15	June 1–Aug. 20	June 1–Sept. 1	June 1–Sept. 15	June 1–Oct. 1.
Squash, winter	June 10–July 10	June 20–July 20	July 1–Aug. 1	July 15–Aug. 15	Aug. 1–Sept. 1	Aug. 1–Sept. 1.
Sweetpotato	June 1–15	June 1–July 1	June 1–July 1	June 1–July 1	June 1–July 1	June 1–July 1.
Tomato	June 1–July 1	June 1–July 15	June 1–Aug. 1	Aug. 1–Sept. 1	Aug. 15–Oct. 1	Sept. 1–Nov. 1.
Turnip	Aug. 1–Sept. 15	Sept. 1–Oct. 15	Sept. 1–Nov. 15	Sept. 1–Nov. 15	Oct. 1–Dec. 1	Oct. 1–Dec. 31.
Watermelon	July 1–July 15	July 15–July 30				

[1] Plants.
[2] Generally spring-planted

Planting Times

Some common vegetables grouped according to the approximate times they can be planted and their relative requirements for cool and warm weather

Cold-hardy plants for early-spring planting		Cold-tender or heat-hardy plants for later-spring or early-summer planting			Hardy plants for late-summer or fall planting except in the North (plant 6 to 8 weeks before first fall freeze)
Very hardy (plant 4 to 6 weeks before frost-free date)	Hardy (plant 2 to 4 weeks before frost-free date)	Not cold-hardy (plant on frost-free date)	Requiring hot weather (plant 1 week or more after frost-free date)	Medium heat-tolerant (good for summer planting)	
Broccoli	Beets	Beans, snap	Beans, lima	Beans, all	Beets
Cabbage	Carrot	Okra	Eggplant	Chard	Collard
Lettuce	Chard	New Zea-	Peppers	Soybean	Kale
Onions	Mustard	land	Sweetpo-	New Zea-	Lettuce
Peas	Parsnip	spinach	tato	land	Mustard
Potato	Radish	Soybean	Cucum-	spinach	Spinach
Spinach		Squash	ber	Squash	Turnip
Turnip		Sweet corn	Melons	Sweet	
		Tomato		corn	

Depth to Plant Seed

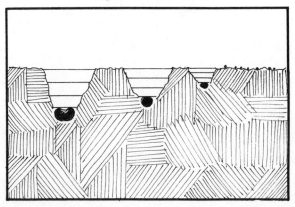

The depth at which vegetable seeds are planted is important for their germination and survival. Follow the directions on the seed package. As a rule of thumb, seed should be planted at a depth 3 times the seed's diameter. Fine seed should be scattered on the surface of the soil and pressed down lightly.

Firming Soil over Seed

If soil over seed is not firmed slightly, it is prone to wash or blow

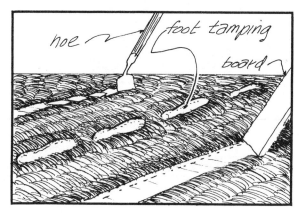

away. You can firm the seed by stepping on it gently or pressing on it with a board or hoe.

✓   ✓   ✓

Vermiculite to Speed Germination

A simple technique can be used to speed the germination of vegetable seeds: sprinkle vermiculite in the row with the seed. The vermiculite will hold moisture and make it available to the seed, thus speeding up the process.

✓   ✓   ✓

Seed Tapes to Space Seed

It is difficult to space seed properly when it is planted. Seed tapes have been developed to simplify spacing and eliminate the need for thinning. Seed is attached to a water soluble organic tape that can be layed in the row. The tape dissolves, leaving the seed properly spaced. The one drawback is the cost of the tape.

✓   ✓   ✓

A Starter Solution for New Transplants

Starter fertilizers are very helpful in getting new transplants off to a good start. A satisfactory solution can be made by stirring 2 tablespoons of such complete fertilizers as 3-12-12, 5-10-10, or 8-16-16 in 1 gallon of water. Mix well and apply 1 cup of this solution on the soil around the roots of each plant at transplanting time. Do not make the solution any stronger or you may burn the plants. Ready-to-use soluble fertilizers are also available. These can be added to the water poured around plants at transplanting time. Follow the directions on the label for recommended concentrations.

✓   ✓   ✓

Vegetables Seeded Directly in the Garden

Vegetables	When to Sow or Plant	Depth In Inches	Seed per 100 feet	Days to Maturity	Planting Distance In Inches		Estimated Yield per 100 feet of Row
					In the Rows	Between Rows*	
Asparagus, crowns	March-April	6–8**	60 crowns	No harvest first year	18	48–60	30 lbs.
Beans, bush snap	May 15 to August 1	½–1	1 lb.	50– 60	3	24	50 lbs.
Beans, green shell	May 15 to July 1	½–1	1½ lbs.	60–100	3	24	
Beans, dry shell	May 15 to June 1	½–1	1 lb.	90–100	3	24	50 lbs.
Beans, bush lima	May 20 to June 10	½–1	1 lb.	65– 85	6	24–30	50 lbs.
Beans, pole snap	May 15 to June 1	½–1	½ lb.	65– 90	24	36	
Beans, pole limas	May 20 to June 1	½–1	¾ lb.	70–100	24	36	
Beets	April 15 to August 1	½	½ oz.	50– 70	3	18	100 lbs.
Cabbage, Chinese	August 1	¼	1 pkt.	80– 90	15	24	80 heads
Carrots	April 1 to July 15	¼	½ oz.	55– 75	3	18	100 lbs.
Chard, Swiss	April 1 to April 10	½	½ oz.	50– 60	8	24	50 lbs.
Collards	April 1 to August 15	¼	1 pkt.	65	15	24	50 lbs.
Corn, Sweet	May 1 to July 1	1–2	4 oz.	64– 90	12	24	100 ears
Cucumber	May 10 to June 1	1–2	½ oz.	50– 70	12	60	12-15 fruit/ plant
Endive	August 1	½	1 pkt.	90–100	15	24	50 lbs.
Kale	April 1 to August 1	½	1 pkt.	50– 70	18	24	75 lbs.
Kohlrabi	April 1 to August 1	½	¼ oz.	50– 70	4	18	100 lbs.
Lettuce, leaf	April 1 to August 1	¼	1 pkt.	40– 50	6	18	50 lbs.
Lettuce, head	August 1	¼	1 pkt.	60	12	24	50 lbs.
Mustard	April 1 to August 15	¼	1 pkt.	40	8	24	50 lbs.
Muskmelon	May 15	1–2	½ oz.	70–100	30	60	50 fruits
Okra	May 1	½	½ oz.	65	15	30	
Onions, seed	April 1	½	1 oz.	110–150	3	18	50-100 lbs.
Onions, sets	April 1	1–2	2 lbs.	100–140	3	18	
Onions, winter	Sept. 1 to October 1	1–2	3 lbs.	—	2	18	
Parsley	April 1 to April 10	⅛–¼	1 pkt.	55– 60	6	18	50 lbs.
Parsnips	April 1	½	½ oz.	130–140	3	24	100 lbs.
Peas	April 1	½	1 lb.	50– 60	1	18	40 lbs. (pods)
Potatoes, early	April 1	3–4	10 lbs.	90–110	9	24	100 lbs.
Potatoes, late	May 15	3–4	9 lbs.	110–140	12	24	
Pumpkin	May 20	1–2	½ oz.	90–110	48	84	75 fruits
Radish	April 1 to August 1	½	1 oz.	25– 35	1	18	25 lbs.
Rhubarb	April	2–3	50 crowns	365	24	36	
Rutabaga	July 1 to July 15	½	¼ oz.	100–120	6	24	150 lbs.
Salsify	April 1 to April 10	½	½ oz.	140–150	2–3	18	75 lbs.
Spinach	April 1 and Sept. 1	½	½ oz.	40– 50	6	18	50 lbs.
Spinach, N. Zealand	April 10 to May 1	½	½ oz.	60– 80	15–18	30	
Squash—							
Bush	May 1 to June 1	1–2	½ oz.	50– 65	36	48	
Summer Vine	May 1 to June 1	1–2	½ oz.	50– 65	60	84	
Winter	June 1 to June 15	1–2	½ oz.	60–110	60	84	100 fruits
Turnips	April 1 to June 1 and Aug. 15	½	¼ oz.	50– 60	3	18	100 lbs.
Watermelon	May 20	1–2	½ oz.	110–130	96	96	

* Adjust row spacing as necessary to accommodate equipment used for cultivation.
** Two inches of soil cover at planting. Gradually fill trench 6-8" deep with soil.

Note: This chart presupposes an average date of last frost of the first week in May. Adjust your own planting dates according to local conditions.

Vegetables Started from Plants

Vegetables	Start	Move Plants to Coldframe	Set Plants in Garden	Days to Maturity from Setting Plants	Planting Distance In Inches		Estimated Yield per 100 feet of Row
					In the Rows	Between Rows*	
Broccoli	Feb. 20	March 15	April 1	80	18	24	50 lbs.
Brussels sprouts	June 1-10	None	July 1	120	24	24	50 lbs.
Cabbage, early	Feb. 20	March 15	April 1	50	15	24	180-240 lbs.
Cabbage, late	May 15-June 1	None	July 15	75–80	18	30	
Cauliflower	June 1-10	None	July 1	100	24	30	45 heads
Celery, early	Feb. 1	None	April 20	90	6	24	200 stalks
Celery, late	April 15	May 15	July 1	110	6	24	
Egg plant	March 20	April 15-20	May 15**	80–90	24	36	150 fruit
Lettuce, head	Feb. 20	March 1	April 1	60	12	24	50 lbs.
Tomatoes	March 20	April 10	May 15	50	24	36	250 lbs.
Peppers	March 20	April 10	May 15	70	18	24	300 peppers
Sweet Potato	April 10	None	May 20	120	12	30–36	

Note: This chart presupposes an average date of last frost of the first week in May. Adjust your own planting dates according to local conditions.

"Harden Off" Greenhouse Plants

When plants are transferred from greenhouses to garden, they experience different light, temperature, and wind conditions; the shock of the change may be too much for them. To prevent damage, place greenhouse plants in a sheltered place outdoors for a week or two before planting in the garden. This "hardening off" period will greatly enhance chances for survival.

✔   ✔   ✔

Cutting Seed Potato Pieces

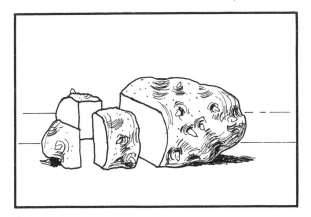

The way seed potato pieces are cut is important. Pieces should be cut so that the vessels that supply the potato's eyes with nutrients are not detached from the eyes. The illustration indicates the way pieces should be cut; the pimpled areas on the surface are the eyes.

✔   ✔   ✔

Growing Potatoes above Ground

Potatoes can be grown above ground if covered by a heavy straw or hay mulch 8 to 10 inches thick. When planting, seed pieces are placed in contact with the soil and are covered with mulch. Using this procedure it is possible to inspect the potatoes during the growing season and harvest new potatoes without disturbing the plants.

✔   ✔   ✔

Protectors Allow Earlier Planting

Paper cups, jars, bottles, etc., can be placed over seedlings to protect them from frost. By using these devices, you can plant and harvest vegetables earlier. Protectors can also be used on crops seeded directly into the garden, such as cucumbers, melons, and squash. If protectors are used on directly seeded vegetables, sow a week to ten days earlier than usual. Protectors are also available commercially under such brand names as "hotcaps" and "hot tents." The next hint provides a means of making your own plant protectors.

✔   ✔   ✔

Bottomless Jugs as "Mini-Greenhouses"

Transplants and some leafy vegetables, such as lettuce, can be grown faster and protected from frosts if grown under transparent covers. An excellent "mini-greenhouse" of this kind can be made by cutting the bottom out of a glass jug. The cap can be removed during the day to allow ventilation and can be replaced at night to provide more warmth.

✔   ✔   ✔

Give Tomato Plants a Cold Treatment

A cold treatment will cause indoor-grown tomato plants to bloom closer to the ground and produce sturdier plants. The cold treatment consists of growing the plants for 3 weeks at night temperatures of about 50-55 degrees F. beginning right after the seed leaves have unfolded.

Deep Planting of Tomatoes

Most plants suffer if they are planted too deeply. Tomato plants actually do better if they are planted deeper than they grew originally. Burying half of the tomato stem will promote root development along the stem. The added roots give the plant a better start.

Tomato Suckers as Transplants

break off sucker plant at foilage level

During the growing season, it is sometimes necessary to replace tomato plants. Consider using "suckers"—branches which grow in the crotch between a regular branch and the main stem—from existing plants to make new transplants. Break off 6-inch-long suckers and plant them up to the foliage. Drench the area with water and shade the sucker with a paper cup. Three out of four suckers should root and produce new plants. This practice is particularly good in areas with longer growing seasons, where it may be desired to plant a second crop of tomatoes. Using suckers eliminates the need to sow new seeds or buy new transplants.

✓   ✓   ✓

Plant Peas Early

Many pea crops fail because they are planted too late. Peas should be planted as early in the spring as possible so that they will mature by June. Peas are cool weather crops and need the cool nights of early spring to germinate and yield. Peas will withstand considerable frost. Plant as early as the middle of March.

Section Four

PRUNING, WEEDING AND OTHER CULTURAL PRACTICES

Pea Vines for Mulch

Peas mature early in the season. When your pea vines are through bearing, they should be removed. Pull them up and use them as summer mulch around tomatoes, green peppers, or cucumbers. Mulch will cut down watering and weeding needs.

✓   ✓   ✓

Using Plastic Film for Weed Control

When rolled into place over soil and properly anchored against the wind, black plastic film, used as a mulch, conserves soil moisture and prevents the growth of weeds. Plastic is particularly useful around difficult-to-weed vine crops such as cucumbers and melons. Three- or 4-foot widths with a thickness of .0015 should be used. To use the plastic film, first prepare the soil for planting in the usual way. Lay 3-foot-wide strips of the film over the row area, making two parallel trenches 3 inches deep, on each side of the row, 30 inches apart (42 inches for the 4-foot width). Place the edges of the plastic film in the trenches and cover it with 3 inches of soil. Make trenches at the ends of each row and cover the film ends with soil. At planting time, cut holes in the plastic just large enough to insert the plants and leave the film intact.

✔   ✔   ✔

Water-Filled Plastic Bags as Mulch

Plastic bags filled with water make an excellent mulch when laid next to plants. The bags conserve soil moisture and reduce soil temperature. String bean yields in Idaho were improved 20% when water-filled bags were used as a mulch. Freezer bags work nicely for this purpose.

✔   ✔   ✔

Blanching Cauliflower

To produce cauliflower heads that are perfectly white, it is necessary to blanch (bleach) them by keeping light away from the head. To accomplish this, bring the outer leaves up over the head and tie them with twine. This should be done shortly after the buttonlike swelling of the head appears. Blanching improves the appearance, flavor, and tenderness of the vegetable.

✔   ✔   ✔

Blanching Celery

Some people prefer celery whose stems are white rather than green. To accomplish this, the celery must be blanched. When the celery is fully grown, place 12-inch-wide rolls of heavy building paper or 10- to 12-inch high boards on each side of the row. In warm weather, the plants will blanch in about 10 days.

✓   ✓   ✓

Blanching Endive

If endive is not blanched, it has a pungent flavor and assumes an un-appealing, dark color. Blanch by placing two 12-inch boards on edge along either side of the fully grown endive row so that their upper edges meet in tent-fashion to exclude light. Anchor with earth and rocks. In 2 to 3 weeks, the endive should be blanched and ready for the salad bowl.

✓   ✓   ✓

Producing Witloof Chicory (Belgian Endive)

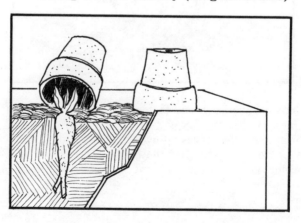

Belgian endive is a gourmet additive for salads. It is produced by "forcing" the roots of Witloof Chicory to sprout tops. In the fall, trim the roots to a length of 8 to 9 inches and place them upright in a box of sand. Place the box in near darkness at a temperature of 60 degrees F. In 2 to 4 weeks, heads of endive are ready for inclusion in a salad.

✓   ✓   ✓

Produce "Tomato-Potato" Plants

"Tomato-Potato" plants can be produced by grafting tomatoes onto potato tubers. Start tomato seeds in flats, as you normally would. When it is time to transplant, set the young tomato seedling in a seed potato with a one-inch-diameter hole cut out and filled with soil. This tomato-potato "graft" will take hold and produce a double crop with tomatoes on top and potatoes on the bottom. Plant the potato at the normal depth in the garden. The result will enthrall children.

✓   ✓   ✓

Sweeter Melons

Tart and tasteless melons are sometimes produced by soil with a low magnesium or boron content. To produce sweeter melons, mix 6½ table-spoons of Epsom salts and 3½ tablespoons of borax (household type) in 5 gallons of water. Spray the melon vines with this mixture when they start to run and, again, when the fruits are between 1 and 2 inches in diameter. The Epsom salts supply the plant with magnesium, and the borax with boron.

✓   ✓   ✓

Preventing Lettuce from "Bolting"

Plants that send up flower stalks instead of forming heads are said to "bolt," or "go to seed." Bolting is a common problem with lettuce when the weather is hot and the plants are planted close together. Lettuce needs cool weather and enough room to head properly. Start seeds early in the spring, or grow as a fall crop. Space or thin plants to at least 12 inches.

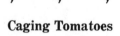

Low Nitrogen for Flowering and Fruiting

The amount and type of fertilizer placed around plants can determine whether most of the growth occurs in the leaves or in the flowers and fruit. Nitrogen encourages leaf growth and should not be added during the flowering and fruiting period of vegetable plants.

Caging Tomatoes

If tomatoes are allowed to develop on the ground, they often rot. Therefore, it is necessary to support most tomato plants off the ground, using stakes or other devices. You might want to try caging rather than staking tomato plants. The cage can be made from a section of wire fencing varying from 30 inches tall and 15 inches in diameter to 50 inches tall and 18 inches in diameter. Caging requires less labor than staking and tying tomato plants, and often results in increased yields.

Prune Okra for Pod Production

Pruning is the secret to good pod production of okra. Snip off approximately 1 out of every 3 leaves throughout the growing season. As a result, the fruit will grow better, and the plant will branch down low.

Pruning Pepper Plants

If pepper plants are pruned, the fruit will increase in size and ripen sooner. Cut out the branches close to the center of the plant so as to open

it up and to promote a more spreading plant. Prune as soon as the plants
are 6 inches tall. Continue to remove inner branches until the plant begins
to flower.

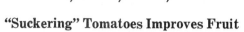

"Suckering" Tomatoes Improves Fruit

"Suckering" of tomatoes improves both fruit set and size. Suckering
consists of removing extra growth that develops at the junction of the leaf
and stem. Leaving suckers reduces the vitality of the plant.

Continuous Watering of Tomatoes

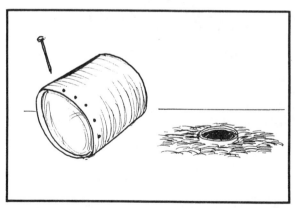

Tomato plants grow faster and produces larger fruits if the soil around
them is amply supplied with water. It is difficult to provide tomatoes with a
constant supply of water by relying on intermittent rain and hand watering.
One solution is to use a coffee or fruit can as a water reservoir. Punch
small soles in the bottom of the can and burrow it in the ground. Water will
drip out of the can slowly, without runoff loss. Plant the tomatoes in a

circle 8 inches away from the can. The result will be similar to the slow-drip irrigation method used in progressive agriculture. Plant food can be mixed with the water.

✓   ✓   ✓

Don't Hoe Too Deeply

Most vegetables have a fine network of roots near the surface that is easily disturbed by cultivation. Be careful to hoe shallowly, thus avoiding root damage that can stunt and kill plants.

✓   ✓   ✓

Make Your Garden Mud Free

Working in a garden can often be a muddy experience. To make a garden mud free, scatter hay liberally between the rows of plants. The hay, unlike straw, will settle in clumps and will not blow away. After a rain, the hay lies flat, making a mud-free floor.

Section Five

PEST CONTROL

Don't Work among Wet Vegetables

Most fungi and bacteria that cause vegetable diseases are carried by water sitting on the surfaces of plants. The gardener will promote the spread of various diseases if he works with garden plants while they are wet. Handle and cultivate plants only when they are dry.

✓   ✓   ✓

Cleanliness to Control Insects

Many garden insects overwinter in plant debris. Dig up old plants in the garden and add them to the compost pile. The cabbage aphid, for example, may overwinter as an egg on the cabbage plant; the adult asparagus beetle persists in the hollow stem of the asparagus plant. By cleaning up and disposing of old plants in the garden, considerable insect control can be accomplished.

✓   ✓   ✓

Stop Early Insect Infestations

Most insects pass through a number of generations in the garden during the course of the growing season. By wiping out the first generation, which appears in the spring, fewer insects will be present during the summer.

✓   ✓   ✓

Safest Insecticides for Home Gardens

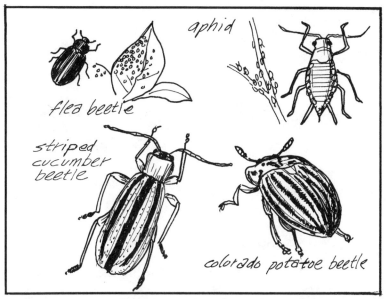

Some common garden pests.

Some insecticides are toxic and are, therefore, dangerous to use around the house or garden. The safest insecticides for home gardens are carbaryl (Sevin) and malathion. Sevin is useful against a wide variety of insects and weakens rapidly. Fifty percent of its activity is gone within 3 days; it is completely ineffective in 2 weeks. Malathion, like Sevin, kills a wide variety of insects. It has a short residual life and disappears completely in about a week. Always apply insecticides strictly according to directions on the label.

✓   ✓   ✓

Purchase One Year's Supply of Pesticides at a Time

Because some pesticides are used in small quantities, it is tempting to buy several year's supply at once and store what you don't need immediately. Resist the temptation. Some pesticides lose their effectiveness rapidly on the shelf. Also, keeping large quantities of pesticides on hand increases the risk of accidental poisoning.

✓   ✓   ✓

SOME BENEFICIAL GARDEN INSECTS

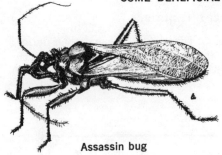

Assassin bug

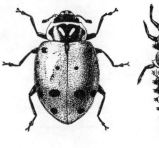

Adult and larva of lady beetle

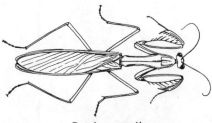

Praying mantis

Tiny wasp depositing egg in an aphid

SOME GARDEN INSECT PESTS

Cabbage looper

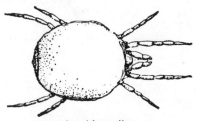

A spider mite

Aphids on underside of leaf

Japanese beetle

Water Sprays for Insects

Water alone can be used to dislodge some insects from plants. Water applied by regular power sprayers eliminates spider mites and aphids.

✓   ✓   ✓

Chemical Control of Aphids

Chemical control of aphids is sometimes necessary. Malathion is most highly recommended. Use as directed on the label.

✓   ✓   ✓

Biological Control of Aphids

Aphids are often a serious garden pest. If you prefer not to use chemicals, consider introducing lady beetles into your garden. Both the adults and larvae feed on aphids. Live lady beetles are available at some garden supply centers.

✓   ✓   ✓

Nasturtiums Repel Aphids

Some plants are useful in that they are attractive and at the same time repel plant pests. Nasturtiums, for example, are repulsive to aphids. Plant nasturtiums between vegetable rows and around fruit trees to reduce the aphid population.

✓   ✓   ✓

Keeping Earwigs out of Head Lettuce

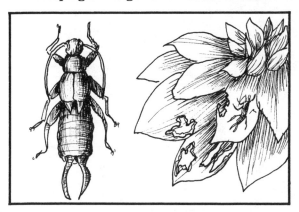

Earwigs can become a problem in head lettuce, disfiguring the leaves and preventing heading. To stop them, place rolled-up newspaper near the plants. Roll the paper snugly and fasten it with a rubber band. The earwigs will crawl into the leaves of paper as if they were lettuce leaves.

Put the paper rolls out each evening and collect and burn them in the morning.

𝄆   𝄆   𝄆

Dry Powders for Insect Control

Dry powders alone can be used to control some insects. Dust from unpaved roads, for instances, gives some control of the striped cucumber beetle. Very fine road dust also works against the cabbage worm. For control, dust the leaves every few days when they are wet with dew.

𝄆   𝄆   𝄆

Controlling Cucumber Beetles Organically

Cucumber beetles can be effectively controlled with insecticides such as Sevin. But if you want to go the organic way, heavy mulches are a time-tested way to reduce populations of this insect. To treat bad infestations organically, mix a handful of wood ashes and a handful of lime in two gallons of water. Apply to both sides of the leaf with a sprayer.

𝄆   𝄆   𝄆

HOW TO CONTROL GARDEN PESTS

Vegetable	Insect or Disease[1]	Description	Damage	Treatment or Control[2]
Beans (dry, lima, shell, or snap)	Fleabeetles	See general pests	Small, round shot-holes in leaves.	General Purpose Mixtures or Sevin.
	Leafhoppers	Up to 1/5" long, light green, wedgeshaped.	Leaves crinkle, turn yellow, then brown.	General Purpose Mixtures or Carbaryl (Sevin) or malathion
	Mexican bean beetle	Adults oval, ¼", copper colored with 16 black spots; Larvae yellow, spiny, up to 1/3" long.	Eat part way through leaves and later make holes.	Carbaryl (Sevin) or malathion. Two or more applications at 7 to 10 day intervals when present.
	Seed corn maggot	Yellowish white, legless, fly maggots, up to ¼", pointed at one end.	Destroy seed. Kill or stunt plants by feeding on seeds, roots and lower stem. Plants wilt.	Buy treated seed. Chlordane or Diazinon to soil at planting or as plants of early plantings emerge particularly in cool, wet seasons.
	Spider mites	See general pests		Kelthane or General Purpose Mixtures.
	Sclerotinia white mold	Fungus	Water soaked spots on stems, leaves and pods which later are covered with a white mold. Plant is stunted and dies.	Plant on land not used for beans, lettuce, potatoes or tomatoes. Zineb.
Beets	Fleabeetles	See general pests	Small, round shot-holes in leaves.	General Purpose Mixtures or Sevin.

[1] For controlling less common pests which may damage crops or pests of vegetables not listed, contact your County Agricultural agent.
[2] Most pesticides can only be used up to a given number of days before harvest. Read the label and follow directions.

Note: The "general pest" description referred to is not included here.

HOW TO CONTROL GARDEN PESTS — Continued

Vegetable	Insect or Disease [1]	Description	Damage	Treatment or Control [2]
Swiss Chard	Spinach leafminer	See under spinach	Circular mines (tunnels) in leaf caused by a white maggot.	Diazinon (first choice) or General Purpose Mixtures.
Broccoli Brussels Sprouts Cabbage Cauliflower Chinese Cabbage Kohlrabi Radish Rutabaga Turnip	Aphids	Two species: 1. grayish and powdery 2. yellow-green See general pests	Leaves become curled and wrinkled. Look for aphids on under surface of leaves and on stems.	General Purpose Mixtures or Malathion, Diazinon or Thiodan. Complete coverage important! Thorough schedule necessary! (5-7 day interval).
	Cabbage root maggot	Yellowish white, legless fly maggots, up to ¼", pointed at one end. Found feeding on roots.	Kill or stunt plants by feeding on roots and lower stem. Plants wilt. Root crops (radish, turnip, etc.) are very susceptible. Damage period may last till August.	Chlordane or Diazinon [3] in transplant water or drench soil at seeding or transplanting. Repeat in 7 to 10 days. Most common in spring, and early summer.
	Cabbage worm	Up to 1½" long, velvety, green. Full grown caterpillars have a yellow stripe down back.	Notches and holes particularly in young leaves or feed at base of the head.	General Purpose Mixtures. Weekly application of carbaryl (Sevin), malathion or methoxychlor. Begin when plants are small or just coming into head. Repeat every 7 days!
	Cabbage looper	Up to 1½" long, light green with white stripes, loops like an inchworm.	Holes in leaves and burrows into the head. Young (smaller) larvae are easier to control.	Thiodan first choice. Same as the cabbage worm. Usually not common before August. Repeat every 7 days. Complete coverage necessary!
	Cutworms	See general pests Plants snipped off at ground level or just below ground level.	Circular, brownish or black caterpillars usually found at base of plant stem in soil. Damage must be anticipated for effective control.	Chlordane first choice. Treat soil and mix well to 3" level before planting. Direct post-plant treatments at soil surface and away from edible plant parts.
	Fleabeetles	See general pests	Shot-holes in leaf.	General purpose Mixtures or Sevin
	Club Root	Slime mold	Swollen, deformed roots. Plants yellowish and stunted.	Rotate plantings in disease free soil or lime soil to pH 7.2
	Damping off	Fungi		Treat soil with fungicide (Captan or Thiram) before planting.
Carrot	Celeryworm	Caterpillar up to 2" long, green with yellow and black bands.	Eats leaves.	Hand picking.

[1] For controlling less common pests which may damage crops or pests of vegetables not listed, contact your County Agricultural agent.
[2] Most pesticides can only be used up to a given number of days before harvest. Read the label and follow directions.
[3] Do not use Diazinon on Rutabagas.

Vegetable	Insect or Disease [1]	Description	Damage	Treatment or Control [2]
Carrot	Carrot rust fly	Yellowish, legless fly maggots, up to ¼" long, pointed at one end.	Burrows in carrot roots.	Diazinon to the furrow at planting time.
	Leafhoppers	See bean pests	Leaves crinkle and turn yellow.	General Purpose Mixtures or Sevin.
	Leaf blight	Fungus	Brown spots on leaves.	Maneb or zineb every 7 days during wet periods.
	Yellows	Virus	Young leaves yellowed, old leaves twisted and reddened. Roots stunted and useless.	Control leafhoppers, See general pests p. 1
Corn (sweet)	Aphids	See general pests	Feed on tassels and destroy pollen, poorly formed ears can result. Sticky, unsightly husks.	General Purpose Mixtures or Malathion, or Diazinon.
Corn (sweet)	Corn earworm	Up to 2" long, green to brown, striped.	Feeds on tips of ears. Damage not noticable till husk removed. Eggs are tiny and laid on Fresh silk. Keep silking corn (mid July and later) treated.	Apply carbaryl (Sevin) or Gardona to fresh silk at 2 to 4 day intervals from mid-July on, particularly in southern half of New Hampshire.
	European corn borer	Up to 1" long, greenish or grayish, black spots and a dark brown head.	Shot-holes in knee high-corn, feed on tassel then enter stalk and/or ear. White egg masses laid on undersides of lower leaves.	Apply carbaryl (Sevin) or Gardona, 2 or 4 applications to corn in the 6 to 8 leaf stage (10-") at 4 to 6 day intervals, and again when ear is present. At 4-6 day intervals till harvest. General Purpose Mixture containing Sevin O.K.
	Seed corn maggot	Yellowish white, legless fly maggots, up to ¼" long, pointed at one end.	Destroy seed and young seedlings. Also a pest on cucumbers and melons.	Buy treated seed or treat soil pre-plant with Chlordane or Diazinon.
Cucumber / Melons	Aphids	See general pests	Suck plant juice. Cause leaves to curl. Transmit Cucumber Mosaic disease.	Malathnion first choice or General Purpose Mixtures.
Pumpkin	Spider mites	See general pests	Suck plant juices.	Malathion or Kelthane
Squash	Spotted cucumber beetle	¼"long greenish yellow with 12 black spots.	Eat flowers, leaves, and stems. Spread Bacterial Wilt Disease organism.	General Purpose Mixtures or Methoxychlor once a week as needed or carbaryl (Sevin) except during bloom because of hazard to bees.
	Striped cucumber beetle	⅕" long usually yellow with three black stripes.	Same as spotted cucumber beetle. Attack plants in very young seedling stage (1"-3").	Same as spotted cucumber beetle. Sevin first choice. Treat very early when seedlings are emerging. Repeat in 4 days.

[1] For controlling less common pests which may damage crops or pests of vegetables not listed, contact your County Agricultural agent.
[2] Most pesticides can only be used up to a given number of days before harvest. Read the label and follow directions.

Vegetable	Insect or Disease [1]	Description	Damage	Treatment or Control [2]
	Squash bug	Up to ¾" long, brown, sucking insects.	Plants wilt and may die. The young nymphs are easier to control.	General Purpose Mixtures Malathion or carbaryl (Sevin) Repeat in 5-7 days.
	Squash vine borer	Up to 1" long, whitish caterpillar.	Bores in stems and larger roots. Plants wilt and die.	General Purpose Mixtures or methoxychlor [3] particularly to the base of plants about June 30, 3 times at 10 day intervals or when vines begin to run.
	Bacterial wilt	Bacteria	Plants turn yellow, wilt and die. Sap from stem milky or sticky.	Control cucumber beetles. Resistant varieties.
	Fruit rots	Fungi	Primarily in stored squash.	Captan or maneb before storage.
	Leaf spots	Fungi	Dead areas on leaves.	Captan, zineb. [3]
	Scab	Fungus	Light green or water soaked spots on leaves, stems and fruit which turn gray to white.	Resistant varieties.
Eggplant	Aphids	See general pests		Malathion or General Purpose Mixtures.
	Colorado potato beetle	See under potatoes		Thiodan or General Purpose Mixtures.
	Fleabeetles	See general pests		Sevin or General Purpose Mixtures
	Tomato hornworm	See under tomatoes		Sevin or General Purpose Mixtures
	Damping off	Fungi, see		Treat soil with Captan before planting.
	Verticillium wilt	Fungus in soil	Plants stunted, wilt; leaves die and drop off. Stem with dark discoloration when peeled.	Disease free seed. Crop rotation. Do not plant after tomatoes or potatoes.
Lettuce (leaf, head, endive, or escarole)	Aphids	See general pests	Suck juice and curl leaves.	Malathion or General Purpose Mixtures.
	Leafhoppers	See bean pests	Same as above.	Sevin or General Purpose Mixtures.
	Yellows	Virus	Yellow green, stunted plants.	Control leafhoppers.

[1] For controlling less common pests which may damage crops or pests of vegetables not listed, contact your County Agricultural agent.
[2] Most pesticides can only be used up to a given number of days before harvest. Read the label and follow directions.
[3] A dust mixture of methoxychlor and zineb is available in some stores.

Vegetable	Insect or Disease [1]	Description	Damage	Treatment or Control [2]
Onion (bulb, green)	Onion maggot	Yellowish white, legless fly maggots, up to $\frac{1}{3}''$ long, pointed at one end.	Destroy bulbs, plants wilt.	Diazinon in the furrow at planting.
	Thrips	Yellowish to brownish insects up to $\frac{1}{25}''$ long.	White stippling or patches on leaves due to feeding. Leaf tips turn brown first.	Malathion at 5 day intervals, or General Purpose Mixtures.
	Purple blotch	Fungus	White spots on leaves which later turn purplish with a yellow margin.	Maneb weekly from late June on, particularly for sweet Spanish type onions.
Parsley	Aphids	See general pests		Malathion
	Celeryworm	See under carrots.		Hand picking.
Parsnip	Aphids	See general pests		Malathion
	Carrot rust fly	See under carrots.		Diazinon applied to soil before planting.
	Parsnip canker	Fungus in soil	Canker — reddish brown, later black areas over most of the root.	Keep roots covered with soil. Control carrot rust fly.
Peas	Aphids	See general pests		Malathion
	Mosaic	Virus	Distorted plants, stunted, mottling of leaves.	Plant early, control aphids.
	Root rots and Fusarium wilt	Fungi in soil	Yellow, stunted plants, wilt.	Rotate location. Resistant varieties.
	Damping off and Seed rots	Fungi in soil	See page 2	Treat seed with chloranil (Spergon).
Pepper	Aphids	See general pests		Malathion or General Purpose Mixtures.
	Fleabeetles	See general pests		Sevin or General Purpose Mixtures.
	European corn borer	Up to 1″ long, greenish or grayish, black spots and a dark brown head.	Bore in stems and fruit.	Carbaryl (Sevin). Begin when fruit begins to form and repeat every 5 days.
	Mosaic	Virus	Mottled, curled leaves, stunted plants.	Control aphids.
Potato	Aphids	See general pests		Thiodian first choice or Malathion. Repeat every 7 days.

[1] For controlling less common pests which may damage crops or pests of vegetables not listed, contact your County Agricultural agent.
[2] Most pesticides can only be used up to a given number of days before harvest. Read the label and follow directions.

Vegetable	Insect or Disease[1]	Description	Damage	Treatment or Control[2]
Potato	Colorado potato beetle	Adults — ⅜" long, yellowish with black stripes. Larvae — brick red with 2 rows of black spots on each side, humpbacked, black head, up to ⅗" long.	Eat leaves and new shoots.	Carbaryl (Sevin) or malathion, or Thiodan. Repeat application every 7 days till good control is attained.
	Fleabeetles	See general pests		Sevin, or Thiodan or General Purpose Mixtures.
	Leafhoppers	See bean pests.		Same as above.
	White grubs	See general pests		Chlordane preplant application to soil.
	Wireworms	See general pests		Same as above.
	Early blight	Fungus	Usually begins on lower leaves as small, irregular brown spots, target-like markings.	General Purpose Mixtures, or Maneb or zineb every 7 to 10 days after plants are up 8-10 inches.
	Late blight	Fungus	Irregular water soaked areas on leaves which turn gray-brown. Entire plant may be killed, may infest tubers.	General Purpose Mixtures, or Maneb or zineb every 7 to 10 days after plants are up 8-10 inches. Most common during cool, wet weather. Resistant varieties. Disease free seed potatoes.
	Scab	Fungus in soil	Rough cankers or lesions on tubers.	Adjust pH between 5-5.3. Crop rotation. Resistant varieties.
	Seed piece decay	Fungi or bacteria	Seed pieces rot	Disease free seed potatoes. Treat seed pieces with captan or Polyram before planting.
	Verticillium wilt	Fungus in soil	Plants turn yellow, wilt and die early in season.	Disease free seed potatoes. Crop rotation. Resistant varieties.
Spinach	Aphids	See general pests		Malathion or General Purpose Mixtures[3]
	Fleabeetles	See general pests		Sevin or General Purpose Mixtures[3]
	Spinach leafminer	Whitish, legless fly maggots up to ⅓" long.	Feed between upper and lower leaf surfaces causing brown blotches.	Diazinon first choice or Malathion at 7 day intervals starting when mines first appear or when leaves are 4" high.

[1] For controlling less common pests which may damage crops or pests of vegetables not listed, contact your County Agricultural agent.
[2] Most pesticides can only be used up to a given number of days before harvest. Read the label and follow directions.
[3] Only one application of Thiodan allowed per season.

HOW TO CONTROL GARDEN PESTS — Continued

Vegetable	Insect or Disease[1]	Description	Damage	Treatment or Control[2]
Tomato	Aphids	See general pests	Suck plant juice and deform the leaves.	Malathion or General Purpose Mixtures.
	Fleabeetles	See general pests	Round shot-holes in the leaves.	Sevin or General Purpose Mixtures.
	Tomato hornworm	Green caterpillar with oblique, white bands on each side and a horn at the tail end. Up to 4" long.	Feed on leaves, can strip plant.	Carbaryl (Sevin) or hand pick, or General Purpose Mixtures.
	Early blight	Fungus	Kills seedlings which damp off or a collar rot may girdle the stem. Also see under potato.	General Purpose Mixtures or Maneb or zineb every 7 to 10 days after plants are up 8 to 10 inches. Resistant varieties.
	Late blight	Fungus	Irregular water soaked areas on leaves which turn gray-brown.	General Purpose Mixtures or Maneb or zineb every 7 to 10 days after plants are up 8-10 inches. Most common during cool, wet weather. Resistant varieties.
	Fusarium and Verticillium wilts	Fungus in soil	Older leaves turn yellow and plant may be stunted or wilt and die. Stem near ground level with dark discoloration when peeled.	Do not plant in infested soil. Resistant varieties.

[1] For controlling less common pests which may damage crops or pests of vegetables not listed, contact your County Agricultural agent.
[2] Most pesticides can only be used up to a given number of days before harvest. Read the label and follow directions.

Salt for Cabbage Worm Control

Insecticides should be avoided on leafy green vegetables. A harmless way to control cabbage worms without insecticides is to use salt. When cabbage worms appear, sprinkle coarse kosher salt down among the leaves. Make 3 applications early in the growing season. The outer leaves may become somewhat dry because of the salt, but the cabbage taste will not be affected.

✓   ✓   ✓

Control Cabbage Maggot with Ashes

Cabbage maggots can get into the leaves of cabbage and destroy the head. One weakness of the cabbage maggot is that it doesn't like alkaline conditions. Create a strongly alkaline area around the cabbage plants by placing a heaping tablespoon of wood ashes around each plant stem. Place some soil on top of the ashes to keep them from blowing away.

✓   ✓   ✓

Organic Maggot Control

Maggot flies have to search out plants in which the insects find it desirable to lay their eggs. Adult maggots can be confused by planting susceptible plants in irregular rows. In the case of onions, the random technique offers added protection to neighboring plants because the onion smell is repulsive to many garden pests.

✓   ✓   ✓

Cutworm Control

Cutworms destroy certain vegetable plants by girdling the stem at the soil line. They are particularly harmful to newly set cabbage and tomato plants. For control, encircle the plants with cardboard collars. The collars should be placed ½ inch from the stem, and should extend 1 inch into the ground and 2 inches above. Cardboard milk cartons make excellent collars around plants to protect them from cutworms. Remove the ends of the cartons and place them around the plant. Burrow them 2 inches deep into the soil.

✓   ✓   ✓

Nonchemical Leafhopper Control

Leafhoppers attack a variety of garden plants, suck out their juices, and weaken them. Since leafhoppers prefer open areas, they are less of a problem to plants near homes or in protected areas. Enclosing garden plants in cheesecloth tents supported by wooden frames also prevents feeding.

✓   ✓   ✓

Control Flea Beetles Organically

Flea beetles can become a pest on a number of vegetables, particularly eggplant. The best nonchemical control involves clean culture, weed control, and removal of crop remnants where the beetles overwinter. Also, cultivation immediately after harvest makes the soil undesirable for egglaying females and destroys eggs already laid.

✓   ✓   ✓

Give Carrots a "Coffee Break"

If you are tired of brown worm trails ruining your carrots, there is a simple solution. Give them a "coffee break" by mixing the carrot seed with a cup of fresh, unused coffee grounds. Plant the coffee with the seed. The coffee repels the carrot flies that lay the eggs which produce the tunneling worms.

✓   ✓   ✓

Squash Bug Control without Chemicals

If you don't want to use chemicals to control squash bugs, you might consider encircling susceptible plants with other plants that repel squash bugs. Nasturtiums, radishes, and marigolds are the most effective. Hand picking eggs, nymphs, or adults is an effective means of control in small gardens.

✓   ✓   ✓

Destroy Corn Stalks in the Fall

Many gardeners have a tendency to leave corn stalks in the garden over winter and plow them under in the spring. The larvae of the European corn borer lives over the winter in corn stalks and adults may emerge in the spring. Destroy your corn stalks in the fall.

✓   ✓   ✓

Avoiding Corn Borers

Since the moths that lay corn borer eggs do so on the earliest planted corn, it is advisable to plant as late as possible. You must, of course, allow enough time for the crop to fully mature.

The surest way to control corn borers is to plant resistant varieties. Your County Agent can suggest the best varieties for your area.

✓   ✓   ✓

Mineral Oil for Corn Earworms

Corn earworms can be effectively controlled without using toxic chemicals. Fill a medicine dropper with clear mineral oil and apply it to the silks at the tip of each ear. Apply only after the silks have wilted and begun to turn brown.

✓   ✓   ✓

Multiple Plantings for Corn Earworm

Corn earworms attack corn during a limited period of the growing season. To reduce earworm damage, make about 4 plantings of sweet corn at 2 week intervals. The first planting will probably be riddled by earworms, the second is likely to be free. The other 2 plantings may have only slight worm feeding at the tips.

✓   ✓   ✓

Keeping Birds out of the Corn

Blackbirds and crows often get first choice in the corn patch. Plant breeders have developed varieties of corn—with long tight husks and deep set ears—that are less subject to bird attacks. The most resistant varieties are: Pioneer 302 A, Pioneer 312 A, DeKalb 837, New Jersey 7, and Connecticut 870.

✓   ✓   ✓

Keeping Raccoons Out of the Corn

Raccoons can be discouraged from eating corn by placing dog manure near corn plants. Raccoons are repelled by the smell. (For additional hints on raccoon control, see information towards the end of this section.)

✓   ✓   ✓

Plastic Covers for Corn Ears

Plastic bags placed over corn ears prevent birds and raccoons from harvesting the corn before you do. Just before the ears reach maturity, cover each with a plastic freezer bag and tie it at the base of the ear.

✓   ✓   ✓

Tomato Hornworm Control

Tomato hornworms are large green worms that devour tomato leaves. They can be killed by handpicking them and placing them in a small can of kerosene. If the back of a worm is covered with a cluster of small white bodies, don't handpick it. The white bodies are parasites which will kill the worm and live to prey on others.

✓   ✓   ✓

Blossom End Rot of Tomatoes

Black blotches on the flesh of the blossom end of tomatoes indicates that they have blossom end rot, a disease caused by uneven water absorption through the roots. The condition can usually be prevented by avoiding over-fertilization with nitrogen, by watering thoroughly once a week during dry weather, and by mulching the plants.

✓   ✓   ✓

Squash Vines That Suddenly Collapse

Squash vines that suddenly wilt and collapse may be infested with stem borers. To reduce borer losses, cut off affected branches, split open the stems, probe for borers with a fine wire, and kill them. Pinch the cut end of each stem back together and mound soil over the wound to stimulate new root growth. To prevent further damage, keep plants sprayed with Rootone or Sevin, as directed on the package.

✓   ✓   ✓

Controlling Bacterial Wilt of Cucumbers

Sometimes, cucumber plants wilt rapidly and die. In most cases, this is due to a disease called "bacterial wilt." When a wilt-affected stem is cut off near the ground, milky sap oozes out of the cut surface. Bacterial wilt is spread by an insect and control is directed toward preventing the carrier insect from feeding on healthy plants. For complete control, an insecticide must be applied to seedlings when they first sprout, and at 2 week intervals throughout the growing season. Sevin is the recommended insecticide. Apply as directed on the label.

✓   ✓   ✓

Avoiding Bean Rust on Pole Beans

Bean rust can become a serious problem on pole beans in years when rainfall is heavy. To reduce the possibility of loss from bean rust, choose varieties that are rust-tolerant (White Kentucky Wonder and Dade). Avoid the highly susceptible varieties (Blue Lake, McCaslan, and Kentucky Wonder).

✓   ✓   ✓

Nematode Control

Nematodes are small, microscopic worms that feed on plant roots and reduce their growth and yield. The most practical nematode control for the average gardener is effected by building up the organic content of the soil. It is also good to interplant with marigolds, especially the French or African varieties, which repel nematodes. If extensive gardening is to be done in a former woodlot or orchard, it would be advisable to have the soil tested for nematodes by a County Extension Service. Such tests run $10.00 to $15.00.

✓   ✓   ✓

Preventing Sowbugs

Sowbugs may become unwanted visitors in the garden. The best control for sowbugs is prevention: eliminate their hiding places in and around the garden area. Because sowbugs thrive on moisture, remove logs, boards, and other objects in contact with the soil.

✓   ✓   ✓

Abrasives for Snail and Slug Control

The bodies of snails and slugs are soft and highly sensitive to sharp objects such as sand. A border of sharp sand or cinders around plants serves as an effective barrier.

✓   ✓   ✓

Trapping Insects in the Garden

A simple but effective way to reduce garden insect populations is trapping and elimination. Flat board and stones placed directly in contact with the soil will attract insects such as the squash bug, snail, wireworm, and harlequin bug—all of which crawl underneath to hide. Examine the traps early in the morning and destroy any insects you find by burning.

↗   ↗   ↗

Bait for Grasshoppers

Grasshoppers are unwelcome garden visitors. They can be attracted to baits of molasses, citrus fruit, lemon or vanilla extracts, apple flavoring, beer, vinegar, saccharin, salt, calcium chloride, and soap.

↗   ↗   ↗

Bait for Ants

Ants are often difficult to locate and exterminate. One technique is to lure them into small paraffin-lined pillboxes or cans baited with sugar, water, bacon rind, fat, or meat. Drop ant-filled traps into a pail of boiling water.

↗   ↗   ↗

Protecting Seed from Birds

Birds sometimes dig up and devour seed before it has a chance to germinate. Newly planted seed can be protected by placing screen doors or windows over the planted area until the seedlings are established.

↗   ↗   ↗

A Raccoon Fence

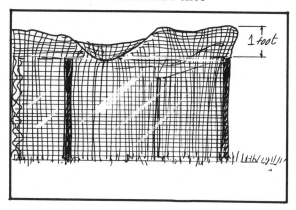

Since raccoons are such good climbers, fences usually do little to deter them. However, there is a special way to construct a "raccoon fence." Make a fence by stapling chicken wire to posts and allow the wire to extend a foot above the posts. The raccoons will find it difficult to climb over the fence because their weight will pull the slack top back over them when they reach the top foot of the fence.

✔   ✔   ✔

Radio Keeps out Raccoons

If your neighbors don't object, a radio playing all night in your corn patch will scare raccoons. Watch the raccoons dance right out of the corn patch.

✔   ✔   ✔

Repelling Groundhogs

Groundhogs can become garden and lawn pests. Spent mushroom soil is an effective repellent for groundhogs. Sprinkle it around your plants as a mulch. You can obtain such soil from mushroom growers in your area.

✔   ✔   ✔

Exterminating Woodchucks

Woodchucks can become garden pests through their digging and destruction of plants. One way to rid yourself of a woodchuck population is to attach a hose to the exhaust of a car and stick it into their burrows. Seal the area where the hose enters the burrow and run the car engine for 20 to 30 minutes.

✔   ✔   ✔

Hot Pepper for Cats and Dogs

Cats and dogs can become a problem in vegetable gardens. A simple and effective way to repel them is to sprinkle hot pepper around the rows you want to protect.

✔   ✔   ✔

Discouraging Rabbits and Deer from the Garden

If you live near a heavy brush or forested area, rabbits and deer can become a pronounced garden nuisance. Dried blood is one of the most effective rabbit and deer repellants. It can be dusted or sprayed on plants without danger of burning them. If spraying, a tablespoon can be added to 2 gallons of water. Plants should be treated about 4 times a year. Dried blood meal is available at garden centers.

Section Six

HARVESTING AND STORING

Pull Tomato Roots to Hasten Fruit Maturity

To get ripe tomatoes as early as possible, try this: When the fruit develops to a good size on the vine, grasp the main plant stem firmly and pull upward until you hear or feel the roots snap. By disturbing the root system, the fruit nearest to maturity will ripen faster. The plant will "reroot" and go on to produce the balance of the crop.

✔   ✔   ✔

Removing Leaves to Ripen Tomatoes

A common problem with tomatoes is that they reach full size but do not ripen. Ripening of tomatoes depends on the fruit temperature. After the fruit has reached its full size, remove 25% of the top leaves and let more sunlight (and heat) reach the fruit. This process will hasten ripening by 3 to 4 days.

✔   ✔   ✔

Harvesting Peas and Lima Beans

The tenderness and flavor of peas and beans vary with when they are harvested. Harvest peas and lima beans when pods are plump but *before* seeds harden or pods yellow. Harvest snap beans when pods are full sized but before seeds cause the pod to bulge. The quality of peas and beans can be preserved if they are cooled as soon as possible after harvest.

✔   ✔   ✔

When to Pick Sweet Corn

Sweet corn is at maximum sweetness just after the kernels have filled out and still spurt "milk" when punctured with the thumbnail. It is not necessary to open the ears to determine the quality of sweet corn. You can tell more by looking at the outside. Look for dark green husks. Yellow or whitish husks indicate that the corn is overmature. Dark brown moist silks indicate well-filled kernels. Old, poor quality corn has dried or matted silks.

✔   ✔   ✔

Deciding When Cantaloupes Are Ripe

Cantaloupes don't develop additional sugar after they are picked. If picked too green, they will only get softer, not sweeter. It is difficult, or impossible, to tell whether a cantaloupe is ripe just by looking at it. However, the "half-slip" method is a reliable way to determine ripeness. Press

Harvest and Save

Vegetable	Harvest When	How to Save
Snap beans	Pods are tender and seeds are still small.	Freeze or can.
Dried beans	Pods turn yellow and dry.	Treat for bean weevil. Store in ventilated glass jar or tin in a cool place.
Lima beans	Seeds show bulges in pod.	Freeze or can.
Beets	1½ to 2 inches in diameter.	Freeze or can.
Carrots	1 to 1½ inches in diameter.	Store in boxes between layers of sphagnum moss, peat moss, or sand at 35° to 45° F.
Rutabaga	3 to 5 inches in diameter.	Store in slatted boxes at 35° to 45° F.
Turnips	2 to 3 inches in diameter.	Store in slatted boxes at 35° to 45° F.
Broccoli	Heads are dark green and before flowers open.	Freeze.
Cabbage	Heads are solid but before they split.	Lift heads and roots and replant in soil in a cool moist cellar. Temperature 35° to 45° F.
Cauliflower	Tie leaves together when head first forms. Harvest when head is bleached white, but before curds begin to separate.	Freeze or pickle.
Sweet corn	Kernels are tender and juicy. Cook immediately after picking.	Freeze or can.
Cucumbers	Slender and dark green and before seeds become large and hard. Pick over-ripe fruits to keep vines bearing.	Pickle.
Lettuce, Endive Other salad greens	Leaves are green and tender.	Keep crisp in refrigerator.
Onions	For scallions, 1 inch in diameter. For storing, stalks turn brown and fall over.	Dry thoroughly, cut off stems, and store in mesh bags or slatted boxes in a cool, dry place above freezing. Temperature 35° to 45° F.
Parsnips	Best to leave in ground until after ground thaws in the spring.	May be dug after first frost in fall and stored in moist sand or sawdust. Temperature 35°–45°.
Peas	Pods are firm with tender green peas. Cook immediately after picking.	Freeze or can.
Swiss Chard	Outer leaves are 12 to 15 inches tall. Break or cut them at plant crown. Plant continues to grow new leaves.	Freeze or can.
Spinach	Plants have 5 or 6 leaves but before seed stems begin to grow. Plants usually go to seed in hot weather.	Freeze or can.
Squash, Summer	Skin is soft, tender.	Freeze or can.
Squash, Winter	Skin is hard, or just before first frost.	Freeze or can.
Pumpkins		Leave stems on. Store on shelves in warm, dry place. Temperature 50° to 60° F.
Peppers	Fruits are solid and dark green.	Pickle or freeze.
Tomatoes	Fruits are ripe red, but before they become soft.	Can or pick green and wrap in paper. Store in box or basket. Temperature 35° to 45° F.
Potatoes	Vines have turned brown and are dry.	Store in boxes, barrels, or bins. Keep dark. Temperature 35° to 45° F. May be stored in outdoor pit.

Note: use recommended directions for freezing or canning. You can get this information from your County Extension Office.

HOW TO USE VEGETABLES FROM YOUR GARDEN

Vegetable	Salads	Cooking	Canning	Freezing	Storing	Other Remarks
Cucumbers	yes	——	yes	——	——	Especially good as pickles.
Tomatoes	yes	yes	yes	yes	——	Green tomatoes picked before frost will ripen indoors during winter.
Zucchini Squash	yes	yes	yes	yes	——	Can be used as substitute for cucumbers in salad.
Peppers	yes	yes	yes	yes	——	Especially good stuffed with meat.
Cabbage	yes	yes	yes	yes	——	Makes good sauerkraut for freezing.
Beans	yes	yes	yes	yes	yes	Dried beans store well for winter use.
Chard	yes	yes	——	yes	——	Very hardy. Lasts into winter months.
Beets	if cooked	yes	yes	yes	yes	Will store through winter in a box of moist sand in cool basement.
Carrots	yes	yes	yes	yes	yes	Will store through winter in a box of moist sand in cool basement.
Spinach	yes	yes	——	yes	——	Grows quickly during cool weather of spring and fall.
Radish	yes	yes	——	——	——	Can be braised to make a cooked vegetable.
Parsley	yes	——	——	yes	——	Used mostly as garnish.
Green Onions	yes	yes	yes	yes	——	Dried onions will keep during winter in a cool dry place.
Leeks	——	yes	——	——	yes	Will store through winter in a box of moist sand in cool basement.
Broccoli	——	yes	yes	yes	——	Plants grow one main head, and side shoots grow smaller heads.
Cauliflower	yes	yes	yes	yes	——	Best grown as a fall crop.
Peas	——	yes	yes	yes	——	Edible podded peas also good to grow.
Brussels Sprouts	——	yes	yes	yes	——	Best grown as a fall crop. Lasts well into winter.

lightly on the stem with your thumb at the point where it joins the fruit. If the attached disc slides off without a great deal of resistance, the melon is ripe. (For gardening purposes, incidentally, cantaloupe should be considered a vegetable.)

Harvesting Brussel Sprouts

Brussel sprouts can be harvested using a procedure that will ensure good flavor and continued productivity of the plant. Start harvesting at the base of the plant where buds mature first. Beginning in September, pick off the lower leaves. This will result in a concentration of the plant's energy in the immature buds. Pick sprouts as soon as they mature; otherwise, they rapidly become tough and flavorless.

Stalk Tipping Signals Onion Harvest

To get a crop with the best possible flavor, harvest onions when the stalks tip over (caused by ripening in the neck region). After the onions are pulled, let them dry outdoors. After the tops are completely dry, cut them off an inch above the bulb and store in a cool, dry place.

Harvesting Asparagus

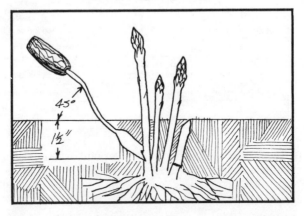

A special knife is available for harvesting asparagus. Hold the knife at a 45-degree angle and cut into the crown of the plant for best results.

The Best Tasting Asparagus

Most of us are accustomed to eating green asparagus heads from the store. If you grow your own asparagus, there is a tastier treat in store for you. The best tasting asparagus heads are the fat, immature, purplish-pink spears about 3 to 4 inches tall. The plants will go on to produce the green heads that we are accustomed to as they mature; but don't let them.

✓   ✓   ✓

Vegetables to Leave in the Garden

Some vegetables can be left in the garden after they have matured to be dug up and used as needed during the winter. The following plants can be stored this way: parsnips, root parsley, salsify, horseradish, and kale. The plants should be mulched to prevent the ground from freezing.

✓   ✓   ✓

Preventing Potatoes from Sprouting

When potatoes are stored, they often sprout and become unusable. Potatoes can be prevented from spouting by interspersing apples with them. Apples produce ethylene gas which halts the sprouting. One apple per bag of potatoes is sufficient. Use about 10 pounds of apples per bushel of potatoes if the spuds are stored loose.

✓   ✓   ✓

How and Where to Store Vegetables

Most vegetable gardens produce more food than the family consumes. A cool, dark storage area in a basement or outbuilding can be used to store the surplus. As a general rule, store vegetables that are mature but not overripe and that are free from insect and disease injury.

Some vegetables should be stored before they reach full maturity. Examples are carrots, beets, turnips, and parsnips. These vegetables tend to become woody at maturity.

Most vegetables will keep best if temperatures are maintained at 32 to 34 degrees F. with humidity as high as possible without creating moisture condensation. Exceptions to this rule include tomatoes, peppers, cucumbers, squash, and melons, which should be stored at higher temperatures (45 degrees F.) to avoid chilling injury. Cabbage, carrots, beets, celery, endive, kohlrabe, parsnips, and salsify store best at low temperatures (32 to 34 degrees F.) with high humidity. Store Irish potatoes at 45 to 50 degrees F. with high humidity.

CHAPTER EIGHT

Home Fruit Gardening

Overview

If you have ample space, fruit trees and fruit-bearing shrubs should be included in your landscape. They add beauty, provide fruit, and make one's garden distinctive. Apples, pears, peaches, plums, nectarines, apricots, sweet and sour cherries, Chinese chestnuts, and walnuts should all be considered as potential shade trees and fruit and nut producers. Small bush fruits, such as currants, gooseberries, quince and blueberries, can function as landscape plants in sunny areas of the yard. Grapes, blackberries, and raspberries can serve as hedges and fences while providing fruit. Strawberry plantings, which are generally replanted every two or three years, can serve as flower beds.

It is important to buy fruit trees and bushes from reputable nurserymen. Be suspicious of extravagant advertising for "super" plants. Extraordinary advertising campaigns are often used to sell very ordinary, often inferior, plants. **In purchasing fruiting plants, it is best to buy 1-year-old stock.** Older stock will generally not bear fruit any more quickly, will be more expensive, and will be harder to establish and train.

Dwarf fruit trees are desirable for small areas. They can be planted 6 to 12 feet apart and, because they grow low to the ground, are easy to prune and spray. **Some fruit trees do not self-pollinate,** and it will be necessary to plant more than one variety.

Fall or **early spring is the best time to plant fruit trees,** with spring the better of the two. *How* you plant the tree is very important. **Most fruit trees are sold bare-rooted. Dig the holes large enough to spread out the roots** without twisting or crowding. Dwarf fruit trees are created by grafting fruit-bearing wood onto special dwarfing root systems. Dwarf and standard size (non-dwarf) trees are planted differently. **For standard fruit trees, dig the hole deep enough to plant the tree 2 inches above where it grew** in the nursery. **Plant dwarf trees 2 to 3 inches** *below* **the graft union,** making sure *not* to cover the union. If the union is covered, the dwarfing effect might be lost.

Before planting, **prune ½ to 2 inches from the tips of all roots.** Soak the tree in water for 2 to 4 hours. Then, set the tree as straight as possible in the planting hole. **Fill the hole** 2/3 full **with a mix of 1/3 peat moss and 2/3 topsoil.** Pour in a bucket of water. After the water has been absorbed, fill the rest of the hole with top-soil mix and **tamp down around**

288

the roots. Remove any tags or wires around the tree and **prune it to a height of between 30 and 36 inches** above the ground. No further pruning will be needed the first year. Subsequent yearly pruning will be geared to training the tree and producing the earliest possible fruit. County Extension bulletins discuss training and pruning goals for each type of fruit. Understand these goals *before* planting.

A complete fertilizer should be applied in April or May of the second year for trees not yet in bearing. Apply ½ pound of 10-10-10 to young apple trees, scattering it around the base of the tree. Pears need 1 pound of 10-10-10. If your soil is sufficiently fertile, fertilization of nonbearing trees might not be necessary. A soil test will tell. **After trees are in bearing, fertilize each year in April or early May** with ¼ pound of 16% nitrate of soda for every year of tree growth. **Do not fertilize fruit trees in the fall.** Fall fertilization may stimulate overproduction of late new growth which can suffer winter injury.

In order to produce edible fruit, **most fruit trees will have to be sprayed.** "All-purpose" formulas for insect and disease control simplify home spraying. A spray formula containing malathion, methoxychlor, captan, and sulfur is particularly effective against most fruit pests. **The timing of spray applications** for fruit pests **is important.** It is generally necessary to make 4 or 5 spray applications during the growing season. The most important times to spray are during the "prebloom" period, when blossom buds begin to show color but before they unfold, and after "petal fall," when the last petals have fallen off the blossoms.

For information on the care of other tree fruits ask your County Agent for special bulletins.

The most popular bush and vine fruits are blackberries, raspberries, blueberries, strawberries, and grapes.

Blackberries should be planted in a well-drained area in the spring or fall. **Blackberry canes grow one season, fruit the next, and then die,** to be replaced by another set of canes. Old canes should be thinned out.

Blueberries generally do not require spraying and can grow in sun or semishade. They need a humus-rich, acid soil. Older bushes must be pruned to avoid small berries. At least two varieties should be planted because cross pollination is required. Buy rooted plants from your nursery. Blueberry roots grow close to the surface, so mulch the plants with an acid mulch, such as sawdust.

Strawberries are generally grown in beds. Plants should be set 18 inches apart in rows 2 feet apart. The plants will produce runners which will increase the bearing population. Allow no more than 6 to 7 plants per square foot pruning out the balance. Most varieties **will bear the second year,** though everbearing varieties, which will bear late the first summer, are available

A few **raspberry bushes** planted in the spring in a corner of the garden **will yield fruit the following year.** They will also produce numerous divisions that can be used to expand the planting. Red, black, and purple raspberry varieties are available.

Grapes can be grown for the table, for juice, or for wine. Ontario, an early white grape, and Buffalo, a midseason blue grape, are useful to home gardeners since they do not require spraying. Grape vines will require training on a trellis or wire. **Grapes need annual pruning.**

Anyone planning home fruit growing would do well to become very familiar with recommended practices before starting. Though fruit gardening is very much a "doable" undertaking, basic mistakes in tree selection and pruning made in the first year of a planting can be very hard to overcome. With a little foreknowledge, fruit growing can be one of the most rewarding aspects of gardening.

Section One

SELECTING AND PLANTING

Care of Newly Arrived Nursery Stock

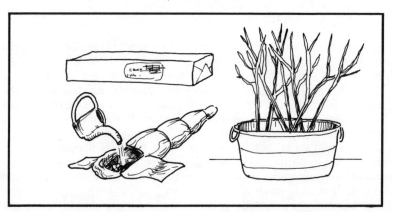

Fruit-bearing plants are usually ordered and shipped through the mail. The plants come in moisture-controlled packing and need immediate attention upon arrival. Moisten the roots immediately, cover them with wet burlap or the like, and store in a cool place. An even better procedure is to unwrap the plants and "heel them in" before planting. "Heeling in" means burrowing the root systems in a temporary hole or trench and later transplanting them to their permanent site. Before planting, it is wise to let the root systems of the plants stand in a bucket of water for up to 24 hours.

Sources of Fruit Trees

Fruit and Nut Trees

*Adams County Nursery & Fruit Farms, RD 1, Aspers, Pa. 17304

*Bountiful Ridge Nurseries, Princess Anne, Md. 21853

Brokaw Nursery, Inc. P.O. Box 4818, Saticoy, Ca. 93003

*C & O Nursery Co., Box 116, Wenatchee, Wash. 98801

Chick-a-dee Nursery, 24130 S.W. Graham's Ferry Rd., Sherwood, Ore. 97140

*Columbia Basin Nursery, P.O. Box 458, Quincy, Wash. 98848

Cumberland Valley Nurseries, Inc., McMinnville, Ten. 37110

Heberle Nursery Co., 478 Browncroft Blvd., Rochester, New York 14610

*Hilltop Orchards & Nurseries, Inc. Hartford, Mich. 49057

*Kelly Bros. Nurseries, 940 Maple St., Dansville, New York 14437

**Henry Leuthardt Nursery, East Moriches, New York 11940

**C. M. Lewis M-VII Nursery, 38875 Mentor Ave., Willoughby, Ohio 44094

McCormick Fruit Tree Co., 1315 Fruitvale Blvd., Yakima, Washington 98902

*J. E. Miller Nurseries, Canandaigua, New York 14424

New York State Fruit Testing Coop. Association, Geneva, New York 14456

*Stark Bro's Nurseries & Orchards Co., Louisiana, Mo. 63353

Small Fruits and Grapevines

Adams County Nursery & Fruit Farms, RD 1, Aspers, Pa. 17304

Ahrens Strawberry Nursery, RR 1, Box 721, Huntingburg, Ind. 47542

W. F. Allen Co., 15 Strawberry Lane, Salisbury, Md. 21801

Boordy Vineyard, Box 38, Riderwood, Md. 21139

Bountiful Ridge Nurseries, Princess Anne, Md. 21853

Bully Hill Vineyards, Inc., Hammondsport, New York 14840

Chalet Du Lac Vineyards and Nursery, Route 1, Box 9F, Altus, Ark. 72821

Dean Foster and Sons, Strawberry Plant Nursery, Hartford, Michigan 49067

Foster Nursery Co., Inc., 69 Orchard, Fredonia, New York 14063

Kelly Brothers Nurseries, Dansville, New York 14437

Lewis Strawberry Nursery, Rocky Point, N.C. 28457

Rayner Nurseries, Salisbury, Md. 21801

Stark Brothers Nurseries and Orchards Co., Louisiana, Mo. 63353

Van Well Nursery, Wenatchee, Wash. 98801

*Also Dwarf   **Dwarf Only

Plant Young Fruit Trees

Some gardeners plant older fruit trees, thinking that they will come into bearing sooner than younger ones. This is a fallacy. Actually, young fruit trees (1 and 2 years old) bear fruit earlier than older ones. Nothing is gained by planting "bearing-age" trees. When purchasing fruit trees, ask for 1-year-old whips (unbranched).

✓   ✓   ✓

Don't Overfertilize Young Fruit Trees

Fruit production by young fruit trees can actually be delayed by over-fertilization. This practice resuts in excessive shoot and leaf growth and pre-vents early bearing by retarding the development of fruit buds. Fertilization is not usually necessary until the spring of the second year. There is some evidence that, with careful mulching, it is not necessary to fertilize fruit trees at all. Fertilization of fruit trees depends very much on the individual situ-ation, as determined by a soil test, and should always be on the conservative side.

✓   ✓   ✓

Fruit Trees Need Full Sunshine

All fruit trees need full sunshine to develop and ripen their fruit properly. Don't make the mistake of planting them in the shade of buildings or other trees. If fruit trees cannot be planted in full sunlight, they should not be planted.

✓   ✓   ✓

Planting Young Grapevines

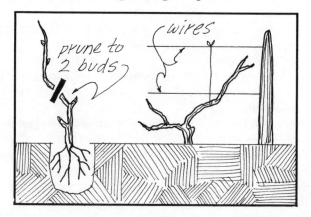

Plant young grapevines in holes larger than their root systems and firm the soil around their roots. Then, cut the vine back leaving only 2 buds. As the vines grow, they should be trained onto a supporting structure. If you use the 2-wire system (see diagram) to train your grapevine, tie a string to the top supporting wire to lead the strongest cane upward.

Building a Support Arbor

A functional and decorative grape arbor can be constructed simply, as illustrated. Wire is stretched between two supports. (It will soften the lines of some buildings and aid in landscaping.) Construct the arbor on the south side of a structure so that the grapes receive ample sunlight.

Don't Plant Blueberries in Alkaline Soil

Blueberries require a soil that is kept constantly acid. If planted in an alkaline environment they will decline and die. Treatment of the soil with acid peat alone prior to planting is insufficient. Plants should be mulched each year with acid peat or composted sawdust.

Strawberries in a Pot

Strawberry plants produce runners that root and produce new plants. These runners can be set to root in a pot if you desire. Simply fill a 4-inch pot with good soil and bury the pot in the soil next to a mother plant. Place the tip of the strawberry runner in the pot and secure the runner to the pot with a clothespin. When the runner is rooted and established in the pot, sever the new plant from the mother plant.

A Strawberry Barrel

If space is limited and you want to grow strawberries, consider a strawberry barrel. Drill planting holes approximately 4 inches apart on the side

of the barrel and construct a central core of wire that contains peat moss for air and drainage, as illustrated. Place the barrel in an open area, where it will receive full sunshine and rainfall. During dry periods it may be necessary to add supplemental water from above.

✔   ✔   ✔

Growing Strawberries in Limited Space

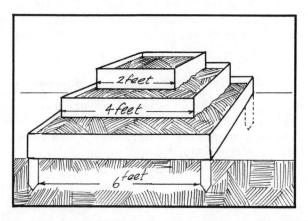

If space is limited, a large number of strawberries can be grown at different levels on square terraces. The pyramidal structure illustrated also makes an attractive addition to the landscape. Space plants 8 inches apart and plant them in good garden soil or in a mixture of ½ peat and ½ soil.

✔   ✔   ✔

Correct Depth to Plant Strawberries

Oftentimes, strawberry plants do not survive or produce well because they are planted improperly. Always plant so that the dividing line between the roots and the top, or crown, is exactly even with the surface of the soil.

Information for Selecting Fruit for Planting

Fruit	Years to Bearing	Approx. No. of Days from Bloom to Harvest[a]	Space Requirement Per Plant	Yield Potential at Maturity[b]	Expected Useful Life with Good Care	Special Considerations
APPLE						
Semi Dwarf						
(Malling 7)	4–5	60–185	625 sq. ft. (25' x 25')	5–10 bu.	15–20 yrs.	Requires 8-15 spray applications, depending upon harvest time and weather conditions. Cross pollination usually necessary for full production.
(Malling 106)	4–5	60–185	750 sq. ft. (30' x 25')	5–12 bu.	15–20 yrs.	
Dwarf						
(Malling 9)	3–4	60–185	150 sq. ft. (15' x 10')	3– 5 bu.	10–15 yrs.	
(Malling 26)	3–4	60–185	216 sq. ft. (18–20' x 12')	3– 5 bu.	10–15 yrs.	
BLACKBERRY (Erect Type)	2	20–40	27 sq. ft. (9' x 3')	1½–2 qts.	10–12 yrs.	Requires 7 spray applications. Sterility can result in poor production. Use healthy stock.
BLUEBERRY	3	55–90	50 sq. ft. (10' x 5')	6– 8 pts.	30–50 yrs.	Requires 6 spray applications. Soil acidification is necessary if soil reaction is above 5.0.
CHERRY **Red Tart** Standard	3–5	60–90	625 sq. ft. (25' x 25')	2– 3 bu.	15–20 yrs.	Requires 5 spray applications.
CHERRY **Red Tart** Genetic Dwarf	2–3	60–90	225 sq. ft. (15' x 15')	½–¾ bu.	10–15 yrs.	Fruit protection against loss to birds.
CHERRY, SWEET Standard	4–7	60–90	900 sq. ft. (30' x 30')	2– 4 bu.	15–20 yrs.	Requires 5 spray applications. Fruit protection against loss to birds. Cross pollination essential.
CURRANT, RED	2	45–70	30 sq. ft. (6' x 5')	5– 8 qts.	12–15 yrs.	
ELDERBERRY	2	50–60	81 sq. ft. (9' x 9')	3– 4 qts.		Subject to some insects, diseases which may or may not be a problem in any given growing season.
GOOSEBERRY	2	45–70	45 sq. ft. (9' x 5')	6–10 qts.	12–15 yrs.	
GRAPE	3	75–120	72 sq. ft. (9' x 8')	20–30 lbs.	25–30 yrs.	Requires 7-9 spray applications. Vines must be supported. Fruit must be protected against loss to birds.
PEACH Standard	2–3	94–150	625 sq. ft. (25' x 25')	3– 5 bu.	10–15 yrs.	Requires 8-10 spray applications. Tree borers and bacterial canker can be serious problems.
PEAR Standard	4–5	110–175	625 sq. ft. (25' x 25')	3– 5 bu.	15–20 yrs.	Requires 9 sprays. Fireblight disease may be a problem.
Dwarf	3–4	110–175	225 sq. ft. (15' x 15')	1– 3 bu.	10–15 yrs.	
PLUM Standard	3–5	105–140	625 sq. ft. (25' x 25')	3– 5 bu.	15–20 yrs.	Requires 8 spray applications.
Dwarf	3–4	105–140	225 sq. ft. (15' x 15')	1– 2 bu.	10–15 yrs.	
RASPBERRY Red	2	40–50	15 sq. ft. (6' x 2½')	1½ qts.	8–10 yrs.	Requires 6 spray applications.
Black	2	40–50	15 sq. ft. (6' x 2½')	1½ qts.	8–10 yrs.	
Purple	2	40–50	20 sq. ft. (8' x 2½')	1½ qts.	8–10 yrs.	
Red, Everbearing	2	40–50	15 sq. ft. (6' x 2½')	3 qts.	8–10 yrs.	
STRAWBERRY June Bearing	1⅓	30	6 sq. ft. (4' x 1½')	1 qt.	2– 3 yrs.	Sprays may or may not be required for insect-disease control.
Everbearing	¼	30	135 sq. in. (no runners)	½ qt.	2– 3 yrs.	

[a] Depends upon variety and growing conditions. Varieties are classified as very early, early, midseason, late and very late. Fruit plant growth and development is accelerated by warm, moist conditions. Development is delayed by cool dry conditions. As seasons vary considerably, dates from bloom to harvest can vary for each variety.

[b] Yield can vary considerably from season to season and depends heavily upon prevailing weather conditions and grower attention to cultural detail.

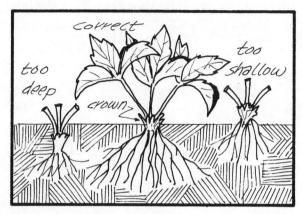

Plants will not do well if planted too deep or too shallow. The center illustration shows the correct planting depth.

✔   ✔   ✔

Variety Descriptions

APPLE: Plant at least two different varieties for pollination.
Uses: Fresh out of hand, Salads, Sauce, Pies, Jams and Jellies and Cider.

Variety	Season	Remarks
Lodi	Summer	Fruit similar in quality and flavor to Yellow Transparent, but larger and firmer. Used as culinary apple.
Tydeman's Red	Late summer	Fruit with good red color and flavor. Ripens about 3 weeks before McIntosh. Apples do not store well.
McIntosh	Early fall	A very high quality, medium sized apple. A good general purpose fruit.
Jonathan	Early fall	A good medium bright red apple of multiple use. Trees subject to fire-blight.
Delicious	Late fall	A highly flavored dessert apple. Trees slow coming into production and sometimes shy producers.
Golden Delicious	Late fall	A very high quality apple for dessert and culinary uses. The trees come into production early and are productive.
Stayman	Late fall	A good general purpose late fruit. Fruit has a tendency to crack in some seasons.

Apricot

A delightful stone fruit but, unfortunately, crops are frequently lost when blooms are killed by spring frost. Growers should keep this in mind before selecting this fruit crop for establishment in the home planting. Trees grown in sheltered areas may prove satisfactory.

Note: So many fruit varieties are available that it is impossible to present an all-inclusive listing. Studying as many growers' catalogues as possible gives the best picture of available varieties.

Blackberry

Uses: Fresh, Jams, Jellies, Preserves, Cobblers, Pies.

Variety	Season	Remarks	
		Plant	Fruit
Hedrick	Early July	Erect habit, hardy, productive, vigorous.	Large, firm, good quality.
Bailey	After Hedrick	Erect habit, not as productive as Hedrick.	Large, firm berries.
Darrow	. . . . . .	Erect habit, hardy, productive, vigorous.	Good quality berries.
Smoothstem[a]	Over an extended season	Thornless stems, erect habit, vigorous and very productive.	Medium to large, good quality, lack firmness.

[a] May not always be winter hardy.

Blueberry: Plant at least 2 different varieties for pollination.

Uses: Fresh, Pies, Pancakes, Dessert Toppings.

Variety	Season	Remarks	
		Plant	Fruit
Earliblue	Early	Vigorous, upright.	Large, firm, light blue berries of high quality.
Stanley	Early Midseason	Hardy, vigorous, upright, little pruning required.	Medium sized, firm, well colored.
Bluecrop	Midseason	Productive, vigorous, hardy.	Very large, light blue, firm, well flavored.
Berkeley	Late Midseason	Hardy, vigorous, very productive.	Light blue, firm, mild flavor.
Jersey	Late	Vigorous, hardy, productive.	Medium to large, of good blue color, average dessert quality.
Dixi	Late	Vigorous, productive, hardy.	Large and attractive but berries do not hold up well because of large scar resulting from picking.
Coville	Late	Vigorous, hardy, productive.	Large and attractive but tart berries.

Cherry, Red Tart

Uses: Pies, Jellies, Jams, Desserts

Variety	Season	Remarks
Standard		
Early Richmond	Early	Fruits of fair quality. Trees productive.
Montmorency	Midseason	Best of the red tart cherry varieties. Fruit red, tart and of good quality.
Dwarf (Genetic)		
Meteor	Midseason	Hardy, high quality fruit. Fruit often small.
North Star	Midseason	Quality less than Montmorency. Small fruit.

Cherry, Sweet: Plant at least 2 different varieties for pollination.

Uses: Eating fresh out of hand, in salads and desserts.

Variety	Season	Remarks
Emperor Francis	See Fig. 25, Page 30.	Fruits pinkish yellow and large. Trees vigorous and productive.
Windsor		Fruits dark red with firm flesh. Trees large, vigorous, productive and reasonably hardy and long lived.
Schmidt		Fruits dark red, firm, large and attractive. Trees late in coming into production and not as productive as desired.

Currant, Red

Uses: Eaten fresh from the cluster, Juice, Wines, Pies, Jams, Jellies.

Variety	Season	Remarks
Wilder	See Fig. 25, Page 30.	Berries attractive dark red and firm fleshed but with a tender skin. Berries are of good flavor but very tart. Plants are large, vigorous, productive, hardy and long lived.
Red Lake		Berries of attractive red color with a fairly tough skin. Berries are of good flavor, but are very tart. Plants are vigorous, productive and hardy.

Elderberry

Uses: Pies, Jellies, Jam, Winemaking.

Variety	Season	Remarks
Nova	See Fig. 25, Page 30.	Plants are vigorous, and very productive.
York		Suitable for planting under Ohio conditions.
Adams No. 2		Suitable for planting under Ohio conditions.

Gooseberry

Uses: As for Red Currant.

Variety		Remarks
Poorman	See Fig. 25, Page 30.	Attractive, large, oval fruits of pinkish red color. Fruit quality is high. Plants are vigorous and productive.
Downing		Ripens a week later than Poorman. Berries green in color.
Pixwell		Plants moderately vigorous and productive. Fruits large, dark red when ripe, excellent quality. Moderately resistant to leaf diseases.

Grape, American

Uses: Eaten fresh from the cluster, Juice, Wines, Pies, Jams, Jellies.

Cultivars	Color[1]	Approximate Season	Approx. Days from Bloom to Harvest[2]	Principle Use[3]	Remarks
Himrod (seedless)	W	Very Early	75	T–H	Best of the seedless.
Van Buren	B	Early	80	T–W	Vigorous, hardy, Concord type.
Buffalo	B	Early	80	T–W–J	Excellent quality, distinctive flavor.
Fredonia	B	Early Midseason	95	T–J	Concord type, vigorous, hardy.
Alden	B	Early Midseason	100	T–W–H	Large berries, non-slipskin type.
Bath	B	Midseason	105	T–H	Productive, hardy, Concord type.
Steuben	B	Midseason	105	T–W	Concord type, vigorous.
Delaware	R	Midseason	100	W	Excellent for wine, high sugar, good keeping quality.
Niagara	W	Late Midseason	110	W–T	Excellent for wine, outstanding white grape of Ohio.
Concord	B	Late Season	115	J–W–T	Standard of quality in Ohio.
Cayuga White	W	Late Season	115	T–H	High dessert quality, tight clusters.
Sheridan	B	Late Season	120	T–H	Needs long season, Concord type.
Catawba	R	Late Season	120	W–J	Principal wine grape of Ohio.

[1] Fruit Color: W = white; B = black or blue; R = red.
[2] Based on data from Southern Branch, OARDC, Ripley, Ohio.
[3] T = table or dessert quality; W = wine; J = juice; H = good for home plantings.

Grape, French Hybrid

Use: Primarily wine making.

Cultivars	Color[1]	Approximate Season	Approx. Days from Bloom to Harvest[2]	Principle Use[3]	Remarks
Foch	B	Very Early	...	W	Extremely vigorous, not fully evaluated.
Seibel 5279 Aurora	W	Very Early	80	W	Holds promise as commercial wine grape.
Seyve Villard 5276	W	Early	...	W	Susceptible to black rot and mildew.
Seibel 9549	B	Midseason	...	W	One of the best wine grapes. Excellent quality; not too hardy.
Seibel 7053	B	Early Midseason	100	W	Very productive, good vigor, moderate hardiness.
Baco #1	B	Midseason	110	W	Extremely vigorous, productive, small berries, small clusters.
Seibel 7053	B	Midseason	115	W	Good vigor, potential for wine.
S.V. 12375	W	Late Midseason	110	W–T	Excellent vigor, productive, hardy.

[1] Fruit Color: W = white; B = black or blue; R = red.
[2] Based on data from Southern Branch, OARDC, Ripley, Ohio.
[3] T = table or dessert quality; W = wine; J = juice; H = good for home plantings.

Pear: Plant at least two different varieties for pollination.

Uses: Eaten fresh out of hand, Salads, Mixed fruit deserts, Canning.

Variety	Season	Remarks
Clapp Favorite	Early	Fruits large and attractive, resembling Bartlett in size. Susceptible to fireblight.
Early Seckel	Early	Trees slow in coming into production, but fruit is of very high quality.
Bartlett	Early Midseason	Susceptible to fireblight, but fruit of very high quality. Leading cultivar.
Beurre Bosc	Midseason	Trees productive and somewhat resistant to fireblight.
Magness	Midseason	Trees very vigorous, spreading growth habit, moderately productive, requires cross pollinating cultivar. Moderate fireblight resistance, fruit lightly russeted, medium size, good quality.

Peach

Uses: Eaten fresh out of hand, Pies, Cobbler, Jams, Jellies, Preserves, in mixed fruit desserts, in and over ice cream.

Variety	Season	Remarks
Harbinger	Varieties listed in order of ripening.	Yellow, clingstone, hardy; good early peaches.
Garnet Beauty		Yellow, semi-freestone, hardy; resembles Red Haven but earlier, red overcolor.
Sunhaven		Yellow, freestone, productive; attractive fruit with red skin color.
Redhaven		Yellow, freestone, hardy; becoming standard early peach variety.
Harken		Yellow, freestone, hardy; good quality.
Reliance		Yellow, freestone, very hardy; medium sized fruit.
Glohaven		Yellow, freestone; large, good quality peach.
Harmony		Yellow, freestone, hardy; fruit large, well colored.
Cresthaven		Yellow, freestone, hardy; large fruit with dark red skin color.
Madison		Yellow, freestone, hardy; high quality, attractive peach.
Redskin		Yellow, freestone, late; very good late season peach.
Belle of Georgia		White, freestone, late, very hardy; one of the oldest varieties still being grown.
White Hale		White, freestone, late; good late white peach.
Dwarf Compact Red Haven		Fruit characteristics similar to Red Haven but fruit are borne on small tree.

Nectarine

Variety	Season	Remarks
Cherokee	Early	Yellow flesh, semi-freestone; productive trees with showy flowers.
Lafayette	Midseason	White flesh; productive trees.
Garden State	Late	Trees vigorous, large attractive fruits of good quality.

Plum

Uses: Eaten fresh out of hand, Canning, Freezing, Jams, Jellies, Pies, Cobblers, Mixed fruit desserts.

Variety	Season	Remarks
European		
Bradshaw*	Early	Trees slow growing and late in coming into production. However, trees are hardy, long lived and productive. Fruits are medium to large in size with yellow flesh and freestone habit. Only fair in quality.
Italian Prune*	Midseason	Trees are large, vigorous and productive. Fruit blue and of fair to good dessert quality.
Stanley	Midseason	Trees vigorous and relatively hardy. Fruit an attractive blue plum of medium size. The variety is self-fruitful and a good pollinator of other plum varieties.
Reine Claude (Green Gage)*	Midseason	Trees only moderately vigorous, but productive. Fruit is greenish yellow in color, of medium size and of high quality. The variety is self-unfruitful.
Bluefre*	Late Midseason	Trees productive, fruit large blue and with yellow flesh. Has a tendency toward split pits.

Japanese*

Generally not recommended for planting in Ohio because of their early blooming habit. Growers should keep this in mind before selecting this fruit crop for establishment in the home fruit planting.

* Plant with another variety for pollination.

Raspberry

Uses: Fresh in desserts, Pies, Jams, Jellies, Preserves.

Variety	Season	Plant Characteristic	Fruit Characteristic	Remarks
Red				
Taylor	See Fig. 25, Page 30.	Vigorous, hardy, productive.	Berries large, bright, attractive, firm, and of high quality.	Matures in same season or slightly before Latham.
Latham		Winter hardy, subject to mosaic but productive.	Berries attractive light red in color, round in shape and medium in size. Berries may crumble in some seasons.	Widely planted in Ohio.
Milton		Erect, vigorous with some mosaic resistance.	Berries large, conic in shape and of good quality.	Ripens near the end of the Latham season.
Black				
Bristol		Tall, vigorous, hardy and productive	Berries medium large, glossy, attractive, firm and of good quality.	Most popular in Ohio.
Allen		Plants productive and vigorous.	Berries large, attractive and of good quality.	Slightly earlier than Bristol.
Black Hawk		Plants vigorous, but not overly productive.	Berries of good size and quality.	Relatively new variety.

Raspberry—continued

Variety	Season	Remarks	
Purple			
Sodus	Plants vigorous, upright, very productive and hardy.	Berries firm and of good quality but quite tart.	
Clyde	Plants vigorous and hardy.	Berries large, firm coherent and tart.	Relatively new variety.
Amethyst	Plants vigorous and hardy.	Berries are moderately firm, shiny, good quality.	Relatively new variety.
Everbearing			
Durham	Plants vigorous and erect.	Fruit large and attractive, but only of fair quality.	
September	Matures after Durham.	Berries large, attractive and of good quality.	
Heritage	Late.	Berries medium sized, very firm, coherent and of fine quality.	One of the newer everbearing varieties.

Strawberry

Uses: Preserves, Jelly, Jam, sliced over shortcake, in and over ice cream, in mixed fruit desserts.

Variety	Season	Remarks
June Bearing		
Cyclone	Early	Productive plants, large, good quality berries. Tends to be soft.
Pocahontas	Early Midseason	Productive plants, large tart flavored berries. Firm and good for freezing.
Surecrop*	Midseason	Plants strong, hardy and productive. Berries medium to large, somewhat rounded and bright, shiny red. Good for freezing. Resistant to Verticillium Wilt.
Redchief*	Midseason	Plants moderately productive of good quality berries. Resistant to Verticillium Wilt.
Midway*	Midseason	Plants healthy and vigorous. Berries conic, firm fleshed, medium to large in size. Good for freezing.
Guardian*	Midseason	Productive plants with good disease resistance. Berries very large, firm and of good flavor. Flesh a little light for a good frozen pack. Some berries tend to be rough.
Raritan	Midseason	Relatively new variety. Plants highly productive of very attractive, solid high quality berries.
Robinson	Late	A longtime standard, large fruited variety.
Vesper	Late	Probably the best of the late season varieties in Ohio.
Marlate	Very Late	Productive plants, large fruit of excellent quality. Promising new variety.
Everbearing		
Ozark Beauty		Plants productive, producing fair amount of runners. Berries large, sweet and of good flavor. Berries suitable for freezing.
Superfection		Highly productive plants. Medium sized, tart berries. A longtime favorite.

* Red Stele resistant.

Characteristics of Quality Nursery Stock

Stock	Age	Caliper[a]	Height	Branching	Remarks
Apple	1 year	⅜-½ in.	3-5 ft.	None (whips preferred)	Larger trees are more difficult to train and sometimes are more difficult to establish.
Blackberry	1 year	....	10-12 in.	....	Use state inspected, virus-free stock with vigorous root systems.
Blueberry	2-3 years	....	1-1½ ft.	2 or more branches.	Plants should have extensive root system.
Cherry, Red Tart	1-2 years	½-⅝ in.	3-5 ft.	....	Should be virus free.
Cherry, Sweet	1 year	¾-⅞ in.	4-6 ft.	....	Should be virus free.
Currant, Red	1-2 years	....	10-12 in.	....	Multi-stemmed plants desirable. Otherwise, well rooted cuttings or mound layers can be used. Plants should have extensive root systems.
Elderberry	1-2 years	....	....	....	One year rooted cuttings are satisfactory.
Gooseberry	1-2 years	....	10-12 in.	....	Multi-stemmed plants desirable. Otherwise, well rooted cuttings or mound layers can be used. Plants should have extensive root systems.
Grape	1 year	....	10-12 in.	With one or more canes.	Plants should have extensive root system.
Peach, Standard	1 year	½-⅝ in.	3-4 ft.	Well branched.	Plants should be well rooted.
Pear	1 year	⅜-½ in.	4-5 ft.	None.	Plants should be well rooted.
Plum	1 year	½-⅝ in.	3-5 ft.	....	Plants should be well rooted.
Raspberry	1 year	....	10-12 in.	Single cane.	Plants should be registered virus-free.
Strawberry	1 year	....	....	....	Dormant strawberry plants that are certified virus-free are most desirable. Plant should have an extensive root system.

[a] Refers to trunk diameter.

Don't Grow Peach Trees from Pits

There is a temptation to save the pits from extremely tasty peaches and attempt to grow your own tree. Don't. The seedling that will result will not be like the parent tree. Peach trees are grown by budding or grafting certain varieties to seedling root stocks. So if you want to produce a particular peach, check the variety and purchase that tree from a nursery.

Currants and White Pines Are Not Compatible

White pine blister rust is a fungus disease that attacks both white pines and currants, particularly black currants. The disease cannot exist unless the two different types of plants are within ½ mile of each other. So, if you have a number of white pines in your area, do not plant currants. This will promote a disease that will be destructive to your white pines as well as to your currants.

Fruit throughout the Growing Season

	JUNE	JULY	AUG.	SEP.	OCT.
JUNE BEARING STRAWBERRY	███				
EVERBEARING STRAWBERRY	█			████████	
GOOSEBERRY		██			
SOUR CHERRY		███			
RED RASEBERRY		██			
BLACK RASEBERRY		███			
SWEET CHERRY		██			
CURRANT		███			
APPLE		████████████████████			
BLUEBERRY		█████████████			
PEACH		█████████			
PEAR			██████████		
PLUM			█████		
GRAPE			████		

Fruit-bearing plants mature at different times during the growing season. In order to have fruit throughout the growing season, select varieties of plants that mature at different times. The chart will be helpful in making your selection.

"Layering" to Produce New Plants

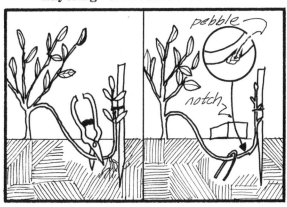

pebble

notch

One method of producing new plants from old ones is "layering." This method works particularly well for grapes and some shrub fruits like gooseberries. It involves cutting a notch in a segment of a branch or vine from a plant and burrowing it in the ground. The notch should be kept open with a pebble or matchstick. The remaining portion of the branch is tied upright to a stake. Roots will develop in the notched area. When they are well developed, sever the new plant from the old. Woody plants take up to 9 months to root.

✓   ✓   ✓

Tree Fruit Seed Needs Cold Treatment

If you plan to grow fruit trees from seed, remember that the seeds need a cold treatment before they will germinate. Plant the seed in a 1 to 1 sand-peat mixture, cover with a screen, and place in a cold frame over winter. The seed will germinate the following spring.

✓   ✓   ✓

Nuts That Need Cross-Pollination

The female flowers of some nut trees (e.g., walnut, hickory, and pecan) are self-fertile and do not require pollen from other trees for pollination and nut production. However, some nut trees require cross-pollination of their flowers from another variety for a satisfactory nut crop. Among the nuts that require cross-pollination are almond, chestnut, and filbert. When planting any of these three, be sure to plant a cross-pollinating variety nearby.

✓   ✓   ✓

Use Budded or Grafted Nut Trees Only

Sometimes seedling nut trees are sold with the indication that they will produce nuts like the parent tree. A seedling is the result of the genetic crossing of two trees, one of which is not identifiable. Therefore, you will not know what kind of nuts a seedling tree will produce until it matures. Plant budded or grafted trees from reputable nurseries for predictable results.

Section Two

PRUNING AND GRAFTING

When to Prune Fruit Trees

In general, fruit trees should be pruned during the late winter months before the buds break. Young trees, not yet bearing fruit, need training to develop a strong, well-balanced structure. Once the trees begin to bear fruit, maintenance pruning is needed to encourage the development of short, bearing laterals and to prevent crowded inner growth.

✓   ✓   ✓

Pruning Fruit Trees

The question of *how* to prune a fruit tree is difficult to answer. Different growers have different preferences and cases can be made for all of them. In all cases, the purpose of pruning is to develop strong lateral branches which will hold the fruiting wood. If you are seriously interested in fruit growing, the best suggestion is to first read several pamphlets on the various approaches and then visit an orchard to see how they are carried out. Your County Extension agent should be able to help you find a fruit farm to visit.

Three basic pruning approaches are currently in use for fruit trees:

In the *open center system,* several strong branches, originating at about the 3-foot mark, are trained to form a bowl-shaped scaffold. There is no leader.

In the *modified central leader system,* 3 to 5 scaffold branches from the main trunk are selected and trained to a wide crotch angle. At the 8 to 10 foot mark, the central leader is *modified* by cutting off the main trunk at a scaffold branch. This scaffold branch becomes the leader and opens up

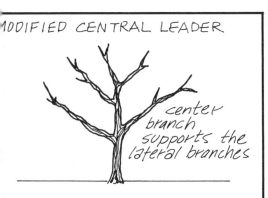

MODIFIED CENTRAL LEADER

center branch supports the lateral branches

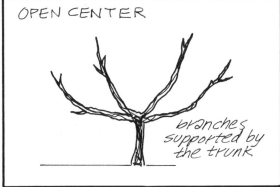

OPEN CENTER

branches supported by the trunk

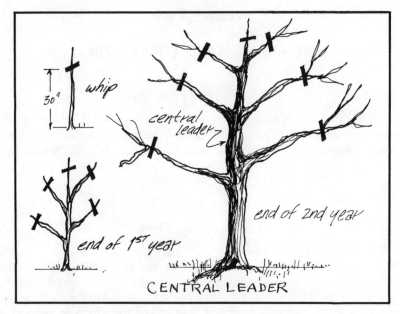

CENTRAL LEADER

the tree as it grows upward *and* outward instead of just upward.

In the *central leader system,* several scaffold branches are trained around the central leader for each year of growth. A gap of 20 to 25 inches is left between the top scaffold branch of one year and the bottom branch of the next. What results after several years is a series of layers of scaffold branches, with each layer a year younger than the one below. The shape of the tree is pyramidal.

The *open center system* is used primarily for peaches, apricots and nectarines. The two *central leader systems* are used primarily for apples and pears.

↗   ↗   ↗

Prune Trees to a Bud

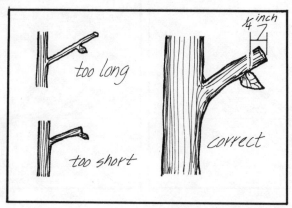

Trees should be pruned so that a bud at the end of the branch will be stimulated to continue growth. If a stub is left beyond the bud, the branch will die back and disfigure the tree. If the pruning cut is made too close to the bud, it will be killed with the same result. Pruning cuts should be made about ¼ inch beyond the bud, as illustrated.

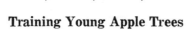

Training Young Apple Trees

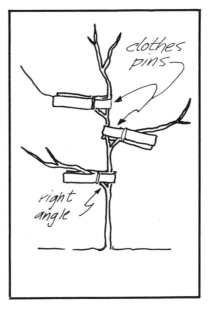

Early training of branches on young apple trees is important. Clothespins can be used to hold small branches at desired positions. Remove the clothespins at the end of the growing season. In pruning, leave branches that make near right angles to the main trunk. Such branches are stronger than those with V-shaped crotches.

Pruning Neglected Apple Trees

Neglected apple trees require considerable pruning to open up the tree so that spray materials and sunlight can penetrate. Don't try to prune a neglected tree all in one year. The bark on newly exposed branches may sunscald. Trees with severe sunscald seldom recover. Schedule reconstructive pruning operations over a 3-year period, gradually exposing inner branches.

Pruning for Growth Direction

The direction in which the last bud is pointing below a pruning cut will

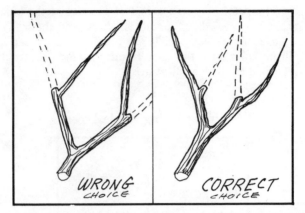

determine the direction of growth of the branch. Prune so that the last bud is pointing outward, not inward. This will result in a better growth pattern.

The plant in the left of the diagram was pruned at inward-growing buds, while the one on the right was pruned correctly, at outward-growing buds. Examine the branch to be pruned before cutting. The difference between outward-growing and inward-growing buds is easy to see.

Kniffin System for Pruning Grapevines

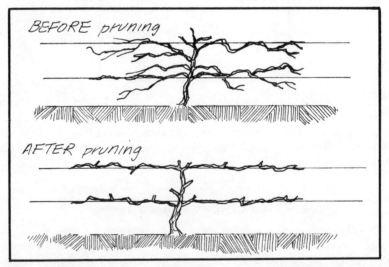

The Kniffin system is the most popular way of pruning American grapevines that fruit on the previous year's wood. First, a single cane is pruned and tied to the top wire of a 2-wire trellis. All canes which sprout between the top wire and the ground are pruned—with the exception of 4. These 4 canes are trained and tied to the wire. Prune grapes in February or March before the sap flows.

Training and Pruning Systems

Fruit	Training System	Pruning
Apple	Central leader for dwarf trees Modified central leader for semi-dwarf trees.	Annual dormant (February-early March). Remove dead, broken branches, crossed limbs and water sprouts. Make cuts to give tree the desired shape and to admit sunlight to the center area.
Blackberry	Hill	Prune three times. (1) Annual dormant, (2) summer topping as shoots reach 30 inches high, and (3) removal of fruiting canes after harvest (see Fig. 11).
Blueberry	Hill	Annual dormant. Moderate pruning to remove dead and broken branches; thin, weak stems; and spindly or bushy twigs.
Cherry (sweet and red tart)	Modified central leader.	Annual dormant. Light pruning to keep tree of desired shape and size.
Currant	Hill	Annual dormant. Moderate pruning to remove dead and broken branches; thin, weak stems; and spindly or bushy twigs.
Elderberry	Hedgerow or hill	Annual dormant. Moderate pruning to remove dead and broken or damaged branches; thin, weak stems; and spindly or bushy twigs.
Gooseberry	Hill	Annual dormant. Moderate pruning to remove dead and broken branches; thin, weak stems; and spindly or bushy twigs.
Grape	4 or 6 cane Kniffen, Umbrella Kniffen.	Annual. Cut to 40-60 buds per plant. Divide the buds among the canes.
Peach	Open center (vase)	Annual dormant. Remove dead or broken limbs. Cut to outward growing limbs. Keep center of tree free of dense growth.
Pear	Central leader or modified central leader.	Prune similarly to apples. Avoid excessive pruning.
Plum	Modified central leader	Annual dormant. Light pruning to keep tree of desired shape and size.
Raspberry (black, purple)	Hill	Prune three times. (1) Annual dormant, (2) summer topping as shoots reach 24 inches high, and (3) removal of fruiting canes after harvest
Raspberry (red) everbearing	Hedgerow or Hill.	Annual dormant for two crops. Mow canes to ground line in spring for fall crop.
Raspberry (red)	Hedgerow or Hill.	Prune twice. First in the spring, removing all dead, weak and damaged canes. Adjust cane stand and reduce cane height. Second pruning to remove fruiting canes after harvest. Do not summer top.
Strawberry, everbearing	Hill	Remove undesired runners as they appear. Remove flowers until July 15 the season of planting.
Strawberry, June Bearing	Matted row.	Remove flowers as they appear the season of planting. matted row. Remove surplus plants.

Note: Recommended training and pruning practices are constantly changing as new research is done. If you wish to keep up with the latest recommendations, stay in touch with your Extension fruit agent.

Pruning Gooseberries and Currants

Prune gooseberries and currants when the fruit is harvested. In pruning, cut all 3-year-old wood to the ground and remove the berries from the stems (an easier way to pick the berries). Berries from 1- and 2-year-old wood are then harvested on the bush. After harvest, prune away all but 3 or 4 of the sturdiest of the current year's growth.

Pruning Red Raspberries

Red raspberries should be pruned twice a year: in the spring and immediately after harvest. The spring pruning, in late March or early April,

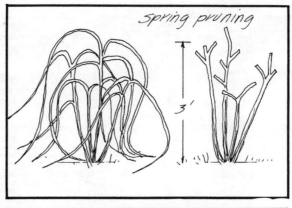

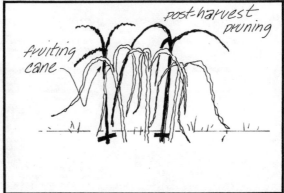

consists of removing all weak canes and cutting back all remaining unsupported canes to a height of 3 feet. Lateral branches should be cut back to 10 inches in length. The second pruning consists of the removal of fruiting canes, at ground level, after harvest.

Prune Raspberries after Fruiting

Raspberry canes should be pruned immediately after they have borne fruit. The fruiting canes should be cut to the ground to make room for new canes which will bear fruit the following year. The next year, the new growth should be pruned to half its length when leaf buds begin to appear on the stalks. This prevents too much top growth and encourages fruiting.

"Summer Top" Black Raspberries and Blackberries

Yields can be increased if you practice "summer topping" of black raspberries and blackberries. In the summer, a succulent top growth develops on these plants. When this growth reaches 24 inches, pinch off the top 3 to

4 inches of the growing tip. This practice will promote greater bushiness and better yields.

✔   ✔   ✔

Grafting and Budding Fruit Trees

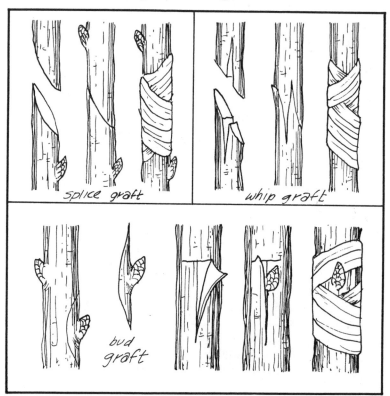

Most commercial fruit trees are grafted or budded on seedling root systems. *Grafting* involves joining stem pieces of different trees together; *budding* involves implanting a bud from one plant onto a branch or stem of another. You can graft and bud your own fruit trees using several different techniques. No matter what the technique, it is always essential that good contact be made between the cambial areas (the thin line between the bark and wood) of the two pieces being joined. Rubber bands or grafting wax can be used to hold the joined pieces together. Four different ways to graft and bud are illustrated .

✔   ✔   ✔

A Good Grafting Wax

Grafting wax is often used to cover grafted and budded areas in order to prevent desiccation. A good grafting wax can be made by mixing together

1 pound of rosin, 3 pounds of linseed oil, and 5 pounds of paraffin. This mixture can be applied with a brush.

Wrap Grafts with Plastic

In order for grafts to become established, it is important that they do not dessicate (dry out). One effective way to keep grafts from drying out is to wrap the grafted area with plastic. Saran Wrap works well for this purpose.

Remove Suckers from below Grafts

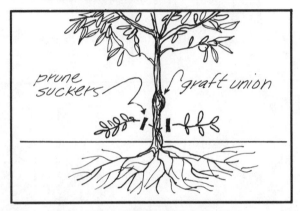

All fruit trees purchased from a nurseryman have been grafted. If suckers develop *below* the graft, they will not form desirable fruit-bearing branches. Therefore, remove all suckers as they develop below graft unions.

Growing Fruit Trees in Limited Space

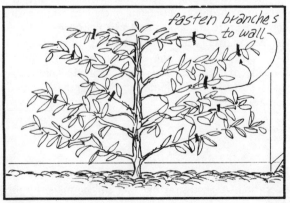

Gardeners with a limited amount of planting area who want to grow fruit trees might try *espalier* training. This method involves cutting the central leader of the tree at a desired height and then fastening and directing selected lateral shoots so that they form a desired shape. Undesired branches are pruned out. Using this method, a home gardener can raise a bearing fruit tree against a stone wall or other structure.

Section Three

CULTURAL PRACTICES

Hastening Fruiting of Young Trees

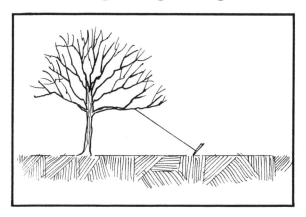

You can hasten fruiting of young trees by spreading branches. This practice encourages the initials that produce fruit to form earlier and more abundantly. Changes induced in the hormonal balance of the tree by the spreading are what encourages fruit formation. To spread branches, drive a stake into the ground, make a slip-knot with a piece of rope, and tie it to the end of an upright branch. Pull the branch down until it is horizontal to the ground and tie it to the stake.

Branches can also be spread by fitting a piece of wood or a rigid piece of wire between the branch and the main stem. The spreader should be long enough to keep the branch from returning to its original position. Spreaders are available commercially.

✸   ✸   ✸

Ringing Bark Hastens Fruiting

Removing rings of bark from apple and pear trees induces early fruiting. When trees are ringed, additional carbohydrates remain in the top of

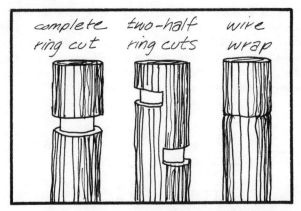

the tree and promote flower-bud formation and development. Ring bark by cutting a complete ring ⅛-inch wide around a fruiting branch, or two half rings ½-inch wide and 4 inches apart. Tight wire wrapped around a branch in the spring will sometimes accomplish the same purpose.

ᚐ   ᚐ   ᚐ

Thin Apples to Improve Quality

Too much fruit on an apple tree one year prevents flower-bud formation the next year and results in bearing in alternate years only. In mid-June, thin your heavy-bearing apple trees to prevent this problem. Leave the best fruit spaced about 4 to 6 inches apart. This will increase the size and quality of the apples. In cases where manual thinning is impractical, Sevin, applied within 3 weeks of petal fall, will accomplish the same purpose.

ᚐ   ᚐ   ᚐ

Remove First-Year Strawberry Blossoms

The first growing season that strawberries are set out should be primarily for the purpose of their becoming established, not for fruit production. To ensure that most of the plants' energy goes into growth rather than fruit, blossoms should be removed the first year. Remove the flower stalks of June-bearing strawberries as soon as they appear. Remove the blossoms of everbearing types as they appear until the middle of July. Then, allow flowers to set fruit for harvest during the remainder of the first season (August-September). Blossoms should not be removed after the first year.

ᚐ   ᚐ   ᚐ

Remove Fruit Blooms the First Year

In the first year, all fruit-bearing plants should be allowed to use their energy for growth rather than the production of fruit. Therefore, it is wise to remove the blooms of newly-planted raspberries, blackberries, and cur-

Indices for Judging Nitrogen Status of Fruit Trees

Index Point	Low Nitrogen	Normal Nitrogen	Excessive Nitrogen
Terminal Shoot Growth	Bearing; Small diameter, less than 4 in. av. length	Av. 4-12 in. long	Av. 12-20 in. long
	Non-bearing; Less than 10 in. av. length	Av. 10-24 in. long	Av. 24-40 in. long
Leaf Size	Small, thin	Medium to average	Large, thick, often puckering at tip
Leaf Color	Uniformly pale, yellowish-green	Normal green	Very dark green
Fall Leaf Drop	Early; leaves show some coloration in veins	Normal time; leaves green to light green	Late; leaves remain dark green until severe frost
Bark Color	Light brown to reddish brown	Gray to dark gray-brown	Greenish gray to gray
Fruit Set	Poor; June drop of young fruit usually heavy	Normal for the cultivar, apples 1 to 3 fruits set per cluster	May have little or no effect; or may reduce set somewhat
Fruit Size	Per tree av. is smaller than normal	Normal for the cultivar	Per tree av. is larger than normal
Fruit Overcolor	Highly colored often earlier than normal	Av. color for the cultivar at picking time	Poor color up to and after normal picking period
Fruit Undercolor	Yellow color develops earlier than normal for the cultivar	Yellow-green to yellow color develops normally for the cultivar	Green to greenish-yellow color at normal picking period for the cultivar
Fruit maturity	Somewhat earlier than normal for the cultivar	Normal picking dates for the cultivar	5 to 10 days later than normal for cultivar

rants during their first year. You will be rewarded the next year with healthier plants and more abundant fruit.

✹   ✹   ✹

Fertilization of Small Fruits

Fertilization of small fruits is often not necessary unless plants appear light green and do not grow well. For strawberries, apply 1½ to 2 lbs. of ammonium sulphate per 100 foot of row about a month after growth begins. For grapes, apply 1/10 lb. of actual nitrogen per vine in early spring. Make a 3 foot diameter circle of fertilizer around the plant. For blueberries, apply ¼ to ½ lb. of ammonium sulphate around each plant in the spring before growth begins. Iron chlorosis may develop in blueberries which requires fertilization with chelated iron as directed on the package. For blackberries, raspberries and other brambles, apply ½ to 1 lb. of actual nitrogen per 100 foot of row before growth starts. When applying fertilizers to small fruit, select a dry day and brush all fertilizer off of the leaves to prevent burning.

✹   ✹   ✹

Fertilizing Fruit Trees

Fruit trees are fertilized somewhat differently than other plants. Since the object in fertilization is to encourage fruit buds instead of lush vegetation, fruit trees are fertilized as little as possible. When fertilization is needed, nitrogen is generally the nutrient which needs to be supplemented. For the home gardener, a good rule of thumb is to apply ¼ lb., or the equivalent, of 10-10-10 each year for all young trees exhibiting low or normal nitrogen symptoms (see chart). For trees over 2″ in diameter, add ¼ lb. per inch of tree diameter per year. Trees in the high normal or excessive ranges should not be fertilized. Spread the fertilizer around the drip line of the tree in early spring.

✹   ✹   ✹

Place Apple Blossoms near Beehives

Bees are the most important pollinators of fruit trees. If you do not have good pollinating plant varieties nearby for your fruit trees, you can cut off branches with blooms from a good pollinator and place them near the entrance of nearby beehives. The bees will walk over the blooms, pick up pollen, and pollinate your trees when they visit them. Fruit tree catalogues and manuals will note those varieties which are poor pollinators.

Support for Weak-Crotched Fruit Trees

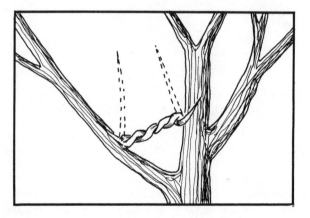

Weak, V-shaped crotches can split away from a tree when branches become overloaded with fruit. A way to strengthen weak crotches is to make the tree support itself. Water sprouts, or "suckers," are entwined around each other as shown in the illustration. These eventually unite and form a bond which will brace the tree for the rest of its life.

Filling of Nut Kernels

The fruits (nuts) of nut-bearing trees are storage organs for food that can be used by the developing embryo when it germinates. Whether or not nuts completely fill with storage materials is affected by a number of factors. If nuts don't fill, consider the following possibilities: (1) not enough foliage per number of nuts; (2) the preceding year's crop may have drained the reserve food needed for this year's crop; (3) the nuts may be injured by diseases or insects; or (4) weather conditions during pollination inhibited good cross-pollination.

Section Four

PEST CONTROL

Clean Area Surrounding Fruit Trees

Do not allow plant debris to collect around fruit trees. Insects and disease organisms are often harbored in fruit and leaves that have fallen to the ground. If an orchard is kept clean, the result will be a reduced incidence of disease and insect attack.

✓   ✓   ✓

Preventing "Southwest Injury" on Fruit Trees

Bark on the trunks of fruit trees is often split open on the southwest side of the tree ("southwest injury"). This damage occurs in the winter when the combination of the sun's rays and freezing temperatures causes stress that cracks the bark. To reduce "southwestern injury," paint trunks and crotch areas of lower limbs on the south and west sides with a good grade of white latex paint. The white paint acts as a reflectant, reducing bark temperatures on the sunny side of the tree. Do not use oil-based paints or latex paints containing oil.

✓   ✓   ✓

Discouraging Birds from Fruit

Often, birds enjoy your fruit crop before you do. To prevent this, just before the fruit becomes ripe, cover the tree, bush, or bed with a lightweight nylon bird screen. Garden centers carry this material, which will keep the birds out but let the light and rain in.

✓   ✓   ✓

Buy Healthy Strawberry Plants

Strawberry plants may already be infected with viruses and fungi when purchased. Such plants are low-yielding and do not survive long. Buy your plants from a reputable nurseryman whose plantings have been inspected and certified disease-free by the government. To avoid loss of plants from red stele root rot, use the following resistant varieties: Sprakle, Midway, Red Chief, Surecrop, and Stelemaster.

✓   ✓   ✓

Organic Control of Codling Moths

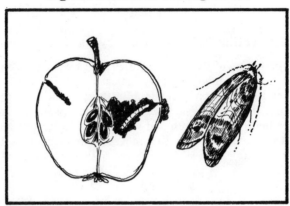

Codling moths lay eggs that develop into larvae. The larvae create "wormy apples." A nonchemical way to partially control codling moths is to place a band of corrugated paper around the main branches and trunk of affected trees. When larvae have spun their cocoons inside the wrinkles in the paper, they can be easily removed and burned. Also, remove loose bark from trunks and limbs where moths like to hibernate.

✓   ✓   ✓

Controlling the Peach Tree Borer

Larvae (worms) of the peach tree borer feed on the inner bark of peach trees at, or just below, the soil line. Several larvae feeding at one time can girdle and kill the tree. If you find globs of gum mixed with bits of chewed wood attached to the trunk of your tree, peach tree borers are almost certainly responsible. A very inexpensive yet effective way to control these borers is to sprinkle moth crystals (paradichlorobenzene) around the base of the stem. The crystals dissolve in air and give off a gas that is lethal to the borers—even those inside the tree. Apply about 1 ounce of the substance per tree and cover it for 1 month with soil until it dissolves.

✓   ✓   ✓

Spray Schedule for Fruit Pest Control

Spray	Apples	Pears	Peaches apricots, nectarines	Plums & prunes	Cherries
Dormant			Bordeaux		
Green tip	Captan or Bordeaux & oil[1]	Bordeaux & oil[1]			
Half-inch green	Maneb/zinc & oil	Oil	Oil	Oil	Oil
Tight cluster	Captan & malathion	Captan & malathion			
Pink	MP	MP	Benomyl & malathion & methoxychlor	Benomyl & malathion & methoxychlor	Benomyl & malathion & methoxychlor
Bloom[3]	Captan or weak Bordeaux[2]	Weak Bordeaux[2]	Benomyl	Benomyl	Benomyl
Petal-fall	MP	MP	MP	MP	MP
First cover	MP	MP	MP	MP	MP
Second cover	MP[4]	MP	MP	MP	MP
Third cover	MP[5]	MP			MP
Fourth cover	MP	MP	MP	MP	Benomyl[5]
Fifth cover	MP	MP			
Sixth cover	MP	MP	MP	MP	
Seventh cover	MP	MP	Benomyl[6]	Benomyl[6]	

NOTE: MP = multipurpose spray mixture containing *captan, malathion,* and *methoxychlor.*

[1]Use the strong Bordeaux mixture plus oil where fire blight has been a problem.

[2]Use the weak Bordeaux mixture during bloom where fire blight has been a problem.

[3]To avoid killing bees, DO NOT APPLY INSECTICIDES DURING BLOOM.

[4]Substitute carbaryl for methoxychlor in this spray if thinning is desired.

[5]Carbaryl can be substituted for or added to the malathion and methoxychlor or to the multipurpose spray mixture in postbloom applications where apple maggot and codling moth are severe problems. See note on carbaryl.

[6]Benomyl is used to control brown rot on stone fruits as the fruit is softening, 2 weeks, 1 week, and 1 day before harvest.

Peach Borer Control

Another way to reduce peach borer populations is to keep the ground beneath peach trees perfectly clean of grass and weeds. This makes poor conditions for borer development in the soil and allows for birds to "get to" the borers on the ground.

Destroying the Raspberry Cane Borer

The adult of the raspberry cane borer is a slender beetle which, in July, makes two rows of egg-laying punctures around the canes, approximately 6 inches below the tips. The tips above the punctures wilt and droop. The distinctive stem girdling makes this pest easy to identify. Control them by cutting off the wilted tips (which contain the eggs) a few inches below the girdle and destroy them immediately.

Traps for Curculio and Pecan Weevils

The larvae of curculios and pecan weevils burrow into and destroy pecan nuts. To eliminate these insects, it is necessary to trap and destroy the

Spray to Runoff

Height (feet)	Gallons per tree	
	Early spring	Summer
4–6	¼–½	1–1½
6–8	½–1	1½–2
8–10	1–2	2–3
10–15	2–3	3–5
15–20	3–5	5–10
20–25	5–10	10–15

Approximate amount of spray required to wet a tree to runoff.

adults. When both species of these insects are disturbed, they will drop to the ground and "play possum." So, jar the trunk and larger branches of the tree; the curculios and pecan weevils will fall to the canvas, where they can be collected and destroyed.

✔   ✔   ✔

Powdery Mildew Control on Blueberries

If a white powdery growth develops on your blueberries, the plants are probably suffering from a powdery mildew disease. The best means of control is to select and plant resistant cultivators, such as Jersey, Roncocas, or Stanley. Karathane fungicide is also helpful if used as directed on the label.

✔   ✔   ✔

Fire Blight Control on Pears

Pears are particularly susceptible to fire blight, a bacterial disease that leaves branches looking scorched, and that leaves dead areas of bark (cankers) that can encircle and kill the tree. The best way to control the disease is to plant resistant strains of Kieffer, Bosc, and Seckel pears. Do not fertilize trees heavily with nitrogen, which favors fire blight. Also, prune out

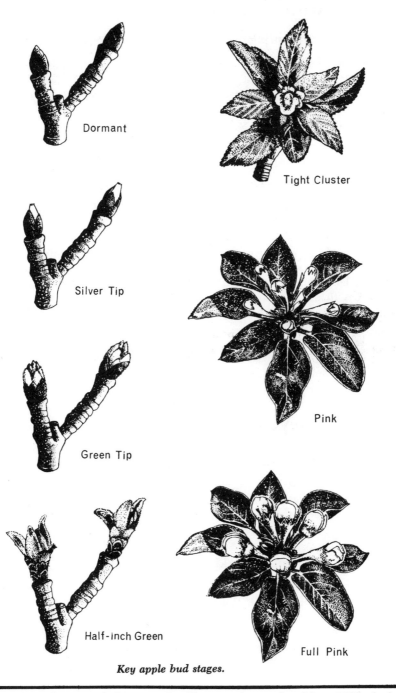

Dormant

Silver Tip

Green Tip

Half-inch Green

Tight Cluster

Pink

Full Pink

Key apple bud stages.

any diseased parts of the tree. Sterilize pruning tools with a 70% alcohol solution to prevent spreading of the disease.

Preventing Mice Damage to Fruit Trees

When mice find their way into fruit orchard, they may girdle young fruit trees. There are practices that will minimize their damage. Orchards that are thoroughly cultivated are relatively free of mice. Mice depend on grass and weeds for protection from predators. Repeated mowing of grass in the fruit orchard during the growing season removes both food and cover for mice, exposing them to such natural enemies as hawks, owls, and weasels.

✓   ✓   ✓

The Latest for Disrespectful Deer

If your property is located in deer country, keeping deer out of your garden can be a problem. This is a particular problem with fruit orchards where a nip in the wrong place can hurt the all important tree shape. Since deer have no trouble jumping over even a 6-foot barrier, fencing is often not the answer. Repellants are available, but are expensive and tend to be washed off by rain. The latest solution, successful in some commercial New York State orchards, is to fill a stocking with human hair and tie the stocking around the tree. The scent of the hair repells the deer. The hair needs to be replaced every 6 to 8 months.

Section Five

HARVESTING AND STORING

Detecting When Pears Are Ripe

How does one determine when a pear is ripe? Here is a handy tip: Check the small freckles (lenticels) on the skin of the fruit. When they have turned from white to brown, the pear is ripe.

✓   ✓   ✓

Harvesting Blackberries and Raspberries

The manner in which blackberries and raspberries are harvested can affect the quality of the fruit. When possible, avoid picking the berries when they are wet. Harvest as often as possible, preferably every second or third day. Pick berries by gently lifting them with the thumb and fingers. Raspberries separate, leaving the receptacle (the center part of the fruit) on the bush. Blackberries separate so that the receptacle and fruit remain intact. Always be careful to prevent bruising of harvested berries. Both blackberries and raspberries should be protected from the sun and cooled to extend their storage life.

✓   ✓   ✓

When to Harvest

Crop	Indication of Maturity	Further Ripening for Quality Development off the Plant
Apple	Fruit increases in size with full color development. Ground color becomes strawy yellow to creamy in color in red varieties. Yellow varieties develop a golden color upon ripening.	Yes, if fully mature prior to harvest.
Blackberry	Berries, upon ripening, become dull black in color and begin to get soft and sweet. The small depression in each druplet should be well filled. The small fruits or druplets are harvested on the central core of receptacle. Harvest every 2 or 3 days.	No
Blueberry	Berries should be dark blue in color and easily removed from the cluster. Taste a few of the harvested berries. Continue harvesting if berries have desired sweetness and flavor; if not, delay harvest for a day or two.	No
Cherry, Red Tart	Cherries increase in size and develop full color as they ripen. They should be left on the tree until juicy and fully flavored. Bird protection is generally necessary.	No
Cherry, Sweet	Cherries increase in size and develop full color as they ripen. They should be left on the tree until fully colored and sweet. Bird protection is generally necessary.	No
Currant	Currants for jelly making should be harvested prior to full ripeness. At this stage of development, the pectin content is high. Fully ripe currants are of full size and color, juicy, and beginning to get slightly soft.	No
Elderberry	Fruit should be plump, of full color and just beginning to soften.	No
Gooseberry	Pick gooseberries when they are still firm.	No
Grape	Grapes change color long before they are fully mature. Therefore, it is possible to pick the clusters before they have reached their peak in flavor, size, and sweetness, if berry color alone is used as a guide to harvest. For best fruit, taste the grapes prior to harvest. If quality is satisfactory, harvest the fruit; otherwise, wait a few days for optimum quality to develop. Protect against loss to birds.	No
Peach	A good guide to correct timing of peach harvest is the ground color. Harvest yellow fleshed varieties when the ground color is changing from green to yellow. Harvest white fleshed varieties when the ground color changes to white. Correlate this color change with a taste sample prior to harvesting many fruit.	Yes
Pear	Pears should be harvested before they are tree ripe. However, they must not be picked too green or they will shrivel in storage and have a poor flavor. Helpful guides as to the right time to harvest pears include observation of the color of the fruit skin, corking of the lenticels, and general finish. Lenticels (small spots on the fruit surface) are white on green or immature pears. When the lenticels become brown in color, the fruit can be picked and will ripen satisfactorily off the tree. Pears ready for harvesting also become more rounded and develop a waxiness on the skin. Pears ready to harvest will separate easily from the tree spur with an upward twist of the fruit.	Yes. For best dessert quality, most varieties of pears should be ripened at 60-70° F. and a relative humidity of 80-85 percent.
Plum	It is difficult to detect by color alone when a plum is ripe. The best guide to plum ripeness is to apply gentle pressure to the fruit with the thumb and determine if the flesh is beginning to soften. If so, the fruit should be ready for consumption.	Yes
Raspberry	Ripe raspberries are of full color and separate easily from the receptacle or center part of the fruit. Harvest frequently, as berries continue to ripen over a period of several days. Pick the berries by gently lifting them with the thumb and fingers.	No
Strawberry	Fully ripe strawberries are uniformly red in color, firm, but beginning to soften slightly. Harvest the fruit with the calyx ("cap") on so that it will keep better. Do this by pinching the stem off about ¼ inch above the "cap."	No

When to Harvest Peaches

In order for peaches to taste "right" and to preserve well, they should be harvested at the proper time. The background color of the peach gives a clue to its ripeness. Harvest yellow-fleshed varieties when the background color is changing from green to yellow. Harvest white-fleshed varieties when the background begins turning white.

✓   ✓   ✓

When to Pick Grapes

The longer grapes stay on the vine, the sweeter they become . . . up to a point. They will not get any sweeter after they are picked. A taste test is the best guide to the ripeness of grapes. Pick them when the flavor suits your taste. White grapes develop a yellowish-green skin color when ripe; blue varieties, a deep blue color; and red varieties, a bright red skin.

✓   ✓   ✓

Eliminating Blanks from Nut Trees

When a nut shell contains no "meat" (is blank), the cause is inadequate cross-pollination. This can be due to bad weather at flowering time or the lack of a "rooster tree" (a tree with fertile pollen). A safe practice with all nut trees is to plant at least 2 varieties together to ensure cross-pollination.

✓   ✓   ✓

Harvesting Black Walnuts

Harvest black walnuts as soon as you can dent the hull of several nuts with your thumb. Hulling quickly after harvest is important if nuts are to be eaten. Black walnuts have a stain in the hull that will penetrate the shell if the hull is left attached for any length of time. The stain discolors the kernels and makes them strong-tasting.

✓   ✓   ✓

Save Hickory Nut Shells

When you hull hickory nuts, save the shells. The next time you cook meat over a charcoal grill fire, add a hickory flavor to the meat by tossing a few of the hulls into the fire.

✓   ✓   ✓

Walnut Hull Juice Will Stain

Be careful when handling green walnut hulls. They contain a chemical-fast stain that is difficult to remove from hands and clothing. So far as is known, nothing will remove it from the hands except time or a good abrasive such as pumice.

✓   ✓   ✓

Store Nuts in Their Shell

If nuts are to be kept for any length of time, they should be kept whole, not as kernels. The nut shell makes an excellent seal against contamination from outside odors and moisture. Store nuts at about 32 degrees F. in a relative humidity of between 70% and 75%. All nuts should be thoroughly dried if they are to store satisfactorily. If the kernels break with a snap when bitten or broken, they are dry enough to store.

✓   ✓   ✓

Remove Walnut Hulls Immediately

Walnut hulls should be removed from around the nut immediately after harvesting. If hulls are left on to turn black and musty, the juice in the hull penetrates the shells and discolors the kernels.

✓   ✓   ✓

Moisten Nuts before Shelling

Before nuts are shelled, they should be moistened in order to toughen the kernels, or the kernels will shatter badly when cracked. Soak nuts in water overnight before shelling to provide the needed moisture.

✓   ✓   ✓

Apples That Store Best

Some apple varieties store better over the winter than others. Varieties that store best are: Northern Spy, Rhode Island Greening, Rome Beauty, and Baldwin. Make sure the apples are free from cuts, bruises, and disease. Damaged apples don't store well regardless of the variety.

✓   ✓   ✓

Storing Apples in a Garbage Can

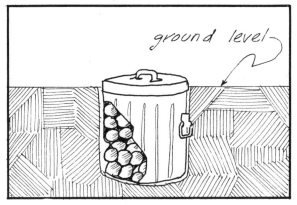

Surplus apples can be stored outdoors throughout the winter. A garbage can sunk into the soil makes an excellent storage place. Dig a hole in a shady spot. Place a clean, galvanized garbage can in the hole just deep enough so that the lip rests slightly above ground level. Place the apples inside and close the lid tightly. Cover the top with straw weighted down with bricks. In most cases this will prevent freezing. In areas of extreme cold, several inches of straw should be placed inside the can, and the can sunk a bit below soil level.

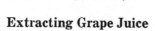

Storing Apples in a Refrigerator

A discarded refrigerator set into the ground makes an excellent place to store apples over winter. In a shady spot, dig a hole big enough to accommodate the refrigerator. Place the refrigerator on its back and insert it into the hole with the door remaining flush with the soil surface. Bushels of apples can be set inside the refrigerator. After the door is closed, cover with a layer of straw and leaves. Remember to knock the latch off the refrigerator door so that a child will not become trapped within.

Extracting Grape Juice

There are a number of commercial presses and devices available for juicing grapes, but there is a simple device one can make, called the "nutcracker press," that works very well. Simply cut out two paddle-shaped boards and attached them with a rope at one end, as illustrated. The grapes can be bagged in cheesecloth and suspended over a container.

CHAPTER NINE

Houseplants

Overview

Houseplants can be divided into three general groups: *tropical plants,* which grow naturally in the hot, steamy tropics; *subtropical plants* from such countries as India, China, Japan, and our own southern states; and *desert plants* (also known as *succulents*) native to the desert. Tropical and subtropical plants require less light and more humidity than desert plants. Many desert plants require a dormancy period.

Before buying a houseplant, inquire about the environmental conditions it requires for growth. If these conditions can't be met, don't buy the plant.

Homes are not natural places for plants, but many will do well if careful attention is given their requirements for light, temperature, humidity, ventilation, and watering.

Houseplants vary in their light requirements. Cacti require direct sunlight while a plant such as the Chinese evergreen *(Aglaonema)* needs hardly any light at all. Flowering plants generally require more light than plants that are grown only for their foliage. Even here, there is variation. Mums will only bloom when the day length is short, which is why their flowers appear in the fall. The day length of some houseplants can be manipulated by use of shades and other devices.

Houseplants vary in their temperature requirements. The ideal temperature for most plants is 70 degrees F. during the day and 55 degrees F. at night. Most homes don't provide the lower night temperature, and for best results special plants should be placed in a cooler room or near a window at night. Heated sunporches with a southwest exposure provide optimum conditions of light and temperature for most houseplants.

The humidity in the house **affects the rate at which water is lost from the leaves** of houseplants. Most houseplants are tropical in origin and are accustomed to high humidities. Therefore, the low humidities in most homes is a problem. This can be remedied by misting the plant leaves with a hand mister, by placing the pots on stones in an open tray containing water, by placing the plants close together, thereby trapping existing moisture, or by adding a humidifier to the heating and cooling system.

If houseplants are not properly ventilated, toxic gases may accumulate

327

and injure them. As little as 1 part methane (cooking gas) in 1,000,000 parts of air is harmful to some flowers. **Place houseplants in well-ventilated areas,** taking care to avoid drafts. It is a good practice during the summer to take houseplants outdoors for an "airing." You can leave them in a shaded area for several days.

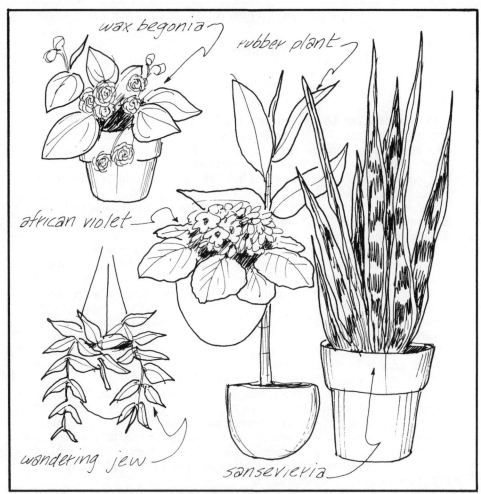

wax begonia

rubber plant

african violet

wandering jew

sansevieria

A selection of houseplants.

More houseplants are killed by improper watering than anything else. **It is important not to overwater or underwater.** The easiest method to determine whether water is needed is to stick your finger into the growth medium to a depth of 1 inch. If it is dry at that level, water is needed. Water so that the entire growth medium becomes damp but is not flooded. The best water to use is rainwater or distilled water. Occasionally, city water and treated well water may be harmful to houseplants.

The root systems of some houseplants outgrow their containers (plants become "potbound"). Such plants should be repotted in larger containers. Remove a portion of the old soil and matted roots when you repot and add new potting soil. If desired, with some potbound plants it is possible to prune both the top and roots and retain the same size container.

Small amounts of liquid plant fertilizer should be applied to the growth medium of houseplants every month to keep them in the best condition. Fertilizer can be incorporated into the water and applied as you water. Apply as directed on the fertilizer container.

Many insects and disease problems of houseplants can be avoided by selecting "clean" plants from a reputable plantsman and using a sterile planting medium in which to grow them. **Spraying houseplants is usually not worth the effort.**

Houseplants need special attention in the winter. The light intensity and humidity in the house is reduced during this period—conditions that work against good plant growth. Plants should be misted more often and placed where there is a greater exposure to sunlight. Supplemental artificial lighting may be required.

Section One

SELECTING HOUSEPLANTS

Learn Scientific Names

The scientific name of a plant consists basically of two Latin words, each designating a category of plants. The first word is capitalized and is called the *genus*. The second word represents a more limited category, is not capitalized, and is called the *species*. Occasionally, a third name is added. Because more than one kind of plant is often referred to by the same common name, when purchasing new plants refer to them by their scientific names.

✓   ✓   ✓

What to Look for in Houseplants

Even when buying houseplants from a reputable dealer, it is necessary to use discrimination in picking the healthiest plant. Avoid plants that have yellowing or ragged leaves. Choose plants with a dense, well-balanced array of leaves that are attached to a straight, sturdy stalk. Choose flowering plants that have many flowering buds at different stages of maturity. Don't choose

plants whose main stem is gangly and whose leaves are sparse or flowering plants that have no developing flower buds.

✓   ✓   ✓

Plants for a North Window

It is recommended that most plants be grown in a sunny south window. If your apartment or house does not have a southern exposure, buy plants that do well in northern exposures. Among these are ferns, ivies, philodendron, African violets, large-leaved begonias, pick-a-back plant, bromeliads, and strawberry-begonia.

✓   ✓   ✓

Plants for Full Light

For rooms that are bathed in sunshine most of the day, the following plants are good candidates: cacti, *Cymbalaria, Dionea, Iresine, Oxalis, Sarracenia,* and *Trifolium.*

✓   ✓   ✓

Plants for Low Light and High Temperature

It is difficult to grow plants in a home where there is little light and high temperatures. Two plants to try in this environment are *Aspidistra elatior* (cast-iron plant) and *Sansevieria* (snake plant). Don't overwater these two plants. They can't take it.

✓   ✓   ✓

Best Indoor Ferns

Ferns make graceful indoor plants. The best adapted ferns for home environments are Boston (*Nephrolepsis*), coarse-leaved polypody (*Polypodium*), brake (*Pteris*), bird's nest (*Asplenium nidus*), maidenhair (*Adiatum*), and rabbit's-foot (*Davallia*). Ferns require warmth, high humidity, and indirect sunlight. A growth medium that drains well is essential. If small raised dots develop on the underside of the fronds, don't be alarmed. These are reproductive structures that produce *spores*.

✓   ✓   ✓

Large False Aralias Need Misting

False aralia (*Dizygotheca elegantissima*) is an attractive houseplant with narrow-toothed leathery leaves. It requires bright, but not direct, sunlight and cool temperatures (60 to 70 degrees F.). Large plants are difficult to grow in the low humidities of home environments and require frequent misting.

✓   ✓   ✓

Misting Helps English Ivy

English ivy (*Hedra helix*) makes an attractive houseplant. Numerous named varieties with unusual leaf shapes and coloration are available. English ivy grows best in full sunlight and high humidity. Weekly misting of the foliage at the sink is highly beneficial. Such baths reduce susceptibility to red spider.

✓   ✓   ✓

Varieties of Dracaena

Draceana is a foliage plant that comes in a variety of shapes and colorations. They are slow growers that tolerate northern exposures and low humidity. Well known species include: *Draceana marginata,* with long, narrow foliage; *Draceana fragrans massangeana* (often called corn plant), with broad cornlike leaves; *Draceana derenensis Warnechi,* with sword-shaped green-and-white-striped leaves; and *Draceana sanderiana,* a small pot plant.

✓   ✓   ✓

Pittosporum Likes It Cold

Pittosporum (*Pittosporum tobira*) is a small tropical tree that can be grown indoors. Pittosporum will grow in average soil and thrives in a cool room (50 to 55 degrees F.). Keep the soil on the dry side and provide plenty of sunlight. Pruning is necessary for a shapely plant.

✓   ✓   ✓

Improper Light Misshapes Norfolk Island Pine

The Norfolk Island pine (*Araucaria excelsa*) makes an excellent houseplant with graceful branches. The branches grow in best proportion if they receive east or west sunlight. Norfolk Island pine should be grown in average soil that is kept moist. It tolerates low humidity.

✓   ✓   ✓

Jade Plants Need Sunlight

The jade plant (*Crassula argentea*) is an attractive succulent for indoors. Insufficient sunlight is the usual cause for this plant's failure. Jades need about 6 hours of sunlight daily. Make sure the soil is well drained and allow it to dry out thoroughly between waterings.

✓   ✓   ✓

Zebra Plant Needs Moist Soil

The zebra plant (*Aphelandra*) is a striking houseplant from Brazil. It has glossy green leaves marked by white veins; yellow-orange flowers appear in the fall. The secret to healthy zebra plants is to pot them in double the usual amount of humus and keep the growth medium moist. Give the zebra plant filtered sunlight and keep it slightly potbound.

✓   ✓   ✓

Indoor Figs

A variety of fig plants make excellent houseplants. Figs grow best in bright, but not direct, light in an average soil which is kept evenly moist. The indoor rubber tree (*Ficus elastica*) is the most popular. Others include the fiddle-leaf fig (*Ficus lyrata*), weeping fig (*Ficus benjamina*), creeping fig (*Ficus pumila*), and Indian laurel (*Ficus retusa nitida*). Don't expect to harvest figs: these plants don't produce fruit.

✓   ✓   ✓

Dieffenbachia a Handsome Houseplant

Dieffenbachia (dumb cane) is a very useful houseplant with large handsome leaves. Given proper care, it grows indoors like a tree. *Dieffenbachia* tolerates low humidity and moderate light but thrives when given more of each. Overwatering will cause root rot. Let soil dry out moderately between waterings. Leaves will cause a painful swelling of the tongue if chewed.

✓   ✓   ✓

Palms Need Warmth

A wide variety of palms (*Palmaceae*) are available that will flourish indoors. Palms should be kept away from direct sunlight and in a warm place. Their soil should be a mixture of 2 parts clay and 1 part each of sand and humus. Keep soil moist at all times and syringe foliage with water occasionally.

✓   ✓   ✓

Special Care for Bromeliads

The leaves of the tropical bromeliad plant meet to form a cup and are accustomed to this cup being filled with water. Bromeliads grow best in shallow containers filled with a fibrous mixture of peat, bark chips, humus, and sand. Although an east or west exposure is most desirable, they will grow in northern light.

✔   ✔   ✔

Chinese Evergreen Good for Trouble Spots

The Chinese evergreen (*Aglonema modestum*) is a waxy-leaved foliage plant that can grow almost anywhere in the house. It tolerates low light and low humidity—conditions that are commonly found indoors. Aglonema grows well in water containing charcoal chips or in humus soil that is kept moist.

✔   ✔   ✔

Moisture Level Important to Schefflera

The umbrella tree (*Brassaia actinophylla*), or *Schefflera,* is a rapid grower that makes a graceful houseplant. Care must be taken in watering this plant; excessive dryness or excessive wetness causes the leaves to drop. *Schefflera* tolerates some shade and low humidity.

✔   ✔   ✔

Bonsai Plants from the Yard

Plants which appear in the yard uninvited can be started and trained as bonsai trees. Seedling of maple, elm, peach, or apple are particularly useful. They make good material to practice methods of dwarfing and shaping.

✔   ✔   ✔

Flowers in Low Sunlight

Most flowering houseplants require considerable sunlight in order to bloom. However, some plants will bloom with exposure to only 2 or 3 hours of sunshine during the winter. The small-flowered begonias are the most dependable. African violets and bromeliads will sometimes bloom without direct sunlight.

✔   ✔   ✔

Blooming Plants for Winter

Nothing brightens the indoors in winter more than blooming flowers. For protracted blooms in the winter, collect the following plants: wax begonia, Riegor Elatior begonia, African violets, scented geraniums, veltheimia, amaryllis, and jasmine.

✔   ✔   ✔

Let Fuchsias Rest in Dry Winter Soil

Fuchsias, or lady's eardrops, are an attractive houseplant with beautiful

Common Houseplants

A list of some of the most common houseplants follows. The scientific name of the plant, together with its origin, is given here. The conversion chart on pages 373-374 gives its common name. Exact temperature, humidity and light information are given on pages 375-383.* Houseplants requiring *bright* light should be placed in a south window, glassed porch or greenhouse. Those requiring *filtered light* should be placed in an east or west window. Plants requiring *shade* need some sunlight, but will tolerate light from a north window or darker areas of the house.

Scientific Name	Origin	Scientific Name	Origin
Abutilon hybridum	tropical	Echinocereus dasyacathus	desert
Adromischus clavifolius	desert	Echinopsis multiplex	desert
Aechmea chantinii	desert	Episcia	tropical
Agave	desert	Euonymus	subtropical
Aglaonema	tropical	Euphorbia	tropical
Allophyton mexicanum	subtropical	Fatsia	subtropical
Aloe	desert	Ficus	tropical
Anthurium	tropical	Fittonia verschaffeltii	tropical
Aphelandra squarrosa	tropical	Gasteria	desert
Araucaria excelsa	subtropical	Gymnocalycium	desert
Ardisia	subtropical	Haworthia	desert
Asparagus	subtropical	Herniaria glabra	tropical
Aspidistra elatior	subtropical	Hoya	subtropical
Asplenium buliferum	subtropical	Hypocyrta numnularia	tropical
Astrophytum myriostigma	desert	Hypoestes sanguinolenta	tropical
Bambusa	subtropical	Kalanchoe	desert
Begonia	tropical	Kleinia	desert
Bertolonia maculata	tropical	Kohleria amabilis	tropical
Bougainvillea	subtropical	Lemaireocereus beneckei	desert
Caladium	tropical	Lithops bella	desert
Calathea picturata		Mammillaria	desert
argentea	tropical	Maranta leuconeura	
Cephalocereus senilis	desert	kerchoveana	tropical
Cereus peruvianus	desert	Monstera	tropical
Chamaecereus silvestrii	desert	Notocactus	desert
Chlorophytum	tropical	Opuntia	desert
Cissus	tropical	Peperomia	tropical
Cleistocactus strausii	desert	Philodendron	tropical
Clerodendrum		Phoenix rœbelenii	tropical
thomsoniae	tropical	Pilea	tropical
Codiaeum	tropical	Pittosporum tobira	subtropical
Coffea arabica	tropical	Plectranthus	
Columnea	tropical	australis	subtropical
Conophytum aureum	desert	Podocarpus gracilior	subtropical
Cotyledon teretifolia	desert	Rebutia	desert
Crassula	desert	Sansevieria	tropical
Crossandra		Saintpaulia	
infundibuliformis	tropical	ionantha	tropical
Ctenanthe	tropical	Sedum	desert
Dieffenbachia	subtropical	Siderasis fuscata	tropical
Dracaena	tropical	Sinningia	tropical
Dryopteris erythrosora	subtropical	Streptocarpus	tropical
Echeveria	desert	Syngonium	subtropical
Echinocactus ingens	desert	Tradescantia	tropical

Abutilon hybridum (tropical origin, temperate temperature, high humidity, bright light), *Bougainvillea* (subtropical, warm temperature, high humidity, bright light), *Dieffenbachia* (subtropical, warm temperature, intermediate humidity, filtered light) and *Monstera* (tropical, temperate temperature, intermediate humidity, shade) are not included in the chart.

bell-shaped flowers. They are excellent for hanging baskets. Colors are shades of pink, red, rose, blue, fuchsia, and white. Sunlight and good air circulation are needed for plants to bloom well. The soil should be left dry during the winter rest period.

✓   ✓   ✓

Geraniums Need Clay Soil

Geraniums (*Pelargonium*) are a universally enjoyed plant both indoors and out. They will bloom almost year 'round indoors. Plant geraniums in soil with a high clay content (2 parts clay to 1 part soil and 1 part humus). Avoid overfertilization, which promotes leaf growth and prevents flowers from developing. And avoid overwatering, which causes leaves to yellow.

✓   ✓   ✓

Watch Sudden Temperature Change with Gloxinia

Gloxinia (*Sinningia speciosa*) is a beautiful houseplant that forms spectacular trumpet-shaped flowers with red, blue, or white petals. Plants are grown from tubers that are planted in February. For blooms in the spring, place plants in moderate sun and mist them frequently. Gloxinias are particularly susceptible to rapid changes of temperature. So, keep them out of drafts.

✓   ✓   ✓

Miniature Roses Indoors

Miniature roses do well in a window garden if properly cared for. They need a sunny spot in a cool room or window (not above 65 F. in the daytime and 10 degrees cooler at night). Water daily, but do not let water stand in the pots. Frequent syringing of foliage is helpful. Recommend selections are Tom Thumb or Pixie.

✓   ✓   ✓

Nasturtiums Indoors in the Winter

Nasturtiums can be made to grow and bloom indoors in the wintertime. They must be grown in a cool, sunny window or plant room. To start nasturtiums, plant seeds in late summer in pots of soil. Do not add fertilizer since its addition tends to delay bloom.

✓   ✓   ✓

Fuchsia That Bloom in Winter

Fuchsia blooms are welcome throughout the year, but particularly in the winter. *Fuchsia magellaniea gracilis* is a winter bloomer. With its ruby red blooms, it makes a beautiful plant in a hanging basket.

✓   ✓   ✓

Morning Glory as a Houseplant

Most people don't realize that morning glories (*Ipomoea horsfalliae*) will bloom profusely indoors. Plant seeds in a pot with equal parts of sand, peat, and loam mixture and you will have blossoms in 2 months. Some form of support for the vines will be needed.

✓   ✓   ✓

Peppers as Houseplants

Some vegetables grow well indoors, producing attractive flowers and fruit. Ordinary bell peppers and dwarf sweet peppers grow well as houseplants in 8-inch pots. Plants can be started from seed or dug from the garden. Place them in a sunny window.

✓   ✓   ✓

Try Some African Violet Relatives

The African violet is the most popular flowering houseplant. Some people don't realize that this plant has relatives whose flowers are equally attractive. Among these plants are the lipstick plant, goldfish plant, peacock-plant, and *Streptocarpus*—all of which are excellent bloomers and require the same care as African violets.

✓   ✓   ✓

The Care of Orchids

Different varieties of orchids require different care. The epiphytes (tree-grown), which are most common, should be potted in either a fir-bark mixture or chopped tree fern preparation, both of which are available at garden centers. In watering epiphytes, make sure that the water passes through the medium easily and that no free water is left standing. The medium should be kept moist at all times. Those orchids with moisture-holding pseudobulbs (*Cattleya*) should have 25% sphagnum moss added to the fir-bark or chopped tree fern media. Allow the growth medium for these orchids to dry out between waterings. Orchids potted in soil, such as the ladyslipper, are watered like other houseplants. Frequent misting and added fluorescent lighting benefits all orchids.

✓   ✓   ✓

Orchids for Your Window

If you wish to grow orchids in a south window, try varieties of *Cattleya* (corsage), *Cypripedium* (lady-slipper type), *Epidendum, Oncidium* (butterfly type), and *Phalaenopsis* (moth orchids). These orchids require medium-warm to warm temperatures; they bloom from winter to late spring.

✓   ✓   ✓

Indoor Citrus Trees

Glossy leaves and fragrant blossoms make citrus trees attractive houseplants; moreover, they also produce ripe fruit. The Ponderosa lemon is the best known of the window-grown citrus houseplant. Others are the Chinotto, King, and Sweet Orange. The dwarf tangerine (*Citrus nobilis deliciosa*) is an attractive houseplant that produces delicious fruit as well.

✓   ✓   ✓

Vegetables for Flower Arrangements

A number of vegetable garden plants are useful for indoor decorations. Kale makes attractive foliage in bouquets. Ornamental kale has multiheaded, crinkled leaves with frilled edges. Dark opal basil with reddish-purple leaves is useful. Bronzed lettuce can be used as greenery with flower arrangements. Some vegetable flowers are also attractive. Try yellow broccoli flowers or cream-yellow blooms of okra.

Section Two

GROWTH MEDIA AND POTTING

Don't "Overpot" Houseplants

It may be hard to believe, but a houseplant can actually be handicapped by being placed in a pot that is too large. In an overly large pot, the plant fails to absorb the water in the soil quickly enough. When water is allowed to stand in a pot for too long a period of time, it fills up the air spaces and encourages the growth of microorganisms that are unfavorable to plants. Place plants in pots that comfortably fit their roots so that they deplete the moisture content at a desirable rate.

✓   ✓   ✓

A Good Potting Mixture

The following is a basic soil mixture that has proven highly satisfactory for houseplants:

4 parts coarse builder's sand
2 parts peat or peat moss
1 part dried cattle manure
1 part vermiculite

Add to each bushel (32 quarts):

8 level tablespoons of superphosphate
8 level tablespoons of cottonseed meal
4 level tablespoons of sulfate of potash
4 level tablespoons of ground limestone (omit for acid-loving plants)

✔   ✔   ✔

Drainage for Houseplant Containers

Good drainage material should be placed in the bottom of pots and other containers used for houseplants. This keeps the potting soil from becoming waterlogged and damaging plant roots. Place 2 inches of broken clay pot material or coarse gravel in the bottom of containers used for houseplants.

✔   ✔   ✔

Add Charcoal to Undrained Pots

If pots do not have drainage holes, a musty odor often develops in the potting mix. Charcoal can be added to the planting mix to prevent this problem. Mix ½ to 1 teaspoon of crushed charcoal (not the barbecue type, but the type you find at garden centers or drug stores) into the soil in each pot. If at all possible, all planting pots should have drainage holes.

✔   ✔   ✔

Best Potting Mix for Bromeliads

Most bromeliads do better in a special mix than in a standard potting soil. A half-and-half mixture of shredded osmunda or tree fern fiber with soil is recommended for most bromeliads. An exception is the terrestrial species—*Cryptanthus*—which grows well in a standard potting mix.

✔   ✔   ✔

When Repotting Is Necessary

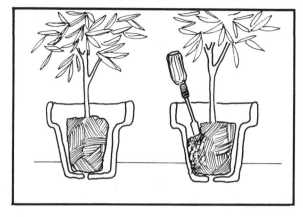

To determine whether plants need repotting, gently knock them out of their pots and examine their root systems. If roots have formed a thick, dry web on the outside of the root ball, the plant should be replanted. Use a pot one size larger than the one in which the plant was growing. Carefully comb out matted roots before adding new potting soil.

✁   ✁   ✁

Top Dressing Houseplants

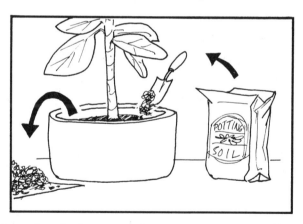

Houseplants benefit from repotting every 2 years even if they have not outgrown their containers. The reason for this is that potting soil tends to become compacted. Further, after 2 years it is pretty much robbed of certain essential nutrients.

Repotting large houseplants can be a rather laborious task. A lazy man's way to reap some of the benefits of repotting without the labor is to top dress house plants. Remove 1 or 2 inches of the soil from the pot or container, taking care not to injure roots. Replace the removed soil with a rich mixture of fresh potting soil.

*   *   *

Low Nitrogen for Geraniums

If geraniums are grown in soil with high nitrogen content, they will make extensive vegetative growth but won't flower. For this reason, avoid heavy feeding with high nitrogen fertilizers.

*   *   *

Good Soil Mix for Ferns

Ferns require a soil mix that is light and porous. For a good medium, mix 2 parts good loamy soil, 2 parts leaf mold, 1 part sand, ¼ part dried cow manure or rich compost, ¼ part broken charcoal, and ¾ of a pint of superphosphate to each bushel of mix.

*   *   *

Making a Fern Ball

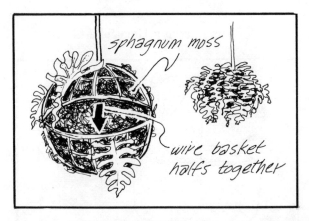

sphagnum moss

wire basket halfs together

Fern balls make attractive hanging plants. They are made by wiring together two wire hanging baskets after each has been stuffed with unmilled sphagnum moss and planted with ferns. The ferns grow out through the openings in the baskets. Keep the balls moist and in a slightly shaded place. The stuffed sphagnum moss can also be planted with begonias and small-leaved ivy. The sphagnum moss ball should be fertilized with a liquid house plant fertilizer. Follow the directions on the label as to concentration and frequency. The root systems of the plants penetrate the moss and hold the plants securely.

*   *   *

Vitamins Don't Help Houseplants

Some manufacturers advertise plant "vitamins" that stimulate vigorous growth. Don't believe it. Plants manufacture most of their own vitamins, and these claims have not been scientifically substantiated.

✓   ✓   ✓

A Simple Hanging Basket

Wire frames can be used as supports for makeshift hanging baskets. A perforated sheet of plastic can be used to hold the potting soil. Sheet moss can be placed on the outside of the basket to give it a natural appearance. The moss will absorb any excess water that may leak through the drainage holes.

✓   ✓   ✓

Proper Medium for Orchid Cactus

The orchid cactus (*Epiphyllum*) needs a more moist and richer growing medium than desert-type cacti. A proper mix for this plant is: 2 parts loam, 2 parts leafmold, 1 part sharp sand, and 1 pint of bone meal to each bushel of mix.

✓   ✓   ✓

Don't Grow Cacti in Pure Sand

Although cacti do well with some sand in their growing medium, they do not grow well in pure sand. Most cacti grow best in a loose, porous soil that does not contain too much nitrogen and is composed of about ¼ sand.

✓   ✓   ✓

Use Unglazed Pots for Cacti

Glazed pots hold moisture within while unglazed pots allow it to evaporate from the planting mix. Don't use glazed pots for cacti; the trapped moisture can kill the plants. Water cacti sparingly.

Totem Poles for Vines

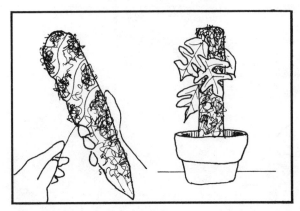

Vining philodendrons, grape ivy, English ivy, and other vines are attractive when trained on posts in pots. "Moss sticks" or "totem poles" can be constructed by wrapping sphagnum moss around slabs of bark. Secure the moss to the bark with copper wire. Place the pointed end of the slab of bark into the soil. Roots from the vine will grow into the totem pole as well as into the soil.

Growing Houseplants in Water

Some houseplants can be rooted and grown in water. The addition of a liquid fertilizer to the water greatly enhances growth. Plants that grow well in water are Chinese evergreen, philodendron, pathos, and nephthytis. Change the water occasionally during the first few months of growth.

Composting in Flower Boxes

Flower boxes lay idle part of the year. One way to put them to work during these periods is to use them for composting. Start with a layer of garbage trimmings (egg shells, fruit rinds, etc.). Add a layer of potting soil. Repeat each layer to form a small pile. The "mini-pile" can be covered with plastic to facilitate composting and reduce any odor.

A Cupboard Full of Flower Containers

If you are in need of new and unique flower containers, look in the cupboard. You may find many containers that are suitable; bean pots, sugar bowls, cream pitchers, and gravy boats are some to consider. Best results will be obtained if drainage holes can be pierced or drilled in the containers.

Section Three

WATERING

Determining the Need for Water

It is sometimes difficult to determine if a particular houseplant needs water. One technique is to tap the side of the pot with a small block of wood. A resulting clear ring means dry soil. A dull, heavy, thumping sound means water is sufficient.

✔   ✔   ✔

Avoid "Softened" Water for Indoor Plants

Ion exchange water softeners produce water that is injurious to plants. If this water is used repeatedly, the soil will accumulate a toxic amount of sodium. Use untreated tap water for all plants. Rainwater or spring or well water is best when available. If you have a water softener, it probably has a bypass which will allow you to draw untreated water.

✔   ✔   ✔

Watering a Very Dry Houseplant

Sometimes, houseplants are allowed to become too dry, almost to the point of killing the plant. In such cases, rapid first aid is in order. Immerse the pot in a bucket of water up to the rim. Allow the plant to water itself for 1 hour. Then, remove the water from the bucket and allow the excess water in the pot to drain back into the bucket.

✓   ✓   ✓

Water Immediately after Repotting

When a plant is repotted, it should be watered immediately to promote good contact between the soil and roots. The plant also needs ample water to help it overcome the shock of transplantation.

✓   ✓   ✓

Increasing Humidity for Houseplants

Most houseplants need a higher humidity then houses provide. To solve this problem, group houseplants together and place a few glasses filled with water among the pots. The water that evaporates will be trapped by the dense canopy of foliage and increase the humidity content of the air surrounding the plants.

✓   ✓   ✓

Self-Watering Pots

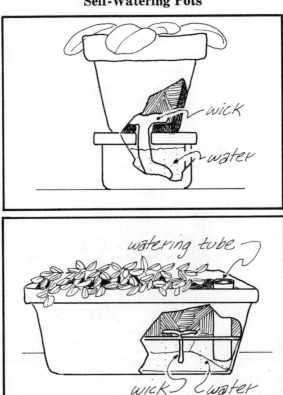

When vacations and work schedules make it difficult to water plants on schedule, you might consider constructing a self-watering device in the bottom of each plant container. If wicks which lead to the water are inserted into the pot, they will carry the water from the reservoir to the soil automatically as needed. To mask the self-watering system, a false bottom can be constructed in a container, as illustrated. Commercial models are available.

Watering Hanging Baskets

Before securing a hanging basket, consider how you will water it. Because hanging baskets are exposed to the atmosphere on all sides, water evaporates rapidly. Baskets can be attached to a pulley arrangement so that they can be lowered for watering. Rigid extensions for hoses are available to water baskets hanging above your head. Do not forget to cover the carpet before watering.

Watering Hanging Plants with Ice Cubes

If it is difficult to reach your hanging plants to water them, one solution is to reach up and place ice cubes on the surface of the soil. The warm room temperature will melt them and water will slowly penetrate the soil. Don't place the cubes against the plant flesh; that could be injurious.

Crown of Thorns Needs Water

The crown of thorns is a house plant with a thick stem and thorns. Because it resembles a cactus, some people make the mistake of giving it very little water. Actually, the crown of thorns (*Euphorbia milii*) should be kept well watered.

Funnel for Hanging Basket

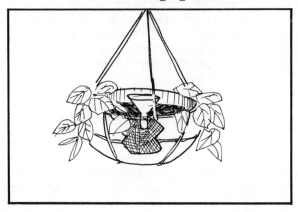

It is difficult to get water to penetrate soil in hanging baskets because much of the water runs down the sides of the container. To ease this watering problem, insert a small funnel into the soil in the center of the basket when you plant it. Water can then be poured into the funnel, where it will sink into the soil rather than run down the sides of the container.

✔   ✔   ✔

Don't Overwater Jade Plant

If a jade plant (*Crassula argentea*) is overwatered, the leaves and stem will wither. Some people interpret this as a need for water and add even more moisture. Jade plants thrive in dry conditions. Because this plant stores considerable moisture in its leaves and stem, let the soil dry out between waterings.

✔   ✔   ✔

Watering African Violets

Water should *not* be poured directly on African violet plants. An accumulation of moisture on the leaves and in the crown promotes disease problems. Water should be supplied through a saucer at the bottom of the pot or poured around the edge of the pot. Let the soil approach dryness between waterings.

✔   ✔   ✔

Best Way to Water Cacti

When watering cacti, it is important not to wet the plants themselves. Submerge the pots nearly to their rims in water and leave them in this position until water entering through the drainage hole reaches the surface. Let pots become dry between waterings.

Section Four

CULTURE AND CARE

Houseplants Need Rest

Even tropical houseplants that come from a fairly uniform climate undergo periods of active growth and periods of rest. In winter, ferns and palms are less active and produce fewer new leaves than in the spring. In early fall, cacti enter a period of dormancy which lasts through the winter. After flowering, some plants (e.g. cyclamens) appear dead for a period of time. When plants are in dormancy, they require water and some warmth. They should not be fed at this time.

✦   ✦   ✦

Giving Houseplants a Summer Vacation

Most houseplants will prosper outdoors during the summer; but if plants are not sunk into the soil, they will turn over from the wind and will quickly dry out. Therefore, dig a hole deep enough to sink the pot containing the plant under a sparsely-leaved tree, such as a honey locust. The leaves of the tree will allow in sunlight while preventing sunscald. Place 3 inches of stone in the bottom of the hole for drainage and fill around the pots, up to the rim, with peat moss. Once placed outdoors, houseplants should not be neglected. Because they are contained in pots, they will need additional watering. Turn the pots periodically to break any roots that may penetrate the soil through the drainage holes. Return plants to the house in early fall before frost threatens.

✦   ✦   ✦

Giving Houseplants a Turn

Plants have a tendency to grow *toward* light. If plants are left in one position, they will become misshapen by the accelerated growth of parts nearer the light. To prevent this, periodically turn your houseplants, each time exposing a different side to the light source.

✦   ✦   ✦

Fertilizing Houseplants

Little fertilization of houseplants is necessary. In fact, once plants are well established, new growth may not be desired. Once the plants have grown to a desirable size, fertilization once a year is satisfactory for foliage plants. Use a liquid fertilizer and follow directions on the label.

✦   ✦   ✦

Avoid Granular Fertilizers

If granular fertilizers come in direct contact with plant tissues, they will burn them. For this reason, use liquid, *not granular,* fertilizer for your houseplants. Follow directions on the label as to time and rate of application.

✓   ✓   ✓

Don't Overfeed African Violets

African violets are more often overfed than underfed. If your African violets are growing well and show no signs of hunger, don't feed them. If hunger signs, such as yellowing leaves, appear, apply a liquid fertilizer as directed on the label. Once a year, repot the plants in fresh, fertile soil. Old soil becomes compacted and unfertile.

✓   ✓   ✓

African Violets with Upright Leaves

Sometimes, the leaves of African violets become elongated, growing upright rather than spreading. This is a sign that the plants are not receiving sufficient light and should be moved to a place with more sunlight.

✓   ✓   ✓

Prune African Violet Blooms

You can prolong the life of remaining African violet blooms if the stems of faded blooms are pruned out as soon as they fall. This also prevents the formation of seed pods, which sap the plant's energy.

✓   ✓   ✓

Don't Prune Tuberous Begonias

Open wounds in tuberous begonias are very susceptible to attack by fungi. For this reason, do not prune tuberous begonias. When you cut the flowers, do so half way down the stem. The remaining half of the stem will heal at the base and fall off, avoiding an open wound.

✓   ✓   ✓

Beware of "Plant-Shine" Compounds

A number of "plant-shine" compounds, claiming to make the surfaces of foliage plants shiny, are available on the market. Repeated application of some of these compounds can injure leaves. If you use any type of polishing compound, don't use it on the undersides of leaves, where most of the stomates (leaf pores) are located.

✓   ✓   ✓

Indoor Citrus Need Pollination

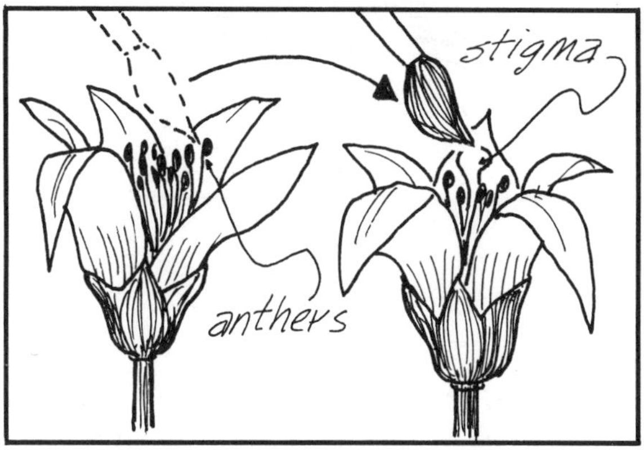

Indoor citrus plants will not produce lemons or oranges unless they are hand-pollinated. Take pollen from the male anther of a flower and place it on the female stigma of the plant to be pollinated. The female blossoms which should be pollinated are easily distinguished by their long protruding stigma. A camel hair brush can be used to transport the pollen.

Inducing Indoor Azaleas to Rebloom

Indoor azaleas require special treatment to induce them to bloom more than once. After the plant has bloomed in the spring, place it in a sunny place and feed it with an acid fertilizer once a month. Azaleas require high humidity, so water the plants freely and spray the foliage. When fall comes, discontinue the fertilization and keep the plant near a cool window (45 to 55 degrees F.). Water and mist during the winter. In the spring, place the plant in a warm, sunny location and water freely. Blooms should form within 3 or 4 weeks.

Making Hoya Bloom

Hoya plants are naturally slow bloomers, sometimes taking 3 or 4 years. What is more, hoya plants require full sunlight before they will form blossoms. Allowing the plants to become potbound often promotes flower bud formation.

Making Bromeliads Bloom

When bromeliads fail to bloom, blossom formation can be hastened by placing a ripe apple in the center of the leaf rosette and sealing the whole plant in a plastic bag. Remove the plastic bag and the apple after 48 hours.

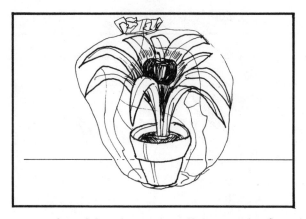

The ethylene gas released by the apple will hasten the flowering process. Flowers should appear within several weeks following this treatment.

✓   ✓   ✓

Making a Christmas Cactus Bloom

The Christmas cactus produces a beautiful flower—*when* it blooms! To encourage the cactus to bloom, place the plants in absolute darkness from 5:00 p.m. to 8:00 a.m. daily, starting around October 20th and continuing for a minimum of 40 days. Either move the plant into a dark closet each night or completely cover it with black cloth for the night. After 40 days, place the plant in a well-lighted window and wait for it to bloom.

✓   ✓   ✓

Cure for Leggy Poinsettias

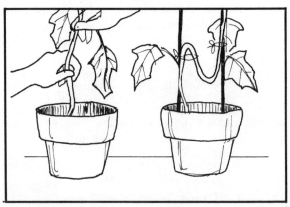

Poinsettias often become leggy and unmanageable. By forming an S curve in the stem, the height of a poinsettia will be reduced. As illustrated in the left of the diagram, compress the stem gently with thumb and index finger at two points on the stem into an S and support with two stakes, as illustrated at the right.

✓   ✓   ✓

Forcing Hyacinth Flowers

When hyacinth bulbs are forced to bloom indoors, the flowers sometimes develop poorly. To ensure good flower development, place a cone of paper over the bulb for 14 days after the flower first starts to appear. This "draws" the flower bud upward and results in a fuller bloom.

✓   ✓   ✓

Pebble Trays for Orchids

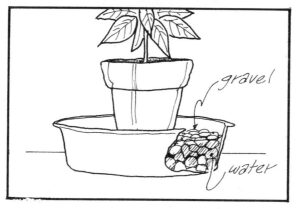

Orchids require high humidity in order to grow and prosper. The dry conditions in most houses are not conducive to orchid culture. One method to provide high humidity content in the air around orchid plants is to place the pots containing the plants on trays filled with gravel and half filled with water. The water will evaporate from the trays, at which time it should be replaced.

✓   ✓   ✓

Forcing Daffodil Bulbs

To force daffodils bulbs to bloom indoors, place them in stones within a small container. Keep the bases of the bulbs moist and place the container in a bright window. The bulbs will produce leaves and flower. Do not attempt to replant the bulbs next year.

✓   ✓   ✓

Encouraging a Rubber Plant to Branch

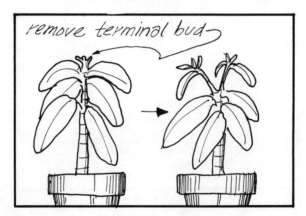

remove terminal bud

The natural habit of the rubber plant is to grow a single stem for many years before branching. If you wish to encourage branching earlier, remove the terminal (top) bud after the plant has 6 to 8 leaves. This will induce 2 or 3 new branches.

✓   ✓   ✓

Fuchsias Need Special Care

Fuchsias are beautiful houseplants that form hanging bell-shaped flowers. They need special care indoors. Fuchsias do not like hot temperatures and will not flower when the temperature rises above 65 degrees F. Overwatering fuchsias to the point that water stands in the bottom of the container will cause plants to wilt and die. After blooming indoors, place plants outdoors in a semishaded area. In the fall, take cuttings from the old plants and start them indoors. Abandon the old plants, which will not regenerate into desirable specimens.

Planting of Potted Easter Lilies

Potted Easter lilies can be saved for future flowering. To accomplish this, after the flowers have died place the plant in a sunny window and water when necessary. In late May, the plant can be removed from the pot and the bulbs planted in the garden. As is true for all lilies, plant in a well-drained area. Dig the holes so that the nose of each bulb is 3 to 4 inches below the surface of the soil. Do not remove the foliage, water regularly, and fertilize the plant monthly until the foliage dies down naturally, at which time it can be clipped. The plant will produce a flower the next spring.

"Gassing" Plants to Force Blooms

Stems cut from a number of flowering plants can be brought into the house in the winter and their blooms forced to open. Cut off 6- to 12-inch twigs with abundant flower buds. The forcing process will be hastened by exposing the twigs for ½ hour to fumes of ammonia (ordinary household type) or carbon tetrachloride (the solvent used in most cleaning fluids). Place the cut branches in a plastic bag (the type used by dry cleaners works well). Soak a cloth with ammonia or carbon tetrachloride and place it in the bag. After ½ hour, remove the branches and place them in a container of water in front of a brightly lit window. The branches will bloom and eventually die.

Forcing Flowering Branches in the House

If you want a breath of spring in the winter, consider forcing branches of early flowering shrubs in your house. Easy-to-force branches include forsythia and flowering quince. Always choose branches that have abundant flower buds. (Usually, the plumper buds are flowering buds and the pointed ones leaf buds.)

To encourage flowering, cut off branches 12- to 24-inches long and soak them overnight in lukewarm water in a bathtub. Then, place them in tall containers of water in a sunny window. It takes about 3 to 4 weeks for flowers to appear from branches collected any time during the winter.

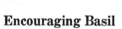

Ferns Can Get Too Much Light

Ferns, like all plants, need light; but they can be injured by direct sunlight. Ferns receiving too much light develop a sickly, yellowish appearance. Avoid placing ferns in spots where they will be exposed to a full day's sun. A lace curtain in front of a sunny window should create the proper light conditions. Ferns will also do well in areas receiving no direct sunlight provided that there is sufficient indirect light.

Encouraging Basil

Basil grows well in pots indoors. Remove the tips of young plants at a uniform height to promote bushiness. As the plants mature, crop as illustrated to promote a rounded form. Leafy clippings (but not flowering stems) of this popular herb can be used for seasoning.

Common Poisonous Houseplants

If consumed, parts of some houseplants are poisonous to children and pets. Common houseplants that may be poisonous include hyacinth, narcissus, gloriosa lily, amaryllis, nerine, oleander, dumbcane, caladium, philodendron, and mistletoe.

Bookshelves for Houseplants

If you have limited space for houseplants, consider putting them on bookshelves. It is simple to attach artificial fluorescent lighting on the bottom of the shelf above the plants. Houseplants grow well in artificial fluorescent light.

✓   ✓   ✓

Labels from TV Trays

Labeling plants is important. Names are often forgotten if plants aren't labeled as soon as they are purchased. One handy way to make permanent labels for plants is to cut TV dinner trays into 1-inch by 4-inch strips. Using a nail or ballpoint pen, impress the name of the plant permanently into the aluminum. This tag can be affixed to the plant or attached to a stake that is placed in the pot.

Section Five

PEST CONTROL

Sterilizing Pots

Contaminated pots can be the source of insect and disease problems. Before placing a plant in a used container, sterilize it. Mix 1 part of household bleach to 10 parts of water. Let pots soak in this mixture for at least 20 minutes and rinse. They will then be sterile.

✓   ✓   ✓

Give Houseplants an Occasional Shower

Give houseplants an occasional shower using any spray device. This cleans the foliage, washes off pests such as aphids and mites, and provides a period of high humidity.

✓   ✓   ✓

Sterilize to Prevent Damping-Off

If your seedlings fall over and die soon after they germinate, they probably are being attacked by damping-off organisms that live in the soil. The best way to eliminate these organisms is to sterilize the soil. An easy sterilization technique is to pour boiling water into the pots or flats, wetting the soil thoroughly several times in quick succession. Seeds may be sown when the soil has dried out sufficiently. Clay pots should be placed in boiling water for 15 minutes before being used. Plastic pots can be cleaned in the same manner as one washes the dishes.

✓   ✓   ✓

Soil Sterilization

If soil used in potting mixes is not sterilized, a variety of disease and insect problems may develop. Soil can be sterilized by baking it in flat pans in an oven at 200 degrees F. for ½ hour, or by pressure-cooking it at 15 pounds of pressure for 15 minutes.

Controlling Mealy Bugs

Mealy bugs, crawling insects that look like bits of cotton fluff, can destroy houseplants by sucking out their sap. For control, dip a cotton-tipped tooth-pick in alcohol and lift off each visible bug. Repeat the treatment each week until bugs are no longer in evidence.

A Hot Bath to Control Aphids

Aphids on houseplants can be eradicated by submerging plants briefly in hot water. Heat a pan of water to between 125 and 135 degrees F. Dip the infested houseplant into the water for a few seconds. The aphids will be eradicated and the plant will not suffer injury.

Spray Houseplants after Being Outdoors

Houseplants are commonly placed outdoors during the summer. Although this practice revitalizes plants, it also exposes them to a number of insect and disease pests. To prevent introducing insect and disease problems into the house, spray plants a week or two before bringing them into the house. An all-purpose garden spray containing malathion and captan will work. Follow the directions on the label.

A Chamber to Spray Plants

When houseplants are sprayed with pesticides, they should either be taken outdoors or placed in a chamber. This eliminates the possibility of pesticide deposits accumulating on house furnishings. A spray chamber can be made by placing the plant in a 4-cubic-foot box laid on its side. Spray the plant at a distance of 18 inches with sweeping motions for 4 seconds. Close the lid of the box for 2 minutes until all the spray has settled on the plant and box.

✓   ✓   ✓

First Aid for Ailing Plants

Sometimes, weak and ailing plants won't respond to normal care and drastic measures are called for. One procedure is to dip ailing plants—roots, leaves, and all—into a liquid plant food such as Ra-pid-gro (23-19-17). This treatment has often been found to retrieve the irretrievable.

✓   ✓   ✓

Mildew on Begonias

One of the major problems to beset begonias is mildew disease. The disease, caused by a fungus that forms a white flower-like growth on the surface of the plant, can be controlled by spraying with Karathane as directed on the label.

Section Six

PROPAGATION

Easy Way to Sprout Fine Seed

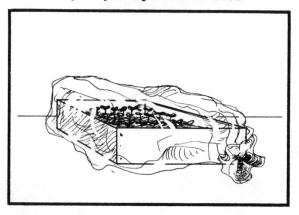

If you want to sprout a *large* quantity of fine seed, obtain a flat box. Fill the "flat" with a starting medium, such as milled sphagnum or horticulture vermiculite. Moisten the growth medium and dust the seeds lightly across the surface. Enclose the flat in a plastic bag and place it in a sunny place. Seed should sprout within a few days or weeks, depending on the variety sown.

✓   ✓   ✓

Sprouting Seed in a Jar

If you want to sprout a *small* quantity of seed, this can be done effectively in a jar. Set the jar on its side and fill it with 1 inch of moist, milled sphagnum moss. Level the growth medium with a knife blade. Sprinkle seeds lightly on the surface and screw on the perforated lid. Seeds should sprout within 2 or 3 weeks.

✔   ✔   ✔

Foliage Plants from Seeds

Most foliage plants are purchased as potted plants from nursery outlets. Some foliage plants can be grown easily from seed. You might want to try the following: *Eucalyptus globulus, Eucalyptus citriodora, Greuillea robusta, Asparagus sprengeri, Asparagus plumosus,* and *Cordyline indivisa.*

✔   ✔   ✔

"Pot in Pot" Method to Germinate Seed

When seed is germinating, it is important that the soil remain constantly moist. A "pot in pot" method of watering ensures good soil moisture during seed germination: Bury a small pot in the soil of a larger pot and use it as a water reservoir. The small pot *must* be porous. When water is placed in the small pot, it seeps through the porous walls and continually "waters" the surrounding soil. After sewing the seeds, the large pot should be covered with a plastic bag. This arrangement also works well in propagating root cuttings.

✔   ✔   ✔

Airplant Plant Easy to Propagate

The airplane plant (*Chlorophytum comosum*) forms small aerial plantlets on its flower branches. If these plantlets are cut off and planted as soon as they form roots in the air, they will produce new plants.

✔   ✔   ✔

Germinating Fern Spores

Ferns can be produced from the spores found on the undersurface of fronds (leaves). When spore cases turn brown, cut the fronds into 2-inch seg-

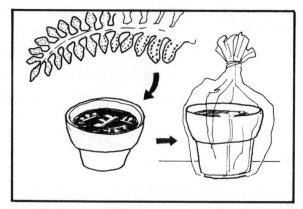

ments and lay them, spore side *down,* on the surface of a pot filled with potting soil. Enclose the pot in a plastic bag with a little water in the bottom of the bag. Loosen the plastic when new plants appear. After 2 weeks, uncover the pot entirely. New plants can be transplanted into individual pots.

ᐟ   ᐟ   ᐟ

Repotting and Dividing a Boston Fern

The best time to divide and repot a Boston fern is in the spring, just as new growth begins. Select younger and stronger crowns from the outside of the plant for replanting. Discard the old woody interior parts.

ᐟ   ᐟ   ᐟ

Pick-a-Back Plant Easy to Propagate

Pick-a-back plants are so called because they develop small plantlets on the back of their leaves. These plantlets will root easily if removed from the plant and placed in close contact with the surface of the soil contained in a pot.

ᐟ   ᐟ   ᐟ

Exacta Knife Good for Cuttings

Cuttings taken from plants for vegetative propogation should be removed "cleanly." If the cut end has ragged edges, there is less chance the cutting will produce healthy roots. A good instrument for making cuttings is an exacta knife. This kind of knife, which can be purchased at hobby centers, is extremely sharp and will not tear or bruise the tissue when cuttings are made.

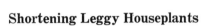

Shortening Leggy Houseplants

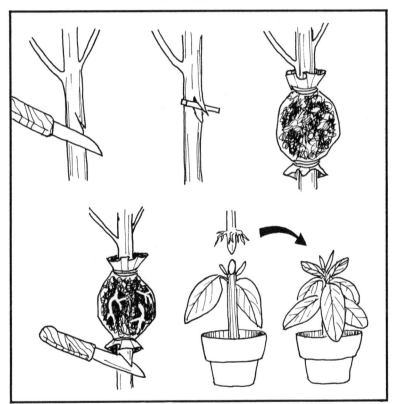

Often, houseplants develop long stems with sparse foliage. A technique to produce more compact plants is called "air layering"—a process whereby roots are induced to grow on the main stem: (1) Notch the stem and prop the notch open with a toothpick. (2) Wrap the wounded area of the stem with wet, wrung-out sphagnum. (3) Tie a piece of plastic around the wrapping. (4) When roots appear in the sphagnum, cut the stem off just below the roots and pot the new, more compact plant.

Shortening Dieffenbachia

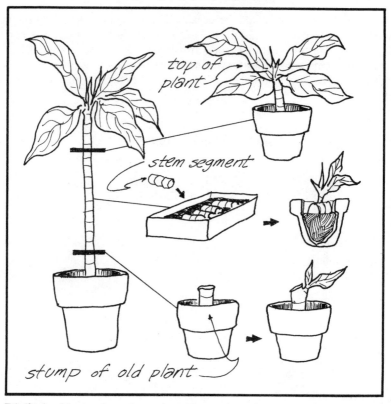

Dieffenbachia tend to become tall and leggy with age. A plant can be easily shortened by cutting off the top of the plant and placing the cut end in water to root. Once roots have developed, place the cut end in a pot of soil. The stump of the old plant will generate a new top, leaving you with two shorter dieffenbachias. Segments of stems will also form new plants if they are partially buried lengthwise in a 50-50 mixture of sand and peat.

✦   ✦   ✦

Easy Ways to Propagate Rex Begonias

Leaf cuttings from rex begonias readily regenerate new plants. Wedges of leaf tissue, including the main vein, can be partially buried (the point of the leaf is buried in the soil) in potting soil to root new plants (upper left and right of diagram). Whole leaf cuttings, placed petiole (leaf stem) down in a glass of water, will also root (center). Or whole leaves can be pinned to the surface of a rooting medium and the veins severed, as indicated by the

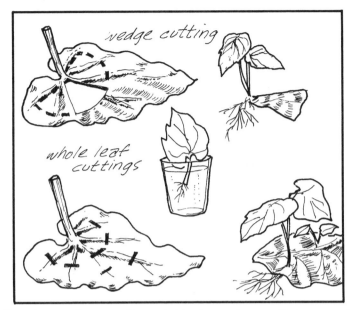

black lines in the diagram (lower left). New plants will form at the cuts (lower right).

✔   ✔   ✔

African Violets from Leaf Cuttings

African violets are easy to propagate from leaf cuttings. Leave 1 or 2 inches of the petiole (leaf stem) when you take the cuttings. Leaf cuttings can be rooted by placing the cut ends in a glass of water. A second method is to put potting soil in the bottom of a closed plastic bag. The bag will serve as a mini-greenhouse. Cuttings will also root in small containers filled with a 50-50 mixture of peat and perlite.

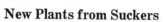

New Plants from Suckers

A number of houseplants send up short suckers from their base. Notable among these are bromeliads. After suckers have grown 2 or 3 inches, they can be cut off and rooted to form new plants. Place the cut ends in potting soil and keep them moist until roots are established.

A Plant from a Pineapple

A houseplant can be produced from pineapples bought from grocery stores. Slice off the top of the pineapple with 1 or 2 inches of fruit attached. Scoop out the meaty part, being careful not to injure the tough little stem in the center. Next, air dry the top for 24 hours. Plant in a pot of soil and place in a sunny window. Keep moist until top growth indicates that the new plant has rooted. Plants may actually produce their own fruit in 18 months to 2 years.

Making a Sweet Potato Vine

A sweet potato vine can be produced indoors from whole sweet potatoes. Select a glass container about 8 inches deep and wide enough to insert a potato. Wash the potato gently to remove any chemicals that might interefere with sprouting. Thrust toothpicks in the middle of either side of the potato and let the toothpicks rest on the rim of the container. Fill the container with water, and make sure that the lower end of the potato is always immersed. After the sweet potato has rooted, it can be potted; a vine will soon develop. Roots should develop within a month. Once the sweet potato has begun to grow leaves, it should receive several hours of sunlight per day.

Houseplants from Your Grocery Bag

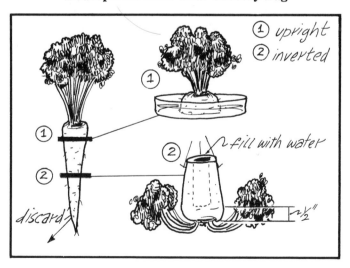

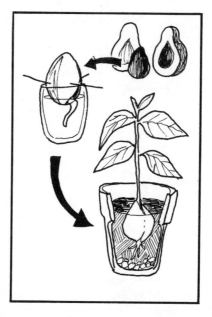

Some fruits and vegetables commonly purchased by homemakers can be turned into attractive houseplants. Carrots (see illustration) can make a "fern" plant. Simply cut off the top at (1) and place it, cut surface down, in a dish of pebbles and water. Alternatively, cut it at (2), hollow out the top half, hang it upside down and fill it with water. Avocado seed (see illustration) can be grown into an attractive houseplant. Thrust toothpicks into the sides of the seed to keep the pointed part out of water. Seeds of grapefruit, orange, lemon, and other citrus can be removed from fruit and started immediately in a pot of loose soil. They will germinate and produce attractive houseplants. These plants should be placed in a sunny window to develop and grow.

🗡   🗡   🗡

Rooting Cactus Cuttings

Most cacti can be rooted readily from cuttings. Spring and early summer is the best time to take the cuttings. Let cuttings "heal" in the sun for a few days; then insert them in moist sand. Keep the sand moist but do not promote a humid atmosphere around the plants as you would for other cuttings. After a good root system develops, cuttings can be planted in a potting mix.

🗡   🗡   🗡

Grafting Cacti

Different cacti can be grafted together to produce interesting and unusual

plants. Two basic grafting techniques are illustrated. In the top diagram, pieces of columnar and globe cacti are removed at the black line and the two cut surfaces are placed together and held in place with rubber bands. In the bottom diagram, a columnar cactus is grafted to a "rabbit ear" cactus (*Opuntia*) by making a cut and inserting the Opuntia cactus into a V made by removing a wedge from the columnar cactus.

CHAPTER TEN

Terrarium and Dish Gardening

Overview

If you lack the time for serious outdoor gardening, you might want to try indoor terrarium or dish gardening. Both types of gardening require little time or space and can be quite rewarding. In terrarium gardening, a transparent container, which partially or wholly encloses the plants is used. In dish gardening an open dish or bowl is used to contain miniature plants.

There are 6 steps to follow when establishing a terrarium or dish garden: (1) selection of a container, (2) selection of plants, (3) designing the landscape, (4) preparation of the growth medium, (5) planting and (6) maintenance.

A terrarium container must transmit light, hold water, and have an opening. Many containers around the house will fit these requirements. Humidity conditions can be modified in terrariums by adjusting the size of the container opening. **Almost any container will do for a dish garden,** with the sole stipulation that it be at least 3 inches deep.

A wide variety of plants will grow well in both terrarium and dish gardens. Many can be purchased in 2-inch pots at florists, nurseries, or garden centers; they are displayed as "houseplants" or "terrarium plants." If you plan on gardening **in a completely enclosed terrarium, choose plants that are adapted to high humidities. Grow plants that require low humidities in open terrarium containers, dishes, or bowls.** For a particular miniature garden, all the plants chosen should require similar environmental conditions.

Terrarium and dish garden landscapes can be designed to resemble a natural scene or can be inspired by your imagination. Plants can be chosen that resemble trees, shrubs, and grass. Numerous artifacts, such as ceramic animals and bridges, are available to add points of interest to the landscape design. Deserts, temperate forests, tropical forests, and bog environments all can be created in terrariums.

To prepare a dish garden for planting, cover the container bottom with ½ to 1 inch of small pebbles for drainage. Then, add a thick layer of activated charcoal. Finally, add at least 2 inches of a commercial potting mix.

Terrariums can be constructed with or without 1 inch of drainage material in the bottom of the container. A good growth medium to accommodate most terrarium plants includes: 1/3 potting soil, 1/3 vermiculite, and 1/3 peat moss. Desert terrariums require a special medium: 1/3 vermiculite, 1/3 potting soil, 1/6 sand, and 1/6 peat moss.

The growth medium can be moistened in a plastic sack *before* or *after* it is placed in the container. Use simple tools to dig planting holes. Place the roots of each plant in a hole and tamp down the medium around the plant. Make sure that the roots make good contact with the growth medium. To plant terrarium bottles, it will be necessary to buy or make special tools to handle the plants through narrow bottlenecks.

If properly constructed, **terrariums and dish gardens require little maintenance.** Many pest problems can be avoided by selecting insect-free and disease-free plants and by planting them in a sterilized growth medium.

Don't overwater! Press your finger 1 inch into the growth medium. If the medium is moist at that level, water is not needed. Fertilizers are not needed since it is best that the plants remain small.

Prune out dead and dying plants parts and remove dead plants as necessary. Make your pruning cuts with a sharp knife or razor blade ¼ inch above the bud.

Most terrarium and dish garden plants grow best in indirect sunlight. Don't place closed containers in direct sunlight or the plants will cook. An exception is desert plants housed in open containers, which should be placed in direct sunlight.

Terrarium and dish gardens hold great fascination for children, who can learn much from watching plants develop before their eyes. Different growth environments (tropical, forest, desert, and bog) can be constructed and studied. Insect-eating plants are particularly fascinating to grow and observe.

Section One

THE CONTAINER

Containers around the House

Many dish garden and terrarium containers can be found around the house. Consider the following: beer mugs, apothecary jars, brandy snifters, cake covers, cheese dishes, cookie jars, decanters, fish bowls, fish tanks, flower vases, fruit jars, glass dishes, goblets, juice pitchers, lighting fixtures, mayonnaise jars, medicine bottles, vinegar jars, water bottles, and wine bottles.

✗   ✗   ✗

Combine Other Hobbies with Terrarium Making

Terrarium enthusiasts can combine other hobbies—such as macramé, glass cutting, making leaded glass, and ceramics—with terrarium making. Ceramic dishes and bowls make attractive bases for dome terrariums. Macramé for hanging terrariums is a natural. Leaded glass terrariums can be very elegant.

Clean Your Container Thoroughly

Some containers have residues on their surfaces that can harm plants. Wash your container thoroughly in warm soapy water. Dry it before planting. A clean container adds to the beauty of the final creation.

A Lamp Terrarium

Terrariums can be made functional as well as attractive. For example, bottle-type terrariums can be used as lamp bases. A large bottle can function in this manner if a hole is cut in the side to allow planting and maintenance. When choosing plants for a lamp terrarium, make sure that they can tolerate the light that the lamp will produce.

A Plexiglass Planter-Aquarium

If you are handy with plexiglass, you can make a great variety of ter-

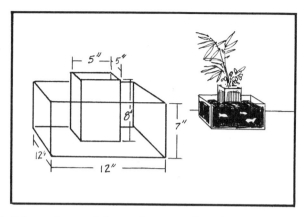

rarium and dish garden containers. An attractive plexiglass aquarium-planter can be made by following the design shown.

✔   ✔   ✔

Tank-Type Aquariums for Terrariums

Tank-type aquariums make excellent terrarium containers. Humidity can be regulated by covering or uncovering the top with a sheet of glass. Often, pet stores and department stores sell aquariums with slight defects at greatly reduced prices. Sealant or epoxy paint can be used to seal leaks.

✔   ✔   ✔

Pots in Terrariums

The terrarium environment is ideal for the care of some potted plants. High humidities are maintained and the plants are protected against drafts and dust. By placing potted plants in tank-type terrarium containers, they will reap the benefits of a terrarium environment. This combination is also pleasing aesthetically. Place gravel in the bottom of the terrarium container to support the pots. The gravel will accommodate excess water and will be decorative. Plants which would do well in such an environment include African violets, *Episcia, Marchantia,* and *Calodium.*

✔   ✔   ✔

Terrarium Kits

Terrarium kits of various sorts are available commercially. They are useful as gifts to introduce a friend to a possible new hobby. However, it is generally less expensive to buy the components of a terrarium separately.

✔   ✔   ✔

Tinted Glass for Terrarium Containers

Plants will grow in terrarium containers made of slightly tinted glass. However, because of the reduced light that is available to plants in such containers, choose shade-loving plants. Make sure to pick plants with bold leaves or interesting foliage that will be observable through the tinted glass.

✔   ✔   ✔

A Simple Hanging Terrarium

Hanging plants are popular these days, but perhaps you haven't seen a hanging terrarium. A simple way to make one is to turn a globular fish bowl on its side and hang it in a macramé sling. Plants can be grown in the container, and ivies can be trained downward out of the opening.

Environmental Compatibility Chart

The environmental compatibility chart which follows will give you a quick indication of the environmental requirements of those plants that are most commonly used in terrariums. The chart is arranged according to each plant's Latin name. If you know the Latin name, proceed directly to the chart. If you only know the plant's common name, the listing below will enable you to determine the correct Latin name.

Temperature is divided into three categories. *Warm* means that the plant prefers temperatures which range to 80-85 degrees during the day and 62-65 degrees at night. *Temperate* plants like temperatures in the 65-70 degree range during the day and 50-55 degrees at night. Plants labeled *cool* will do well in temperatures of 55-60 degrees during the day provided that there is sufficient sunlight, and 40-45 degrees at night.

Humidity requirements are broken into high, intermediate, and low. The conditions for *high* humidity can be created by completely enclosing the terrarium; a partially open terrarium will provide *intermediate* humidity conditions; and a completely open container will provide *low* humidity conditions.

Light requirements are classified as *bright* (full sun), *filtered* (indirect sunlight), and *shade* (away from the sun).

This chart can also be used for information about houseplants.

COMMON NAME	SCIENTIFIC NAME	COMMON NAME	SCIENTIFIC NAME
AFRICAN BOXWOOD	*Myrsine africana*	CONE PLANT	*Conophytum aureum*
ALUMINUM PLANT	*Pilea cadierei minima*	CORAL-BEAD PLANT	*Nertera depressa*
ARTILLERY PLANT	*Pilea microphylla*	CORAL BERRY	*Ardisia crispa*
ASPARAGUS FERN	*Asparagus plumosus*	CORKSCREW PLANT	*Pandanus veitchii*
AUSTRALIAN SILK OAK	*Grevillea robusta*	CREEPING CHARLIE	*Pilea nummulariifolia*
BABY SMILAX	*Asparagus asparagoides myrtifolius*	CREEPING PEPEROMIA	*Peperomia fosteriana*
BABY'S TEARS	*Helxine soleirolii*	CROTON	*Codiaeum variegatum pictum*
BARREL CACTUS	*Echinocactus ingens*	CURIOSITY CACTUS	*Cereus peruvianus*
BASKETBALL PLANT	*Euphorbia obesa*	CYCLAMEN	*Cyclamen coum*
BEAD PLANT	*Nertera grandadensis*	DEVIL-IVY	*Scindapsus aureus*
BEARD TONGUE	*Penstemon rupicola*	DWARF BALSAM FIR	*Abies balsamea nana*
BELLFLOWER	*Campanula*	DWARF CENTURY PLANT	*Agave filifera senilis*
BIRDSNEST SANSIVIERIA	*Sansevieria trifasciata 'Hahnii'*	DWARF CLUB MOSS	*Selaginella kraussiana brownii*
BISHOP'S CAP	*Astrophytum myriostigma*	DWARF GLOXINIA	*Sinningia concinna*
BLEEDING HEART	*Clerodendrum thomsoniae*	DWARF KANGAROO IVY	*Cissus antartica 'Minima'*
BLOODLEAF	*Iresine herbstii*	DWARF MAIDENHAIR FERN	*Adiantum hispidulum*
BLOOD ROOT	*Sanguinaria canadensis*	DWARF MYRTLE	*Myrtus communis microphylla*
BLUE CHALK STICK	*Kleinia repens*	DWARF PERIWINKLE	*Vinca minor*
BLUE CLUB MOSS	*Selaginella erythropus*	DWARF POMEGRANATE	*Punica granatum nana*
BOX-LEAF EUONYMUS	*Euonymus japonicus microphyllus*	DWARF SPIDER PLANT	*Chlorophytum bichetii*
BRAWN'S CREEPING CLUB MOSS	*Selaginella kraussiana*	DWARF STRAP FERN	*Polypodium lycopodioides*
BRILLIANT STAR	*Kalanchoe blossfeldiana*	EASTER LILY CACTUS	*Echinopsis multiplex*
BRITTLE FERN	*Cystopteris fragilis*	EBONY SPLEENWORT	*Asplenium platyneuron*
BROMELIAD	*Aechmea chantinii*	EMERALD IDOL	*Opuntia cylindrica*
BUGLE WEED	*Ajuga reptans*	EMERALD RIPPLE PEPEROMIA	*Peperomia caperata*
BUNCHBERRY	*Cornus canadensis*	ENGLISH IVY	*Hedra helix*
BUNNY EARS	*Opuntia microdasys*	FALSE CYPRESS	*Chamaecyparis*
BUTTERWORT	*Pinguicula lutea*	FALSE HOLLY	*Osmanthus ilicifolius variegatus*
BUTTON FERN	*Pellaea rotundifolia*	FEATHER CACTUS	*Mammillaria plumosa*
CALADIUM	*Caladium humboldtii*	FERN PINE	*Podocarpus gracilior*
CALICO HEARTS	*Adromischus clavifolius*	FIG	*Ficus pumila minima*
CAST IRON PLANT	*Aspidistra elatior*	FIRECRACKER VINE	*Manettia bicolor*
CHALK CANDLE	*Lemaireocereus beneckei*	FIRE FERN	*Oxalis hedysaroides rubra*
CHINESE EVERGREEN	*Aglaonema commutatum*	FITTONIA	*Fittonia verschaffeltii*
CLUB MOSS	*Selaginella uninata*	FLAME VIOLET	*Episcia cupreata*
CLUB MOSS CRASSULA	*Crassula lycopodioides*	FLAMINGO FLOWER	*Anthurium scherzerianum*
CLUSTERING CACTUS	*Gymnocalycium brichi*	FLOATING FERN	*Salvinia auriculata*
COBRA PLANT	*Arisaema tortuosum*	FLOATING MOSS	*Azolla caroliniana*
COBRA PLANT	*Darlingtonia californica*	FRECKLE FACE	*Hypoestes sanguinolenta*
COFFEE TREE	*Coffea arabica*	GASTERIA	*Gasteria hybrida*
COLEUS	*Coleus rehneltianus*	GOLD DUST PLANT	*Aucuba japonica 'variegata'*
COLUMNAR CRASSULA	*Crassula columnaris*	GOLD DUST PLANT	*Codiaeum aucubaefolium*
COMMON PIPSISSEWA	*Chimaphila umbellata*	GOLDFISH PLANT	*Hypocyrna nummularia*

COMMON NAME	SCIENTIFIC NAME	COMMON NAME	SCIENTIFIC NAME
GOLD THREAD	Coptis groeolandica	RAINBOW CACTUS	Echinocereus dusyocathus
GRAND LEAF PILEA	Pilea grandis	RAINBOW PLANT	Ctenanthe tricolor
GRAPE IVY	Cissus striata	RAINBOW VINE	Pellionia pulchra
GREEN BURRO TAIL	Sedum rubrutinetum	RATTLESNAKE CRASSULA	Crassula teres
GREEN CARPET PLANT	Herniaria glabra	RATTLESNAKE PLANTAIN	Goodyera pubescens
HARTS TONGUE FERN	Phyllitis scolopendrium cristatum	RED FLOWERING CRASSULA	Crassula schmidtii
HEDGE FERN	Polystichum tsus-sinense	RESURRECTION FERN	Polypodium polypodioides
HEMLOCK	Tsuga canadensis	ROCK POLYPODY	Polypodium virginianum
HOLLY FERN	Cyrtomium falcatum	SAGO PALM	Cycas revoluta
HOUSELEEK	Semperivum calcareum	SCREW PINE	Pandanus utilis
HUNTER'S HORN	Sarracenia	SCRUBBY YEW PINE	Pandanus macrophyllus maki
INDIAN HEAD	Notocactus ottonis	SEERSUCKER PLANT	Geogenanthus undatus
INDOOR OAK	Nicodemia diversifolia	SENSITIVE PLANT	Mimosa pudica
IRISH SHAMROCK	Trifolium repens minus	SHINLEAF OR WINTERGREEN	Pyrola elliptica
IVY PEPEROMIA	Peperomia griseo argentea	SICKLE-THORN ASPARAGUS	Asparagus falcatus
JACK-IN-THE-PULPIT	Arisaema triphyllum	SILVER LACE	Pteris quadriaurita 'Argyraea'
JADE NECKLACE	Crassula 'Mamieriana hybrid'	SNOWBERRY	Chiogenes hispidula
JADE PLANT	Crassula arborescens	SPANISH SHAWL	Schizocentron elegans
JAPANESE ARALIA	Fatsia (Arabic) japonica	SPIDER PLANT	Chlorophytum cosmosum vittatum
JEWEL PLANT	Pachyveria haegei	STAR PLANT	Cryptanthus acaulis
JOSEPH'S COAT	Alternanthera bettzichiana	ST. AUGUSTINE GRASS	Stenotaprum sedundatum variegatum
KENILWORTH IVY	Cymbalaria muralis	STONE FACE	Lithops bella
LEMON BALL	Notocactus lninghausi	STRAWBERRY BEGONIA	Saxifraga sarmentosa
LILY-TURF	Ophiopogon joburan	STRIPED PIPSISSEWA	Chimophila maculata
LIVERWORT	Marchantia polymorpha	SUNDEW	Drosera filiformis
MAIDENHAIR FERN	Adiantum cuneatum	SUNDEW	Drosera rotundifolia
MAIDENHAIR FERN	Adiantum bellum	SWEAT PLANT	Selaginella emmeliana
MAIDENHAIR SPLEENWORT	Asplenium trichomones	SWEDISH IVY	Plectranthus australis
MEXICAN FIRECRACKER	Echeveria setosa	SWEDISH IVY	Plectranthus oertendahli
MEXICAN FOXGLOVE	Allophyton mexicanum	SWEET BOX	Sarcococca ruscifolia
MEXICAN SNOWBALL	Echeveria elegans	SWEET FLAG	Acorus gramineus pusillus
MINIATURE BAMBOO	Bambusa multiplex	SWEET OLIVE	Osmanthus fragrans
MINIATURE FERN	Polystichun tsus-sinense	SWEET VIOLET	Viola odorata
MINIATURE HOLLY	Malpighia coccigera	SWORD FERN	Nephrolepis exaltata
MINIATURE PILEA	Pilea depressa	TABLE OR BRAKE FERN	Pteris cretica wilsonii
MINIATURE WANDERING JEW	Tripogandra multiflora	TABLE FERN	Pteris tremula
MINIATURE WAX PLANT	Hoya chaffa	TIGER JAW	Faucaria tigrina
MING ARALIA	Polyscias fruticosa 'Elegans'	TIGER JAWS	Aloe brevifolia
MISTLETOE FIG	Ficus diversifolia	TOUCH-ME-NOT (BALSAM)	Impatiens walleriana
NEEDLE HAWORTHIA	Haworthia radula	TRAILING ARBUTUS	Epigea repens
NEPHTHYTIS	Syngonium podophyllum	UMBRELLA PLANT	Cyperus alternifolius
NORFOLK ISLAND PINE	Arancaria excelsa	VELVET PLANT	Gynura auranthiaca
OLD MAN CACTUS	Cephalocereus senilis	VENUS FLYTRAP	Dionaea muscipula
ORANGE GLORY	Crossandra infundibuliformis	VICTORIA FERN	Pteris ensiformis 'Victoriae'
PAINTED LADY	Echeveria derenbergii	VOGEL CLUB MOSS	Selaginella vogeli
PANAMIGA	Pilea involverata	WALKING FERN	Adiantum caudatum
PANDA PLANT	Kalanchoe tomentosa	WALLIEH CLUB MOSS	Selaginella wallichi
PARROT'S FEATHER	Myriophyllum proserpinacordes	WANDERING JEW	Zebrina pendula
PARTRIDGE BERRY	Mitchella repens	WART PLANT	Haworthia 'Margaritifera'
PARTRIDGE BREAST	Aloe variegata	WATER CLOVER	Marsilea
PEANUT CACTUS	Chamaecereus silvestri	WATERCRESS	Nasturtium officinale
PEARLY DOTS	Haworthia papillosa	WATERMELON PEPEROMIA	Peperomia sandersii
PEPPER FACE	Peperomia obtusifolia variegata	WATER LETTUCE	Pistia statiotes
PHILODENDRON	Philodendron adreanum	WATER PENNYWORT	Hydrocotyle rotundifolli
PIGGY-BACK PLANT	Tolmiea menziesii	WATER POPPY	Hydrocleys commersonii
PIGMY DATE PALM	Phoenix roebelenii	WAXLEAF PRIVET	Ligustrum japonicum 'Texanum'
PINK LADY-SLIPPER ORCHID	Cypripedium acaule	WAX PLANT	Hoya carnosa
PITCHER PLANT	Nepenthes; sarracenia; Darlingtonia	WHORLED HAWORTHIA	Haworthia limefolia
PLAIN CACTUS	Gymnocalyirum mihanovichii	WILD GINGER	Asarum shuttleworth
POWDERPUFF CACTUS	Mammillaria bocasana	WINDOWED HAWORTHIA	Haworthia cymbiformis
PRAYER PLANT	Maranta leuconeura kerchoveana	WOOD ANEMONE	Anemone quinquefolia
PROPELLER PLANT	Crassula perfossa	WOOD BETONY	Pedicularia canodensis
PURPLE HEDGE HOG	Echinocereus purpureus	WOOD FERN	Dryopteris erythrosora
PURPLE-LEAVED SWEDISH IVY	Plectranthus purpuratus	YEW	Taxus
PUSSYTOES	Antennaria	ZEBRA HAWORTHIA	Haworthia fasciata
PYRAMIDAL CRASSULA (Large)	Crassula pyramidalis	ZEBRA PLANT	Aphelandra squarrosa 'louisae'
PYRAMID CRASSULA	Crassula imperialis		

Environmental Compatibility Chart

SCIENTIFIC NAME	Creeping	Grasslike	Shrublike	Treelike	Succulent	Flowering	Desert	Trop. Forest	Temp. Forest	Bog	Cool	Temperate	Warm	Low	Intermediate	High	Shade	Filtered	Bright
	Growth Habit						**Ecosystem**				**Temperature**			**Humidity**			**Light**		
Abies balsamea nana				•					•										
Acorus gramineus pusillus	•							•	•	•	•				•			•	
Acorus gramineus variegatus	•							•	•	•	•					•		•	
Adiantum bellum			•						•				•			•		•	
Adiantum caudatum			•						•				•			•		•	
Adiantum cuneatum			•						•				•			•		•	
Adiantum hispidulum			•						•				•		•			•	
Adromischus clavifolius					•		•						•	•					•
Aechmea chantinii		•						•	•				•	•	•			•	
Agave filifera senilis					•		•						•	•					•
Aglaonema commutatum			•					•	•				•	•	•		•	•	
Aglaonema modestum			•					•	•				•	•	•		•	•	
Aglaonema pictum			•					•	•				•	•	•		•	•	
Aglaonema treubii			•					•	•				•	•	•		•	•	
Ajuga reptans	•							•	•		•				•			•	
Allophyton mexicanum		•							•		•				•			•	
Aloe brevifolia					•		•						•	•					•
Aloe variegata					•		•						•	•					•
Alternanthera bettzichiana		•							•				•	•			•		
Anemone quinquefolia						•			•		•				•			•	
Anthurium crystallinum			•					•					•		•		•		
Anthurium scherzerianum			•					•					•		•		•		
Aphelandra squarrosa			•					•					•	•				•	
Araucaria excelsa			•					•	•				•	•				•	
Ardisia crenata		•				•		•	•		•				•			•	
Ardisia crispa		•						•	•		•				•			•	
Arisaema tortuosum						•			•			•			•			•	
Arisaema triphyllum						•			•		•				•			•	
Asarum shuttleworth						•			•		•				•			•	
Asparagus asparagoides myrtifolius	•							•	•			•			•			•	
Asparagus densiflorus			•					•	•			•			•			•	
Asparagus falcatus	•							•	•			•			•			•	
Asparagus japonica			•					•	•			•			•			•	

Groups — **Growth Habit:** Creeping, Grasslike, Shrublike, Treelike, Succulent, Flowering · **Ecosystem:** Desert, Trop. Forest, Temp. Forest, Bog · **Temperature:** Cool, Temperate, Warm · **Humidity:** Low, Intermediate, High · **Light:** Shade, Filtered, Bright

Species	Creeping	Grasslike	Shrublike	Treelike	Succulent	Flowering	Desert	Trop. Forest	Temp. Forest	Bog	Cool	Temperate	Warm	Low	Intermediate	High	Shade	Filtered	Bright
Asparagus plumosus			•					•	•		•				•				•
Aspidistra elatior			•					•	•		•				•			•	•
Asplenium			•						•		•					•		•	
Asplenium buliferum			•					•			•					•		•	
Asplenium trichomones			•						•		•					•		•	
Astrophytum myriostigma					•		•					•			•				•
Aucuba japonica 'Variegata'			•					•				•				•			•
Azolla caroliniana	•									•	•				•			•	•
Bambusa multiplex nana				•				•	•		•	•			•				•
Begonia						•		•				•			•				•
Bertolonia maculata			•					•				•				•		•	
Buxus microphylla japonica			•						•		•				•				•
Caladium humboldtii			•					•				•				•			•
Calathea picturata argentea			•					•				•				•			•
Campanula						•			•		•				•				•
Cephalocereus senilis					•		•					•			•				•
Cereus peruvianus					•		•					•			•				•
Chamaecereus silvestrii					•		•				•				•				•
Chamaecyparis			•					•			•					•			•
Chimaphila maculata	•								•		•				•				•
Chimaphila umbellata	•								•		•				•				•
Chlorophytum bichetii	•							•			•				•				•
Chlorophytum cosmosum vittatum	•							•			•				•				•
Cissus antartica 'Minima'	•							•					•			•			•
Cissus striata	•							•					•			•			•
Cleistocactus strausii					•		•				•				•				•
Clerodendrum thomsoniae						•		•					•		•				•
Codiaeum aucubaefolium			•					•	•			•			•				•
Codiaeum variegatum pictum			•					•	•			•			•				•
Coffea arabica			•					•	•			•			•				•
Coleus rehneltianus	•							•	•			•			•				•
Columnea hirta						•		•				•	•			•			•
Columnea microphylla						•		•				•	•			•			•
Conophytum aureum					•		•					•			•				•

	Growth Habit						Ecosystem				Temperature			Humidity			Light		
	Creeping	Grasslike	Shrublike	Treelike	Succulent	Flowering	Desert	Trop. Forest	Temp. Forest	Bog	Cool	Temperate	Warm	Low	Intermediate	High	Shade	Filtered	Bright
Coptis groeolandica	•									•	•				•		•		
Coptis trifolia	•								•		•				•		•		
Cornus canadensis						•			•		•				•		•		
Cotyledon teretifolia					•		•						•	•					•
Crassula arborescens				•	•		•						•	•					•
Crassula columnaris					•		•						•	•					•
Crassula cooperi					•		•						•	•					•
Crassula imperialis					•		•						•	•					•
Crassula lycopodioides					•		•						•	•					•
Crassula mamieriana hybrid					•		•						•	•					•
Crassula perfossa					•		•						•	•					•
Crassula pyramidalis					•		•						•	•					•
Crassula schmidtii					•		•						•	•					•
Crassula teres					•		•						•	•					•
Crossandra infundibuliformis		•						•					•			•	•		
Ctenanthe opperheimiana			•					•					•			•	•		
Ctenanthe opperheimiana tricolor		•						•					•			•	•		
Cuphea hyssopifolia			•						•		•				•				•
Cycas revoluta			•				•	•			•				•		•		
Cyclamen coum						•	•	•			•				•		•		
Cymbalaria aequitriloba	•						•	•			•				•		•		
Cymbalaria muralis	•							•			•				•		•		
Cyperus alternifolius			•							•	•				•		•		
Cryptanthus acaulis		•					•					•				•	•		
Cryptanthus zonatus 'Zebrinus'							•					•				•	•		
Cypripedium acaule						•			•		•	•		•	•		•		
Cypripedium pubescens						•		•	•			•		•	•		•		
Cyrtomium falcatum				•					•		•				•				•
Cystopteris fragilis				•					•			•			•				•
Darlingtonia californica				•					•	•	•					•	•	•	
Dionaea muscipula		•							•	•	•	•			•				•
Dracaena fragrans	•							•	•				•		•			•	
Dracaena godsettiana	•							•	•				•		•			•	
Dracaena sanderiana	•							•	•				•		•			•	

	Growth Habit						Ecosystem				Temperature			Humidity			Light		
	Creeping	Grasslike	Shrublike	Treelike	Succulent	Flowering	Desert	Trop. Forest	Temp. Forest	Bog	Cool	Temperate	Warm	Low	Intermediate	High	Shade	Filtered	Bright
Drosera filiformis			●							●	●	●			●				●
Drosera rotundifolia			●							●	●	●			●				●
Dryopteris erythrosora				●					●			●			●			●	●
Echeveria derenbergii					●		●						●		●				●
Echeveria elegans					●		●						●		●				●
Echeveria setosa					●		●						●		●				●
Echinocactus ingens					●		●						●		●				●
Echinocereus dasyacathus					●		●						●		●				●
Echinocereus purpureus					●		●						●		●				●
Echinopsis multiplex					●		●						●		●				●
Epigea repens	●								●		●	●			●			●	●
Episcia cupreata	●							●					●		●			●	
Episcia dianthiflora	●							●					●		●			●	
Euonymus fortunei uncinatus	●								●	●	●				●			●	
Euonymus japonicus medio-pictus			●						●	●	●				●			●	
Euonymus japonicus microphyllus			●						●	●	●				●			●	
Euphorbia 'Bojeri'				●			●						●		●				●
Euphorbia obesa					●		●						●		●				●
Exacum affine			●					●					●			●		●	
Fatsia japonica				●					●		●				●			●	
Faucaria tigrina					●		●						●		●				●
Ficus diversifolia				●				●					●			●		●	
Ficus pumila minima				●				●					●			●		●	
Fittonia verschaffeltii				●				●					●			●		●	
Gasteria hybrida					●		●						●		●				●
Gasteria lilliputana					●		●						●		●				●
Geogenanthus undatus			●										●			●		●	
Goodyera pubescens		●							●	●	●					●		●	
Gymnocalycium brichi					●		●				●				●				●
Gymnocalycium mihanovichii					●		●				●				●				●
Gynura auranthiaca				●				●	●				●		●				●
Haworthia cymbiformis					●		●						●	●				●	
Haworthia fasciata					●		●						●	●				●	
Haworthia limifolia					●		●						●		●			●	

	Growth Habit						Ecosystem				Temperature			Humidity			Light		
	Creeping	Grasslike	Shrublike	Treelike	Succulent	Flowering	Desert	Trop. Forest	Temp. Forest	Bog	Cool	Temperate	Warm	Low	Intermediate	High	Shade	Filtered	Bright
Haworthia 'Margaritifera'					•		•						•	•				•	
Haworthia papillosa					•		•						•	•				•	
Haworthia radula					•		•						•	•				•	
Haworthia tessellata					•		•						•	•				•	
Hedra helix	•								•	•	•				•				•
Helxine soleirolii	•								•				•			•	•		
Hepatica americana						•			•		•				•		•		
Herniaria glabra	•								•				•			•	•		
Hoya carnosa			•						•	•			•	•					•
Hoya chaffa			•						•	•			•	•					•
Hydrocleys commersonii						•				•			•			•	•		
Hydrocotyle rotundifolia										•	•					•	•		
Hypocyrta numnularia	•								•				•			•	•		
Hypoestes sanguinolenta			•						•	•			•		•		•		
Impatiens walleriana						•			•				•		•				•
Iresine herbstii			•						•		•				•				•
Juniperus			•						•		•				•		•		
Kalanchoe blossfeldiana					•		•						•	•					•
Kalanchoe pumila					•		•						•	•					•
Kalanchoe tomentosa					•		•						•	•					•
Kleinia mandraliscae					•		•						•	•					•
Kleinia repens					•		•						•	•					•
Kohleria amabilis						•	•						•			•	•		
Lemaireocereus beneckei					•		•						•	•					•
Ligustrum japonicum 'texanum'			•						•		•			•					•
Lithops bella					•		•						•	•	•				•
Malpighia coccigera		•						•					•	•					•
Mammillaria bocasana					•		•						•	•	•				•
Mammillaria elongata					•		•						•	•	•				•
Mammillaria plumosa					•		•						•	•					•
Manettia bicolor	•									•			•	•			•		
Maranta leuconeura kerchoveana		•							•				•			•	•		
Marchantia polymorpha	•									•	•					•		•	
Marsilea		•								•			•			•	•		

	Growth Habit						Ecosystem				Temperature			Humidity			Light		
	Creeping	Grasslike	Shrublike	Treelike	Succulent	Flowering	Desert	Trop. Forest	Temp. Forest	Bog	Cool	Temperate	Warm	Low	Intermediate	High	Shade	Filtered	Bright
Mimosa pudica					●			●					●			●	●		
Mitchella repens	●								●	●	●			●			●		
Myrsine africana			●						●			●		●					●
Myrsine nummularia			●						●			●		●					●
Myrtillocactus cochal					●		●					●		●					●
Myrtus communis microphylla			●						●			●		●					●
Nasturtium officinale	●									●	●				●		●		
Nepenthes										●			●		●		●		
Nertera depressa	●								●		●					●	●		
Nertera grandadensis	●								●		●			●					●
Nephrolepis exaltata			●						●			●		●			●		
Nicodemia diversifolia			●						●				●	●					●
Notocactus leninghausi					●		●					●		●					●
Notocactus ottonis			●				●					●		●					●
Ophiopogon joburan		●							●			●		●					●
Opuntia cylindrica					●		●					●		●					●
Opuntia microdasys					●		●					●		●					●
Osmanthus fragrans			●						●		●			●					●
Osmanthus ilicifolius variegatus			●						●		●			●					●
Oxalis hedysaroides rubra			●						●		●			●					●
Oxalis henrei	●								●		●			●					●
Oxalis martiana 'aurfo-reticulata'	●								●		●			●					●
Pachyveria haegei					●		●						●	●					●
Pandanus utilis	●												●	●			●		
Pandanus veitchii	●												●	●			●		
Pedicularia canadensis						●			●		●			●			●		
Pelargonium						●			●		●			●			●		
Pellaea rotundifolia				●			●					●			●			●	●
Pellionia daveauana	●							●					●			●	●		
Pellionia pulchra	●							●					●			●	●		
Pellionia repens	●							●					●			●	●		
Penstemon rupicola						●			●		●			●					●
Peperomia bicolor			●					●	●				●	●			●		
Peperomia caperata			●					●	●				●	●			●		

	Growth Habit						Ecosystem				Temperature			Humidity			Light		
	Creeping	Grasslike	Shrublike	Treelike	Succulent	Flowering	Desert	Trop. Forest	Temp. Forest	Bog	Cool	Temperate	Warm	Low	Intermediate	High	Bright	Filtered	Shade
Peperomia fosteriana	•							•	•				•		•				•
Peperomia griseo argentea	•							•	•				•		•				•
Peperomia incana			•				•						•		•				•
Peperomia magnoliaefoliae			•					•	•				•		•				•
Peperomia marnorata					•			•	•				•		•				•
Peperomia metallica					•			•	•				•		•				•
Peperomia obtusifolia			•					•	•				•		•				•
Peperomia obtusifolia variegata			•					•	•				•		•				•
Peperomia ornata					•			•	•				•		•				•
Peperomia nummularifolia	•							•	•				•		•				•
Peperomia rubella			•					•	•				•		•				•
Peperomia sandersii			•					•	•				•		•				•
Peperomia verticillata			•					•	•				•		•				•
Philodendron adreanum			•					•	•				•		•				•
Philodendron micans	•							•	•				•		•				•
Philodendron sodiroi					•			•	•				•		•				•
Philodendron verrucosum					•			•	•				•		•			•	
Phoenix roebelenii					•			•	•				•		•			•	
Phyllitis scolopendrium cristatum					•			•	•		•					•		•	•
Pilea cadierei minima			•					•	•				•		•				•
Pilea depressa	•							•	•				•		•				•
Pilea involverata			•					•	•				•		•				•
Pilea grandis			•					•	•				•		•				•
Pilea microphylla			•					•	•				•		•				•
Pilea nummularifolia	•							•	•				•		•				•
Pilea serpillacea					•								•		•				•
Pinguicula lutea										•	•					•	•	•	
Pistia statiotes	•									•			•			•	•		
Pittosporum tobira				•				•	•			•			•				•
Plectranthus australis	•							•	•			•			•			•	
Plectranthus oertendahli	•								•			•			•			•	
Plectranthus purpuratus	•								•			•			•			•	
Podocarpus gracilior				•				•	•			•			•				•
Podocarpus macrophylla Maki				•				•	•			•			•				•

	Growth Habit						Ecosystem				Temperature			Humidity			Light		
	Creeping	Grasslike	Shrublike	Treelike	Succulent	Flowering	Desert	Trop. Forest	Temp. Forest	Bog	Cool	Temperate	Warm	Low	Intermediate	High	Shade	Filtered	Bright
Polypodium virginianum			●						●		●				●		●		
Polyscias filicifolia			●						●			●			●			●	
Polyscias fruticosa 'elegans'			●						●			●			●			●	
Polyscias quilfoylei victoriae			●						●			●			●			●	
Polystichum tsus-sinense			●						●		●				●			●	
Pteris cretica albo-lineata			●						●			●			●			●	
Pteris cretica wilsonii			●						●			●			●			●	
Pteris ensiformis 'Victoriae'			●						●			●			●			●	
Pteris quadriaurita 'Argyraea'			●						●			●			●			●	
Pteris tremula			●						●			●			●			●	
Punica granatum nana			●						●				●		●			●	
Pyrola elliptica						●			●		●				●		●		
Rebutia kupperiana					●		●					●			●				●
Rebutia senilis crestata					●		●					●			●				●
Rosa chinensis						●			●			●			●				●
Ruellia makoyana	●								●			●			●		●		
Salvinia auriculata	●									●			●			●			●
Sansevieria trifasciata 'Hahnii'		●							●				●		●		●		
Saintpaulia ionantha						●			●				●		●		●		
Sanguinaria canadensis						●			●		●				●		●		
Sarracenia										●	●					●		●	
Saxifraga sarmentosa	●								●		●					●		●	
Scilla violacea						●			●			●				●	●		
Scindapsus (Pathos) aureus	●								●				●		●		●		
Scindapsus pictus	●								●				●		●		●		
Sedum adolphii					●		●					●			●				●
Sedum confusum					●		●					●			●				●
Sedum jepsonii					●		●					●		●					●
Sedum kraussiana brownii					●		●					●			●				●
Sedum lineare variegata					●		●					●			●				●
Sedum multiceps					●		●					●			●				●
Sedum rubrutinetum					●		●					●			●				●
Sedum spurium					●		●					●			●				●
Selaginella emmeliana	●								●	●	●	●				●		●	

Species	\	Growth Habit \	\	\	\	\	\	Ecosystem \	\	\	\	Temperature \	\	\	Humidity \	\	\	Light \	\
	Creeping	Grasslike	Shrublike	Treelike	Succulent	Flowering	Desert	Trop. Forest	Temp. Forest	Bog	Cool	Temperate	Warm	Low	Intermediate	High	Shade	Filtered	Bright
Selaginella erythropus	•								•	•			•			•	•		
Selaginella kraussiana	•								•	•		•	•			•	•		
Selaginella uninata	•								•	•		•	•			•	•		
Selaginella vogeli	•								•	•		•	•			•	•		
Selaginella wallichi	•								•	•		•	•			•	•		
Semperivum calcareum					•		•				•			•					•
Sarcococca ruscifolia		•							•				•	•			•		
Siderasis fuscata		•							•				•		•		•		
Sinningia concinna						•			•				•	•			•		
Sinningia pusilla						•			•				•	•			•		
Stenotaptrum sedundatum variegatum	•								•			•		•					•
Streptocarpus rexii						•			•			•				•	•		
Streptocarpus saxorum						•			•			•				•	•		
Syngonium erythophyllum			•						•				•	•				•	
Syngonium podophyllum			•					•	•				•	•				•	
Tillandsia ionantha	•						•					•				•		•	
Tolmiea menziesii		•							•			•		•			•		
Tradescantia flumensis 'variegata'	•								•			•		•			•		
Trifolium repens minus	•								•		•			•					•
Trillium grandiforum						•			•		•			•			•		
Trillium undulatum						•			•		•			•			•		
Tripogandra multiflora	•								•				•	•			•		
Tsuga canadensis				•					•		•			•			•		
Vinca minor						•			•		•			•			•		
Viola odorata						•			•		•			•					•
Viola orbiculata						•			•		•			•					•
Zebrina pendula	•								•			•		•				•	

Section Two

PLANT SELECTION

Quarantine Your New Plants

If you plan on extensive terrarium and dish gardening, it would be wise to designate one large terrarium as a "quarantine." As you purchase new plants, place them under quarantine for a month or so and watch for the development of disease and insect pests. The high humidity of an enclosed terrarium will greatly accelerate disease and insect development. This will enable you to identify and eliminate any pest-ridden plants before they affect an entire terrarium.

✓ ✓ ✓

Clean Nurseries Mean Clean Plants

If the outlet from which you obtain your plants practices good sanitation, you are less apt to have pest problems with your plants. Inspect the nursery or other plant outlet before buying. Is there a general air of cleanliness? Are the plants vigorous, properly watered, and neatly arranged? If the answer is affirmative, the odds are that good sanitation is being practiced. If dead or dying plants are for sale, or if soil is scattered around and a general air of uncleanliness exists, there is a good possibility that the plants will have disease or insect problems.

✓ ✓ ✓

Bring Your Container When Shopping for Plants

If you have already chosen your container, take it along when you shop for plants. This will make it easier to choose the number and size of plants that can be accommodated by the container.

✓ ✓ ✓

Flowering Plants for Terrariums

Flowering plants add much to the attractiveness of terrariums. The African violet is one of the flowering plants best adapted to terrarium environments. They can be grown in almost completely closed terrariums, or in completely closed terrariums if the lid is removed periodically for ventilation. Ventilation is necessary to control excessive accumulation of moisture on the foliage and, thereby, to prevent disease.

✓ ✓ ✓

Bromeliads for Terrariums and Dish Gardens

The best bromeliads for terrariums and dish gardens are those forming compact, low rosettes of stiff colorful foliage. Try *Cryptanthus bivittatus minor,* a 3- to 6-inch rosette with pink overtones and white stripes on spring leaves. Another bromeliad that makes a good terrarium plant for an uncovered container is the 2- to 4-inch dwarf *Tillandsia ionantha.*

✓   ✓   ✓

Native Plants for Terrarium and Dish Gardens

Native woodland plants can be collected and grown in temperate forest terrariums. Some good plants to collect are: Jack in the pulpit, bluebell, pipsissewa, spring beauty, trailing arbutus, checkerberry, partridge berry, Solomon's seal, and wild violets.

✓   ✓   ✓

Plants Requiring Low Light

If your terrarium or dish garden is going to be placed in a low light area, such as in the darker corners of a room, or if your container has tinted glass, choose low-light plants. Some good examples are: *Aglaonema, Chamoedorea, Dracanea, Philodendron, Sansevieria, Scindapsus,* and *Syngonium.*

✓   ✓   ✓

Orchids for Terrariums

A variety of miniature orchids are beautiful when displayed in terrariums. Recommended are: *Angraecum falcatum, Bulbophyllum barbigerum, Cirrhopetalum cumingii, Ornithochallis chrysantha,* and *Resptrepia elegans.* The following jewel or gold lace orchids are also recommended: *Haemaria, Anoectochilus, Goodyearea, Microstylis, Erythrodes,* and *Macodes.*

✓   ✓   ✓

Succulents Add to Desert Landscapes

Cacti are "stiff" plants with geometrical shapes. The addition of other succulents to desert landscapes tends to soften the sharp lines and make the landscape more appealing. Try varieties of *Crassula, Echeveria, Sedum,* and *Haworthia.*

✓   ✓   ✓

Plants for a Bottle Terrarium

Plants in a bottle terrarium need to be relatively carefree because they are difficult to manipulate once they have been planted. The following are recommended: baby tears, dwarf palm, prayer plant, peperomia, umbrella sedge, and Chinese evergreen.

✓   ✓   ✓

Good Ground Cover Plants

A terrarium landscape appears more natural if ground cover plants are used to fill in the bare spots between the plants. Some good candidates are: *Helxine soleirolii, Pellionia davesuana, Episcia dianthiflora, Ficus pumila minima, Peperomia nummularifolia, Pilea depressa,* and *Selaginella.*

✓   ✓   ✓

Animals for Your Terrarium

Although animals are generally destructive to terrarium plants, some can be managed in the miniworld of terrariums. Horned toads and geckos live in relative harmony with desert plants. Chameleons, salamanders and turtles can be added to tropical terrariums. Newts and wood toads will survive in temperate forest terrariums. *Remember:* animals need a source of water and food.

Section Three

THE GROWTH MEDIUM

The Amount of Growth Medium Needed

A good rule of thumb for planting terrariums that are largely enclosed is to allot one quarter of the space for the growth medium and drainage material. For example, a 12-inch bottle should contain 3 inches of growth medium and drainage material. Open terrariums and dish gardens should have 50% to 75% of their space occupied by planting material.

✓   ✓   ✓

Purchase Sterilized Soil

Sterilizing your own soil can be difficult and burdensome. Purchasing pre-sterilized soil is an easy solution. Most garden centers sell pre-sterilized growth media for various types of dish and terrarium gardens. If these media are marked "sterilized," they should be free of insects and disease organisms.

✓   ✓   ✓

Make Uneven Landscapes

Flat landscapes are generally uninteresting. Add additional growth medium to your terrarium or dish garden to form slopes, knolls, and terraces.

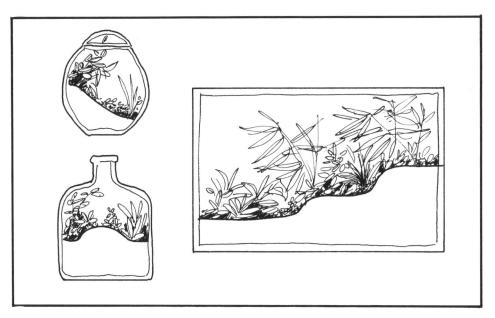

More possibilities for plant arrangements exist for uneven landscapes than for flat ones.

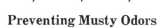

Preventing Musty Odors

Containers for dish gardens should be at least 3 inches deep. If containers without drainage holes are used, add a layer of charcoal to the medium. The charcoal will prevent a musty odor from developing. In dishes about 3 inches high, place a ½-inch layer of gravel at the bottom. Cover it with a ½-inch layer of charcoal, and top with 2 inches of good potting soil.

Charcoal can also be added to the terrarium medium to reduce odor. Add a ½-inch layer between the gravel and the growth medium or mix an equal amount into the medium.

✓   ✓   ✓

Gravel for Container Bottoms

Gravel should be placed in the bottom of dish gardens and may or may not be placed at the bottom of terrarium containers. The size of the gravel to use depends on the size of the container. Pea gravel is suitable for large containers, such as tank-type aquariums. Aquarium gravel can be used for small containers. About ½ to 1 inch of gravel in the bottom of a container is sufficient.

✓   ✓   ✓

Growth Medium for Bog Plants

Some bog, or swamp, plants can be grown in dish gardens and terrariums. The growth medium for such plants should be acid. The following is a good acid mix: ½ peat moss, ⅜ potting soil, and ⅛ sand. The mixture should be passed through a ¼-inch screen and moistened until it has an even, granular texture.

✓   ✓   ✓

Growth Medium for Bottle Terrariums

The planting medium in a bottle terrarium should not exceed ¼ the total volume. A typical container should have about 2 inches of gravel at the bottom. Cover it with a ½-inch layer of charcoal, and top with a 2½-inch layer of potting soil. Add dry planting ingredients to the bottle so that they won't stick to the sides. Water can be added later.

✓   ✓   ✓

Growth Medium for Desert Plants

A good growth medium for desert terrarium and dish garden plants includes: $\frac{1}{3}$ vermiculite, $\frac{1}{3}$ potting soil, 1/6 sand, and 1/6 peat moss. Mix thoroughly and pass the mixture through a $\frac{1}{4}$-inch screen. Moisten it until it has an even, granular texture. Planting should be made in this mixture; the surrounding terrain may be formed with pure sand.

Section Four

PLANTING

Remember That Plants Will Grow

When planning terrariums and dish gardens, remember that plants will grow. Space them so that they will have room to realize their natural form and to eliminate the need for future replanting and rearranging.

✓   ✓   ✓

Arrange Plants Outside the Container

Before planting a terrarium or dish garden container, experiment with arrangements *outside* of the container. Planning the arrangement before planting gives you a preview of how the garden will appear. Once you have decided on your arrangement, sketch the design on a piece of paper. Follow the design when planting.

✓   ✓   ✓

Accents for Miniature Gardens

Just as statue figures and fountains add to outdoor gardens, similar accents can add to miniature gardens. Small ceramic animals or mushrooms can function well as a center of interest in a terrarium or dish garden.

✓   ✓   ✓

Paper and Aluminum Foil Funnels

To aid in adding planting medium through narrow-necked terrarium containers, an improvised funnel can be made out of paper or aluminum foil, as

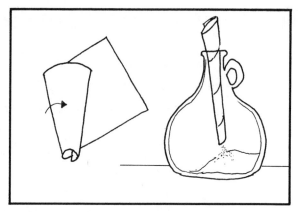

illustrated. Material will not stick to the sides of the bottle and thereby require cleaning.

Sterilize Natural Materials before Use

Natural materials, such as rocks and driftwood, make excellent additions to terrariums and dish gardens. When using such materials, remember the possibility of introducing insect and disease pests. To prevent this, place natural materials in an airtight container containing Vapona pesticide strips for several days. Or, soak materials in a 1-10 dilution of household bleach for at least 10 minutes to kill disease organisms. Wash objects in running water for 5 minutes after a bleach treatment.

Tools to Handle Plants

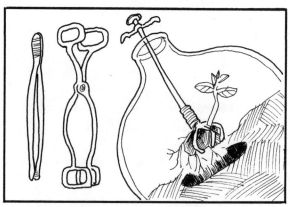

Fingers are the best tool with which to handle terrarium and dish plants. However, special tools are sometimes needed if the container opening is narrow. Forceps and tongs can be used to set plants in place. If you need tools with long handles, auto supply stores sell "grabber" or pickup tools designed to pick up objects in inaccessible places. Such tools work well for manipulating plants through narrow openings.

✓   ✓   ✓

Coathanger Tool for Planting Bottles

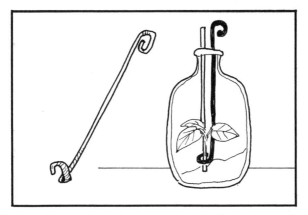

It is difficult to insert plants into narrow-necked containers. A simple tool to do this job can be fashioned out of a coathanger, as illustrated.

✓   ✓   ✓

Digging Tools

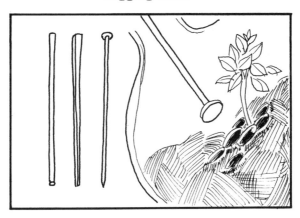

Chopsticks or wooden dowels are useful for digging planting holes and for tamping down the growth medium around the plants. The "wrong" end of a knitting needle also works well for this purpose.

✓   ✓   ✓

Don't Plant Cacti in Enclosed Containers

Cacti and other suculents should be planted only in open terrariums or dish gardens. If planted in enclosed containers, they will soon rot. Cacti also need direct sunlight.

Tamp Medium Tightly around New Plants

Often, newly planted indoor garden plants die because good contact was not established between the root system and growth medium at planting time. Tamp the growth medium firmly around the root system of new transplants. Also, water the planting site thoroughly to establish good root-growth medium contact.

Removing Indoor Garden Plants from Pots

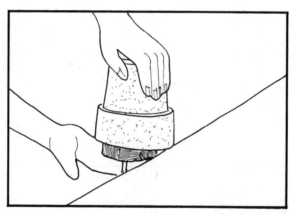

Most plants for terrariums and dish gardens are sold in small plastic or clay pots. Plants should be removed from these pots and the soil gently washed away from the roots. To remove the growth medium and plant roots from the pot, turn the pot upside down and tap its rim on a table edge. The plant, medium, and roots will separate from the pot. Be prepared to "catch" the plant and root system.

Remove Soil from Plant Roots before Planting

Because of the limited space in most containers, it is best to remove the soil from the plant roots before you plant them in dish gardens and terrariums. If this is not done, the large holes required to accommodate the plant and growth medium restrict the number of plants you can use as well as their arrangement. Soil can be gently washed away from the roots under a cold water faucet or plant roots can be soaked in a pan of water until the roots are freed from the soil. The removal of soil before planting also reduces the possibility of introducing soil-borne disease organisms and insects into your indoor garden.

Don't Let Roots Dry Out during Planting

Although it is good practice to remove the soil from terrarium and dish garden plant roots before planting, be careful that the roots don't dry out before they are secured in their new planting site. The root systems of indoor garden plants are very delicate and die rapidly when they become dry. To prevent this, place the root system in a glass of water after the soil has been removed, until it is time to plant.

Planting in a Bottle

After the growth medium has been placed in a bottle container, special care is needed in planting. (1) Set the roots of the plant loosely in the grabbers of a "pick-up" tool. (2) Ease the plant, roots first, through the neck of the bottle, gently twisting the leaves with your hand so that they will fit through the narrow opening. (3) Place the plant in a hole you have previously prepared with a knitting needle or piece of doweling. (4) Cover the roots with ½ inch of soil and tamp around them firmly with a blunt tool. (5) Remove the "pick-up" tool and the tamper through the neck. (6) Water until good contact is established between the roots and the growth medium.

Leave Plants in Pots in Large Containers

In large tank-type containers in which there is much space, terrarium plants can be left in their pots when they are planted. Simply bury the pots so that only the plants are visible. This eliminates transplanting shock and allows easy rearrangement of the plants at a future time.

Section Five

MAINTENANCE

Fertilizing Terrariums and Dish Gardens

Since it is desirable for miniature gardens to stay small, fertilization is generally not necessary. If plants show hunger signs, such as a general yellowing, use a dilute liquid fertilizer when you water. Dilute it to ¼ of the manufacturer's instructions and apply the fertilizer at no more than ½ the recommended frequency.

✓   ✓   ✓

Don't Overfeed Carniverous Plants

Carnivorous plants can be fed insects and crumbs of lean, uncooked hamburger. However, be cautious not to overfeed; excess food that plants do not digest will promote the growth of plant decaying bacteria. Feed carnivorous plants insects and meat only once or twice a month. Some carnivorous plants that do well in enclosed terrariums include: the pitcher plants (*Sarracenia, Darlintonia,* and *Nepenthes*), the butterworts (*Pinguicula*), the sundews (*Drosera*), and the venus-flytrap (*Dionaea muscipula*).

✓   ✓   ✓

Don't Use City Water for Terrariums and Dish Gardens

Most city water has sufficient chlorine and salts to injure terrarium plants. For this reason, use distilled water or rain water for watering your terrarium or dish garden. Filtering devices that can be attached to faucets, and which will produce the equivalent of distilled water, are available.

✓   ✓   ✓

A Handy Cleaning Tool

Sometimes, special tools are needed to clean the insides of containers. A useful tool can be made by attaching a piece of sponge or paper toweling to the end of a dowel or wire. Artist brushes also work in some cases.

✓   ✓   ✓

Keep Enclosed Terrariums out of Direct Sunlight

Do not place enclosed terrariums in direct sunlight to "rejuvenate" the plants. The result will be "extermination." Radiant heat builds up rapidly within enclosed containers, and the plants are, literally, cooked.

✓   ✓   ✓

Artificial Lights for Terrariums and Dish Gardens

Terrariums and dish gardens can be grown under artificial light. Artificial light (fluorescent, mercury vapor, or incandescent) can be used as a total substitute for natural light or as a supplement to weak natural light in the darker corners of a house. Place the plants no farther from the light source than 18 inches. The light can be turned on in the morning and off at nights manually, or a timer can be purchased to do this job automatically. Light should be provided for approximately 12 hours per day.

✓   ✓   ✓

Watering Dish Gardens

Water dish gardens by misting the foliage and growth medium. This increases the humidity around the foliage, cleans the leaves, and provides even watering of the growth medium.

✓   ✓   ✓

Watering Terrariums

More problems result from overwatering than underwatering terrariums. The amount and frequency of moisture condensation on the sides of the container are an adequate clue to the moisture level in the terrarium. If moisture condenses and streams down the sides, the terrarium has been overwatered. Leave the cover off for a few days to allow the excess water to evaporate. A light fog should form on the inner walls of the container after it has been properly watered.

✓   ✓   ✓

Watering Tool for Narrow-Necked Terrariums

When watering terrariums with a narrow opening, the water should be directed down the sides of the container. A funnel with a short piece of rubber tubing attached makes a useful tool to accomplish this task. To operate, pinch the rubber tubing near the funnel and fill the funnel with water. Insert the tube into the container and direct it with your fingers. Shut the water supply on and off by pinching the tubing. By watering this way, you cleanse the inside of the container and avoid displacing the plants with the water.

✓   ✓   ✓

Growth Control by Pruning

Most plants chosen for terrariums are not true miniatures, and they soon outgrow their containers. The most direct way to control this growth is by

Diagnosing Plant Problems

Symptoms	Possible Causes
General loss of leaves.	Sudden changes in temperature. Shock from transplanting. Sudden change in intensity—moved from strong sunlight to a dark location. Overwatering.
Browning of leaf tips.	Improper watering. Exposure to cold drafts. Insect attack. Burning from excessive fertilizer.
Yellowing or loss of normal foliage color.	Overwatering. Lack of adequate nutrients. Insect attack.
Gray, moldy appearance on leaf in blotches.	Gray mold promoted by excessive humidity.
Leaves take on a watersoaked, cooked appearance in blotches.	Excessive heat from exposure to direct sunlight.
Lower leaves turn yellow and stem becomes soft and dark. Green scum forms on medium.	Excessive water.
Yellow or dark localized areas develop on the leaves.	Leaf spotting fungi or bacteria.
Plants become spindly and stretch toward light. Leaves on new stems are pale yellow.	Too little light.
Leaf edges look scorched and leaves eventually die and fall off.	Too little humidity and inadequate watering.
Yellowing and decline of plant with roots showing decay.	Root rot probably associated with overwatering.
Chewed up leaves.	Chewing insects or slugs.

pruning. If pruning is done properly, it helps retard growth and shape the plants. The terrarium environment is excellent for the healing of pruning wounds and the regeneration of growth. Do not be overly concerned about hurting the plants. Be more concerned about keeping them under control. Pruning cuts should be made with a sharp tool about ¼ inch above a bud.

✓   ✓   ✓

Pruning to Prevent Disease

Most disease-causing organisms are encouraged by dead and decaying plant debris. Pruning out dead and dying plant parts is a helpful way to keep plant diseases from building up and spreading. Simply pinch or cut out dead or dying plant parts as they develop.

✓   ✓   ✓

Use Pesticides Outdoors

If you decide to use an insecticide or fungicide to control pests in your indoor garden, take it outdoors to do the spraying. This eliminates possible spray accumulation on floor and furniture, and keeps harmful spray fumes out of the house. Before applying a pesticide, make sure you have identified the problem correctly and that you have chosen the right pesticide. Labels on pesticides tell you the pest against which they are effective and the proper amount to use. Follow the labels carefully. White flies, mealy bugs, aphids, and spider mites are common pests of indoor gardens.

✓   ✓   ✓

CHAPTER ELEVEN

Home Greenhouses

Overview

A greenhouse allows you to grow your favorite flowers and vegetables at any time of the year. Available greenhouses range from the elaborate prefabricated ones costing hundreds or thousands of dollars to the simple, inexpensive ones with plastic coverings. Special window units are available for people with limited space.

Before choosing or constructing a greenhouse, **determine whether you have an appropriate site.** Greenhouses must be exposed to full sun for at least half the day in the fall and winter. **If you don't have a proper site, don't set up a greenhouse.**

There are two basic greenhouse designs: *lean-to* and *even-span.* The lean-to greenhouse has one side, two ends, and a roof. A house or garage serves as the second side. The even-span greenhouse has two sides, one or two ends, and a roof. Lean-to greenhouses can be built as extensions of living areas, preferably on the south side of the house. Even-span greenhouses can be attached to a building, eliminating the need for one end.

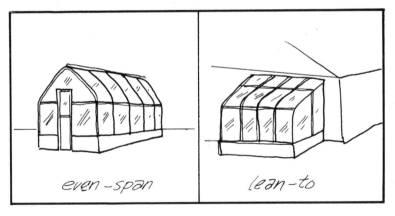

even-span   lean-to

Check local building restrictions before ordering or constructing a greenhouse. Urban or suburban areas often have building codes that must be considered. A building permit may be necessary. Also check with your tax assessor: an elaborate greenhouse might raise your proper-

397

ty value and, hence, your taxes.

The benches on which plants rest **inside the greenhouse should be made of rot-resistant wood,** such as cedar, cypress, or redwood. Corrugated asbestos or fiberglass can also be used. Benches need drainage holes so that water will not accumulate. Shelves can be installed along the upper walls of the greenhouse to make maximum use of space. Hanging baskets also help maximize use of greenhouse space.

Greenhouses should be equipped with heating, hot and cold water, plumbing, electricity, and ventilators. The type of heating to install will depend on what is most economical locally. Gas and oil heating units should be properly ventilated or their fumes will damage plants. Circulating fans are necessary to distribute the heat.

The optimum temperature for greenhouses varies with the kinds of plants being grown. A cool house (containing cool-loving plants) is usually kept at 45 to 55 degrees F. at night, with a rise of 10 to 15 degrees in the daytime. A moderate to warm house (containing warm-loving plants) varies from 55 to 70 degrees F. It is wise to install an alarm system that will go off if the heat fails and temperatures approach freezing. The alarm will allow you time to correct the situation before plants are injured.

Greenhouses should be ventilated to keep temperatures down during the summer and to provide for adequate gas exchange for the growing plants. Ventilation should be sufficient to provide the maximum amount of air exchange without affecting the temperature or humidity of the greenhouse. Opening roofs and windows in greenhouses facilitates ventilation. In order to allow enough air exchange, you may have to add heat and moisture at times since opening up the greenhouse may allow warmth and moisture to escape.

Greenhouses should be shaded in the spring to prevent scalding of the foliage due to the strong sunshine at that time of the year. Cheesecloth or plastic screening hung parallel to the glass or plastic inside or outside the house will work. Also, greenhouse glass or plastic can be sprayed with whitewash. If excessive heat in your greenhouse becomes a summertime problem, it may be necessary to move plants outdoors during extremely hot periods.

Greenhouse plants are grown in a soil mixture placed in pots or "flats" (flat wooden boxes). Different soil mixtures suit different plants. However, **most plants will grow well in a mixture containing 2 parts soil, 1 part peat moss, and 1 part perlite, vermiculite, or coarse sand.** Add 4 ounces of a complete fertilizer (5-10-5) to each bushel of mix.

Disease and insects can cause much trouble in a greenhouse: the ideal growing conditions present are also ideal for pests. To avoid problems, **the soil should be sterilized.** One of the most common soil sterilants is Vapam. Vapam is very potent and should only be used in an empty greenhouse or out-of-doors. Vapam is mixed with water which is poured over the soil mixture. Treated soil must be aerated 2 weeks before planting. If peat, perlite, vermiculite, and sand are used in the mix, without any natural soil, sterilization is not necessary; these materials are free of pests. Use of only artificial ingredients in the mix will, of course, increase costs.

Good sanitation (keeping a greenhouse clean) **reduces disease and insect incidence.** Remove all plant and soil debris, including dead leaves and shriveled flowers. Don't allow mosses and algae to cover the exteriors of pots. Remove weeds from the pots, benches, and ground. Wash all surfaces, thoroughly. The addition of Consan-20 to the wash water will help control algae, fungi, and bacteria.

If your greenhouse is moderate to large in size, **you will find it necessary to spray against insects and disease.** Inexpensive hand sprayers can be used. Chemicals suited to the plants grown are sold at garden centers.

The frequency of watering for greenhouse plants depends on the type of soil, the size of the container, and the demand of the plant. During the warm months, and also during periods when artificial heat is used, many plants require watering daily. During cool or cloudy weather, several days may elapse before water is needed. Newly potted or transplanted plants should always be watered with a can equipped with a fine nozzle spray head rather than with a stream of water.

Any garden plant—vegetables as well as flowers—**can be grown in a greenhouse** if conditions are favorable. When growing plants in a greenhouse, try to create the optimum conditions for growth, bloom, and fruiting for the plants selected. Select plants that have similar temperature and humidity requirements. Soil and light conditions can't always be varied within an individual greenhouse. Don't attempt to grow a wide variety of plants in the same greenhouse unless the proper growing conditions can be provided.

Section One

GREENHOUSE CONSTRUCTION

Situate Greenhouses away from Trees

Greenhouses should not be erected close to trees. The shade of trees lessens plant growth, and falling tree debris presents a hazard to both glass and plastic houses. Avoid small trees as well; they grow into big ones.

✓   ✓   ✓

Locating Attached Greenhouses

Where a greenhouse is attached to another structure is important. It is better to locate a greenhouse on the south or east side of a house rather than on the north or west side. Southern exposures provide the strongest sun in the winter.

✓   ✓   ✓

Use Glass for Permanent Greenhouses

Plastic film, a substitute for glass, has become a popular covering for greenhouses. But remember that the greenhouse structure is only part of the initial cost. Heating, electricity, and other operating costs are approximately the same for both glass-covered and plastic-covered greenhouses. Glass out-lasts plastic film and the replacement cost of plastic film soon brings its cost up to that of glass. Use glass for a more permanent greenhouse.

✓   ✓   ✓

Location of Greenhouse Floors

Erect greenhouse floors above ground level. If floors are below ground level, drainage is poor and flooding may result from rain or snow.

✓   ✓   ✓

Partition Long Greenhouses

A greenhouse that is 20 feet or more in length can be divided into 2 sec-tions to provide separate areas for cool-loving and warm-loving plants. If one section is maintained at 50 degrees F. at night and the other at 60, a great variety of plants can be grown successfully.

✓   ✓   ✓

Hot and Cold Water Is Essential

It is desirable to supply both hot and cold water and a mixing faucet to greenhouses. This allows you to obtain water of optimum temperature (60 degrees F.) to water plants. Extremely cold water in the winter can shock plants and retard growth.

✓   ✓   ✓

Shade Part of the Greenhouse

You can grow both sun-loving and shade-loving plants in the same green-house by shading a portion of the greenhouse. The shaded part also makes a good place to store cuttings until they are rooted and to store newly potted plants until they recover from the shock of transplanting. Although it is unwise to plant trees to supply cover from the sun (for reasons mentioned previously), a portion of a greenhouse can be shaded by painting the glass with Garland White Shading Compound as directed on the label.

✓   ✓   ✓

Plant Benches and Shelves

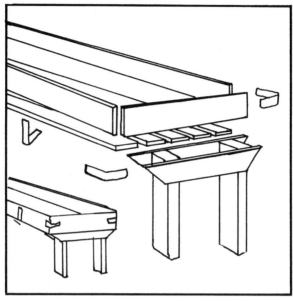

Never set up small flimsy benches or tables. Buy the prefabricated type from a greenhouse manufacturer or make your own. California redwood or a good grade of cypress are the only suitable woods to use. They are durable under conditions of moisture and should last from 10 to 15 years. Only an occasional bottom board will need to be replaced. A coat of copper-naphtenate wood preserver will add years to the life of the bench. The sketch shows a time-tested bench design.

Organize Your Greenhouse

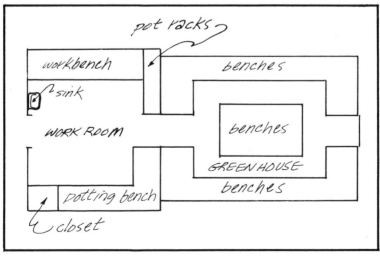

The first thing to do after erecting a greenhouse is to organize the space available. A greenhouse can fast become a very cluttered place if all available space is not put to best use. The floor plan shown in the diagram contains a work area and a growing area. Space is set aside for work benches, a sink, and a closet.

✦   ✦   ✦

Alternative Greenhouse Shapes

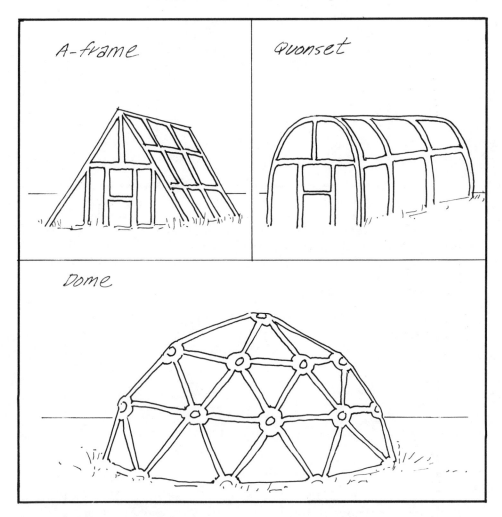

In addition to the more conventional even-span and lean-to home greenhouses, home gradeners will find several alternative shapes. Illustrated are

A-frame, quonset, and dome greenhouses.

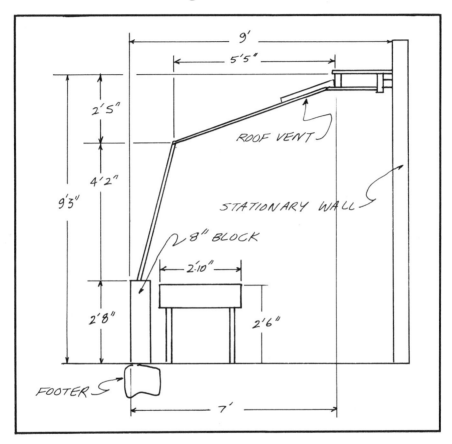

Constructing Your Own Greenhouse

Plans for a lean-to greenhouse.

If you are handy, it is possible to construct your own greenhouse at a considerable savings. Illustrated are cutaway plans for even-span and lean-to greenhouses. Each can be as long as desired. In order to simplify your construction effort, you might purchase the assembly manuals produced by many of the manufacturers of prefabricated greenhouses. By reading several of these, you will get a feel for the types of materials that can be used. Reading such manuals will also help you decide if you really want to do the job yourself from scratch.

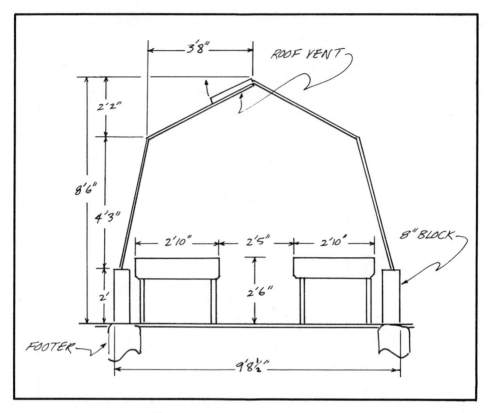

Plans for an even-span greenhouse.

Section Two

COLD FRAMES AND HOTBEDS

Cold Frames

A cold frame is an unheated, boxlike, glass-covered structure for protecting young plants. Cold frames, which extend the growing season of plants, can be converted into miniature greenhouses by constructing them against basement windows, allowing the heat from the house and the rays of the

sun to keep them warm. Minigreenhouses of this kind can be used the year 'round.

Homemade Cold Frames

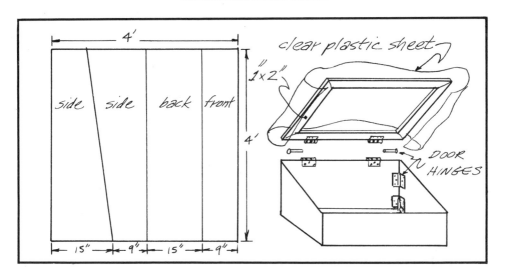

Cold frames are useful for storing plants during the winter and for starting plants early in the spring. The sides of a simple cold frame can be cut from a 4-foot-square piece of ½-inch exterior-grade plywood, as shown at the left of the diagram. Cut the sides, back, and front as illustrated and assemble the base and sides with removable-pin hinges for easy assembly. For the cover, fasten lengths of 1 inch by 2 inch lumber with angle irons. Wrap clear polyethylene sheeting, 4 to 6 mils thick, over the top; secure it with staples. The hinged top can be propped open with a wooden block for ventilation.

🌱   🌱   🌱

Simple Hotbeds

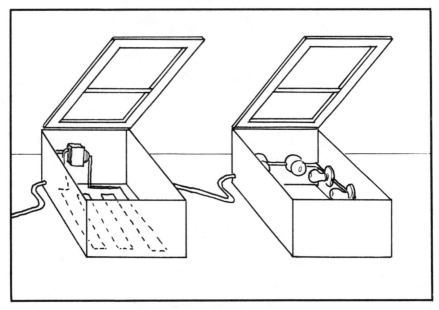

Hotbeds and cold frames are both boxes that let in light and provide a place for plants to grow. Whereas cold frames depend somewhat on the sun's rays for heating, hotbeds are supplied with an artificial source of heat. Hotbeds are heated by placing heating coils along the bottom of the structure (as illustrated, left of diagram) or by installing light bulbs on the sides of the structure (as illustrated, right of diagram). The light bulbs also serve as a source of light.

Section Three

PLANTING AND PROPAGATION

Filling Standard Wooden Flats

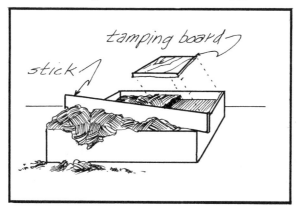

Flat boxes, filled with a growth medium, are the standard place to start seedlings in the greenhouse. Once the medium has been placed in a flat, level it with a board and tamp it down firmly.

Planting Seed in Flats

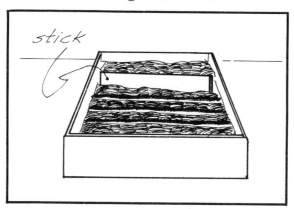

Once a flat has been filled with a suitable growing medium, planting the seed is an easy operation. First, mark off the rows by making indentations with a stick, as illustrated. Then, drop seed in the rows as directed on the package and cover lightly with vermiculite, milled sphagnum moss, or sifted peat moss.

Avoiding Sterilization of Greenhouse Soil

A sterilized growth medium free of weed seed, insects, and pathogens should be used in greenhouses. But sterilization can be a laborious process, and there is a way to avoid it: use ingredients for the growth media that are relatively sterile in themselves. Sand, vermiculite, perlite, or a sand-peat mix are suitable. Avoid soil.

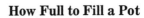

How Full to Fill a Pot

The depth to which you fill a pot with soil affects future watering. If you fill the pot too high (diagram, left), water will spill over the side and not penetrate the soil. Too little soil (center) causes you to add too much water to the remaining soil and possibly injure the plants. The correct level (right)—about ½ inch from the top for small pots—helps provide the right amount of water. Leave 1 inch for pots 6 inches or larger in diameter. When watering, fill the entire space at the top of the pot with water.

A Row Marker for Flats

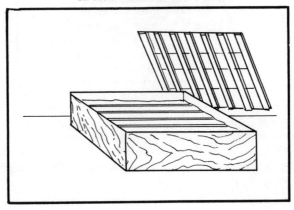

If a large number of seeds is to be planted in rows, it is wise to construct a row marker. One can be made easily by tacking 1-inch strips of wood to a piece of plywood the same size as the flat (as illustrated). Press the plywood onto the medium to establish the planting rows.

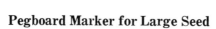

Pegboard Marker for Large Seed

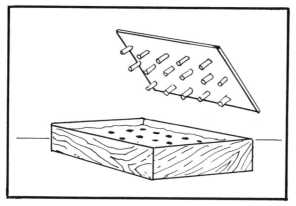

It is impossible to plant seed uniformly in a flat without a guide of some kind. A convenient guide can be made for large seed and seedlings by inserting short pieces of doweling into a piece of plywood as pictured. When the board with the peg is pressed onto the medium, a proper planting pattern will emerge.

Salt Shaker for Fine Seed

Fine seed is difficult to sow evenly on a growth medium. To solve this problem, mix the seed thoroughly with dry sand and place it in a salt shaker. The sand and seed can then be dusted evenly over the planting medium.

Proper Wetness of Potting Soil

Seed and seedlings get a better start if the potting soil has the proper wetness. Potting soil should be neither too wet nor too dry: it should be damp enough to adhere to itself and not crumble when a handful is gently squeezed, but not so moist that it drips.

Jiffy Pots for Transplants

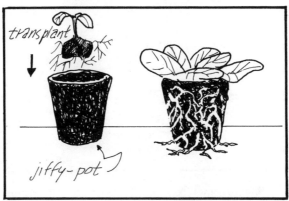

Jiffy pots are made out of peat and allow you to plant pot and plant together at transplanting time. Roots can easily penetrate the soil through the peat pot, and the peat itself becomes part of he growing medium. Vegetables and flowers can be started in these pots in the greenhouse and transplanted in them at planting time. This procedure avoids transplanting shock by not disturbing the root system.

When Seedlings Are Ready to Transplant

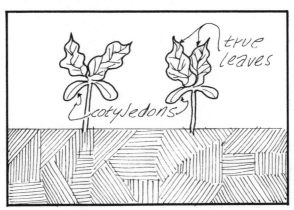

Guidelines for Germination of Annual, Pot Plant and Ornamental Herb Seeds

Common name and cultivar	Genus and species	Approximate number seeds/ oz.	Group	Optimum temperature for best germination	Continuous light or dark	Usual time required for uniform germination (days)
Ageratum Golden	Lonas annua (L.) Vines & Druce	128,000	I	70	D	5
Ageratum Blue Mink	Ageratum houstonianum Mill.	200,000	VI	70	L	5
Alyssum Carpet of Snow	Lobularia maritima (L.) Desv.	90,000	I	70	DL	5
Amaranthus Molten Fire	Amaranthus tricolor L.	47,000	III	70	DL	10
Anise	Pimpinella anisum L.	9,600	IV	70	DL	10
Aster Ball White	Callistephus chinensis (L.) Nees.	12,000	I	70	DL	8
Balsam Scarlet	Impatiens balsamine L.	3,300	III	70	DL	8
Basil Dark Opal	Ocimum minimum L.	20,000	III	70	DL	10
Basil Lettuce Leaves	Ocimum basilicum L.	9,600	III	70	DL	10
Begonia, fibrous-rooted, Scandinavia Pink	Begonia semperflorens Link & Otto	2,000,000	V	70	L	15
Begonia, tuberous-rooted, Double mix	Begonia X tuberhybrida Voss.	2,000,000	VI	65	L	15
Borage	Borago officinalis L.	2,100	VIII	70	D	8
Browallia Blue Bells and Silver Bells	Browallia speciosa Hook. (B. Major Hort.)	130,000	VI	70	L	15
Browallia Sapphire	Browallia viscosa HBK Compacta	340,000	V	70	L	15
Calceolaria multiflora nana	Calceolaria X herbeohybrida Voss.	600,000	VI	70	L	15
Calendula Orange Coronet	Calendula officinalis L.	3,000	VIII	70	D	10
Companula—Annual Mix	Campanula medium L.	50,000	III	70	DL	20
Candytuft Giant White	Iberis amara L.	9,500	I	70	DL	8
Carnation Chaband's Giant and Imp. Cardinal Red	Dianthus caryophyllus L.	14,000	IV	70	DL	20
Celosia Toreador	Celosia argentea L.	28,000	III	70	DL	10
Centaurea Blue Boy	Centaurea cyanus L.	7,000	VIII	65	D	10
Centaurea Dusty Miller	Centaurea gymnocarpa Moris & deNot.	7,000	VIII	65	D	10
Centaurea—yellow	Centaurea moschata L.	7,000	VIII	70	D	10
Chives—Grass onion	Allium schoenoprasum L.	22,000	IV	60	DL	10
Christmas Cherry Masterpiece	Solanum pseudocapsicum L.	12,000	III	70	DL	20
Cineraria Maritima Diamond	Senecio cineraria DC.	65,000	VII	75	L	10
Cineraria—Vivid	Senecio cruentus DC.	150,000	III	70	DL	10
Clarkia—Florist mixture	Clarkia elegans Dougl.	90,000	I	70	DL	5
Cobaea—Cup-and-Saucer Vine, purple	Cobaea scandens Cav.	375	I	70	DL	15
Coleus Red Rainbow	Coleus blumei Benth.	100,000	VII	65	L	10
Coriander—annual	Coriandrum sativum L.	1,240	VIII	70	D	10
Cosmos Radiance	Cosmos bipinnatus Cav.	5,000	II	70	DL	5
Cynoglossum—Firmament	Cynoglossum amabile Stapf & Drummond.	5,000	IV	60	D	5
Cuphea Firefly	Cuphea llavea Llave & Lex. var. miniata Koehne	7,000	VI	70	L	8
Cyclamen Pure White	Cyclamen persicum Mill.	2,500	IX	60	D	50
Dahlia—Unwins dwarf mix	Dahlia pinnata Cav.	2,800	I	70	DL	5
Dianthus Bravo	Dianthus chinensis L.	25,000	I	70	DL	5
Didiscus Blue Lace	Trachymene caerulea R. Grah.	10,000	IV	65	D	15
Dill	Anethum graveolens L.	6,300	IV	60	L	10
Dimorphotheca Orange Improved	Dimorphotheca sinuata DC.	9,500	II	70	DL	10
Euphorbia—annual poinsettia	Euphorbia heterophylla L.	5,000	I	70	DL	15
Exacum Tiddly-Winks	Exacum affine Balf.	1,000,000	V	70	L	15
Fennel, sweet	Foeniculum vulgare Mill.	4,000	IV	65	D	10
Feverdew Ball Double White Improved	Matricaria capensis L.	145,000	VII	70	L	15
Freesia White Giant	Freesia (garden cultivars)	3,000	IV	65	DL	25
Gaillardia Tetra Red Giant	Gaillardia pulchella Foug. var. picta Gray	14,000	III	70	DL	20
Gazania—Mix	Gazania rigens R. Br.	12,000	IV	60	D	8
Gloxinia Emperor Wilhelm	Sinningia speciosa Benth. & Hook.	800,000	V	65	L	15
Gomphrena Rubra	Gomphrena globosa L.	5,000	III	65	D	15
Grevillea (Australian Silk Oak)	Grevillea robusta Cunn.	3,000	VI	80	L	20
Gypsophila Covent Garden	Gypsophila elegans Bieb.	2,400	I	70	DL	10
Helichrysum (Everlasting)	Helichrysum bracteatum Andr.	36,000	VII	70	L	5
Heliotrope Marine	Valeriana officinalis L.	50,000	IV	70	DL	25

Hollyhock Powderpuffs Mix	Althaea rosea (L.) Cav.	2,000	IV	60	DL	10
Hunnemannia (Bush Escholtzia) Sunlite	Hunnemannia fumariaefolia Sweet	8,000	III	70	DL	15
Impatiens Holstii Scarlet	Impatiens holstii Engler & Warb.	44,000	VI	70	L	15
Kalanchoe Vulcan	K. blossfeldiana v. Poelln.	2,500,000	V	70	L	10
Kochia Bright Green	Kochia scoparia (L.) Schrad. var. culta Farwell	45,000	I	70	DL	15
Larkspur White Supreme	Delphinium ajacis L.	8,000	IX	55	D	20
Lobelia Crystal Palace	L. erinus L. var. compacta Nich.	700,000	III	70	DL	20
Lupine Giant King Oxford Blue	Lupinus hartwegii Lindl.	1,300	IV	55	DL	20
Marigold Doubloon	Tagetes erecta L.	10,000	I	70	DL	5
Marigold Spry	Tagetes patula L.	9,000	I	70	DL	5
Marjoram, sweet	Majorana hortensis Moench.	100,000	II	70	DL	8
Mesembryanthemum criniflorum	Dorotheanthus bellidiformis (Burm.) N.E. Br.	100,000	IX	65	D	15
Mignonette Early White	Reseda odorata L.	27,000	I	70	DL	5
Mimosa (Sensitive Plant)	Mimosa pudica L.	4,500	VIII	80	D	8
Morning Glory Heavenly Blue	Convolvulus sp.	650	III	65	DL	5
Myosotis Ball Early	Myosotis sylvatica Hoffm.	44,000	IV	55	D	8
Naegelia Art Shades	Smithiantha X hybrida Voss.	1,500,000	V	70	L	15
Nasturtium Golden Giant	Tropaeolum majus L.	175	IV	65	D	8
Nemesia Fire King	Nemesia strumosa Benth. var. suttonii Hort.	90,000	IX	65	D	5
Nicotiana Crimson Bedder	Nicotiana alata Link & Otto var. grandiflora Comes	400,000	VII	70	L	20
Nierembergia Purple Robe	Nierembergia hippomanica Miers	175,000	III	70	DL	15
Pansy Lake of Thun	Viola tricolor L. var. hortensis DC.	20,000	IX	65	D	10
Parsley—Extra triple curled	Petroselinum crispum (Mill.) Nym.	18,500	IX	75	D	15
Penstemon Sensation Mixture	Penstemon X gloxinioides Hort.	55,000	VIII	65	D	10
Perilla Burgandy	Perilla frutescens Britt. var. crispa Deane	20,000	VI	65	L	15
Petunia Maytime	Petunia hybrida Vilm.	200,000	VI	70	L	10
Phlox Glamour	Phlox drummondii Hook.	14,000	VIII	65	D	10
Plumbago, blue	Plumbago capensis Thunb.	2,000	IV	75	DL	25
Poppy Nudicaule Iceland	Papaver nudicaule L.	275,000	I	70	D	10
Portulaca, yellow	Portulaca grandiflora Hook.	280,000	IV	70	D	10
Primula Chinese Giant Fringed	Primula sinensis Sabine	18,000	VIII	70	D	25
Primula malacoides White Giant	Primula malacoides Franch.	385,000	VI	70	L	25
Primula Fasbender's Red	Primula obconica Hance.	130,000	VI	70	L	25
Rosemary, perennial	Rosmarinus officinalis L.	30,000	IV	60	DL	15
Rudbeckia Single Gloriosa Daisy	Rudbeckia laciniata L.	40,000	III	70	DL	20
Sage, perennial	Salvia officinalis L.	3,250	VIII	70	D	15
Saintpaulia Blue Fairy Tale	Saintpaulia ionantha Wendl.	750,000	V	70	L	25
Salpiglossis Emperor Mix	Salpiglossis sinuata Ruiz & Pav.	125,000	III	70	D	15
Salvia St. John's Fire	Salvia splendens Sello	7,500	VI	70	L	15
Savory, Bohnenkraut	Satureia hortensis L.	15	VI	65	L	15
Scabiosa Giant Blue	Scabiosa atropurpurea L.	4,500	III	70	DL	10
Schizanthus Ball Giant Mix	Schizanthus pinnatus Ruiz & Pav.	60,000	VIII	60	D	20
Shamrock, True Irish	Trifolium dubium Sibth.	28,000	IX	65	D	10
Smilax	Asparagus asparagoides (L.) Wight	4,000	VIII	75	D	30
Snapdragon Orchid Rocket	Antirrhinum majus L.	180,000	VII	65	L	10
Statice Iceberg	Limonium sinuatum (L.) Mill.	350	I	70	DL	15
Statice suworowii Russian	Limonium suworowii (Reg.) Kuntze	12,000	VIII	70	D	15
Stock, Lavender column stock	Matthiola incana (L.) R. Br.	16,000	I	70	DL	10
Streptocarpus	Streptocarpus X hybridus Hort.	750,000	V	70	L	15
Sweetpea Ruth Cuthbertson	Lathyrus odoratus L.	350	IV	55	D	15
Thunbergia gibsoni	Thunbergia gibsonii S. Moore	500	III	70	DL	10
Thyme, perennial	Thymus vulgaris L.	96,000	IV	75	DL	10
Tithonia Torch	T. rotundifolia (Mill.) Blake	3,500	VIII	70	D	20
Torenia	Torenia fournieri Lind.	375,000	III	70	DL	15
Verbena Torrid	Verbena hybrida Voss.	10,000	VIII	65	D	20
Viola Blue Elf	Viola cornuta L.	24,000	IX	65	D	10
Vinca, Periwinkle—alba aculata	Vinca rosea L.	21,000	VIII	70	D	15
Wallflower Golden Standard	Cheiranthus cheiri L.	14,000	I	70	DL	5
Zinnia Isabellina	Zinnia elegans Jacq.	2,500	III	70	DL	5

When seedlings are grown in flats in the greenhouse, the proper time for transplanting to pots or to the garden is always questioned. Seedlings first develop seed leaves (cotyledons) and, later, true leaves. Once a full set of true leaves has developed, a seedling is ready to be transplanted.

Propagation by Root Cuttings

Some plants, such as oriental poppy, are easier to root from root cuttings than stem cuttings. Cut roots into a 2- to 4-inch segments and lay them on a rooting medium. Mulch and cover the cuttings during the winter; they will produce shoots in the spring. Alternatively, set 3-inch root pieces singly in 4-inch pots of sandy soil. Submerge the pots into sand in a cold frame over winter. When leaves appear in the spring, transplant to the garden.

Hardware Cloth for Greenhouse Benches

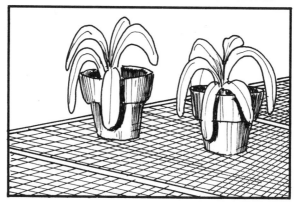

A material often used to support plants on greenhouse benches is a wire mesh known as hardware cloth. This arrangement allows for better air circulation and water drainage than a solid bench. Use ½-inch hardware cloth for this purpose.

When to Take Cuttings from Plants

The time of year that cuttings are taken from plants affects their chances of rooting successfully. Plants such as geraniums, which are relatively "juicy," are in the best stage of development for cutting when new growth snaps readily when broken. Shoots of woody shrubs—such as lilacs, mock-orange, and azaleas—should be taken when they are pliable, not stiff. Take cuttings from flowering shrubs and perennials in late spring or early July, when the new growth is almost complete.

WOODY ORNAMENTAL PLANTS REPRODUCED BY CUTTINGS

Name	Time to Take	Type of Cutting	Rooting Powder Strength	Rooting Time
Deciduous Shrubs and Trees				
Japanese Quince	June–July	Heel	3 or C	45 days
Flowering Dogwood	Early June	Softwood-tip	3 or C	30 days
Cotoneaster	August	Half-hardened tip	3 or C	75 days
Forsythia	June	Tip	2 or B	30 days
Ginkgo	Mid-June	Tip	2 or B	45 days
Beautybush	July	Tip	2 or B	45 days
Magnolia	June	Tip	2 or B	40–60 days
Mock Orange	June	Tip	2 or B	60 days
Lilacs	May	Tip	2 or B	60 days
Viburnums	June–Early July	Tip	2 or B	55–70 days
Wisteria	July	Tip	2 or B	60 days
Roses	After 1st bloom	Tip	2 or B	60–75 days
Narrow-Leaf Evergreens				
Chamaecyparis	July	Heel	3 or C	30–45 days
	March or Sept.	Hardwood Heel	2 or B	90 days
Junipers	November	Hardwood Heel	3 or C	110 days
Yews (taxus)	August–Sept.	Tip, with a piece of last year's wood at base	3 or C	120 days
Thuja (white cedar)	Mid-June	Heel	3 or C	90 days
	Nov.–Mar.	Hardwood Heel	3 or C	120 days
Broad-Leaf Evergreens				
Japanese Spurge	June–July	Tip	2 or B	60 days
Euonymous (big leaf wintercreeper)	July	Tip	2 or B	40 days
Rhododendron	August	Tip or leaf-bud	3 or C	120 days

Note: All flower buds are removed when rhododendron cuttings are made. A large basal wound also encourages rooting.

Selecting Wood for Cuttings

Most cuttings root better if taken from immature wood (soft-wood) which has yet to form much bark. Softwood cuttings can be taken from deciduous or evergreen shrubs and trees, as well as from herbaceous or ever-

HERBACEOUS PLANTS TO GROW FROM CUTTINGS

Name	Time to Take	Type of Cutting	Rooting Powder Strength	Rooting Time
		Annuals		
Ageratum	Anytime	Tip or leaf-bud	1 or A	10–14 days
Lantana	Anytime	Tip or leaf-bud	1 or A	10–14 days
Petunia	Anytime	Tip or leaf-bud	1 or A	10–14 days
Periwinkle	Anytime	Tip or leaf-bud	1 or A	10–14 days
Pinks	Anytime	Tip or leaf-bud	1 or A	10–14 days
		Perennials		
Balloon Flower	June–July	Tip	2 or B	30 days
Basket of Gold Alyssum	June–July	Tip	2 or B	30 days
Bee Balm (Monarda)	June–July	Tip	2 or B	21 days
Butterfly Weed	June–July	Tip	2 or B	30 days
Perennial Candytuft	June–July	Tip	2 or B	30 days
Chrysanthemum	Spring, New Growth	Tip	2 or B	21 days
Fall Aster	Spring, New Growth	Tip	2 or B	30 days
Loosestrife	Spring, New Growth	Tip	2 or B	30 days
Mountain Bluet	June	Tip	2 or B	21 days
Perennial Phlox	June	Tip	2 or B	21 days
Perennial Pinks	June	Tip	2 or B	21 days
Stonecrop (sedum)	May	Tip	2 or B	14 days
Veronica (speedwell)	June	Tip	2 or B	21 days

Note: Flowers and flower buds should be removed from perennial cuttings at the time the cuttings are taken.

green perennials. Lateral or side branches that have formed after the growing tip of the main stem has been pinched back generally make good cuttings.

✓   ✓   ✓

Plant Easter Lily Bulbs Deep

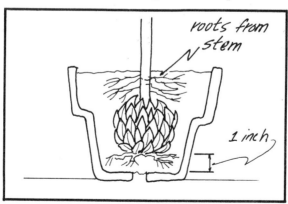

Easter lilies are a popular greenhouse plant. When planting an Easter lily bulb, place a handful of sterilized stones at the bottom of the pot to provide drainage. Place 1 inch of potting soil on top of the small stones. Then place the bulb—nose up—on the soil in the center of the pot. Add soil until it is even with the edge of the pot and press it down slightly. Easter lily bulbs are planted deep (1 inch above the bottom of the pot) so that roots will develop on the stem to help anchor the plant and prevent it from drooping.

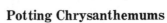

Potting Chrysanthemums

Chrysanthemums are generally started by planting 4 or 5 rooted cuttings in a ¾-inch pot. Cuttings should be potted shallowly to ensure good aeration in the root area. Plant at an angle so that the top of the cutting extends over the edge of the pot. This encourages more shoots per cutting and larger and better-formed plants. The illustrations show how to produce rooted

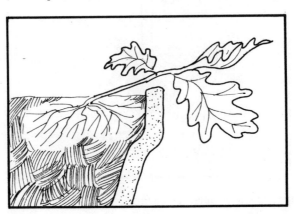

chrysanthemum cuttings and how to transplant them into pots. Dipping the cuttings into a root hormone prior to potting aids in root formation.

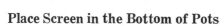

Label Newly Planted Seed

Since seedlings are difficult to identify, label all newly planted seed. Stick a wooden stake into flats. Write the planting date and variety planted on the stake. Use a pencil, *not* ink. Ink may run when wet.

Place Screen in the Bottom of Pots

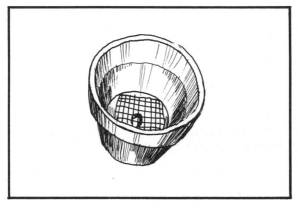

Slugs and other chewing insects can enter pots through drainage holes in their bottoms. To prevent this, line the bottoms of pots, just under the drainage material, with a piece of fine mesh screen.

Section Four

PLANT SELECTION AND CARE

Greenhouse Roses

Roses not only provide cut flowers, but add much to the color of a greenhouse. Rose plants can be grown in 7-inch pots filled with a standard soil mixture. Recommended cultivars for the greenhouse are: Bright Pink Garnett, Carol Amling, Dick Koster, Garnette, Orange Rumba, Margo Koster, Mother's Day, Pink Marvel, Scarlet Marvel, Skylark, Summer Snow, Thunderbird, and Triumphe d'Orleans.

Roses in Bloom for Easter

Roses are becoming more popular as an Easter flower. To produce blooming roses at Easter, use the following greenhouse schedule: transfer plants from the cold frame to the greenhouse on January 15th; keep at a temperature of 45 to 48 degrees F. until February 15th; then, raise the temperature to 54 to 56 degrees F.; in early March, increase the temperature to 60 degrees F.

✶   ✶   ✶

Plants for Warm or Cold Greenhouses

Most plants should be grown in either a warm (58 to 70 degrees F.) or cold (45 to 57 degrees F.) greenhouse. Some plants, however, will grow well in both. Among these are: *Begonia tuberhydrida, Billbergia windii, Bouvardia humboldtii, Campanula isonphylla, Clivia miniata, Cobaea scandens, Manettia bicolor, Plumbago capensis, Stephanotis floribunda, Thumbergia alata,* and *Tiboushina semidecandra.*

✶   ✶   ✶

Plants That Will Bloom at Any Time of the Year

Some plants require special light and nutrition in order to bloom in a greenhouse. Among the plants that will bloom *without* special treatment are: *Saintpaulia ionantha, Impatiens sultanii, Abutilon megopotamicum, Begonia semperflorens,* and *Tagetes patula* 'Spy.'

✶   ✶   ✶

Orchids Can't Take Cold Drafts

Orchids, being a tropical plant, are easily injured by cold winter drafts that may come through the greenhouse vents. To deal with this problem, mechanical ventilators containing heating devices can be purchased. These devices can be installed at either end of the house.

✶   ✶   ✶

A Greenhouse with a Permanent Look

Many greenhouses have an antiseptic appearance. Decorate your greenhouse by "landscaping" its interior and exterior. Once possibility is to train a nasturtium vine, as a frame, over one of the doorways. Another is to place hanging baskets at various points inside the greenhouse. The outside of the greenhouse can be landscaped with flowers and shrubs—but remember not to plant anything that will obstruct the sun.

✶   ✶   ✶

Don't "Overpot" Bulbs

If you use an oversized pot for bulbs, the roots tend to dry out, possibly killing the plant. Bulbs have a better chance of survival in a pot that is too small rather than too large. Pot bulbs as soon as you purchase them; they dry out rapidly in storage.

⚡   ⚡   ⚡

Ornamental-Leaved Plants

Various ornamental-leaved plants make attractive additions to a greenhouse. Some to consider are: ornamental-leaved begonias (*Begonia rex*), the colored-leaved *Coleus* family, *Chlorophytum elatum variegatum,* and *Cyperus alternifolius.*

⚡   ⚡   ⚡

Evergreens for the Greenhouse

Evergreen plants provide a nice visual background for the flowering plants in a greenhouse. Two evergreens that can be grown inside the greenhouse for this purpose are *Araucaria excelsa* and asparagus ferns.

⚡   ⚡   ⚡

Tomatoes for the Greenhouse

Tomatoes can be grown in greenhouses throughout the winter. Some of the more popular greenhouse varieties are: Michigan-Ohio hybrid, Ohio W-R7, Pink Globe, Waltham hybrid, Spartan Red 8, and Spartan Pink 10.

⚡   ⚡   ⚡

Vegetables in the Greenhouse

Various vegetables can be grown in the greenhouse if they mature in a short time, have compact growth, and are not root crops. (It is difficult to provide containers suitable for root crops.) The easiest vegetables to grow are cucumbers, lettuce, tomatoes, peas, and beans. Plants can be grown in large clay pots. It will be necessary to provide support for vining crops such as tomatoes, cucumbers, and beans. In general, the flavor of greenhouse-grown vegetables is not as good as that of vegetables grown outdoors.

⚡   ⚡   ⚡

Carbon Dioxide Enrichment of Greenhouses

It has been found that by increasing the amount of carbon dioxide in the greenhouse atmosphere, plants grow more rapidly and become more productive. Carbon dioxide enrichment is important during the shorter days of autumn and winter; it compensates for reduced growth due to reduced light. Special lamps for producing carbon dioxide, along with instructions for their use, are obtainable from makers of greenhouse equipment.

⚡   ⚡   ⚡

Disbudding Chrysanthemums

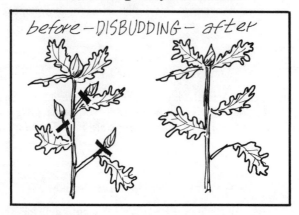

Chrysanthemum shoots have one large flower bud at the end of the stem and many smaller side buds. So that each stem produces a single large flower, chrysanthemums should be "disbudded." If the side buds are not removed, a bulky-looking flower stem results. Side buds should be pinched off with the fingers as soon as the buds can be grasped (as illustrated).

✓   ✓   ✓

Pinching Chrysanthemums

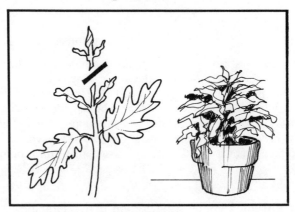

By pinching young chrysanthemum plants you can cause 4 to 6 new shoots to develop from the point where the leaf joins the stem (the axil of the leaf). The result is a bushier and more attractive plant with a greater number of blooms. Pinch out the top ¼ to ½ inch of the shoot tip by breaking it off with the fingers. Best results are obtained if rooted cuttings are allowed to grow for about one week before they are pinched.

✓   ✓   ✓

Precool Your Easter Lily Bulbs

Easter lily bulbs will produce flowers earlier if they are precooled. To precool bulbs, store them at 33 to 35 degrees F. for a minimum of 5 weeks. Bulbs can be potted and then precooled by plunging them into straw-covered cold frames that have temperatures ranging from 32 to 50 degrees F.

Encouraging African Violets to Bloom

African violets fail to bloom for a number of reasons. The most common of which is insufficient light for flower bud formation. To alleviate, move the plants to the brightest side of the greenhouse. The addition of a solution of aluminum sulfate (1 teaspoon per quart of water), applied once a week until flower buds appear, will encourage some plants to flower.

Handle Bedding Plants by Their Leaves

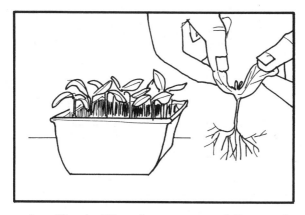

The roots of seedling bedding plants are very delicate and can be easily damaged when handled. To reduce root damage and increase chances of survival, handle seedlings by the leaves when transplanting.

Watering on Hot Days

Although it is customary to water a greenhouse once a day, it may be necessary to water twice a day in the heat of summer. During such periods of extreme heat, extra watering can be reduced by dampening the walks and areas under benches, thereby raising the humidity level in the house and reducing plant water loss.

Use Low Analysis Fertilizers

It would seem that high analysis fertilizers would be more efficient than low analysis fertilizers. This isn't the case for greenhouse plants. Since growth media for greenhouse plants are largely synthetic, they don't contain many of the microelements essential for plant growth. High analysis fertilizers are so refined that they contain *reduced* amounts of needed microelements. To ensure that your plants are supplied with a sufficient amount of microelements, use low analysis fertilizers (e.g. 5-10-5 as opposed to 10-20-10).

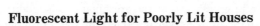

Fluorescent Light for Poorly Lit Houses

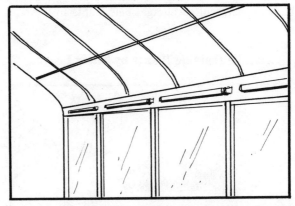

Some greenhouses, due to their location or construction, are poorly lit. Strips of fluorescent lights installed along the sides of such houses will improve the growth and flowering of plants. Buy special fluorescent bulbs that emit the type of light most needed by plants.

Insulate House Plants from the Cold

Sometimes it is necessary to carry houseplants outdoors from the greenhouse in cold weather. Do not expose houseplants to sudden changes in temperature. You may cause them to lose their leaves or even be killed. To prevent this, wrap plants in 3 or 4 layers of newspaper, as illustrated, before taking them outdoors.

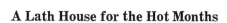

A Lath House for the Hot Months

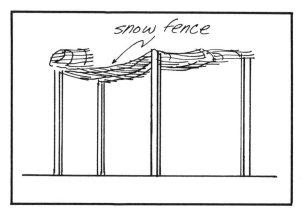

A lath house is an unenclosed shading structure in which greenhouse plants can be placed during the hot summer months. A simple lath house can be constructed by stretching several lengths of snow fence over 4 stakes tall enough to allow working space underneath.

Section Five

PEST CONTROL

Damping-Off Control

Damping-off is a disease that results in the death of seedlings. Seedlings may be killed before they sprout, or they may bend over at the soil line and die soon after sprouting. Because damping-off is caused by fungi that live in the soil, the best means of prevention is to use sterilized soil or a sterilized growth medium. Once the disease has appeared, prevent further contamination by maintaining good sanitation.

Thrips Control

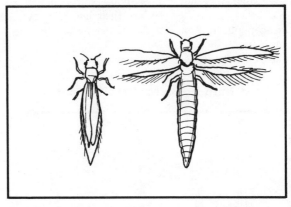

Thrips (illustrated) are slender gray or cream-colored insects about ¼ inch in length. Commonly found on roses, carnations, and chrysanthemums, they cause streaks on petals and may prevent flower buds from opening. For control, spray the tops of plants with malathion, as directed on the label, when thrips first appear. Repeated application will probably be necessary.

✓   ✓   ✓

Greenhouse White Fly

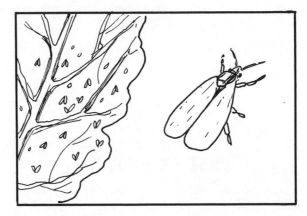

White flies, the size and color of dandruff, are pests which commonly afflict chrysanthemums, tomatoes, ageratum, and poinsettias, causing blotches to appear on the leaves. Attacked leaves sometimes turn black because of the growth of a sooty mold fungus on excrements left by the insect. Thiodan 50 will give adequate control when applied according to the directions on the label.

✓   ✓   ✓

Botrytis Blight Control

Botrytis blight is particularly troublesome to chrysanthemums and carnations from spring through fall. The botrytis fungus, which attacks flowers when the air is too moist, can blight entire flowers. The disease can be recognized by the gray fungus growth that covers the blighted tissue. To control the disease, reduce moisture content in the air by using fans to increase air movement in the greenhouse. Destruction of all diseased flowers and removal of mature flowers as soon as they appear reduce spread of the blight. Spraying with Zineb or Captan, as directed on the label, is also helpful.

✓ ✓ ✓

Powdery Mildew Control

Powdery mildew is caused by a fungus that forms a powdery white growth (that looks like flour) on the leaves and stems of plants. This disease can be eliminated in large part by increasing air circulation, thus reducing the accumulation of moisture on leaf surfaces. Karathane will give control. Apply as directed on the label.

Section Six

HANDY MAINTENANCE TIPS

Automatic Ventilation for Greenhouses

Ventilating greenhouses requires much time and attention. The temperature has to be checked and the ventilators opened if it is too hot or

closed if it is too cold. Automatic ventilation devices (illustrated) available at greenhouse suppliers can eliminate this burden. They monitor the temperature, and open and close the ventilators with an electric motor when required.

✓   ✓   ✓

Grandstand Arrangements for Plants

If plants are arranged on ascending steps of a greenhouse bench, they will receive more light. A grandstand arrangement also allows better display and easier inspection of plants.

✓   ✓   ✓

Use Water Breaker and Wand to Water Plants

Important: when watering greenhouse plants, do not allow water to strike plants and soil with great force. Plants can be uprooted and damaged by excessive force. Instead, attach a water breaker to the end of a rigid watering wand. The wand will enable you to direct the water to the less accessible parts of the greenhouse.

✓   ✓   ✓

Keep Good Records

Keep good records of your greenhouse operations. Record the source of your plants and how they were cared for. Fertilization, temperature, and light records are invaluable when analyzing growth problems. Also record such facts as the time seed was sown, when cuttings were made, and when plants were pinched.

Hang Pots to Create Space

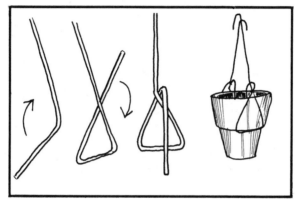

Create more space in your greenhouse by hanging pots on the sides of the house. Simple hangers can be made with galvanized wire, as illustrated.

Glass Shelves Add Room

Greenhouses soon become crowded and extra space for pots is usually needed. Create additional space by installing glass shelves on the greenhouse walls. The glass shelves minimize shading of the plants below.

Watering Hoses for Individual Plants

A number of devices that can be attached to hoses are now available to help in your watering chores. Spikes can be inserted into the hose to release water around individual plants. Another arrangement, called "spaghetti hose," can be run from a main hose to individual plant containers or individual plants in the ground. By attaching your watering hose to a timing device it is possible to water plants in the greenhouse automatically. Watering by this method prevents wetting of the leaves, which promotes disease development.

✓   ✓   ✓

Getting Your Hose out from Underfoot

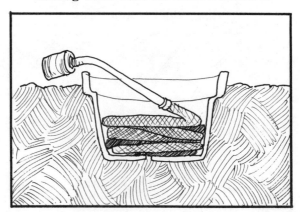

Hose left on the greenhouse floor is easy to trip over and difficult to manipulate. Coil your hose and store it in a large sunken clay pot. It will always be easy to reach, but will be out of the way.

✓   ✓   ✓

Syringing Greenhouse Plants

Many plants—orchids, carnation, snapdragons, cyclamen, and chrysanthemums—benefit from being syringed with a mist of water during the hotter hours of bright days. The spray reduces leaf temperatures and transpiration. Nozzles that break water into a fine mist are available. When syringing, wet the foliage but do not fill the pots or containers. Syringing is not a substitute for regular watering.

✓   ✓   ✓

Keep Leaves away from Glass in Winter

During the winter, leaves resting on the glass of a greenhouse may become frozen as heat is rapidly lost from the leaf surface to the cold glass. To avoid this, keep leaves away from the glass or put up insulating material. Polyethylene plastic fastened 1 inch away from the glass provides an air space for added insulation.

✓   ✓   ✓

Don't Overcrowd Greenhouses

Overcrowding, common to most greenhouses, is foolish. Crowding causes plants to shade one another; the reduction in light results in spindly growth and poor flowering. Overcrowding also makes watering difficult and increases chances of insect and disease infestation. Be wise: grow fewer plants and give them proper care and space.

✓   ✓   ✓

Reducing Greenhouse Fuel Costs

Fuel costs are increasing each year. The cost of heating a greenhouse can be reduced 20% to 40% by installing polyethylene film inside the greenhouse 1 to 2 inches below the glass. The dead air space that is created makes an excellent insulation.

✓   ✓   ✓

Checking Roots in a Pot

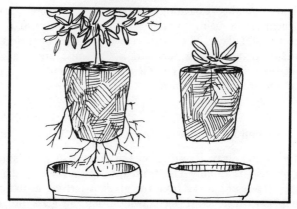

Greenhouse plants in pots should be checked periodically to see if plant roots have outgrown their containers or if the roots have not fully permeated the growth medium. To check root growth, turn the pot upside down and carefully remove the plant from the pot. If there is extensive root development outside the growth medium, repot in the next size pot. If the roots of the plant have not permeated the growth medium, repot it in a smaller pot. Carefully comb out matted roots before repotting.

🗡   🗡   🗡

Reduce Night Temperatures 10 Degrees

Plants do much of their growing at night. Since the higher the temperature, the greater the amount of food a plant burns through respiration, if night temperatures are too high, too much food will be burned and little or none will be available for growth. For this reason, keep night temperatures about 10 degrees lower than during the day.

CHAPTER TWELVE

Gardening Equipment

Overview

Gardening is more pleasurable if you have the right tool to perform each specific task. If you are a beginning gardener, **choose and accumulate tools slowly,** according to the jobs that need to be done. This will enable you to avoid filling your garage with useless tools.

Before buying any tool, **check the tool for weight and balance.** Also, test the grip on small hand tools such as pruning shears to see whether they "feel" right.

In purchasing all tools, manual or power, **always buy good quality products.** Avoid cheap tools. A good tool, properly maintained, will last many years. A poor tool, made of inferior metal, might not even survive one year's use.

Hand Tools

The following hand tools are necessary for basic gardening:

- A *shovel* for digging, transplanting, and excavating. A good shovel should have a strong handle, a curved or straight tip, a sharp edge, and a broad surface for your foot to push. You will eventually need more than one shovel to handle various tasks.
- A *digging fork* (pitchfork) for turning over a small patch as well as for lifting clumps of lilies, irises, potatoes, and dahlias without cutting roots.
- A *hoe* for cultivating and cutting out weeds as well as for making and covering rows. Hoes are available with a fork or pronged cultivating implements on the opposite face of the hoe.
- A *bow rake* made of steel-tined teeth for smoothing out freshly tilled ground and raking up debris.
- A *wire* or *bamboo leaf rake* to sweep leaves off the lawn and gather grass clippings.
- A *pronged cultivator* to loosen soil crusts and do light weeding.
- A *trowel* for small planting jobs. One with a rounded wooden handle is less apt to raise blisters.
- A *garden cart* for carrying loads. A cart is better than a wheelbarrow since you can carry more with less effort.
- A *spreader* to distribute chemical fertilizers, grass seed, peat moss, and other soil conditioners.

You will eventually need a variety of cutting tools:

* An *ax*—a 4-pound head is recommended.
* A *pruning saw* that has 5 or 6 teeth to the inch.
* *Pruning shears*—a snap-cut type makes a cleaner cut.
* *Hedge shears*—the larger and heavier, the better.
* An *asparagus knife*—a long steel shank with a V-shaped, pronged, sharp blade. Used for digging out deep-rooted weeds.
* *Grass clippers*—buy a set that can be squeezed easily.

Take care of your tools. Don't store garden tools until soil and plant debris have been removed and metal surfacess have been wiped dry with an oily cloth. Soil does not cling to a clean tool as much as to a dirty one.

Bent tools should be straightened in a vise by bending them gently. Spades and hoes should be sharpened by clamping them in a vise and filing toward the edges of the blade at a 45-degree angle.

All **hand tools with movable parts should be oiled** occasionally. Tools with grease fittings, such as some wheelbarrows, should occasionally be given a shot of grease. When storing tools for the winter, it is good practice to coat metal surfaces lightly with grease. This will prevent rust.

Eventually, **you will need a sprayer and duster.** Dusters are less expensive. One of the simplest and least expensive sprayers is the "trombone type." Since a bucket serves as the tank in this type of sprayer, materials are easily mixed and washed out. If you only have a few plants, start with a duster. For a big yard with a lot of plants, start with a sprayer and get the duster later. A duster can be used for small jobs in a big yard. Spraying is cheaper than dusting and does a better job for pest control. Keep a separate sprayer for weed killers. Weed killer residue in the spray tank may kill plants when the same sprayer is used to apply insecticides or fungicides. If it is impractical to keep a separate sprayer for weed killers, rinse several times with warm, soapy water after use, taking care that the sprayer mechanism as well as the tank is flushed.

Power Equipment

There is no limit to the number of power tools now available to make your gardening chores easier. Most cutting tools are now available in power models. Your decision to buy a power tool will depend on your budget and the size of your task. Power tools require more maintenance and, unless you plan to get sufficient use out of them, they are often not needed.

Power tools are generally available with three power sources: (1) cord outlet-operated electrical motors, (2) battery or power-pack-operated electric motors, and (3) gasoline engines. Electric models are easier to maintain and cheaper to operate. If your garden is close enough to a house outlet and your task is not too difficult, a cord-operated model is best. Battery operated models gives the maintenance advantage of the cord-operated model without the nuisance of the cord. The mobility advantage has to be weighed against the need to constantly recharge the battery. If your task is extensive or far from the house, you will probably want to choose a gasoline engine model.

Before purchasing any power tool, read brochures and talk to neighbors to learn of their experiences. Advertisements are often misleading, and it pays to study the subject before spending a lot of money.

The only power tool which has become a necessity is the power lawn mower. A garden tractor is recommended only if your area justifies it. Most suburban lawns would do best with a walk-behind mower, which offers greater mobility in corners and around plants. An advantage of garden tractors is that attachments can be purchased that are operable using the tractor power plant (or PTO—power take-off).

Lawn mowers come in reel and rotary models. The reel type is best for fine lawns mowed close to the ground. A rotary mower is recommended for the average lawn. In either case, keeping the blade sharp—something you can do yourself with a rotary blade—is very important.

Most power tools come with basic maintenance instructions. **The most important maintenance steps are to grease the machine, change the oil, and replace the filters at required intervals.** Many owners neglect these steps, resulting in the destruction of tens of thousands of machines each year.

Follow manufacturer's directions for maintenance and storage of all power tools. In all cases, tools which are not used during the winter should be run until all remaining fuel is consumed before storage.

Handy Devices and Gadgets

Since such a large part of gardening involves improvising, as would be expected, a large number of devices and gadgets have become commercially available to assist you in your gardening. Some of these are very useful; others are a needless expense. Experience will make you discriminating in your purchases. In your own gardening, you will doubtlessly come up against many tasks which will require you to invent a tool or gadget. The last section of this chapter contains a selection of unusual and improvised tools which may prove useful.

Section One

HAND TOOLS

Judging Metal Quality of Hand Tools

Poor quality metal hand tools often become worthless after a single use. Difficulties develop because of the poor quality metal used in the tool. Test a hand trowel or shovel by placing the point into a board and applying pressure onto the handle. If the metal bends or buckles easily, don't choose that tool. Choose a tool with unbendable metal. It is good economy to spend a little bit more money and buy good quality hand tools. Good quality tools can last a lifetime.

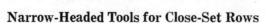

Narrow-Headed Tools for Close-Set Rows

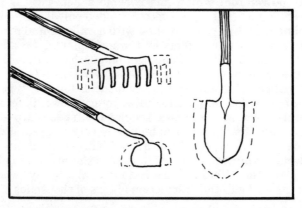

Digging, weeding, and other garden operations between close-set rows are difficult with standard sized garden tools. Keep in mind that narrow-headed rakes, shovels, and hoes are available. Such tools have heads that are 6 to 8 inches wide. They are particularly useful for flower gardening.

A Good Planting Hoe

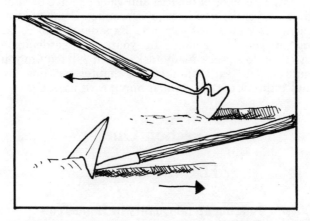

Pointed hoes are available that are useful in planting a garden row. The point can be turned face down to make furrows for seed and plants. The other face can then be used to hill soil over newly sown seeds, as illustrated.

Special Hoes for Shallow Digging

When hoeing a garden, it is important not to dig too deeply to avoid injuring vegetable roots. There are special hoes that prevent you from digging too deeply. Conventional hoes have a blade that is approximately 5 inches wide and 4 inches deep. Special hoes with blades 7 inches wide and 1¾ inches deep are better for weeding between garden rows. These hoes are sometimes sold under the name "onion hoe."

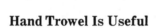

Using a Hoe or a Motorized Cultivator

Garden plants can be damaged by deep cultivation. Most plants in the garden have rather shallow roots. Deep cultivation can destroy roots and injure or even kill plants. If only a few weeds are present, remove them by shallow hoeing. If there are a lot of weeds and you prefer to use a cultivator, make sure that it is set to just skim off the top layer of soil.

Hand Trowel Is Useful

A trowel is a small hand tool consisting of a short handle and a blade that resembles a miniature curved spade or shovel. Hand trowels are useful for anything for which a shovel is useful, but on a smaller scale. They can be used for digging and filling holes, moving soil and cleaning up. The best style hand trowel is one that has one piece of steel with a cone-shaped socket into which a wooden handle is inserted and held by a riveted pin extending through both sides. Such a trowel usually costs more than the one piece pressed metal type or any of the double-ended combination trowel-and-weeders. It is, however, worth the extra money because of its greater usefulness and durability. Wooden handled trowels are also less apt to raise blisters than those with metal handles.

Rakes for Different Purposes

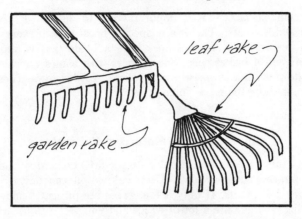

Two basic types of garden rakes are needed for gardening: a lawn rake and a rake with solid steel tines. Lawn rakes are used like a broom to sweep up leaves and other debris. A rake with solid steel tines should not be used for this purpose because it will destroy young grass plants. Steel-tined rakes can be used to break up soil clods and to level and smoothe soil surfaces. They are particularly useful in preparing seed beds for planting.

✓   ✓   ✓

Thatch Removing Rake

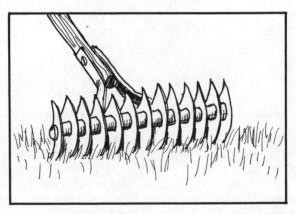

Thatch is the brown layer of plant debris that accumulates at the base of your grass blades. It should be removed to promote grass vigor and reduce the chances of disease. Special machines can be rented to remove thatch from large lawn areas. But for smaller lawn areas, a special dethatching rake can be purchased.

✓   ✓   ✓

Edgers for Grass Borders

Lawns look neater and are easier to maintain if a narrow 1- or 2-inch strip of sod is removed around sidewalks, paths, driveways, and buildings. Edging devices are made to perform this job. Two of the most useful are pictured here.

✓   ✓   ✓

A Useful Sod Plugger

Plugs of sod are used to start some lawns, particularly Zosia and Bermuda grass lawns. The chore of digging up sod plugs and digging holes to plant them can be a laborious one if you do not own the right tool. Illustrated is a handy sod plugger that will perform these tasks. The plugger is operated in "pogo stick" fashion and can speed up plugging operations considerably.

✓   ✓   ✓

Long-Handled Bulb Planters

Planting bulbs can be backbreaking work. One way to reduce the stooping

necessary when planting bulbs is to purchase a long-handled bulb planter. The planter illustrated on the left of the diagram has wings on which you can place your foot and force the planter into the soil. After a core of soil is removed, the bulb is placed in the hole and the soil is replaced. Marks sometimes found on the sides of bulb planters will tell you the exact depth of the hole you have made. Shorthandled bulb planters (right) are available for small plantings.

✧   ✧   ✧

Special Flower-Picking Shears

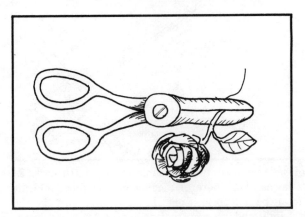

Picking flowers can sometimes become frustrating because it is difficult to hold a flower, cut it, and prevent the flower from falling to the ground. There are special "flower-picking shears" that solve this problem. The flower is cut and also held by the shears until you transfer it to a receptacle. Some ordinary pruning shears also have this "cut-and-hold" feature.

✧   ✧   ✧

Curved Pruning Saws

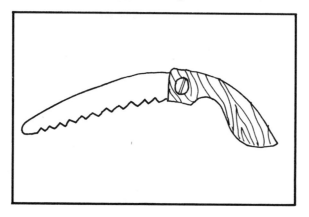

Hand pruners can be used to cut away small branches, but a pruning saw is required to remove larger branches from trees and shrubs. A handy tool for larger branches is a curved pruning saw. The teeth of this saw are designed to cut on the pull stroke, unlike most saws, which are designed to cut on the push stroke.

🗸　　🗸　　🗸

Pole Pruners for Tall Trees

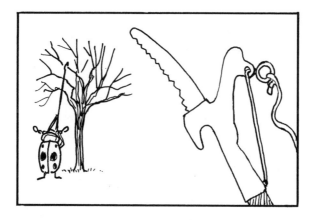

Pruning small branches out of trees at heights above 6 feet is difficult. Even if a ladder is used, some branches are impossible to reach. Pole pruners equipped with pruning shears and saw blades are available for these difficult pruning jobs. Pruning can be performed from the ground without having to climb the tree or a ladder. Pole pruners come with sections that can be fitted together to reach a height of 18 feet.

🗸　　🗸　　🗸

Taking Care of a Digging Fork

Digging forks are very useful for digging flower bulbs, separating flower roots, and turning over soil for a garden. Through improper use, though, digging forks can lose their usefulness rapidly. If only one of the tines on a digging fork is bent out of shape, the fork becomes difficult to insert in the soil. Try to avoid using digging forks in rocky soil or for any job that might bend the tines. If a tine does bend, straighten it out before further use.

Lopping Shears for Powerful Pruning Cuts

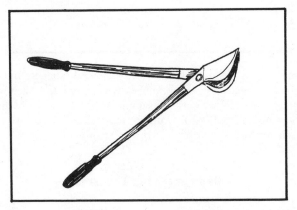

Pruning cuts that cannot be made with hand pruners are best done with lopping shears. These long-handled pruners allow you to make powerful cuts because of the added leverage provided. They work well for thinning hedges or shrubs, removing low sprouts and reducing the number of pruning operations required.

Cyclone vs. Axle Spreaders

Two basic types of spreaders for distributing granular fertilizer, seed and weed killers are available: *cyclone* spreaders and *axle* spreaders. Cyclone spreaders feed the material onto a revolving plate that broadcasts it by centrifugal force. Axle spreaders drop the material through holes in the bottom of a bin with the aid of a rotating axle. In most cases, the spreading mechanism is activated by the turning of the wheels of the device. Cyclone spreaders (pictured) in which the operator provides the power for activating the mechanism are available.

The openings at the bottom of the bin of axle spreaders tend to corrode. When these spreaders are not in use, all material should be removed from the bin and a light coating of oil placed on the axle. Cyclone spreaders are more desirable than axle spreaders because they are less apt to corrode and

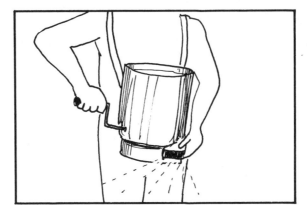

will deliver a more even spread. Axle spreaders deliver in a distinct band and can cause uneven stripes in the yard if the spreader is not precisely lined up.

✓   ✓   ✓

Fruit Pickers

Apples, peaches, and pears are sometimes difficult to reach and harvest even with a ladder. Shaking the tree is not desirable because the fruit falls to the ground and bruises. A number of fruit-picking devices that can help solve this problem are available. The one illustrated has rake-like projections that can be used to pull the fruit loose in such a manner that it will fall into the basket. A long pole can be attached to reach high up into the tree.

✓   ✓   ✓

Choosing a Garden Sprayer

You have a choice between 2 different types of manual garden sprayers: the *continuous pressure* type, which requires physical effort whenever spray

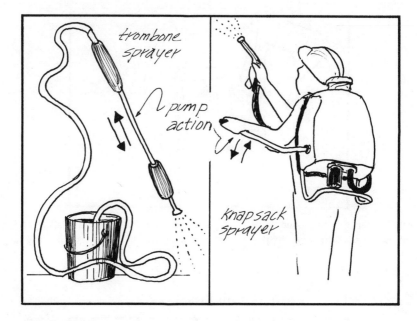

is required; and the *stored pressure* type, in which compressed air sufficient for several minutes of spraying is stored in a tank.

The continuous pressure sprayer is probably the best choice for the casual gardener who has a limited number of plants. In this category, the trombone sprayer is very satisfactory for most tasks. As illustrated in the left of the diagram, this sprayer consists of a hose that takes up spray material from a bucket. Spray pressure is generated by the trombonelike action of the spray gun. The bucket makes mixing and cleaning up much easier than with other types of sprayers.

If your gardening is extensive enough that lugging around a pail would be difficult, consider a continuous pressure *knapsack* sprayer. The one illustrated on the right is activated by moving an arm attached to the sprayer upward and downward, generating compressed air in the tank. No compressed air is stored.

For very limited tasks, such as attending to a few rose plants, squeeze type continuous pressure sprayers are available. These sprayers generally hold about a quart of material. They are useful indoors as well as outdoors. Every gardener should have one of these handy sprayers.

Sprayers that store compressed air in their tanks are most desirable for large jobs since they produce a more powerful spray. A number of hand and power-driven models are available. If you choose a stored compressed air model as your basic sprayer, be aware that this type of sprayer often handles several gallons of material and can become quite heavy. A set-up which allows you to wheel the mechanism is desirable.

Cleaning Sprayers after Herbicide Use

If you have used a herbicide such as 2,4-D in your sprayer, the sprayer tank and hose should be thoroughly cleaned before using it to apply insecticides or fungicides. Herbicide residues may remain in the spray tank and damage plants. Activated charcoal or household ammonia can be used as cleaning agents. If activated charcoal is used, thoroughly mix 1 ounce of charcoal with 1 to 2 ounces of household detergent in 2½ gallons of water. Fill the sprayer with this mixture and operate for about 2 minutes. If ammonia is used, make a solution of 2 tablespoons of ammonia in a quart of water. Fill the sprayer with the solution and spray a small amount through the nozzle. Let the rest of the solution stand in the sprayer overnight. Then, pour out the solution and rinse the sprayer twice with clean water. Spray part of each rinse through the nozzle.

✓   ✓   ✓

Problems with Hand Pump Sprayers

Most hand pump sprayers have galvanized tanks. Because the interiors of these tanks react with the spray chemicals and form substances which tend to gum up sprayer hoses and nozzles, always wash out spray tanks thoroughly after use. Make sure to spray clean water through the hoses and nozzle after use as well. Newer sprayers with plastic tanks are less apt to clog up from corrosion.

✓   ✓   ✓

Earth Auger for Fertilization Holes and Drainage

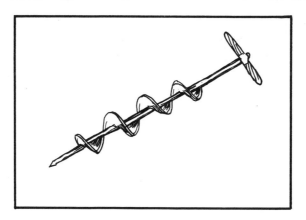

It is sometimes desirable to drill deep holes in the soil to add fertilizers or improve drainage. An earth auger bit has been designed for this purpose. It can be powered manually or by a gasoline-driven motor. The bit lifts the soil out of the hole. The auger comes in a variety of diameters.

✓   ✓   ✓

Seeders Aren't Necessary

Garden catalogs advertise seeders that can be adjusted to plant different types of garden seeds. These machines are really not necessary for the home garden. Most gardening time is spent in preparing the soil and cultivation. Very little time is required for seeding. Seeding by hand can be a pleasurable experience and is more reliable than seeding with machines. If you do buy a machine seeder, you will find yourself spending a great deal of time resetting the seeder as you go from crop to crop.

Section Two

POWER TOOLS

Differences between 2- and 4-Cycle Engines

Some garden tools are powered best by 2-cycle engines; others are powered best by 4-cycle engines. Two-cycle engines are lighter and can run at faster speeds than 4-cycle ones. They are useful for tools such as power chain saws and portable power sprayers that need to be lightweight and run at high speeds. Four-cycle engines are useful where weight and high engine speeds are not factors, as is the case with riding lawn mowers. Four-cycle engines don't require as much maintenance as 2-cycle engines because the engine is less apt to become clogged with carbon. Gas-oil mixtures are needed for 2-cycle engines; gasoline alone is needed for 4-cycle engines. In cases where an option exists as to which engine to purchase—as with power lawn mowers—the 4-cycle model is the better choice.

Two-Cycle Engines Can Be Bothersome

Two-cycle engines require that you use a mixture of gasoline and oil as fuel. Lubrication of internal parts depends on the presence of oil. Mixing the oil and gas in the right proportion can be bothersome. It is easy to forget to add the oil, and gasoline alone can ruin the engine. For this reason, 4-cycle engines are preferable to 2-cycle engines where there is a choice. Because 2-cycle engines are more compact than 4-cycle engines, certain tools, such as chain saws, come only with 2-cycle engines.

Mix Gas and Oil before Adding to 2-Cycle Engines

Some people pour gas and oil into the tanks of 2-cycle engines and mix them in the tank. Don't do this. The oil will clog filters and may even work into the carburetor before the gas has a chance to mix with it thoroughly.

✓   ✓   ✓

Check Oil Level of Engines Regularly

If oil is not maintained at the proper level in gasoline engines, extra stress is placed on engine parts. Check the oil level every 3 operating hours or every week—whichever is sooner. To avoid contaminating oil with dirt and grass clippings, always clean the area around the oil filler plug before removing the plug. The oil level should reach the overflow point in the fill hole or between the "full" and "add" marks on the dipstick.

✓   ✓   ✓

Changing Oil in Gasoline Engines

Changing oil is the single most important step in gasoline engine maintenance. If the oil is not changed periodically, the oil becomes dirty to the point where engine parts begin to wear and the engine's life is shortened. Change the oil in new engines after 2 hours of operation and every 25 hours thereafter—and more often if it is operated in extremely dirty areas.

To drain the oil, first run the engine so that the oil is hot and will run out easily. Next, position the equipment so that the engine oil drain plug is at the lowest point. Allow the oil to drain completely. Replace the oil drain plug and tighten securely before refilling the engine with new oil of the proper viscosity.

✓   ✓   ✓

Put in the Right Oil

Different parts of gasoline-powered machines require oils with different viscosities. The motor's crankcase usually requires 20 or 30 weight oil. The wheels and lighter mowing parts require a 20 weight oil. The gear box requires a 90 weight oil or higher. Though some manuals call for 140 weight gear oil, this is not always available and 90 weight must be used.

✓   ✓   ✓

Don't Put a New Engine Right to Work

New engines need to be broken in slowly. If you have a new engine, run it for an hour or so at idling speed with occasional bursts of full throttle. This allows the engine to "wear in" properly before being strained by a work load.

✓   ✓   ✓

Run Gasoline Engines at Recommended Speeds

Some people think that you can add to the life of a gasoline engine by running it at half speed. For best performance and longest engine life, a gasoline engine should be run at its recommended speed—generally 80% of its top speed. Running an engine slower than recommended actually causes more wear since air intake, cooling, and oil circulation are engineered for the recommended speed.

✦   ✦   ✦

When Engines Overheat Quickly

If your engine overheats quickly after it starts up, the problem may be due to debris clogging air cooling fins. Heat is dissipated through these external fins. When debris becomes clogged between them, heat is trapped and cannot escape fast enough. Clean these fins with a brush.

✦   ✦   ✦

Don't Start Motors in Closed Areas

Never start or operate a gasoline engine in a closed area such as a garage. Even small lawn mower engines can emit deadly amounts of carbon monoxide fumes.

✦   ✦   ✦

Use Your Gas Shut-Off Valve

Most engines have a gasoline shut-off valve located between the gas tank and the carburetor. A way to prevent future carburetor troubles is to use the gas shut-off valve usually located near the gas tank. When you have finished operating the engine, close the gas shut-off valve and run the engine until it stops. This will prevent gummy products from building up in the carburetor. It will also reduce the flooding problems common to some small engines.

✦   ✦   ✦

Check Engine Air Filters

Never operate a gasoline engine without checking the air filter. Clogged air filters reduce engine efficiency and may prevent the engine from running. Do not run an engine without an air filter; doing so can ruin the engine.

✦   ✦   ✦

Check Spark Plugs

The failure of a gasoline engine to run can often be traced to an inoperative spark plug. Periodically take out the spark plugs and remove the debris in the gap with a knife. Gap the plug according to manufacturer recommendations.

✦   ✦   ✦

Oil-Gas Mixtures Not for 4-Cycle Engines

The oil-gas mixtures used for 2-cycle engines won't work for 4-cycle engines. Oily gas fouls the plugs and builds up heavy carbon deposits in 4-cycle engines. Use regular gasoline. If you have 2-cycle equipment as well as 4-cycle equipment, it is a good idea to label the fuel cans to avoid confusion.

✓   ✓   ✓

How to Check Belts

Many pieces of garden equipment depend on belts to run them. For efficient operation, these belts should be checked periodically. Check to see whether there is proper tightness between the belt and the pulleys. There should be about ½-inch play under light finger pressure. Belts tighter than this wear faster and do not improve engine efficiency. Over-tightened belts also put strain on the engine bearings.

✓   ✓   ✓

Storing Gasoline Engines

If gasoline engines are to be stored for more than 30 days, take the following precautions: (1) Remove all gasoline from the carburetor and fuel tank. (2) Run the engine until the fuel tank is empty and the engine stops. (3) Remove the spark plug and pour a few drops of engine oil through the spark plug hole into the cylinder. (4) Crank the engine several times to distribute the oil and replace the spark plug. (5) Remove any clippings, dirt, or chaff from the exterior.

It is good procedure to put an engine in perfect condition *before* storing it. Most owners are in a hurry when taking the machine out of storage and don't take the trouble to check it thoroughly.

✓   ✓   ✓

Self-Propelled vs. Manually-Propelled Mowers

Lawn mowers are available in self-propelled and manually-propelled models. If your lawn is relatively level, there is little advantage in purchasing a sef-propelled model. The less costly manual model should be your choice. However, if you need to negotiate a number of grades, a self-propelled model can reduce your work load considerably.

✓   ✓   ✓

Proper Horsepower for Power Walking Lawnmowers

The horsepower that you choose for a power walking lawnmower should be matched with the mower's cutting width. The wider the cut, the more horsepower required. If the cutting width is less than 20 inches, a 3½-horsepower mower is satisfactory. If the cut is 22 inches or above, don't settle for less than a 4-horsepower engine.

↗   ↗   ↗

Don't Buy Riding Mowers under 7 Horsepower

When buying a riding lawnmower, keep in mind that the power required to carry the rider is usually greater than the power required to cut the grass. Relatively inexpensive riding mowers are on the market with engines rated at low horsepowers. Such mowers are not satisfactory because they do not generate enough power to propel the mower and a rider without considerable strain on the engine. Such mowers do not perform well when they are operating and will need frequent repair. When purchasing a riding mower, never buy one with an engine rated at less than 7 horsepower.

↗   ↗   ↗

Sharpening Rotary Mower Blades

Rotary mower blades can be sharpened using a file or a grinder. The blade should be removed from the mower to sharpen it properly. It is not necessary to sharpen more than the outer three inches of the cutting edge of the blade since this area does all the cutting. Sharpen the cutting edge at an angle of 30 degrees. The two cutting edges should be sharpened as symmetrically as possible to keep the blade balanced. If you have an electric drill, you will find grinding wheels available which mount to the drill as would a drill bit. Devices are available which will hold the drill while you are grinding.

↗   ↗   ↗

Balance Rotary Mower Blades

When sharpening rotary mower blades, make sure that you also balance them. If a blade is unbalanced, it will cause undue wear on the engine. You can check the balance by supporting the blade at the center and observe whether it tips one way or the other. If one side is heavier, remove more metal with your sharpening equipment. Sharpening wheels can be mounted on electric drills and radial saws. Inexpensive bench grinders are also available.

↗   ↗   ↗

Replace Bent Rotary Mower Blades

Bent mower blades not only cut unevenly, but they can also damage the mower by causing vibrations. Check your rotary mower blade before each use. If the blade is bent, replace it.

↗   ↗   ↗

Never Tip a Mower While It Is Running

Never tip a mower for inspection without first stopping it. Remove the spark plug wire before looking under the mower. Turning the blades with the spark plug attached can start the mower.

✤   ✤   ✤

Never Leave a Running Mower Unattended

Never leave a running mower unattended. Besides obvious injuries that can be caused to curious children, a running mower will often move by itself, destroying everything in its path.

✤   ✤   ✤

Clean under Your Lawn Mower

Debris that builds up under a lawn mower can place a strain on the engine and result in poor cutting. Clean under your mower periodically. First, remove the wire from the spark plug to prevent the mower from accidentally starting. Then, use a flexible broadbladed putty knife or a wire brush to scrape all the grass clippings and soil away from the undercarriage and shaft mounting.

✤   ✤   ✤

Keep Reel Type Mowers Clean and Oiled

Reel type lawn mowers are more apt to become fouled than rotary mowers because of the closer clearances between the blades and frame. For this reason, keep reel mowers extra clean and rust free, using oil liberally.

✤   ✤   ✤

Dethatching Attachment for Rotary Mowers

Lawns should be periodically dethatched to reduce disease and facilitate soil aeration. There is a simple dethatching device that can be attached easily to the blade of a rotary lawn mower to perform this function. This device spares you the expense of purchasing separate dethatching equipment.

✤   ✤   ✤

The Best Type of Roto-tiller

A roto-tiller is a machine which churns up the soil. Roto-tillers are very convenient for preparing soil for planting as well as for cultivation. Two basic types of roto-tillers are available: those with wheels *in front of* the tiller and those with the wheels *behind* the tiller. Tillers with wheels in the front are much easier to manipulate when in operation. Holding onto and turning tillers with wheels in the back can be a backbreaking job.

✤   ✤   ✤

Cleaning Roto-tillers

Clean the undercarriage and tines every time you use a rotary tiller. Weeds often wrap themselves around the shaft, putting undue strain on the engine. Wads of clay soil may work themselves into the transmission housing if not removed.

✓   ✓   ✓

Storing Power Sprayers

If sprayers are not stored properly, they can be ruined during the winter by freezing or corrosion. Don't leave any liquids in the sprayer tank or spray lines over winter. Freezing can cause these materials to expand and burst the tank and lines. Thoroughly wash and rinse the spray tank after its last use for the season. Add a cup of kerosene to the tank, slosh it around, and pour it out. This reduces rust and corrosion. Add oil to the suction parts of the sprayer for the winter. If possible store sprayer tanks upside down.

✓   ✓   ✓

Undercapacity Extension Cords Are Dangerous

If undercapacity extension cords are used for electric-powered gardening equipment, both the cord and the equipment will heat up and possibly ignite. In addition, the equipment will not run at full efficiency. Check the instructions on the equipment that you are using for the proper capacity extension cord to use. Most garden equipment requires cords that are rated for 7-8 amps. Cords rated to carry 3-5 amps are not satisfactory. All electric cords carry a rating as to their current carrying capacity. A 16-gauge wire will carry up to 10 amps at a distance of 100 feet. A 14-gauge wire will carry up to 13 amps at 100 feet.

✓   ✓   ✓

Don't Cut Your Extension Cord

Every year thousands of people end up cutting their extension cords with electric hedge trimmers. This can be a literally shocking experience. When cutting a hedge, keep the electrical cord over your shoulder and behind you. Make a conscious effort to know where the cord is at all times. Battery operated hedge trimmers do not present this problem.

✓   ✓   ✓

Nylon Line Grass Trimmer

A new type of grass trimmer is available that utilizes a piece of nylon line rotating at high speed to cut grass. This tool is useful in touching up those hard-to-get-at places after mowing. It efficiently cuts grass and weeds along fences, against walls, and around trees. For the best cutting action, move the trimmer slowly so that grass and weeds are cut with the tip of the high-speed nylon line. With this type of trimmer, you will reduce the danger of bruising trees and avoid the unpleasant scraping sound when blade hits rock. Both electric and gasoline models are available.

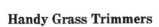

Handy Grass Trimmers

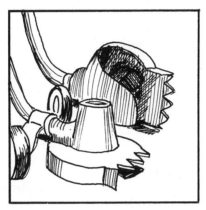

After you have finished mowing the lawn, the trimming of grass around the edges is what gives it that "finished" look. This can be a laborious task, but there are a number of devices that can make it easier. An adjustable electric lawn trimmer is one that will do the job well.

Lightweight Chain Saws Not for Pruning

Lightweight chain saws are useful for a number of tasks around the home and garden, including removing dead branches, cutting fire-wood, and clearing out brush. However, unless you are very skillful, these saws should *not* be used for pruning. They generally leave ragged cuts, and a slip can cause extensive injury to the plant. Pruning saws and shears are preferable to chain saws for good pruning.

Paint Sprayers Work as Garden Sprayers

If you have a compressor-driven paint sprayer, it can be used as an effective garden sprayer. Spray materials can be mixed in the paint container and sprayed on plants. Be sure that the paint container is thoroughly cleaned before and after you apply pesticides with it. Paint residues can injure plants and pesticide residues can ruin a paint job. With a little ingenuity you should be able to find a larger container that will fit the compressor and thereby increase your spraying capacity.

"Shredder-Bagger" for Compost Material

Much potentially good compost material—such as branches, vines, and other plant debris—will not break down in a compost pile because it is too bulky. The "shredder-bagger" is a useful garden apparatus that reduces all plant material down to good composting size and bags it up for you at the same time. Plant debris is fed into a shredder; the shredder spits it out into a bag. Both electric and gasoline models are available. The electric model might require a 220-volt power source.

✓   ✓   ✓

Rechargeable Batteries for Garden Tools

Electric power tools for gardening have been available for some time. They are useful but require long extension cords to reach electrical outlets. The recent development of rechargeable batteries for garden tools has lessened this problem. Some manufacturers make an interchangeable garden workshop battery source that can be used with a variety of tools, including grass and hedge trimmers.

Section Three

HANDY DEVICES AND GADGETS

Waterproof Cushions to Spare Knees

Knees can suffer greatly from a full day of outdoor gardening. To avoid this, a waterproof cushion can turn out to be the gardener's best friend. Any old pillow wrapped in polyethylene will work. You can sit or kneel on it. Why not be comfortable and relatively clean while you cultivate, seed, or weed?

✓   ✓   ✓

Gardening Stool

A simple gardening stool, like the one illustrated, can be very useful. Besides providing a handy seat, it has a place to conveniently store hand tools. A movable gardening stool is particularly useful when performing such tasks as tying up tomatoes.

✓   ✓   ✓

Row Marking Line-and-Reel

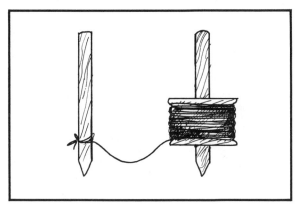

It is very important that garden rows be straight and properly spaced. If they are not, gardening equipment cannot be operated between the rows without disturbing plants. The simplest way to mark garden rows is to stretch a string between two stakes and to use the edge of a hoe to dig a small furrow along the line of the string. A handy, easy-to-make gadget with which to stretch the string is illustrated. The spool provides a place to store excess string and to "reel up" the string after it is used.

✓   ✓   ✓

Use a Shovel as a Sled

Don't lift heavy sacks of fertilizer and plant material unnecessarily. One simple way to move such materials a short distance is to use your shovel as a sled. Snow shovels work particularly well.

*   *   *

Support Ring for Large Plastic Bags

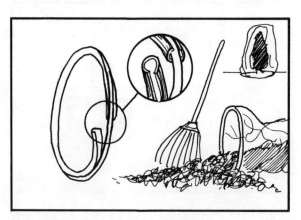

Large plastic bags are used for a variety of gardening chores, including picking up leaves and covering plants. The filling of plastic bags can become a two-man operation—one man to hold the bag open and another to fill it. If you are working alone, purchase a plastic ring known as a "Ring-Dang-Do" to hold plastic bags open. The "Ring-Dang-Do" can also serve as support for a plastic bag used to cover plants.

*   *   *

A Useful Hand Truck

Hand trucks, used in business deliveries, are useful for hauling such things as plant containers, sacks of fertilizer, and concrete. A hand truck fitted with a hoop and plastic bag holder (see previous hint) is particularly useful for gathering leaves and other plant debris.

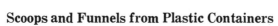

Disposable Plastic Gloves for Handling Pesticides

Some pesticides are dangerous if allowed to come in contact with one's skin. To prevent contamination of skin and clothing, wear disposable plastic gloves when handling pesticides. After use, they can be discarded. If you can't locate plastic gloves, plastic sacks placed over your hands will suffice. Don't use regular cloth gloves since pesticide residue can build up in the glove and penetrate your skin.

Scoops and Funnels from Plastic Containers

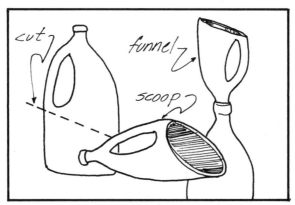

Scoops and funnels are helpful when handling pesticides and fertilizers. Make your own scoop-funnel device by cutting away portions of plastic containers as illustrated below.

Hose Reels Are Useful

Garden hoses are cumbersome to handle and store. A variety of hose reels are available to ease this problem. The garden hose can be reeled up like a fishing line when it is not being used. Some reels can be mounted on the side of a house; others can be mounted on hand trucks for easy movement from one area to another. If you are mechanically inclined, it is possible to convert on old tire rim into a hose reel.

Flame Thrower for Weed Control

Weeds are often difficult to control on walkways and greenhouse floors. Because of potential damage to surrounding plants, chemical herbicides should not be used for these purposes. A novel and effective way to kill these weeds is to use a "flame thrower." Available from some garden suppliers, the "jet rod" flame thrower can be used to actually burn out weeds. The flame thrower burns kerosene and is relatively safe to use.

🔥   🔥   🔥

Lawn Sweepers

Modern lawn mowers have attachments that gather lawn clippings as they are produced. Most gardeners, however, do not own these attachments and still clean up their clippings manually. Raking does the job, but requires considerable muscle. A compromise is to purchase a lawn sweeper, a device that acts much like a carpet sweeper in picking up clippings.

🔥   🔥   🔥

Quick Couplers for Outdoor Hoses

Connecting lawn hoses with the conventional screw-on type of fitting is time-consuming and often unsatisfactory because of leaks. As a timesaver, install "quick coupling connections" on your garden hoses and outdoor faucets. These devices, which snap on and off readily, are widely available at hardware stores and garden supply centers.

⟡   ⟡   ⟡

Siamese Hose Connectors

In gardening, you might occasionally need to connect two hoses to the same outdoor water outlet. The "siamese hose connector" allows you to operate two hoses at the same time. It is equipped with a shut-off valve when only one hose is needed.

⟡   ⟡   ⟡

Stickle-Back Drill for Pots

Sometimes, clay plant pots do not have a hole in the bottom for drainage,

or need additional holes. Hardware and garden centers can supply you with a "stickle-back" drill for this purpose. Simply twist the drill through the point where the hole is wanted. Do not use conventional drill bits, which may crack the pots.

✦   ✦   ✦

Shovel to Dig Trees and Shrubs

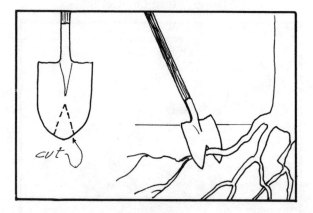

Digging trees and shrubs for transplanting can be a laborious job. One major difficulty is severing the roots around the tree with a shovel before the tree is lifted out of the hole. Roots tend to "run" from the shovel edge and are difficult to cut. By a simple modification of a regular digging shovel, these difficulties can be avoided. Cut a V-shaped wedge out of the center of your shovel with a hack saw or any other cutting tool; sharpen the remaining V in the shovel with a file. Roots are easily corralled and cut in the V as you dig around the tree.

✦   ✦   ✦

Ice Scraper Good for Cleaning Garden Tools

Soil and debris stick closely to garden implements and should be removed before the implements are stored after gardening. A simple device that can be used to remove this material is the common ice scraper designed to remove ice from car windows.

✓   ✓   ✓

Sweeper Nozzles to Clean Garden Equipment

Cleaning the soil from garden equipment can be a laborious job when done by hand. Special "sweeper nozzles" can be purchased for a garden hose that will make this job easier. These nozzles produce a powerful spray that knocks soil particles and other debris off of garden equipment.

✓   ✓   ✓

Hose Guides around the Garden

Dragging garden hose across the garden can cause considerable damage to plants. A simple way to prevent this is to place hose guides around the edge of the garden. This can be done by driving 18-inch stakes into the ground about 6 inches, leaving about 12 inches of the stake above ground. Place the stakes so that the garden hose will slide around them and not enter the garden. The stakes can be removed after watering if they prove to be an eyesore.

✓   ✓   ✓

Weed Killer Applicator on a Stick

Herbicide sprays to kill weeds sometimes cause damage to wanted plants in the vicinity of the weeds. One way to avoid this is to dab the weed killer directly onto the weed rather than spraying it. Simply tie a piece of sponge onto the end of a stick. Keep the sponge wet with concentrated herbicide and touch the weeds that you wish to kill with the sponge.

✓   ✓   ✓

Measuring Foot Candles with a Camera Light Meter

The light requirements of different plants varies and is recorded in foot candles. If you have a light meter that measures light directly in foot candles, it is easy to check the light intensity at various locations in your home. If you don't have a meter of this kind, the light meter that you use with your camera will work. Set the film speed at ASA 100 and aim the meter at a white card placed approximately where the plant will be. The shutter speed reading (taken as a whole number) that appears opposite f4 will correspond to the approximate foot candles of illumination. For example, if the indicated exposure is 1/250 seconds at f4, the light available is 250 foot candles.

LOW LIGHT	MEDIUM LIGHT	HIGH LIGHT
15-25 foot candles	*25-50 foot candles*	*50-100 foot candles*
Aspidistra	Boston fern	Crotons
Chinese evergreen	Bromeliad	English ivy
Diffenbachia amoena	Cissus rhombifolia	Ficus elastica decora
Diffenbachia picta	Holly fern	Ficus elastica doescheri
Nephthytis	Peperomia	Ficus exotica
Philodendron cordatum	Philodendron dubia	Ficus pandurata
Philodendron panduriforme	Devil's ivy	Geraniums
Philodendron pertusum		Japanese fatsia
Sansevieria		Kangaroo ivy
Schefflera		Mountain acanthus
		Velvet plant

Colander Useful to Spread Fertilizer

A colander, which is used in the kitchen to wash and drain vegetables, can be used to spread chemical fertilizers by hand. Simply fill the colander with fertilizer and shake. The material will be released evenly through the holes.

Consider an Aluminum Storage Shed

After you have been involved in gardening for a while, you will find that you have accumulated a wide variety of tools and supplies. They are usually stored in a variety of places, including the garage, basement, and mud room. After a while it becomes difficult to determine what is where. So, consider construction of an aluminum storage shed to store all of your garden tools and supplies. Many styles and sizes are available. You will find that a shed will add much to your gardening pleasure and will take pressure off the garage and basement storage areas. Remember to remove any substances (such as liquid sprays) from the shed for the winter if freezing is likely.

✓   ✓   ✓

L-Shaped Hand Weeder

Sometimes it is difficult to get close to seedlings without damaging them when cultivating. An L-shaped hand cultivator with a blade ½ to ¾ inches wide and a trowel-sized handle is available for this purpose.

✓   ✓   ✓

Ice Cream Scoop for Digging Transplant Holes

A number of homes have old-fashioned ice cream scoops around that are no longer being used. These can be converted into handy tools to dig holes for transplants in your garden. The ice cream release serves well as a soil release.

✓   ✓   ✓

Giant Dust Pan

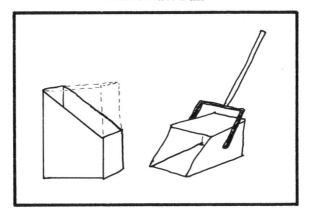

Lawn work often involves picking up and transporting small piles of debris. A giant dust pan similar to the one illustrated is excellent for these jobs. Make one out of a 5-gallon can by cutting it as illustrated and punching holes in both sides about halfway between top and center. Buy a strip of metal and bend it into a U-shape to fit the can. A straight piece of metal can be attached to the U to serve as a handle.

Appendix

Kinds of Fertilizers

Apply fertilizer to soil that is moist (not dripping wet). If applied to dry soil, fertilizer can burn roots. The table below gives directions on amounts to use:

Name of Fertilizer	Analysis	Rate of Application pounds per 100 square feet	Liquid	General Reaction
Ammonium nitrate	33-0-0	1/2	1 oz to 5 gal	Acid
Ammonium sulfate	20-0-0	1	1 oz to 2 gal	Acid
Calcium nitrate	15-0-0	1	1 oz to 2 gal	Alkaline
Sodium nitrate	15-0-0	1	1 oz to 2 gal	Alkaline
Urea or Nu Green	45-0-0	1/2	1 oz to 7 gal	Acid
Urea-form nitrogen Borden's 38, Nitro-form, Uramite	38-0-0	1 to 2	Insoluble	Acid
Superphosphate	0-20-0	5	Insoluble	Neutral
Treble superphosphate	0-45-0	5	Insoluble	Neutral
Muriate of potash	0-0-50	1	1 oz to 2 gal	Neutral
Muriate of potash (trona)	0-0-60	1	1 oz to 2 gal	Neutral
Sulfate of potash	0-0-50	1	1 oz to 2 gal	Neutral
Ammonium phosphate (mono)	11-48-0	1	1 oz to 2 gal	Acid
Ammonium phosphate (di)	21-53-0	1/2	1 oz to 5 gal	Acid
Potassium nitrate	13-0-44	1	1 oz to 2 gal	Neutral
Complete	Varies with Manufacturer	Follow manufacturer's directions		Varies with manufacturer
Chelated Iron	Iron	Not recommended	1 oz to 10 or 15 gal	Neutral
Iron sulfate (ferrous sulfate)	Iron	1	1 oz to 2 gal	Very Acid
Lime, Limestone or Dolomite	Calcium	5	Insoluble	Alkaline
Gypsum (calcium sulfate)	Calcium	5	Insoluble	Neutral

Some Organic Fertilizers

Name of Fertilizer	Analysis in Percent			Pounds Per 100 sq. ft.	Remarks
	N	P	K		
Blood	10	1.5	0	3	/A very rapidly available organic fertilizer
Fish scrap	9	7	0	3 to 4	/Not to be confused with fish emulsives which generally are quite low in fertilizer content.
Guano, Bat	6	9	3	3 to 4	/Partially decomposed bat manure from caves in southwestern U.S.
Bird	13	11	3	3 to 4	/Partially decomposed bird manure from islands off coast.
Kelp or seaweed	1	0.5	9	5	
Leather (Processed)	8	0	0	3 to 4	/Unless steamed under pressure, leather is valueless as fertilizer. See process tankage.
Meal					
Bone, raw	4	22	0	5	/Main value is nitrogen since most of the phosphorus is not soluble.
Bone, steamed	2	27	0	5	/As a result of steaming under pressure, some nitrogen is lost, but more phosphorus is soluble for use by plants.
Cocoa shell	2.5	1	3	5	/Primarily a conditioner for complete fertilizers.
Cotton seed	6	2.5	2	3 to 4	/Generally very acid. Quite useful for bed-grown azaleas and other acid soil plants.
Hoof and Horn	14	0	0	2	/The steam treated and ground material is a rather quickly available source of nitrogen.
Linseed	6	2	1	3	
Mustard Seed	4	2	1	5	
Peanut Hull	1	0	1	5	/Surprisingly low in nitrogen considering the plant is a legume.
Rape Seed	5	2	1	5	
Soybean	7	2	2	3 to 4	
Tung nut	4	2	1	5	

Name of Fertilizer	Analysis in Percent N	P	K	Pounds Per 100 sq. ft.	Remarks
Manure					
Cattle	0.5	0.3	0.5		/Although manures in general are low in fertilizer, when used in relatively large amounts to improve soil struc- ture, damage may occur because of too much fertilizer parti- cularly after steaming
Chicken	0.9	0.5	0.8		
Horse	0.6	0.3	0.6		
Sheep	0.9	0.5	0.8		
Swine	0.6	0.5	0.4		
Mushroom Manure (spent)	1	1	1	5	
Oyster Shells	0.2	0.3	0	5	/Because of their alkalinity these are best used for raising pH rather than as a fertilizer.
Peat (reed or sedge)	2	0.3	0.3	5	/Best used as a soil condi- tioner rather than as a fer- tilizer. Breaks down too rapidly.
Rice Hulls (ground)	0.5	0.2	0.5	5	
Sludge					
Sewage	2	1	1	5	
Sewage, activated (special micro- organisms added)	6	5	0	3 to 4	/Examples of activated sludge are Milorganite (Milwaukee, Wisc.), Hu-Actinite (Houston, Tex.), Chicagrow (Chicago, Ill.) and Nitroganic (Pasadena, Calif.)
Tankage					
Cocoa	4	1.5	2	5	
Garbage	3	3	1	5	
Process (leather, hair, wool, felt, feathers, etc.)	8	1	0	3 to 4	
Tobacco Stems	2	1	6	5	/An excellent organic material high in potash. Has an alka- line reaction.
Wood ashes	0	2	6	5	/Quite alkaline.

FERTILIZER APPLICATION RATES

Fertilizer Grade	Amount required to supply rate of ¼ pound each of N, P_2O_5 and K_2O per 100 sq. ft.		
	On 50 sq. ft.	On 100 sq. ft.	On 200 sq. ft.
	(lb.)	(lb.)	(lb.)
8-8-8	1½	3	6
10-10-10	1¼	2½	5
13-13-13	1	2	4
15-15-15	5/6	1⅔	3⅓

	Amount required to supply rate of ¼ pound N per 100 square feet		
	On 50 sq. ft.	On 100 sq. ft.	On 200 sq. ft.
	(lb.)	(lb.)	(lb.)
Sodium nitrate	¾	1½	3
Ammonium sulfate	⅝	1¼	2½
Ammonium nitrate-lime mixture	⅝	1¼	2½
Ammonium nitrate	⅜	¾	1½
Urea	¼	½	1

Diameter of Area Needing Fertilizer (ft.)	Area Requiring Fertilizer (sq. ft.)	Approximate Amount of Fertilizer Needed for Rate of 2 lb./100 sq. ft.
1	¾	¼ oz. or 1 teaspoon
2	3	1 oz. or 4 teaspoons
3	7	2¼ oz. or 3 tablespoons
4	13	4 oz. or ½ cup
5	20	6 oz. or ¾ cup
6	28	9 oz. or 1 cup
8	50	1 lb. or 1 pint
12	100	2 lb. or 1 quart
35	1000	20 lb. or 10 quarts

CONVERSION TABLE FOR USE OF MATERIALS ON SMALL AREAS

LIQUID MATERIALS			DRY MATERIALS		
Rate/Acre	Rate/1000 Sq. Ft.	Rate/100 Sq. Ft.	Rate/Acre	Rate/1000 Sq. Ft.	Rate/100 Sq. Ft.
1 pt.	¾ tbsp.	¼ tsp.	1 lb.	2 ½ tsps.	¼ tsp.
1 qt.	1 ½ tbsps.	½ tsp.	3 lbs.	2 ¼ tbsps.	¾ tsp.
1 gal.	6 tbsps.	2 tsps.	4 lbs.	3 tbsps.	1 tsp.
25 gals.	4 ½ pts.	1 C.	5 lbs.	4 tbsps.	1 ¼ tsps.
50 gals.	4 ½ qts.	1 pt.	10 lbs.	½ C.	2 tsps.
100 gals.	9 qts.	1 qt.	100 lbs.	2 ¼ lbs.	¼ lb.
200 gals.	4 ½ qts.	2 qts.	200 lbs.	4 ½ lbs.	½ lb.
300 gals.	6 ¾ gals.	3 qts.	300 lbs.	6 ¾ lbs.	¾ lb.
400 gals.	9 gals.	1 gal.	400 lbs.	9 lbs.	1 lb.
500 gals.	11 ¼ gals.	1 ¼ gals.	500 lbs.	11 ¼ lbs.	1 ¼ lb.

These are approximate since materials vary with their density or bulk.

Optimum pH Range for Vegetable Crops*

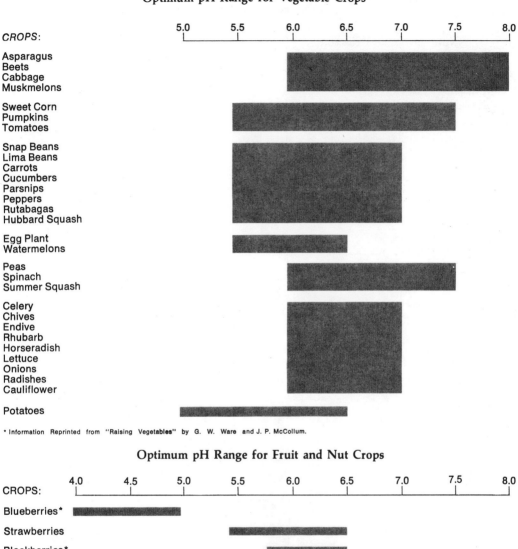

CROPS:

5.0 5.5 6.0 6.5 7.0 7.5 8.0

Asparagus
Beets
Cabbage
Muskmelons

Sweet Corn
Pumpkins
Tomatoes

Snap Beans
Lima Beans
Carrots
Cucumbers
Parsnips
Peppers
Rutabagas
Hubbard Squash

Egg Plant
Watermelons

Peas
Spinach
Summer Squash

Celery
Chives
Endive
Rhubarb
Horseradish
Lettuce
Onions
Radishes
Cauliflower

Potatoes

* Information Reprinted from "Raising Vegetables" by G. W. Ware and J. P. McCollum.

Optimum pH Range for Fruit and Nut Crops

CROPS:

4.0 4.5 5.0 5.5 6.0 6.5 7.0 7.5 8.0

Blueberries*

Strawberries

Blackberries*
Raspberries*

Apples
Apricots
Cherries
Grapes
Peaches
Plums
Pecans

Walnuts

Currants
Gooseberries

Twenty Common Weeds and Controls

TWENTY OF THE MOST COMMON GARDEN WEEDS AND CONTROLS FOR EACH	2,4,D	Dalapon Dowpon	Methane Arsenate	Eptam	Sodium Tea	Atrozine Monuron	Vapam Mylone Cyanamid	Betasan Tupersan	Annual pre-emolient Enide	Shade out Mow higher
Annual Blue Grass Germinates summer and fall Needs light; good turf retards			■				■			
Bermuda Grass Deplete carbohydrate reserve Shade out; selective in dichondra		■			■					■
Burr Clover High nitrogen in soil retards	■									
Chick Weed Rake and mow; Enide	■								■	
Crab Glass Many controls; timing and several applications			■					■		
Dandelion Use concentrate on prods to localize treatments	■									
Dodder Strong Amm. Sulf. (Woody plants recover; not dodder)										
English Daisy Spot treatment in dichondra	■									
Johnson & Dallis Grass Not selective at effective rates; spot treat later, 2-3 wks.		■	■		■					
Morning Glory Root storage, several treatments	■									
Nut Grass Regular cultivation weakens Sterilize with Vapam, Cyanamid				■			■			
Oxalis Difficult in grasses; Silvex, Oxalis-kil (sodium cyanide)	■						■			
Pig Weed (amoranthus) Vertical mowing Close mowing	■								■	
Plantain Several varieties; spot kill in dichondra	■									
Poison Oak Several applications during spring or fall	■									
Puncture Vine Silvex (245 Tp)	■								■	
Purslane Annual Monuron, pre-emergence						■			■	
Spurge Pre-emergent Jan.; repeat as needed. Spurge-ex; shade-out	■									■
Thistle Annual weed	■								■	
Wire Weed (Polgonum vicular)	■							■	■	

PEST	PLANT	MATERIALS per 100 gallons water	TIME
ANTHRACNOSE	Oak, Sycamore, Walnut, Butternut, Hickory, Maple	2 pounds 76% Ferbam	When leaves are unfolding; again when leaves are half grown; and when leaves are full grown.
APHIDS black rosy green	Crabapples, Corylus, Barberry, Elm, Lonicera, Alder, Viburnum, Euonymus, etc.	1½ pints 57% Malathion emulsion *or* 1 pint 25% Diazinon emulsion	When aphid colonies appear on the new leaves and shoots — usually starting during late May.
APHIDS Spruce gall	All spruce	1½ pounds 25% Lindane or 1½ pints 57% Malathion emulsion	Hand-picking galls during early summer and destroying them is effective in controlling this insect on small trees. On large trees apply a chemical spray before plant growth begins in the spring — during April.
BEETLES Japanese	Crabapples, Linden Elm, Horse Chestnut, etc.	2 pounds 50% Sevin wettable powder	When beetles appear, about July 1; and repeat again in 10 days. It may be necessary to treat sod in sandy areas (see Grubs).
BEETLES Leaf Rose Chafer, etc.	Maple, Willow, Oak, Poplar, Clematis, Grape, Hydrangea, Rose	2 pounds 50% Sevin wettable powder	When small worms appear, about June 1, or other times.
BLACK SPOT	Rose	1½ pounds Phaltan or Folpet 50% wettable powder	Apply once a week before rain, or often enough to cover new growth.
BLISTER RUST	White Pine	Remove black currant for radius of 1 mile; other currants 900 feet	Any time of year when found.
BORERS	Mountain Ash, Crabapple, Dogwood, Pine, Spruce, Birch, Linden	4 pounds 50% methoxychlor wettable powder	Paint or spray on trunks and/or main branches (½″ plus), when adults appear; and twice again at 2 week intervals.
CANKER WORM	Most deciduous shade trees	2 pounds 25% Malathion or 2 pounds 50% Sevin	Mid-May.
CEDAR-APPLE RUST	Crabapple, Hawthorn, Quince, Juniper (Red Cedar)	1½-2 pounds 76% Ferbam Acti-dione (as recommended on package)	Eliminate Red Cedar within 1 mile; four applications on Crabapple, etc. weekly, beginning about April 25. When orange masses appear on cedar galls; or eliminate Crabapple, Apple, Hawthorn, Quince, within 1 mile.
FIREBLIGHT	Crabapple, Cotoneaster, Pear, Hawthorn, Pyracantha, Quince	2-6-100 Bordeaux, or Streptomycin (as recommended on package)	When 25 percent of blooms open; again when 75 percent of blooms open.
GRUBS (in soil) Japanese beetle White grubs European chafer	Any soil, conifers, turf	2⅔ lbs. 5% Chlordane per 1,000 sq. ft.	Before planting on turf early spring or fall. Do not exceed one application per year. Treatment is effective for 4-5 years.
LEAF BLOTCH	Horse Chestnut, Witch Hazel	2 pounds 76% Ferbam	Three applications at 2-week intervals after buds open.
LEAFHOPPERS — PLANT BUGS	Flowering Cherry, Apple, Grape, Plum, Viburnum and Honey Locust	1½ pints 57% Malathion emulsion or 2 pounds 50% Sevin wettable powder	General application to control injury due to the feeding of these pests. With repeated treatments include a miticide.
LEAF MINER	Birch, Arborvitae, Lilac, Elm, Alder	1½ pints 57% Malathion emulsion or 2 pounds 50% Sevin or 1 pint 25% Diazinon emulsion	Mid-May; again mid-June; again late summer, spray tree and soil under the tree.

PEST	PLANT	MATERIALS per 100 gallons water	TIME
LEAF SPOT	Lonicera, Cornus, Coton-easter, Kerria, Philadel-phus, etc.	2 pounds Captan 50% wet-table powder, or Zineb 80%	2-week intervals; through July and August.
MAPLE BLADDER GALL	Leaves of silver and red maple	2 pounds 50% Sevin wet-table powder or 1½ pints Malathion emulsion	In the spring as the buds begin to open or in the fall after all leaves have fallen.
MILDEW	Lilac, Rose, Phlox, Privet, Cornus, Euonymouns, Hy-drangea, etc.	2 pounds wettable sulfur 95% WP or 4 ounces Kara-thane or Acti-dione (as recommended on package)	Once a week through July and August.
RED SPIDER (Mite)	Oak, Maple, Locust, Box, Rose, Spruce, Juniper, Ar-borvitae, etc.	Kelthane, and/or Tedion for mite eggs (as recommended on package)	Late May before injury; repeat every 2 weeks or if injury is severe, use miticide alone or include ovicide with miticide.
ROSE CHAFER	Apple, Blackberry, Cherry, Elder, Elm, Hydrangea, Peach, Pear, Peony, Rose	2 pounds 25% Malathion or 2 pounds 50% Sevin	When beetles are present.
SAWFLIES	Pines, Mountain Ash	1½ pints 57% Malathion emulsion of 2 pounds 50% Sevin wettable powder	Mid-May, or when worms appear.
SCAB apple	Hawthorn, Pyracantha, Cotoneaster	2 pounds Ferbam 70% WP	3 or 4 applications at 10 day intervals beginning when buds open.
SCALES (crawlers of) Oyster shell Euonymous Cotoneaster San Jose Lecanium and Cottony scales	Lilac, Poplar, Pachysan-dra, Elm, Pine, Quince, Snowberry, Taxus, Juni-pers, Arborvitae, Coton-easter, Rhododendron, etc.	1½ pints 57% Malathion emulsion or 2 pounds 50% Diazinon emulsion or 2 pounds 50% Sevin	For Euonymus, oystershell, San Jose scales — late May early June. For lecanium, cottony maple and other soft scale — early July. Repeat treatment in 7-10 days.
SHOOT BLIGHT Tip blight Needle cost	Pine, Junipers	2-6-100 Bordeaux	When new growth begins; and at 10-day intervals while new growth develops.
SHOOT MOTH	All pines	4 pounds 50% Sevin wet-table powder	July 1, and again mid-July.
SOIL INSECTS Ants Wire worms	Any soil	2⅔ pounds 5% granular Chlordane/1,000 sq. ft.	Whenever present, not oftener than once a year. Work and water into soil.
TAR LEAF SPOT	Maple	2 pounds 76% Ferbam	3 applications at 10-day intervals beginning when buds open.
TARNISHED PLANT BUGS	Maple, Willow, Oak, Pop-lar, Clematis, Rose, Grape, Hydrangea	2 pounds 50% Sevin wet-table powder or 1 pint 25% Diazinon emulsion or 1½ pints 57% Malathion	Spray when bugs are seen.
TENT CATERPILLARS and FALL WEBWORM	Cherry, Apple, Birch and most deciduous shade trees	2 pounds 50% Sevin wet-table powder or 1½ pints 57% Malathion emulsion	Mid-May or when tents are first noted.
THRIPS	Roses, Gladiolus, Iris	1½ pints 57% Malathion emulsion or 1 pint 25% Dia-zinon emulsion	Begin in May and continue treating to keep new growth covered.
WEBWORM	Juniper, Barberry, Elm, Oak, Maple, Willow, Pop-lar,	2 pounds 50% Sevin wet-table powder	During early May or in October.
TAXUS WEEVIL	Taxus, Hemlock, Retino-spora, other evergreens	2 pounds 50% Sevin wet-table powder	Apply the last week of June and re-peat in 7-10 days. Thoroughly treat plant and soil beneath it.
WORMS striped Oak and Maple	Most deciduous shade trees	2 pounds 25% Malathion or 2 pounds 50% Sevin wet-table powder	When first worms appear, about June 1.

Index

A-20 grass 105, 106
A-24 grass 105
abelia 52, 186, 189
acacia 116
achimenes 55
acidity 20, 22, 73, 169, 171, 239, 288
acid peat 22
acid phosphate 174
Actidione 103
adhesive disks 109
aerating 84-89
African tuliptree 134
African violet 55, 56, 328, 333, 336, 346,
    348, 363, 372, 421
Agriform tablets 149
ailanthus (tree of heaven) 134
air filter 446
airplane plant 359
ajuga 110, 114
alder 140, 142
algae 107, 399
alkalinity 22, 73, 169, 239, 293
"All-American" selection 200
altagrass 80
aluminum 174
aluminum sulfate 22
alyssum 203, 204
amaryllis 55, 333, 354
Amur maple 44, 172
andromeda 44, 172, 187
anemone 117, 195, 205
annuals 18, 51, 54, 194, 195, 198, 201, 203,
    204
anther 17
anthericum 55-56
anti-desiccant 184
ants 281
aphelandra 55
aphid 168, 232, 267, 268, 269, 356
apple 142, 177, 288, 289, 325, 326
apple bud stages 321
apple trees 307
    training 307
apricot 288
aralia 172, 189
Arasan 167, 425
arbor 293
arborvitae 44, 52, 134, 165, 172, 184
arbutus 385
ardisia 55
aronsbeard 114
arrowhead 55-56
artemisia 195
artificial lights 394
ash 44, 134, 140

asparagus 233, 286
asparagus fern 55
asparagus knife 432
aspen 134
assassin bug 268
aster 245
athletic courts 34
auger 443
Australian umbrella tree 55-56
autumn 169, 189, 203
auxiliary bud 151
avocado 55, 366
ax 432
axle spreader 440
azalea 44, 52, 55-56, 169, 171, 172, 175,
    182, 187, 192, 349

baby's breath 67
baby tears 55, 385
bachelor's buttons 229
bacteria 399
bacterial wilt 280
bagworm 165
Bahai grass 77, 78, 81
balancing blades 448
bald cypress 135, 141
"balled and burlapped" (B & B) 142, 145,
    149
banded maranta 55
bank 66, 117
barbecue 35, 158
barberry 172, 187, 193, 245
bare-root stock 11, 144, 146-148, 190, 288
bare spots 83
bark 8, 12
bark wounds 154
Baron grass 106
basil 337, 354
bayberry 114, 116, 118, 172
beach plum 139
beach wormwood 114
bean rust 280
beans 233, 241, 280, 316
bearberry 110, 114, 115, 116
beautyberry 189
bedding plants 421
beech 135, 140, 163
beech, purple leaf 25
bees 246, 316
beet 233
begonia 55, 197, 207, 212, 213, 328, 333,
    348, 357, 362, 419
bellflower 114
bellwort 117
belts 446

471